# The Great Guano Rush

*Also by Jimmy M. Skaggs*

Broadcloth and Britches:
The Santa Fe Trade (*with Seymour V. Connor*)

The Cattle-Trailing Industry:
Between Supply and Demand, 1866-1890

Clipperton:
A History of the Island the World Forgot

An Interpretive History of the American Economy

Prime Cut:
Livestock Raising and Meatpacking in the United States, 1607-1983

# The Great Guano Rush

## Entrepreneurs and American Overseas Expansion

Jimmy M. Skaggs

St. Martin's Griffin
New York

THE GREAT GUANO RUSH

 For information, address St. Martin's Press, 175 Fifth Avenue, New York, N.Y. 10010.

Design by Acme Art Inc.

**Library of Congress Cataloging-in-Publication Data**

Skaggs, Jimmy M.
The great guano rush : entrepreneurs and American overseas expansion / Jimmy M. Skaggs.
p. cm.
Includes bibliographical references and index.
ISBN 0-312-12339-6 (paperback)
1. Guano industry—United States—History. 2. Fertilizer industry—United States—History. 3. United States—Insular possessions—History. 4. United States—Territories and possessions—History. 5. Islands of the Pacific—History. 6. Caribbean Area—History. I. Title.
HD9484.G9U67 1994
338.4'76686366'0973—dc20 93-26784
CIP

First St. Martin's Griffin Edition: May, 1995
10 9 8 7 6 5 4 3 2 1

*for*

*The breakfast bunch*

## CONTENTS

# PREFACE

I have long contended that the popular notion which attributes American economic success to "free enterprise" or "free-market economics" is patent poppycock,[1] for it pointedly ignores the paternalistic role that the public sector has historically played in the United States. From the very beginning of this republic's existence as an independent nation, local, state, and federal governments have striven to promote prosperity for their people. However justifiable such measures as protective tariffs, subsidies, bounties, tax abatements, and a myriad of other governmental actions designed to encourage economic growth and development, they are hardly *neutral*—which is what Adam Smith talked about in 1776 when he first described a pure market organization of society.[2]

Somehow over the years the American public has mistakenly come to view aid to enterprise as a natural part of capitalism but regulation as unnatural, even socialistic. Such misconceptions are often encouraged and perpetuated by politicians whose rhetoric seldom matches their actions, including the Founding Fathers. For all of his vocal support of limited government, even Thomas Jefferson was hardly the unabashed champion of *laissez faire* that some historians have made him out to be. He consistently advocated governmental help for American farmers, especially cheap land, and, as president, he was not above using the national economy to further his foreign policy goals, as with the Embargo Act (1807-1809), or, for that matter, so committed to constitutional procedures that he forwent the chance to add resources to the commonwealth, as with the Louisiana Purchase (1803). Unequivocally in favor of an activist public sector was Jefferson's political and intellectual rival, Alexander Hamilton, whose fiscal, monetary, and business policies as George Washington's secretary of the Treasury laid the philosophical foundation of a political economy in the United States.[3]

The events that encompass what I call "the great guano rush" comprise a case study in activist public economic policy designed to encourage growth and development, both figuratively and literally. As historian Larry Gara has observed, "the droppings of birds played an important role in the history of U.S. imperialism."[4] The great guano rush demonstrates that however clearly public policy may be conceived, it is often confused and inconsistent in execution and sometimes thwarted by bureaucrats who arbitrarily or even purposely rewrite regulations and even negate laws with little or no regard for constitutional procedures.

I first became aware of America's guano empire while researching *Clipperton: A History of the Island the World Forgot* (1989). Once briefly a part of that empire, Clipperton offered me insight into an obscure episode in American history that, while somewhat known to diplomatic and political historians, has not been seriously examined by those scholars interested in the vital role of public policy as it influences economic growth and development. Nonetheless, I have been able to build upon the work of many historians whose directly relevant and even tangential investigations preceded mine and whose studies I gratefully acknowledge in the Bibliography. My research has also been aided by numerous individuals associated with public and private agencies and repositories, some of whom probably would prefer not be openly identified with a book about bird droppings.

Therefore, I express general, albeit sincere, appreciation to countless unnamed persons at the American Philosophical Society, Philadelphia; Boston Public Library; Brooklyn Historical Society, Brooklyn, New York; John J. Hay Library, Brown University, Providence; Special Collections, Baker Library, Graduate School of Business Administration, Harvard University, Boston (and for permission to quote from its Pacific Guano Company Collection); Center for Cryptological History, National Security Agency, Fort George G. Meade, Maryland; Connecticut Historical Society, Hartford; Connecticut State Library, Hartford; Library, University of Chicago; Department of History, Columbia University, New York; Columbus Memorial Library, Organization of American States, Washington, D.C.; Special Collections, the Library, University of Delaware, Newark (and for permission to reproduce graphics in its possession); Special Collections, Hawaii State Archives, Honolulu; Massachusetts Historical Society, Boston (and for permission to quote from Edward Everett's Papers); Maryland Historical Society, Baltimore; Maryland State Archives, Annapolis; Public Library, New London, Connecticut; New York Genealogical and Biographical Society Library, New York; New York Historical Society, New York; New York (City) Public Library; New York State Archives, Albany; Southern Historical Collection, University of North Carolina, Chapel Hill; Pennsylvania Historical Society, Philadelphia; Philadelphia Maritime Museum, Philadelphia; Department of History and the Seeley G. Mudd Manuscript Library, Princeton University, Princeton; Government Group Media Relations, Raytheon Company, Lexington, Massachusetts; Sedgwick County Law Library,

Wichita; Government Documents Library, Texas Tech University, Lubbock; Office of the Commandant, U.S. Army Chemical Materiel Destruction Agency; U.S. Coast Guard, Washington, D.C.; Administrative Office, United States Courts, Washington, D.C.; Defense Nuclear Agency, Alexandria; Federal Judicial Center Historical Office, Washington, D.C.; Office of the Clerk, U.S. House of Representatives, Washington, D.C.; the Bureau of Land Management and the Office of Territorial and International Affairs, U.S. Department of the Interior, Washington, D.C.; Pacific/Remote Islands National Wildlife Refuge Complex, Fish and Wildlife Service, U.S. Department of the Interior, Honolulu (including permission to reproduce its maps of Baker, Howland, and Jarvis islands); Federal Bureau of Prisons, U.S. Department of Justice, Washington, D.C.; Library of Congress, Washington, D.C.; Marine Corps Historical Center, Washington Navy Yard, Washington, D.C.; National Archives and Records Center, Washington, D.C.; Naval Historical Center, Washington Navy Yard, Washington, D.C.; Office of the Chief of Naval Operations, U.S. Navy, Washington, D.C.; Office of the Secretary, U.S. Senate, Washington, D.C.; and the Library, the Office of the Geographer, and the Office of the Legal Adviser, U.S. Department of State, Washington, D.C.

Nevertheless, I would be remiss if I did not identify certain individuals whose assistance has been indispensable: Señor Miguel González Avelar, member, Mexican Chamber of Delegates, provided me with relevant material from Mexico's Archivo Gubernación and graciously entertained me in Mexico City; Professor William Lane Harris, Department of History, The Citadel, Charleston, North Carolina, helped me obtain a copy of his master's thesis; friend Toni Jackman, U.S. Information Agency, Washington, D.C., located valuable material for me in the U.S. State department's Library; attorney Jon E. Krupnick of Fort Lauderdale, Florida, shared with me parts of his extensive collection of information on the Swan islands; Lt. Col. Richard J. O'Brien, U.S.M.C. (Ret.), Paso Robles, California, helped me to locate his research files on Navassa island amid voluminous Marine Corps Records; attorney Rachael K. Pirner, Wichita, guided me through a maze of legalese; Professor Earl Pomeroy, Department of History, University of Oregon, Eugene, traded information on the American cattle industry for data on the Pacific (he and I in effect switching research emphases); Dr. Gale Raymond, Houston, provided much information on America's island claims and possessions and suggested other sources to explore; and Professor David P. Werlich, chairman, Department of History, Southern Illinois University, lent me his department's copy of an otherwise unavailable master's thesis and suggested other sources relevant to my research.

Numerous people at Wichita State University, my academic home for more than two decades, have assisted me in my work. Foremost among these are Thoburn (Buck) Taggart, interlibrary loan librarian emeritus, and his staff whose amiable assistance procured hundreds of research items from the nation's libraries. My labor was further abetted by government documents librarian Arlene Moore and her staff who patiently helped me locate innumerable published documents reposing in the public record. I am very grateful to research assistants in the Department of Economics: Cynthia Engel, Shelley Anne Savoy and especially Charles Mark Clark, whose diligence uncovered numerous sources that otherwise might have been overlooked. Geologist Salvatore J. Mazzullo helped me find information on marine phosphates that I would never have located on my own, and his wife, Heidi, an expert cartographer, prepared original maps of America's guano empire. I also wish to thank my colleagues in the W. Frank Barton School of Business for a research grant that provided travel funds and financial resources with which to duplicate numerous research materials.

Many friends and colleagues at WSU have substantially assisted this project by clarifying technical points and by reading and criticizing all or parts of the manuscript. I am indebted far beyond what mere words could ever repay because the perceptive comments of educator Robert D. Alley, chemist William R. Carper, constitutional historian James C. Duram, geologist John C. Gries, business historian Billy Mac Jones, labor economist Martin M. Perline, political scientist James Sheffield, and economist William T. Terrell have greatly improved this work. Nevertheless, I alone am responsible for whatever errors of fact or interpretation that may remain.

Finally, I dedicate *The Great Guano Rush* to them and the half dozen others who constitute the "breakfast bunch" at WSU—academics representing both genders and a myriad of disciplines who regularly gather to begin the day with camaraderie and convivial discourse. Their encouragement (amid innumerable tasteless scatological puns truly worthy of pedants) has lightened my load and brightened my outlook.

Jimmy M. Skaggs<br>Wichita, Kansas<br>June 15, 1993

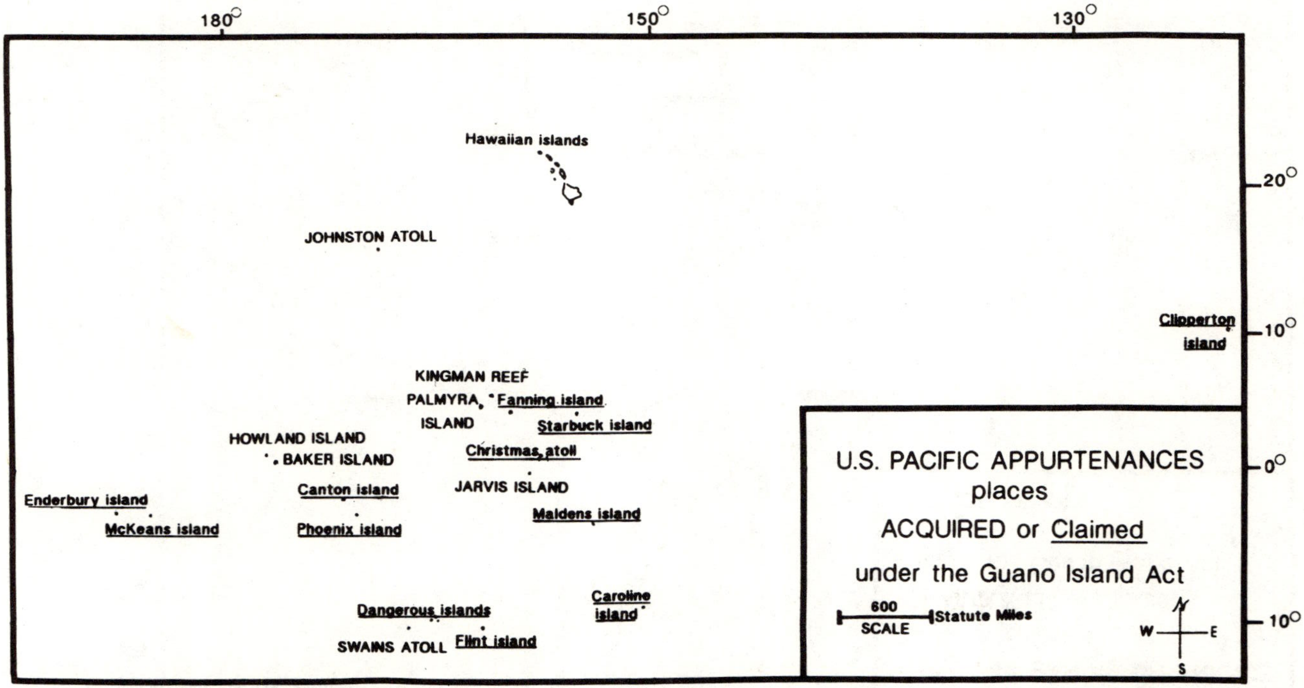
180°
150°
130°
20°
10°
0°
10°
Hawaiian islands
JOHNSTON ATOLL
Clipperton island
KINGMAN REEF
PALMYRA ISLAND
Fanning island
Starbuck island
HOWLAND ISLAND
BAKER ISLAND
Christmas atoll
JARVIS ISLAND
Canton island
Enderbury island
McKeans island
Phoenix island
Maldens island
Caroline island
Dangerous islands
SWAINS ATOLL
Flint island
U.S. PACIFIC APPURTENANCES
places
ACQUIRED or Claimed
under the Guano Island Act
600
SCALE
Statute Miles
N
W
E
S

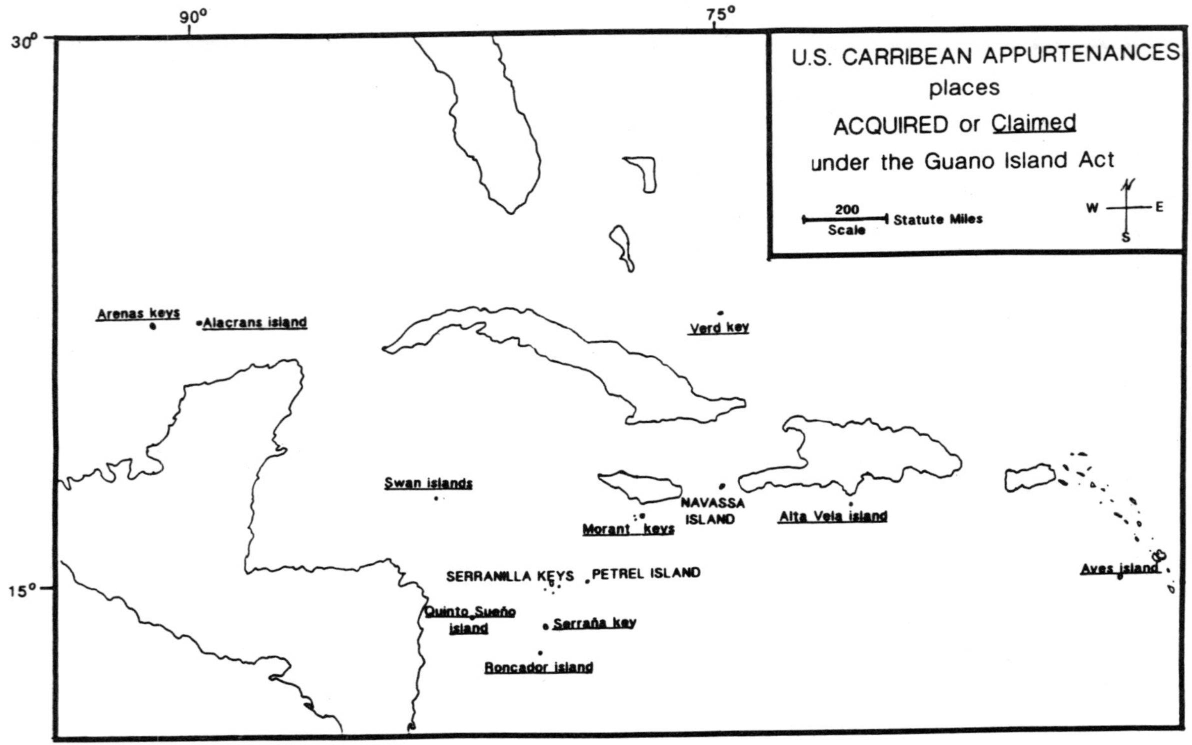
U.S. CARRIBEAN APPURTENANCES
places
ACQUIRED or Claimed
under the Guano Island Act
200
Scale
Statute Miles
W
E
S
90°
75°
30°
15°
Arenas keys
Alacrans island
Verd key
Swan islands
NAVASSA ISLAND
Morant keys
Alta Vela island
SERRANILLA KEYS
PETREL ISLAND
Quinto Sueño island
Serraña key
Roncador island
Aves island

# The Great Guano Rush

# 1

## Supply, Demand, Price, and Politics

Declining agricultural productivity in the United States prior to the Civil War fostered an ever-increasing need for fertilizers. The resulting demand was partially filled by bird droppings, especially "guano" from Peru; however, this exotic and powerful soil additive was in short supply, leading to rapidly rising prices. Guano, or more correctly *huano* (a Spanish word of native American derivation originally meaning the dried excrement of seafowl),[1] came to be so highly prized by farmers in western Europe and North America that the commodity precipitated a veritable global rush among both nations and entrepreneurs who eagerly sought to provide it on a seller's market.

Disgruntled farmers in the United States pressured their elected officials to procure the fertilizer cheaper, thereby setting into motion an overpowering momentum that culminated in the permanent addition of national territory thousands of miles from the mainland of the United States long before the purchase of Alaska. The consequences of this little-known episode in American history were far-reaching and offer insight into U.S. economic growth and development—not the myth of *laissez faire* but, rather, the reality of a paternalistic public sector that, whatever else it may pretend, routinely practices political economy.

As with all acts of production, farming is subject to the unyielding Law of Diminishing Returns. Intensively used land inevitably wears out. Although paleolithic planters worldwide used fertilizers such as animal manures (including bird droppings), bone, chalk, humus, marl, and wood ash (potash) as early as 10,000 B.C., it was not until the early nineteenth century A.D. that systematic scientific study sought to explain how and why assorted soil additives enhanced agricultural output, as well as to suggest why some nutrients worked better than others.[2]

About 1804 Swiss scientist Nicholas Theodore de Saussure demonstrated that plants derive carbon and oxygen from the atmosphere and nitrogen as well as assorted minerals (calcium, magnesium, phosphorus, and potassium) from the soil. For a time his important work was largely ignored because German scientist Albrecht Thaer's rival "humus theory," which insisted that fertility was derived entirely from organic matter in the soil, held sway among most researchers. Englishman Humphrey Davy's *Elements of Agricultural Chemistry* (1813) reconciled these conflicting views insofar as possible and, for the first time, offered farmers a practical handbook of contemporary practical wisdom. In 1834 French chemist J. B. Boussingault built upon de Saussure's base by measuring nutrient input/output, thereby analyzing the chemical constituency of plant growth.[3]

German scientist Justus von Liebig soon offered an even more practical application of his predecessors' work by simultaneously publishing in Germany and Great Britain *Organic Chemistry in Its Application to Agriculture and Physiology* (1840), which was revised and updated the following year expressly for the American market. In time it became a veritable bible for progressive farmers. Liebig stressed the value of nitrogen, phosphate (a salt of phosphoric acid), and potassium (such as in potash) to overcome soil infertility; he also demonstrated that the value of bone meal as fertilizer was greatly enhanced when treated with sulfuric acid, a commodity only recently available in commercial quantities. In 1842 English entrepreneur John B. Lawes applied Liebig's research by treating rock phosphate ("apatite," or mineralized phosphorus) with sulfuric acid, thereby producing the world's first commercial fertilizer, Superphosphate.[4]

Basic research and commercial applications were especially beneficial to American farmers who—seduced since colonial times by the initially bountiful yields of virgin lands—practiced primitive agricultural techniques that, over time, proved to be very destructive of the soil. Productivity declined. For instance, in the once fantastically fertile Genesee valley of New York, corn yields averaged about eight bushels per acre in 1845, down from thirty bushels in 1775. In middle and southern states such as Maryland and Virginia, farmers (growing crops such as tobacco and cotton, both of which are especially hard on the land) faced bleak futures as soil exhaustion became increasingly pronounced.[5]

Worse, eastern farmers in the United States confronted increasing competition from fellow citizens, their contemporaries who had migrated westward to work new, fertile fields, thereby contributing to agricultural overproduction that, in turn, depressed commodity prices. Thus, not only were eastern farmers growing less, but the prices they received for their ever-decreasing yields were steadily declining. Furthermore, whereas the land area of the United States had doubled between 1800 and 1840, primarily because of the Louisiana Purchase (1803), it increased by another two thirds between 1840 and 1850—with the annexation of Texas (1845), the division of the Oregon Territory with Great Britain (1846), and the Mexican Cession (1848). Hence, eastern farmers could reasonably expect fiercer competition in the future by an economic rivalry made even more immediate by the advent of railroads.[6]

Progressive farmers looked for solutions, and an agricultural press that had developed early in the century to serve this important segment of the economy eagerly sought to help—as would the U.S. government, eventually. Private publications such as the *American Farmer* and *Plough Boy,* both begun in 1819, supplemented by more recent journals such as the *New England Farmer* (1822) and the *Genesee Farmer* (1831), urged crop diversification and rotation as well as the generous application of fertilizers. Readers responded by trying animal manures (solid and liquefied), putrefied animal remains, ashes, blood, bones (treated and not), coal tar, chalk, charcoal, assorted composts, crushed cotton seeds, feathers, fish, gypsum, hair, hay, horns, "night soil" (human excrement), saltpeter, sawdust, seaweed, soot, straw, urine (animal and human), vegetable molds, weeds, and wood fibers, among other things.[7] Some worked better than others.

In 1824 John S. Skinner, editor of the *American Farmer,* informed his subscribers of "Guano, a celebrated manure used in South America, . . . possessing astonishing fertilizing properties," a sample of which his son-in-law, a sailor, had recently procured in Peru. Skinner had it analyzed by a "professor of agricultural chemistry" who observed that the stuff contained many of the elements (carbon, nitrogen, phosphorus) known to be important to plant life. Equally significant to Skinner was guano's low price—eighty cents per *fanega* (about 1.5 bushels), or approximately $30 a ton, "making it, as may be perceived, a very profitable business" for both purveyors and users.[8]

Despite his lavish praise of the commodity's extraordinary enriching powers, almost a decade would pass before more samples were imported into the United States and even longer before planters began to use it extensively enough to verify Skinner's report. By then guano was a tightly controlled Peruvian monopoly, and its price (according to American consumers) was outrageously high, which many people in and out of the U.S. government blamed, in part, on the British.

Europeans in general and English farmers in particular were far quicker than Americans to apply the new exotic fertilizer to their fields, and with impressive results. The celebrated German explorer and scientist Baron Alexander von Humboldt is generally credited with introducing guano to Europe at the outset of the nineteenth century following his travels throughout Central and South America in the company of French botanist Aime Bonpland. Humboldt and Bonpland observed bountiful crops in bleak and barren coastal Peru where native farmers had used *huano* for more than a thousand years, and they acquired samples that they eventually presented to chemists François de Foureroy and Nicolas Louis Vauquelin of France and Martin Heinrich Klaproth of Germany for analyses that confirmed an ancient Peruvian proverb, "Guano, though no saint, works many miracles."[9]

For countless eons, sea birds in vast numbers (especially the guanay cormorant but also gannets, gulls, pelicans, and other seafowl) had exploited the cold oceanic current (first described by Humboldt and eventually named for him) that sweeps northward along the west coast of South America from Antarctica and that supports an ocean brimming with anchovies, herring, and other cold-water fishes. After gorging themselves from a bountiful sea, birds roosted and nested by the millions on dozens of small, barren islands just off the coast of South America. Their droppings (calculated to be 1.5 ounces a day per bird) steadily accumulated over time in an arid, desiccating climate that preserved the naturally high nitrogen content of bird feces in a smelly, yellowish concretion that was also very rich in phosphate. By the time Humboldt visited Peru in 1803, guano on some of its islands, especially the Chincas, was more than a hundred feet deep.[10]

Prehistoric Mochian people, inhabitants of Peru about A.D. 500, regularly mined the islands for what they called *huanu,* enabling them to grow foodstuffs and live in one of the least hospitable climates on earth. Their stair-stepped terraces clinging to craggy mountainsides literally stole moisture from fog that enveloped them; with some irrigation, and generous dustings of *huanu,* potatoes and other crops thrived. Quechuans, who established the fabled Incan empire about A.D. 1200, readily embraced these practices, dividing offshore islands among regions and communities in their domain to facilitate the distribution of *huanu* among farmers. Its widespread use allowed them to free manpower for other pursuits, such as road building and gold mining, and to sustain a population of perhaps ten million people by the time of the Spanish conquest in 1532. So valuable were bird droppings to Incas that they ranked *huanu* alongside gold as gifts of the gods and forbade anyone on penalty of death to molest nesting birds.[11]

Although Spaniards observed and even marveled at the phenomenal fertilizing power of what they called *huano, conquistadores* were far more interested in the personally enriching qualities of gold. As attention and manpower shifted increasingly to precious metals during the colonial period, the mining of offshore islands declined, and, over time, Peruvian agriculture suffered. Throughout the seventeenth and eighteenth centuries sporadic and individual runs to the islands in small boats by natives ferried back only modest amounts that invariably found a ready market on the mainland.[12]

Following independence the Peruvian government in 1830 exempted *huano* from taxation because it was "very useful and necessary for the development and prosperity of agriculture,"[13] and, as a consequence, a small domestic trade developed, but, as had been the case at the time of Humboldt's visit, *huano*'s remarkable properties remained mostly unknown to the rest of the world. Samples turned up in North America and Europe, as with John Skinner of *American Farmer* in 1824 and in England two years later, eliciting favorable reviews. A few casks of the pungent yellowish powder were even offered for sale in Baltimore as early as 1832 and in England three years later, but there was no regular international commerce in the commodity before 1840.[14]

About 1838 two Peruvian businessmen, Carlos Barroilhet and Aquiles Allier, sought to change that. They asked English merchant Horace Bland, a resident of Valparaíso, Chile, to forward samples of *huano* to his associate in Liverpool, William Myers, with the simple request that Myers should have local farmers try it. He did, "and the results were most encouraging,"[15] prompting the Liverpool merchant to request larger samples of what the English called "guano" with which to undertake even more sophisticated tests. Once conducted these experiments demonstrated that the stuff was far more powerful than barnyard manure—results that caused Myers to offer to buy into any scheme to import the commodity into England. He said he thought he could sell it for £24 ($120 U.S.) or more a ton.[16]

Consequently, on November 10, 1840, Don Francisco Quirós, a well-connected Lima businessman (acting on behalf of himself and Peruvians Barroilhet and Allier, as well as the French firm of Dutez & Co. and William Myers & Co. of Liverpool) bought for £2,400 ($12,000 U.S.) from the government of Peru the exclusive right to mine and export *huano* for the next six years. Such monopolies, holdovers from days of the Spanish empire, were commonplace throughout Latin America.[17]

For Quirós and his associates, the deal proved to be fantastically profitable, albeit briefly. In 1840 and 1841 they loaded twenty-two ships (all but three bound for Britain) with almost eight thousand tons of bird droppings.[18] Of this initial venture historian Frederick Pike says, "The stench was so foul that, it is reported, when the first guano shipment arrived in Southampton the entire town took to the hills."[19]

Despite the smell, English farmers eagerly applied the new fertilizer. The Earl of Derby purchased an entire shipload of guano for his fields in central England, and the results were so impressive that he soon extolled its powers before the Royal Agricultural Society. Other early users were likewise favorably impressed. Scottish farmer Robert Bell of County Kerry sprinkled it on oats, wheat, potatoes, and turnips resulting in increased yields of between 30 and 300 percent. He even tried it on apple trees and raspberry bushes, causing both to blossom twice in a single year.[20]

Such startling news doubtlessly encouraged other farmers to try guano, some of them so determined to buy the genuine article that they reportedly tasted it,[21] a potentially dangerous practice. One English farmer was so impatient to have a bag of the exotic fertilizer that he sacked it himself, holding the corner of a burlap bag in his mouth as he scooped in powder by hand. In the process he inadvertently ingested some that, he later said, burned him internally as he swallowed. He soon suffered increasing distresses, at first a sore throat that quickly swelled and constricted, followed by hemorrhaging which became so acute overnight that a physician was consulted. According to the doctor, it was too late: "no combination of astringents . . . had the least effect," and the man died about forty-eight hours later. "After [his] death, the blood continued to exude for several hours, till the entire sanguineous system . . . had become emptied of its contents." The attending physician wanted to perform an autopsy, "but [the man's] friends would not permit it."[22]

Yet, neither noxious odor nor deadly danger dissuaded most buyers. Myers & Co. sold each shipload as it arrived at an estimated average wholesale price of £18 ($90 U.S.) a ton. Its cost, delivered dockside at Liverpool, was calculated at £6 ($30) a ton, including all expenses related to mining and loading in Peru, freight, insurance, and warehousing. This left Myers and his Peruvian associates with a handsome profit of £12 per ton, or about £100,000 ($500,000) total.[23]

All across Europe farmers began experimenting with guano. In remote, agriculturally backward Bohemia (present Czech Republic), a scarcity of fertilizers due to relatively few livestock (and their poor diets) typically allowed farmers to manure their fields only once every six years. Consequently, as early as 1843 the Prague Agricultural Society began promoting the use of guano, which eventually led to widespread use of assorted artificial fertilizers on large estates.[24]

Alexander Cochet, a Frenchman living in Peru, somehow caught scent of escalating European demand and in 1841 announced that he had "discovered" the fertilizing properties of guano. He filed claim to a one-third interest in all the nation's bird droppings under an 1833 Peruvian law designed to encourage domestic business development, thus alerting officials to guano's export value. Not long thereafter the British merchantman *Dyson* arrived with a load of coal and news that Chinca island guano commanded as much as £28 ($140 U.S.) a ton in England, retail. Criticism of the Quirós contract had already surfaced in Peru because most of the payment due the government had been remitted in the form of sharply discounted Peruvian bonds, and word of lofty cash prices abroad led President Manuel Menéndez to cancel the 1840 agreement and call for new bids. Only one was submitted, by Quirós, Allier & Co. It offered two thirds of all profits to Peru, payable in cash, in return for a one-year concession, with an option for another four. Quirós and associates also offered 287,000 pesos (£11,480), cash, against future sales. Facing war with Bolivia, Menéndez agreed and released *Dyson* to sail, her cargo hold now full of bird droppings.[25]

Within weeks President Menéndez reconsidered this latest agreement and formally nationalized guano reserves. For the next forty years the Peruvian government would earn most of its foreign exchange from selling feces abroad. It commenced in February 1842 by creating a corporation composed of itself, Quirós, Allier & Co., Puymerol Poumarroux (a French firm), and Gibbs Crawley & Co. (the Lima subsidiary of Antony Gibbs & Sons, London). In return for an additional advance of 200,000 pesos (£8,000) from its partners, a sum to be charged against the government's share of the proceeds, Peru gave the combine a monopoly on exports for five years. In 1847 Gibbs succeeded to sole control of British and North American markets, the continent going to Michel Montané et Compagne, Paris.[26]

Says historian W. M. Mathew, chronicler of the Gibbs mercantile house:

> The way in which this relatively small and initially rather unambitious family enterprise dominated one of the great trades of the international economy in the mid-nineteenth century is probably without precedent. . . . The English merchants were visibly enriched by the guano business, and by the later decades of the nineteenth century were deporting themselves with much poise and confidence in the elevated world of merchant bankers.[27]

Some of the firm's success was obviously attributable to its American monopoly, a lucrative outlet that came to be roundly resented by American farmers, entrepreneurs, and politicians.

Unable to supply adequately even its English market, Gibbs & Sons might never have shared any of the prized commodity with the United States had not a business rival, Andrew Livingstone of Liverpool, in 1842 suddenly dumped onto the British market three shiploads of cheap guano from Ichaboe, a mile-square rock lying off Africa's arid southwestern coast and said to be covered to a depth of twenty-five feet in bird droppings. So many ships sailed for relatively nearby Ichaboe from English ports, coincidentally idled by a slump in the carrying trade, that some observers thought surely the little place would soon be picked clean, which is almost precisely what happened. Ichaboe's guano reserves, estimated to be two hundred thousand tons, were mostly depleted within fifteen months.[28]

Although African guano ultimately proved to contain substantially less nitrogen than the Peruvian variety and therefore was less valuable, its sudden appearance in early summer, after the demand for fertilizer had waned for the year, greatly depressed the market. So too did the nearly simultaneous discovery of numerous other guano islands in Ichaboe's vicinity, as well as additional islets off the coast of Arabia, where the fertilizing properties of bird droppings had been recognized as early as the twelfth century. However well known these places may have been locally, none was closed to alien exploitation; consequently, African and Arabic guano islands were free to anyone who would mine them. Prices in England promptly plummeted, African guano (Chinca's first competitor) stabilizing at about £7 ($35 U.S.) a ton, dragging down with it the superior Peruvian product, to a low of £10 ($50).[29]

Seeing its home market all but disappear, Gibbs imported into Britain merely 1,527 tons in 1843, down from 14,123 tons the year before. Seeking other customers for the feces it had already purchased, that year the firm sent a shipload of unknown quantity to Baltimore where it fetched a phenomenal seven cents a pound, or about $150 (£30) a ton. Encouraged, in 1844 Englishmen allotted two more shiploads (seven hundred tons) to merchant-representatives in the United States, Samuel E. George of Baltimore and Edwin Bartlett of New York, who in turn quickly disposed of their whole inventory to local farmers and to other dealers throughout both the Chesapeake bay region and New England.[30]

By then many farmers in the United States had heard of the fabulous fertilizer and were eager to try it. According to historian Richard Wines, "The widely read *American Farmer* had no references to guano in 1840, one in 1841, twenty-seven in 1845, and eight-five in 1851. Other journals followed the same pattern, although the number of articles were less."[31] Moreover, German chemist Justus Liebig had repeatedly mentioned South American bird dung favorably in his popular *Organic Chemistry,* the progressive farmers' bible. As historian Weymouth Jordan has written, agriculturalists everywhere quickly converted to a "guano gospel," especially in the South.[32]

Among early disciples was John A. Washington, master of Mount Vernon and nephew of the first president. Having first used guano in 1845, John Washington informed the editor of the *Prairie Farmer* in 1852, "I have never seen a worn out or poor soil on which it would not, if properly applied, bring good crops of wheat, corn and grass. . . . Guano can, in my opinion, be used with unquestionable profit."[33] One of Washington's contemporaries, a Virginia tobacco grower, experienced similar results, claiming that "his guanoed lands brought 600 pounds more to the acre than his unfertilized land." Additionally, a South Carolina cotton planter said he netted "over a hundred per cent on the amount expensed in guano."[34]

Likewise experiencing miraculous results, Yankees also converted. Long Island farmers reportedly sprinkled the wonderful stuff on their crops as early as 1845.[35] William P. Cleveland, who raised vegetables outside New London, Connecticut, said he "received a remarkable yield using guano."[36] Maine and Massachusetts farmers happily testified that applications had quadrupled their output of rutabagas and turnips. A chorus of hallelujahs echoed throughout the Chesapeake bay region where, by some accounts, Peruvian bird droppings were found to be thirty-five times as powerful as common barnyard manure. At that time no one knew precisely why (or how) guano worked its wonders, just that it did.[37]

Precise figures for the first few years of what historian Lewis Gray has called the "guano mania" in the United States are unavailable because the Department of the Treasury did not commence compiling import data on the commodity until 1847; however, economist Frank Rutter estimates that between 1844 and 1851 approximately sixty-six thousand tons (aggregating in value $2.6 million, at an average price of $49 a ton, wholesale) entered the United States, the port of Baltimore handling 58 percent of the traffic, with the balance going to New York. Rival products, at first feces from African Ichaboe in 1844, then both phosphates and nitrates from Chilean Patagonia in 1848, also appeared on the American market, but neither was considered equal in potency to Peruvian bird droppings; however, import statistics about them (or the numerous other varieties that later appeared) were never systematically compiled by any government agency. Little matter. American farmers demanded mostly Peruvian guano that was in such short supply before the late 1850s that, by some accounts, four times as much would have been consumed had it been available in the United States.[38]

Because demand for Peruvian guano was substantially greater than supply throughout the early years of the traffic, prices in the United States steadily rose. Gibbs's shipments to Great Britain consistently increased after the initial Ichaboe glut had passed through the market (cresting in 1850 at

199,732 tons, up from 22,410 tons in 1846). By comparison, shipments to the United States were erratic and relatively minuscule: 1,803 tons in 1848, 21,243 tons in 1849, 11,740 tons in 1850, and 23,153 tons in 1851. Prices in the United States peaked at about $76 a ton on strong, early spring demand in 1850, then stabilized at $50 by summer.[39]

Volatile, high prices naturally encouraged a serious search for substitutes and even prompted outright fraud. By 1854 more than a score of alternative bird droppings had been imported from Africa, Atlantic islands off the coast of Spain, Central America, the Caribbean, and assorted Pacific islands, but, according to one contemporary U.S. government study, "they were either found to be worthless or far inferior in quality" to those of Peru.[40] Disreputable businessmen also mislabeled assorted products as pure Peruvian. Fast-talking itinerant peddlers sold near-worthless sacks of sand and gravel (made pungent with assorted animal droppings and urine) to naïve backwoods farmers. Such practices were so prevalent by 1846 that the Maryland legislature mandated oversight of all guano sold in its jurisdiction, a charge of forty cents per ton being tacked onto the retail price by the state's "guano inspector," William S. Reese, who officially poked his nose into sacks at the port of Baltimore and issued grade stamps.[41]

To protect consumers further, Maryland also created the post of "state chemist," who was charged with determining the constituent value of fertilizers offered for sale. In 1851 Dr. James J. Higgins, the state's first such assayer, declared a typical sack of Peruvian guano to be worth $45 a ton. By then such regulatory practices were commonplace. For example, Maryland routinely inspected beef, coal, flour, grain, leather, lumber, pork, tobacco, and other commodities offered for intrastate sale. Nor was that state alone in seeking to safeguard its citizens from crooks selling "fertilizers." Indeed, potash adulterers had forced New York to require inspection as early as 1832.[42]

Mostly, though, American farmers objected to high prices. By all accounts Peruvian guano fostered fabulous yields, but at a cost so dear as to prevent its general use. In 1850, at a time when a single dollar could purchase a man's tailor-made suit, median agrarian income in the United States stood at about $690 annually, representing the return on a hypothetically average farm of 202 acres; yet, most American farmers—north, south, and west—actually tilled far smaller tracts of land, fewer than 100 acres, and earned substantially less than $200 annually. To expend half that annual income for merely enough bird droppings to fertilize 20 acres was an extravagance many farmers simply could not afford.[43]

The reason for high prices, it was widely believed, was the Gibbs monopoly. To "bring about an abolition of the monopoly of the export of guano from Peru which is now enjoyed by British subjects" would be highly advantageous to the United States, or so contended Richard Pollard, one-time American chargé d'affaires in Chile.[44] "A free trade in *guano* would bring the price down from $50 to something like $10 the ton with us," he asserted.[45] Pollard, who had left the diplomatic service to farm land in Albermarle County, Virginia, believed that his government should do something about the situation. So too did members of the State Agricultural Society of Maryland who urged the U.S. Department of State to open negotiations to secure whatever agreement was necessary to provide the commodity "on the same terms" as the citizens of other nations.[46]

Many members of Congress agreed. Given the size and significance of the agrarian sector in the U.S economy at mid-nineteenth century, it would have been unnatural for politicians not to pay particular attention to farmers and their complaints. In 1850 eight of every ten Americans lived on farms, and agriculture accounted for three fourths of the nation's economic output. Although that dominance rapidly eroded as the United States industrialized (the nonfarm proportion of the private sector overtaking agriculture in terms of economic output about the time of the Civil War, and accounting for twice as much of Gross National Product as the farm by the 1870s), it was not until 1920 that the country's urban population was larger than its rural.[47]

As early as 1844 American farmers had begun besieging their representatives in Washington to do something, anything, to assist them in acquiring guano cheaper. For instance, dozens of Marylanders asked that the duty on the commodity, a 20 percent excise tax that also applied to a wide array of other imports, be eliminated entirely.[48] Congress responded, adding guano to the duty-free list by 1847.[49] Many legislators were undoubtedly convinced that bird droppings held great promise for farmers because some of them had personally used it. For instance, Senator Daniel Webster reportedly had "paid a high price for it to improve the fertility of his fields at Marshfield."[50]

Probably no one in Congress was more mindful of bird feces than Senator Thomas G. Pratt of Maryland who could count numerous interested constituents, such as those persons conducting business at the port of Baltimore through which most of the commodity then passed as well as thousands of farmers throughout his state. On June 10, 1850, as the Senate paused in momentous debate about slavery and the territories that eventually resulted in the Compromise of 1850, which forestalled civil war for a decade, Pratt introduced a resolution asking the Taylor administration if "the government of Peru . . . place[ed] the citizens of the United States on an equal footing with the citizens or subjects of other countries in regard to the [guano] trade,"[51] and, if not, would a bilateral trade agreement be an appropriate remedy? The Senate passed the resolution unanimously and directed it to Secretary of State John M. Clayton.[52]

Guano had in fact been a matter of ongoing official discussion between the United States and Peru for much of the past year. Relations between the two countries, says Pulitzer Prize-winning historian Roy Nichols, "at that time were highly unsatisfactory."[53] Peru had reneged on an 1841 agreement to compensate American citizens for damages suffered in its revolution against Spain two decades earlier, and one of those claimants, L. S. Suarez of New York, had even suggested that Peru "discharge its obligations . . . [with] Chinca islands guano," an idea that Zachary Taylor's Department of State actively pursued, to no avail.[54]

Moreover, in 1848 a commercial treaty between the two nations (intended to replace one negotiated ten years earlier between the United States and the short-lived Peru-Bolivia Confederation, but which had been repudiated by the Congress of Peru) was likewise rejected, allegedly the victim of political intrigue. Peruvian president Ramón Castilla was said to be eager to be rid of a powerful and popular opponent, José Manuel Tirado, and Castilla reportedly had the wholly acceptable treaty killed in order to create an important foreign mission on which to send Tirado and "remove him from the field."[55]

Once in the United States, Minister Tirado apparently practiced some Machiavellian politics of his own. When Secretary Clayton suggested that "a free trade in guano between the United States and Peru would materially strengthen the good understanding between the two countries,"[56] Tirado (while insisting the commodity was "not monopolized") replied,

> Happily, however, as the time approaches for the final liquidation of the mortgage [held by Gibbs and others] . . . I flatter myself with the hope, that, as your excellency desires it, the day is not very far off when the United States, as well as the rest of the world, will be supplied with guano through the government of Peru directly—said guano being sold in Peruvian ports to those who go there in search of it, or a moderate duty being imposed upon the exportation of the same. . . .[57]

With no personal stake "in the existing arrangement [which] lined the pockets of [Castilla] administration officials,"[58] and no doubt delighted to embarrass Castilla, Tirado agreed to include in the new treaty a proviso that, should Peru ever open the guano trade to direct export, "Peru shall not exact from citizens or vessels of the United States that may go there in search of guano, in competition with those of other nations, a higher price or higher duties than what they may exact from . . . the most favored nation."[59] Signed on July 13, 1850, and promptly ratified by the U.S. Senate, the Clayton-Tirado Treaty was summarily repudiated by Castilla's government in Peru, and Tirado was abruptly recalled—amid widespread suspicions in the United States that Gibbs had bribed Castilla.[60]

Clayton also soon left office, his departure occasioned by Zachary Taylor's sudden death four days before the doomed treaty was signed by Clayton and Tirado. Taylor's successor, Millard Fillmore (often derided by historians as shallow and weak) exercised what one biographer has characterized as "relatively mild revenge" on political enemies in his predecessor's cabinet who had snubbed, even ridiculed, him by firing them all—including "the able and vigorous, . . . if occasionally intoxicated John Clayton. . . ." The new president replaced him with Daniel Webster who "gradually became for Millard Fillmore little more than a prestigious figurehead." Webster, elderly and often ill, soon was frequently retreating to his estate at Marshfield, thereby forcing Fillmore "to take a more active role in determining foreign policy."[61]

Although ailing, Secretary Webster nevertheless kept his hand in what Roy Nichols has called America's "guano diplomacy."[62] Webster instructed J. Randolph Clay, American chargé d'affaires in Lima, to revive the dead treaty if at all possible, including the section devoted to bird droppings. Clay tried, especially after Castilla was succeeded in office by General Rufiro Echenique, but the new president refused to discuss the matter. Clay reported to Washington in the fall of 1851 that the Clayton-Tirado Treaty was beyond resuscitation.[63]

Aware that "there was no possibility of negotiating a modification of Peruvian policy," says diplomatic historian Kenneth Shewmaker, Secretary Webster for a time allowed the subject to lapse even though "he had become fully aware of the importance of Peru's fertilizer to the South Atlantic states. . . ." He was "well versed on bird lime, even to the extent of how many pounds to use per acre and how to plow it in. . . ." About then he even tried "to purchase several tons of 'good Peruvian guano, at a reasonable rate,' for his estate at Marshfield," but apparently without success.[64]

Meanwhile, Webster had also dutifully forwarded to the U.S. Senate the views of J. Randolph Clay from Lima, to whom Secretary Clayton (just before departing office) had addressed a request for more information about the guano trade. Clay reported that the house of Gibbs, in return for frequent loans to Peru, had been given an extension in its "consignment of this article until the year 1855 . . . with reference to shipments of guano to England." Technically, Gibbs no longer held the franchise for the United States, but it "continues to make shipments for account of the government, under special license from the [Peruvian] President."[65]

The American diplomat estimated that the guano trade aggregated in value $3 million annually, "about one-third of which is clear profit to the State, . . . [and] I feel perfectly assured that [the Peruvian] government will not consent to make any change in its present method of disposing of the article." He doubted that Gibbs had bribed President Castilla, as had been alleged,[66] and dismissed as "essentially erroneous" the assertions of persons such as Richard Pollard that a free trade in guano would reduce its cost to American farmers from $50 to $10 a ton because Peru collected between $12 and $17 for each ton exported. When the costs of mining, shipping, handling, and merchandising were added, Clay thought a price of $47 a ton, f.o.b. Baltimore, was not exorbitant.[67]

The new American president believed otherwise. On December 2, 1850, in his first state of the union message, Fillmore called particular attention to guano. Amid remarks about such monumental matters as slavery, the increasing significance of foreign trade and commerce to the well-being of the national economy, and the growing importance of the United States in the international arena, he said,

> Peruvian guano has become so desirable an article to the agricultural interests in the United States that it is the duty of the Government to employ all the means properly in its power for the purpose of causing that article to be imported into the country at a reasonable price. Nothing will be omitted on my part toward accomplishing this desirable end. I am persuaded that in removing any restraint on this traffic the Peruvian Government will promote its own best interests, while it will afford a proof of a friendly disposition toward this country, which will be duly appreciated.[68]

However, he offered no specific proposal to Congress, and the commodity's price continued to soar.[69]

According to Samuel E. George of Baltimore, a dry-goods merchant and agent for Gibbs & Sons since 1844, the situation was unlikely to improve, because

> a new contract has been effected by the Peruvian Govt, with a party of "Nacionales" (native Peruvians) for the period of ten years to take affect [sic] next April and to extend over the *whole world,* except Gt Britain and such portions of Europe as are now included in Mesr Gibbs & Co.'s contract made last May for a period of five years at the expiration of which time, the native party are also empowered to supply these Countries—of course, [with] the same powers of exclusive export [as] are now granted, which have always existed under the contract of my

> principals. . . . the "monopoly" will therefore merely change hands without any modification.[70]

Unless President Fillmore was prepared "to buy the Chinca islands or to capture them," George saw little "our Gov[ernmen]t can do . . . towards cheapening the article, unless it provides a Bounty for the importer, to be deducted from the price charged to the Farmer, thus benefiting the Farmer."[71]

Samuel George and Edwin Bartlett of New York, who likewise had handled guano for Gibbs, were replaced as agents under a new agreement in 1851 between the Peruvian government and Felipe and Federico Barreda whose firm (Felipe Barreda and Brother) had offices in Lima, Baltimore, and, later, New York. The international enterprise was very well connected. The Barredas were brothers-in-law of Juan Ignacio de Osma, the new Peruvian envoy to the United States; indeed, Osma and his brother Joaquin, the Peruvian foreign minister, were silent partners of the Barreda brothers in the guano business. Soon after he moved to Baltimore to oversee operations there, Federico Barreda recruited Solon Robinson, an agricultural journalist whose articles praising guano had appeared in *De Bow's Review, Southern Agriculturalist,* and *Soil of the South,* to be their chief salesman. After becoming associated with the Barredas, Robinson penned a treatise on the fertilizer that he published in 1852, perhaps with the financial backing of his employers. In any case, he was soon selling $20,000 worth of Peruvian guano a month.[72]

The Barreda franchise reflected the first serious attempt by that government to free itself from dependence upon foreign firms such as Gibbs of London and Montané of Paris, both of which lent it money in return for guano concessions. Lima wished to encourage in their place *hijos del pais* (native sons) as entrepreneurs, who nevertheless offered no prospect of lower prices for foreign consumers, as in the United States. As merchant Samuel E. George of Baltimore had observed, the monopoly merely changed hands.[73]

Even though the price of Peruvian guano continued to climb, averaging $52.60 a ton over the ensuing decade, its popularity nonetheless steadily increased among American farmers. By 1850 it accounted for 22 percent of all commercial fertilizer consumed in the United States; ten years later, by which time planters had tripled their use of fertilizers in general, guano represented 43 percent of the total, despite an average price of $73 a ton.[74]

Strong demand and rising prices naturally attracted entrepreneurs who readily perceived the opportunity for profit, especially with governmental assistance.

# 2

## The Entrepreneur and Daniel Webster

Convergence of supply, demand, price, and politics produced the scent of scandal in 1852 when Brooklyn businessman Alfred G. Benson allegedly attempted to loot a Peruvian island of its bird droppings with the help of American officials. Before the air had cleared, the distinguished secretary of State, Daniel Webster (publicly accused of misconduct in the matter), found himself splattered with muck. Coincidentally, the ponderous machinery of the United States government was nudged into motion, inexorably toward empire.

What contemporary journalists eventually dubbed the "Guano War"[1] originated with Benson's desire to fill the cargo holds of his clipper ships that were returning empty to the East coast from the gold fields of California. Perhaps unfairly, some writers have cast him as villain in what is also known to diplomatic historians as the "Lobos affair." As Roy Nichols once dryly observed, "The guano business was apt to be a dirty one. . . ."[2]

Not much is known of Benson, except that he was "a prominent New York merchant"[3] said to be engaged "in several enterprises of value to New York and Brooklyn." He was obviously alert to business opportunities, to the prospect of profit. Born about 1807 in Maine,[4] Alfred Grenville Benson had moved to bustling Brooklyn, New York, while still "in his youth."

About 1829 he engaged "with a Mr. Buck" in the shipping trade as Buck & Benson. When Buck retired, Benson took over, eventually bringing his brother, Arthur, into the business, which styled itself as A. G. & A. W. Benson.[5]

In 1841 on "the advice of Mr. Webster,"[6] then secretary of State, John Tyler's administration approached Alfred Benson "in confidence . . . to establish a line of transport ships to the Oregon Territory, conveying fifty passengers each trip without charge, upon the condition that [the Bensons] should have the benefit of transporting all the government supplies to the Pacific at the rate of $3 per barrel freight."[7] Eager to reinforce American claims to the Oregon Territory without alerting the British by soliciting open bids, "the President has deemed that considerations of state policy" justified the clandestine arrangement.[8]

A. G. & A. W. Benson promptly sent agents to Oregon, California, and Hawaii and launched numerous "ship loads of merchandise and passengers, both overland and round the Cape, . . . to Oregon,"[9] which then included everything between California and Alaska and which was jointly claimed and occupied by citizens of both the United States and Great Britain. Company ships also were soon hauling Pacific Northwest timber back to shipyards along the American East coast, thereby supplementing the Bensons' revenues. For a time the arrangement appears to have been profitable and mutually beneficial. In fact, in 1845 U.S. Secretary of the Navy John Y. Mason judged that the Bensons had "fully complied with their part of the agreement . . . [and were] entitled to the freight."[10]

Entitled or not, they encountered problems. Bound ultimately for Manila, their bark *Xylon* sailed from New York in 1846 with supplies for the U.S. Navy's Pacific squadron that was said to be at anchor in the Mexican port of Mazatlán. When the merchantman arrived, its captain discovered that the United States was at war with Mexico, that the American squadron had vanished without trace, and that he best depart enemy waters. Expecting to deposit his cargo with the resident American government agent in Honolulu, where the Yankee fleet regularly called to maintain order among American vessels that frequented the port, he sailed to Hawaii only to have the agent refuse to accept the goods. Thus, before proceeding to Manila, *Xylon*'s skipper was forced to detour to San Francisco, trusting that the squadron was there, as reported in Honolulu, annexing Mexican California for the United States. It was, but American sailors demanded delivery in Monterey, which took additional time. Although the Navy department in due course dutifully paid regular freight charges, it refused to compensate the Bensons for the lost time of a broken voyage or for the risks they had unwittingly undertaken.[11]

Alfred Benson also alleged that he had been "abandoned by the Government [in Oregon] . . . and left . . . to take care of myself in opposition to the powerful influence of the Hudson Bay Company, to protect me from which, was one of the prime objects of the contract."[12] Worse, after the Democrats won the White House in the election of 1844, "a subsequent Secretary of the Navy, . . . without any notice . . . deprived [the Bensons] of the right of transporting a large part of the supplies destined for the Pacific, and to the transportation [business] to which they were clearly entitled." As result, they reportedly suffered substantial damage.[13] Even though they successfully appealed to Congress to redress their grievances and even though Daniel Webster (back in the Senate and acting as their attorney) intervened with the Navy, they collected merely $18,000 of the $100,000 that Alfred Benson calculated they had lost.[14]

Fortunately for the Bensons, who operated a fleet of clipper ships, "California gold fever broke out . . . [about then and] many of the earliest emigrants to San Francisco were transported in them."[15] Alfred Benson also held numerous other business interests, including a partnership in a New York City river ferry. During the early 1850s he contracted to build dry docks and a marine railway in Honolulu and, in association with Dr. Gerrit P. Judd (an American medical missionary and, frequently, a minister of the royal Hawaiian government), Benson attempted to establish a steamship line between Hawaii and San Francisco that promised a far faster, more direct connection than the circuitous sail necessitated by currents and prevailing winds out of Hawaii, but the venture failed to materialize. Neither did Benson's 1850 proposal to establish a steamship line (with financial underwriting from Washington) between the United States and China.[16] "Shipping magnate" Benson even once offered "to buy the [Hawaiian] Islands for five million dollars . . . [which], it was understood, would lead to annexation by the United States,"[17] an offer apparently declined by the king.

Benson seems to have been very well connected politically. He was either a "long-time friend of [Daniel] Webster,"[18] or, at the very least, was "familiar with him on a social basis."[19] They probably were introduced by Charles March, the Woodstock, Vermont, attorney with whom Webster once practiced law, and who, reportedly, was one of Benson's many business associates.[20] Whatever the circumstances of their acquaintance, in 1837 Benson offered to take Webster's son and namesake into a land development scheme that promised to yield "a little fortune,"[21] but apparently nothing came of the proposition. Perhaps Secretary Webster returned the gesture in 1841 by recommending Benson to President Tyler as the administration's clandestine merchant-shipper to the Pacific. In any case, when the arrangement soured, Senator Webster became Benson's lawyer and represented his interests with the government.[22]

Webster and Benson obviously shared views, and values. Both favored aggressive commercial development of the United States as well as avoidance of a costly conflict over slavery. A Whig, Benson was one "of one hundred outstanding [New York] merchants" who banded together as the Union Safety

Committee in support of the Compromise of 1850 "to strengthen Union forces in the Empire State, and in this way to consolidate the Union movement throughout the nation." As a member of its Committee on Correspondence, he wrote Senator Webster, the Compromise's principal proponent in Congress, to urge perseverance.[23]

It was the legendary lawmaker's last great achievement. A larger-than-life political leader, Daniel Webster (1782-1852) burst onto the national scene during the War of 1812 as an outspoken opponent of the conflict, a view that had swept him from the backwoods of New Hampshire into Congress where he faithfully represented New England's current commercial and maritime interests by opposing, among other things, the protective features of the Tariff of 1816. Webster's positions then were entirely parochial (strict constructionist, states' rights, and *laissez faire*) but, like the region he represented, his position evolved over time to become more nationalistic and more Hamiltonian, which meant that he came to support the public assistance of private enterprise.[24]

In 1816 Webster moved to Boston to seek his fortune. He quickly established a lucrative legal practice, representing business clients mostly, and soon was the nation's premier authority on constitutional law. Before the U.S. Supreme Court he argued and won many of the era's landmark decisions—*Dartmouth College* v. *Woodward* (1819), *McCullough* v. *Maryland* (1819), *Gibbons* v. *Ogden* (1824)—which sanctified contracts and upheld federal rather than state powers. His successful clients who helped reelect him to Congress in 1822 also "allowed him to buy stock . . . in their rather exclusive corporations . . . and paid him fat fees. . . . During the 1820s he was probably the most highly paid lawyer in the United States,"[25] and, as lore and literature would eventually insist, one fully capable of besting the devil himself in debate.

By the time formidable Daniel Webster had entered the Senate from Massachusetts in 1827 he was an ardent nationalist and unabashed protectionist, and, with such giants as Henry Clay and John C. Calhoun, came to dominate the upper chamber of Congress. While Webster steadfastly opposed secession and states' rights, he strongly supported protective tariffs, government-sponsored internal improvements, and the Bank of the United States. He also vehemently criticized the fiscal and monetary policies of Presidents Andrew Jackson and Martin Van Buren. Acquiring a reputation second to none as orator, three times (in 1836, 1840, and 1852) Webster tried but failed to win the Whig nomination for president.[26]

Twice he served as secretary of State, first under presidents William Henry Harrison and John Tyler (1841-43), then under Millard Fillmore

(1850-52). Secretary Webster's signal achievement during his first stint in the cabinet was the Webster-Ashburton Treaty (1842) that fixed the Maine-Canada border, a long-standing irritant in British-American relations. At the end of his second term, he became mired with Benson in the Lobos mess. "All my concerns in this department," he remarked not long before his death, "have never given me so much disturbance as this Lobos business."[27]

Situated between fourteen and twenty-four miles off Peru's Punta Negra, the Lobos (or Seal) islands (Lobos de Afuera and Lobos de Tierra, respectively) are usually uninhabited dots of land comprising less than one square mile each. Rugged, metamorphic islets of slate-gray schist that had been glazed white by eons of bird droppings, the Lobos (save for occasional raids by American seal hunters) were largely undisturbed rookeries and nesting sites for countless seafowl, especially cormorants, gannets, pelicans, and terns, throughout the mid-nineteenth century. Bird deposits were forty feet thick in places, and the islands' mostly arid climate caused avian feces to aggregate into cementlike layers that, eventually, had to be mined with dynamite and pickaxes. Total reserves for the Lobos islands apparently were never calculated, but the Peruvian government once estimated that Lobos de Tierra alone contained more than a half million cubic yards of guano, approximately eight hundred thousand tons. In 1842 Peru officially closed these islands to foreign ships, thereby reserving them for future exploitation once deposits on the prized Chincas had been exhausted.[28]

While Alfred Benson was probably unaware of this action, in 1851 he unquestionably "obtained information that heavy deposits of excellent Guano existed on the uninhabited Islands of Lobos de Afuera, lying some forty miles [*sic*] off the coast of Peru," and he asked James C. Jewett, master of the bark *Philomela* in which Benson held an interest, to inspect them when next on the Pacific coast.[29] By the time Jewett returned the following spring, Benson had also learned of British interest in the islands. In 1851 an English entrepreneur, T. Wentworth Butler, had written Viscount J. H. T. Palmerston, the foreign minister, to call his attention to the Lobos islands and their guano, which he said he had read about in American mariner Benjamin Morrell's memoirs. Butler believed the islands sufficiently offshore to be unclaimed and unoccupied, and he asked Palmerston to send her majesty's navy to verify this fact and to protect British vessels that might wish to load its bird droppings.[30]

Palmerston declined, saying he thought the islands probably belonged to Peru. They certainly were not British property. Nevertheless, the issue did not immediately die, for English farmers and shippers were soon petitioning Parliament for action. The clamor reached the House of Commons on May 14, 1852, when Prime Minister John Russell was asked to explain his cabinet's reluctance to procure this cheap fertilizer for the realm's agrarian sector. In response, he had printed all his government's correspondence on the subject, which reiterated the official British view that the Lobos were Peruvian property.[31]

The matter was widely reported in the British and American press about the time Captain Jewett returned from the Pacific following his inspection of the islands.[32] Because journalists had "intimated that American citizens had acquired a right to said islands by their long and uninterrupted occupancy of them [*sic*]," Benson later said, he "resolved to be early in the field, and to fit out a number of vessels to go to said islands for loads of Guano," provided his government (unlike the British) did not object.[33]

Given his longstanding personal acquaintance with Webster, Benson's decision to be a silent partner in the venture seems especially peculiar. Rather than inquire personally, he directed Captain Jewett to contact the secretary of State. Without mentioning Benson, Jewett dutifully wrote Webster on June 2, 1852, explaining that he had "recently returned from the Pacific" where he might have "proceeded to the Island of Lobos, adjacent to the coast of South America, for a cargo of Guano," had he known whether or not the stuff might be "rightfully taken by a citizen of the United States. . . ." Jewett added that he was "informed that no Government has any rightful claim to these islands," but he hesitated to act because he was "unwilling to violate any treaty the Government of my own country may have entered into, or any provision of the law of nations. . . ."[34]

What followed has evoked assorted explanations. Perhaps, as historian Roy Nichols has speculated, Webster was still suffering from a recent spill from his carriage—the victim of concussion complicated by age and infirmity: addled thinking. Perhaps, distracted that summer by interest in and failure to capture the presidential nomination, he and President Fillmore (both of whom were rejected by the Whigs) were merely inattentive. Perhaps, as eventually speculated about in the press, Webster stood to gain personally. Or, perhaps, as he later claimed, Webster was misled by Jewett.[35] More likely, as diplomatic historian Kenneth Shewmaker has asserted, Webster was poorly served by an understaffed State department that was composed mostly of unprofessional bureaucrats who should have but did not challenge the secretary's thinking that by "affording naval protection to guano entrepreneurs both American shippers and American farmers would be greatly benefited."[36]

Probably for a complex combination of reasons and circumstances, the secretary questioned any possible Peruvian claim to the Lobos islands. After soliciting a White House review of his proposed response to Jewett (which elicited the marginal note, "Approved June 5, M. F.") Webster immediately advised the mariner by letter that "it may be considered the duty of this government to protect citizens of the United States who may visit the Lobos islands for the purpose of obtaining guano." The secretary cited three reasons for his view: that the Lobos "lay five or six times" more distant from the continent than a marine league, or the three-mile territorial limit then recognized by the United States and many other nations; that the State department was unaware "that the Lobos were [ever] discovered or occupied by Spain or Peru, or that the guano on them" had ever been exploited by anyone; and that since American mariner "Benjamin Morrell . . . visited those islands in September, 1823, [he] may justly claim to have been their discoverer."[37]

Webster informed Jewett that he would send a copy of his "letter to the Secretary of the Navy [William Alexander Graham], and suggest that a vessel-of-war be ordered to repair to the Lobos islands, for the purpose of protecting from molestation any of our citizens who may wish to take guano from them." Scribbled by Webster's own hand was a postscript he would come regret: "It is considered important that this letter should not be made public at present."[38]

Benson was incredulous. Having dealt unsatisfactorily with politicians before, he later mused,

> You will ask why, under such circumstances, I trusted the Government again, and I answer that I thought if it said I had a right to go and take guano from the Lobos Islands, and would send a force there to protect me, [that] there would be no change during the present administration, and that the business would be settled before the next came to power; but I did not trust to the letter of Mr. Webster alone, but directed Captain Jewett to go to Washington and ascertain if the orders referred to in Mr. Webster's letter had gone.[39]

On June 9 Jewett met with Navy secretary Graham, who "rather reproved [Jewett] for [even] asking such a question, stating that 'Mr. Webster's letter was the act of the Government. . . .' "[40] The U.S. Navy's Pacific squadron, commanded by Commodore F. S. McCauley, regularly patrolled Peru's Chinca islands "to maintain order among the unruly merchant seamen" loading guano there, "as well as to make sure that American interests did not suffer unduly from the whims of the Peruvian government."[41] Graham informed Jewett that orders had already been dispatched by mail steamer to McCauley. Jewett wired Benson: "Orders issued yesterday to Commodore for full protection."[42]

That confirmation apparently changed everything. Instead of merely filling the holds of ships regularly returning from California and the Pacific as originally contemplated, Benson obviously saw the chance to make a fortune. He quickly laid plans to import two hundred thousand tons of feces that he proposed to sell at $35 per ton, or about 40 percent below current prices, which he calculated would gross $7 million; after deducting loading costs estimated at $5 a ton and freight expense of about $15 a ton, he anticipated a $3 million profit.[43] He solicited investors, reportedly including "some of Fillmore's wealthy political friends."[44] Joining Benson "were numerous Wall Street entrepreneurs, including the politically active Hiram Ketchum, one of the city's largest capitalists."[45]

Reassured by Secretary Graham, Benson later said, and "relying implicitly on the faith of the Government, I proceeded immediately to fit out a commercial expedition, which in point of magnitude . . . would be at once honor to American enterprise, and a source of profit and wealth. . . ." He loaded the three hundred-ton bark *Sarah Chase* with mining tools and provisions, installed a nine pound cannon on her deck, provided small arms and cutlasses for a crew of forty men, and dispatched it from New York to Lobos de Afuera, simultaneously directing his agent in Honolulu to outfit another ship similarly and to employ a hundred Hawaiian laborers. Benson then chartered all the vessels he could find to sail for the Lobos to load guano, eventually contracting the services of ninety-two ships from eastern U.S. ports and from Honolulu. He also sent agents to England where they contracted to deliver one hundred thousand tons of guano to wholesale merchants over the next two years. All told, he and his associates claimed to have expended about $1 million in the enterprise.[46]

Despite Webster's desire that the matter "not be made public at present,"[47] it soon became common knowledge. Citing an article in the *Boston Daily Advertiser,* prominent Boston merchant and shipbuilder Thatcher Magoun wrote Secretary Webster on June 7 to inquire if it was true "that the government of the United States had offered to protect American ships in procuring 'Guano' from the recently discovered 'Lobos de Fuero' [*sic*]. . . ." Webster promptly replied that "the Navy Department has ordered a vessel of war to those Islands for the purpose of protecting such vessels of the United States as may wish to load guano there."[48] Similar inquiries were directed by Magoun and by Dana & Company of Boston to Navy secretary Graham, who quickly confirmed Webster's stated policy. These replies were published in various American newspapers, leading more ships to sail for the Lobos.[49]

News reports also attracted the attention of Juan Ignacio de Osma, Peru's chargé d'affaires who, as a silent partner with the Barreda brothers in the guano business, had a vested interest in maintaining the Peruvian monopoly. Osma sent newspaper clippings to Lima to alert his brother Joaquin, the Peruvian foreign minister and likewise a Barreda investor. J. I. de Osma also wrote Secretary Webster on June 25 to assert his nation's authority over the Lobos islands, adding that he intended to publish "a warning to ship owners and other merchants . . . [of] the laws of Peru on the subject."[50]

On July 2, J. I. de Osma saw Fillmore and Webster separately. To each he expressed his concern over reports of American commercial raids on Peruvian territory. Fillmore listened politely but expressed no opinion on the matter; however, Webster bluntly told Osma that the United States did not recognize Peruvian claim to the Lobos and would protect its citizens who gathered guano there. The following day Osma wrote Webster to request that the secretary's views "on so serious a subject"[51] be expressed in writing so that he might convey them to his government in Lima. Osma repeated the request on August 9 that was accompanied by a lengthy discourse on his nation's claims to the islands as well as a blistering denunciation of American violation of Peruvian sovereignty. By then Osma's warning to mariners had appeared in numerous American newspapers. Alerted to the issue, the U.S. Senate asked to see the State department's correspondence on the Lobos islands.[52]

Webster's health was deteriorating, and for much of the summer he retreated to Marshfield to escape Washington's oppressive heat; therefore, he did not reply to Osma until August 21. By then the circumstances had changed appreciably. For one thing, the State department had received a dispatch "rich in historical irony" from J. Randolph Clay, U.S. envoy in Lima. "Disturbed by reading in the London *Times* that British adventurers were sending vessels to the Lobos Islands," says historian Shewmaker, "Clay stated that Peruvian sovereignty over those islands was incontestable and that Lima would probably seize the English intruders."[53]

As yet unaware of Clay's report, President Fillmore already was questioning his secretary's foreign policy. Failing to remember either Webster's letter to Jewett or his own initials of approval on it, Fillmore (while Webster was away from the capital) reviewed a draft of the State department's proposed response to J. I. de Osma that questioned Peruvian sovereignty over the Lobos on a variety of grounds, including occupancy and proximity. The president understood the diplomatic argument (that, being so far to sea, the islands "must, like the ocean, be deemed common property to all nations, to be used by each in its own convenience in such a way as not to prejudice the rights of all others") but he confessed to being squeamish about the matter. Because "of the weakness of Peru," he confessed, "I shall be very unwilling to extract from her what I would be unwilling to claim, under similar circumstances, from Great Britain or France. . . ."[54] Nevertheless, he did not immediately order Webster to alter course.

More than a month passed before Secretary Webster returned to Washington. Meanwhile, J. Randolph Clay in Lima had again written the State department regarding the Lobos islands, this time to convey a warning from Peruvian foreign minister J. J. de Osma regarding American vessels, which had been reported by Washington chargé d'affaires J. I. de Osma to be sailing toward the islands "to load with huano" under U.S. Navy protection. Minister Osma had informed Clay that the islands were Peruvian property and "closed to foreign commerce. . . ."[55]

Clay said that when Webster's letters to Jewett and others had been published in Peru anti-American riots erupted in Lima, and, meeting in secret session, the Peruvian Congress authorized the government to increase the size of the army, to arm steamers, and to send troops to the Lobos, if necessary. Calling attention to his recent dispatch on the subject, the American chargé repeated his opinion that the Lobos were "incontestably . . . Peruvian." He added that, should the U.S. government "recognize the title of Peru to those islands, the vessels which may have sailed from the United States, to take huano at them, will not be seized or confiscated; but can at the option of their Captains . . . be chartered by Agents of the Peruvian Government [the Barreda brothers] to carry huano to the United States or England."[56]

About then, Jewett (still fronting for Benson and others and apparently angry at accusations that he had fabricated the pledge of U.S. naval protection) gave Webster's letter of June 5 (with its damaging postscript in old Daniel's own hand) to the *New York Herald,* which printed it on August 11. Jewett also wrote Webster to inform him that, having heard of threats from the Peruvian government, twenty ships in which he held an interest with friends had already departed for the Lobos; the bark *Sarah Chase* that had sailed on July 23 carried a copy of Webster's letter as authority, was armed, and was prepared to resist molestation with force, if necessary—U.S. Navy or no.[57]

Meanwhile, prospects of cheap guano from the Lobos had greatly excited journalists. The *New York Times* opined that Webster's declaration along with naval protection meant that soon "our farmers may expect to obtain this wonderful renovator of worn-out soils—more precious to them than California gold—at a moderate price."[58] The *Salem* (Massachusetts) *Gazette* reported that the frigate USS *Raritan* was already on station to protect the thirty or so local vessels en route "under the guarantee of Mr. Webster's letter."[59]

Yet, eyebrows were raised by Webster's postscript that seemed to afford Jewett and his still mute associates great advantage and, to some observers, implied that "Godlike Daniel" stood to profit personally, thereby justifying his other popular nickname—Black Dan. In Webster's defense the *Boston Journal* pointed to previously published epistles from both secretaries Webster and Graham to firms in its city that had openly spelled out U.S. policy. It was hardly secret. There was no conspiracy.[60] When merchant Hiram Ketchum, an acquaintance of both Benson and Webster[61] and, allegedly, a silent partner in Jewett and Benson's venture, offered Webster proof of intermittent American occupation of the Lobos, the secretary eagerly replied, "If there is any proof of that, for Mercy's sake let us have it."[62]

Until publication of the Jewett letter, Fillmore was unaware that "orders had been issued to our fleet," or so he claimed.[63] This revelation prompted his visit to the State department upon Webster's return to the capital to review relevant correspondence, including Clay's dispatches, which "left 'no reasonable doubt' in the president's mind that the Lobos belong to Peru. . . ."[64]

With no recollection of either having reviewed or approved Webster's letter to Jewett, as the secretary (and his assistant) insisted had been the case, Fillmore asked to see the original,which could not be produced because Webster had inadvertently taken it to Marshfield with him and left it behind—to be discovered among his personal papers after his death. Those copies in departmental files that were available for Fillmore's scrutiny also failed to carry Webster's curious postscript, which the secretary could neither recall having appended nor explain. Fillmore ordered Webster to change course, and the aging secretary complied. He also offered his resignation, but Fillmore—still a great admirer of the old man—refused to accept it.[65]

On August 21 Secretary Webster finally answered Peruvian chargé J. I. de Osma's repeated requests for a formal explanation of the American position. After a lengthy review of Peruvian claims based upon rights of discovery and use, which the secretary continued to question, and after a rejection of Peru's claims by virtue of proximity, which he dismissed because of American adherence to the concept of a three-mile territorial limit, Webster nevertheless acknowledged that his government "was prepared to give due considerations to all facts tending to show possession or occupancy of the Lobos islands by Peru. . . ." He added, "the President thinks it is most advisable . . . that proper orders be given to the naval forces of the United States . . . to prevent collision until further examination of the case." Furthermore, Webster said the U.S. government would not support its businessmen who resorted to force "in the prosecution of any commercial enterprises to those islands. Such acts would be acts of private war, and their authors would thereby forfeit the protection of their own government."[66]

Fillmore included Webster's letter to Osma in copies of the Lobos correspondence that he dutifully forwarded to the Senate that same day in compliance with its recent request for information. Within the week Webster's letter to Osma had also been published by numerous American newspapers, alerting shippers to impending peril. On August 25 John P. Kennedy, Fillmore's new Navy secretary, ordered Commodore McCauley "to abstain from aiding or abetting any citizen of the United States who may forcibly resist the execution of the laws of Peru. . . ."[67] Furthermore, Chargé Clay in Lima was instructed to tell McCauley "to prevent any attempt . . . to take away guano forcibly from those islands." Clay was also directed to try to repair the damage to U.S.-Peruvian relations.[68]

Later that same day Webster notified Jewett that since the secretary's most recent letter he had learned that "the Peruvian Government claims jurisdiction over those Islands," which by its laws were closed to foreign vessels. He warned that any resistance to Peruvian authority under force of arms, as implied by Jewett's letter of August 16, "would be an act of private war, which can never receive any countenance from this Government." Moreover, Webster charged that "Some of the statements contained in your letter of the 2d of June had a tendency to mislead us. . . ."[69] Jewett was outraged and wrote Fillmore demanding to know, "Will the government of my country compel me and my associate to the abandonment upon our part of the enterprise, and thus consign us to hopeless insolvency as a penalty for confiding in the protection of our government freely tendered?"[70]

Although Benson did not identify himself as the unnamed associate until early September, word of his involvement reached Webster about the time of his most recent letter to Jewett. On August 24 William Miles, one-time American commercial agent in Peru, had written the secretary somewhat cryptically from New York,

> I have heard with extreme interest the agitation of the Lobos Islands question, & have heard of Mr Bensons conduct during the whole of it, ie remarking how among the *traders to Peru* & their Bankers Alsop & Co &c that "he (*Benson*) had the government foul any how, & that it must see him out, & that he supposes that if Mr Webster knew Jewett's letter was for *him,* he would have seen him in a very bad place I can't mention before he would have given it," &c.[71]

There is no evidence whatsoever that Webster had previously been aware of Benson's involvement.

Benson broke the silence himself when he wrote President Fillmore on September 8 to complain of repeated shabby treatment by his own government, first in Oregon, then during the Mexican War, and now in the Lobos. He said that he, Jewett, and others had invested "nearly a million dollars" on the word of public officials, and Benson thought "the Government of the United States is bound to fulfill its obligations for all of the vessels which have been engaged to go there relying on its protection." If Peru required compensation for the guano under these circumstances, the U.S. government should pay for it because Benson and others had engaged in the enterprise at public encouragement, incurring large expenditures "in preparations to load hundreds of ships. . . ."[72] Fillmore sent the letter to Webster, who returned it with merely an expression of "concern about the Lobos business, but we will do as well as we can, & must trust to fortune." Webster expressed neither surprise nor dismay at Benson's involvement in the affair.[73]

Then, on September 24, the *New York Evening Post* charged that "A. G. Benson . . . has been speculating in guano with Mr. Webster,"[74] an allegation that hurt Webster deeply. Back at Marshfield and virtually on his death bed, he apparently chose not to refute the allegation; however, Benson sent emissaries and personally visited the newspaper repeatedly. He categorically denied any wrongdoing, trying in vain to convince an editor that the accusation was baseless and that it should be retracted. According to Benson, he and Webster "had quarreled, . . . and they had not spoken with each other for more than a year,"[75] which might explain Benson's original decision to hide his connection with the Lobos enterprise from Webster.

When Benson's visits failed to persuade the editor of his and Webster's innocence, the merchant offered his views to the rival *Daily Times,* which garbled Benson's disclaimer by stating that the businessman had personally spoken to *Evening Post* editor William Cullen Bryant when, in fact, Benson had merely identified "an editor." This evoked an angry letter to the *Times* from Bryant who said he had never met or talked with Benson about anything, much less Daniel Webster. Webster sympathetically wrote to Benson on September 30: "A portion of the Public Press of the United States has become, indeed, awfully wicked and corrupt."[76]

A few days before his death on October 24 Webster remarked that the thought of dying with such a serious but specious charge soiling his reputation "was exceedingly painful." He again professed his innocence, expressing hope "that when Mr. Bryant stands on the brink of the grave, as I do now, his conscience will be as clear of having performed the duty of justice toward my name."[77]

Not long after Webster's death, by exchange of correspondence with Peru, the United States seemingly settled the Lobos affair. On November 17 the new secretary of State, Edward Everett, formally conceded Peruvian sovereignty over the islands.[78] In return, Peruvian foreign minister J. J. de Osma reassured Everett that vessels which had sailed on Webster's word between June 5 and August 25 would be allowed to load Chinca island guano for $20 a ton under recharter to the Peruvian government's American consignee, Felipe Barreda and Brother of Baltimore and New York. Moreover, mining equipment and supplies carried by American vessels would "be taken on account by the government. . . ."[79]

The understanding effectively blocked any chance Benson had of recovering his investment—perhaps as punishment for having precipitated the affair. Secretary Everett observed that, under the circumstances, "the arrangement" was as advantageous as possible for ship owners. As for speculators and "their extravagant expectations of immense profits," it would likely be otherwise. He instructed Chargé Clay in Lima to be watchful for "frauds . . . attempted . . . on the Peruvian government" by bogus charter contracts.[80]

Benson's guano fleet met assorted fates—all of them disastrous for the Brooklyn businessman. Notwithstanding Jewett's bravado in his second letter to Webster, *Sarah Chase* surrendered meekly when confronted by the Peruvian Navy which, after confiscating tools and cannon, detained the ship in port at Callao for months; when she finally sailed for home, her cargo hold was empty. Upon being informed that they might take Chinca guano at $20 a ton ($7 higher than the usual Peruvian severance fee, and $15 more than Benson had guaranteed to pay upon delivery), many of Benson's other "charter parties" renounced their agreements with the businessman, sailed to ports of opportunity for such freight as could be found, then returned home. Benson (whose signature adorned their contracts) was held personally "responsible for the full amount due on their charters."[81]

Other ships rechartered with the Peruvian government and paid $20 a ton, cash, to take on board guano destined for the Barreda brothers with the understanding that the consignee would reimburse carriers for the severance tax as well as pay an additional $20 a ton freight. Upon arrival in the United States, many captains discovered instead that the Barredas "refused to pay twenty silver (or hard) dollars a ton freight in any instance, and upon such ships as they chose to pay at all, they have paid a freight of only nineteen paper dollars a ton." Many shippers sued Benson, some "for additional pay," others for "an absolute breach of charter party." He reportedly lost most of these cases and consequently faced "complete ruin."[82]

Contending that he had been "induced" into the mess "by the pledges of his Government" and forced to rely upon newspaper reports for essential details of the arrangement with Peru, Benson besieged the State department for information and assistance that might extricate him. Fair was fair, he argued: if he must pay for the guano, he should either receive it or be reimbursed by the Barreda brothers for the $20 a ton his charter parties had paid in Peru. Secretary Everett sent Benson's plea to Lima, where Minister J. J. de Osma rejected it out of hand.[83]

Soon after Democrat Franklin Pierce was inaugurated president in 1853, Benson again begged the State department for help. Secretary William L. Marcy consequently asked Peru to reconsider, at least insofar as those ships that had rechartered with the Barreda brothers and had been shorted on freight payments. The Barredas eventually agreed to pay Benson about $35,000, only two thirds of which they actually remitted. Benson once more complained, and in April 1855 Marcy advised the businessman to pursue "a suit at law. . . ."[84]

Benson chose instead to exercise his First Amendment right to petition Congress for a redress of grievances. In January 1855 he compiled and printed a twenty-eight page *Memorial of Alfred G. Benson to the Senate and House of Representatives of the United States* that included his version of events as well as his (and others') correspondence with public officials about the Lobos islands. He asserted that he had been lured into "a disastrous expedition . . . by pledges of his Government to support him," which were not kept; therefore, in consideration of his losses, he asked Congress to "award him such compensation and repayment thereof as may be just and proper."[85]

Such petitions, mostly praying public action for private relief, were increasing at such a rate that, in time, they very nearly clogged the machinery of American government. While the First Congress of the United States (1789-91) enacted merely ten "private bills" (8.6 percent of the total legislation that session), all of which were signed into law by President George Washington, their numbers thereafter increased proportionally and absolutely. In the Twentieth Congress (1827-29), 101 laws (43 percent) were private relief measures, and by the time Benson's bill first came before Congress in 1855 an estimated one half of all legislation was private. In fact, the problem had become so pronounced that Congress created the U.S. Court of Claims in 1855 expressly for the purpose of studying and reporting on such matters; however, most legislators could not bring themselves to refer more than a handful of constituents' complaints to the bench for adjudication. Therefore, not until 1911 was there any meaningful reform designed to unstop the legislative process by mandating most "memorials" to the court.

Before that occurred, much legislative time and energy had been expended on constituents' causes.[86]

A few legislators considered private claims to be an anathema. In 1832 Massachusetts Congressman John Quincy Adams, who had vetoed no private legislation while president (1825-29), complained that "One-half the time of Congress is consumed by it, and there is no common rule of justice for any two cases decided."[87] Yet, most of his colleagues obviously reveled in such seeming trivia, for it provided inexpensive opportunities to earn plaudits from constituents, most of whom mistakenly believed that the introduction of private bills was an onerous burden for lawmakers. Much to the contrary, even relief measures that failed of passage often gained the gratitude of interested voters. Furthermore, as a matter of common courtesy, rarely did legislators raise serious objections to private matters proposed by their colleagues, for to do so was to court their wrath (and obstruction) in retaliation.[88]

Like Adams, most nineteenth-century American presidents were reluctant to block private legislation, the majority of which provided pensions for widows, aid for orphans, citizenship for those who otherwise did not qualify, or direct financial relief for some terrible calamity. Not until James Madison (the nation's fourth chief executive) vetoed two private bills in 1811 was any private legislation turned aside. Thereafter, until U. S. Grant (1869-77) nixed sixty-six measures (only three of which were overturned by congressional votes), did any chief executive demur more than twice to provide public assistance for private problems. Not even President Abraham Lincoln (who urged Congress in his 1861 state-of-the-union message to refer more private matters to the Court of Claims, which had been expressly created to adjudicate such matters) could bring himself to exercise more than a single pocket veto.[89]

Thus, when Senator William H. Seward of New York presented Benson's memorial "praying indemnity for losses" in the Lobos affair to his colleagues on February 1, 1855, it seemed destined for prompt approval. The measure was routinely referred to the Committee on Claims which on February 24 requested that President Pierce share with it relevant correspondence related to Benson and the Lobos islands. For reasons that are not entirely clear, the administration failed to respond to that request for more than a year.[90] Meanwhile, apparently having anticipated a lack of White House cooperation, on February 17, 1855, Seward had introduced Senate bill 42, a proposed joint resolution of the Thirty-third Congress, "authorizing the Secretary of the Treasury to settle" Benson's claim "on the principle of equity and justice." The proposition was referred to the Committee on Foreign Affairs.[91]

Chaired by Senator John Clayton of Delaware (Zachary Taylor's secretary of State and negotiator of the ill-fated Clayton-Tirado Treaty that had tried to procure Peruvian guano for American farmers inexpensively), the Foreign Affairs committee was apparently familiar enough with the issues involved that members saw no need for a detailed staff report. Thus it merely asked the State department for a copy of Peruvian foreign minister J. J. de Osma's promise to American vessels that had sailed before August 25, 1852.[92]

That document in hand, three days later Clayton's committee reported favorably on Senate bill 42, recommending its passage without amendment. It provided that the secretary of the Treasury be authorized to settle Benson's claims of losses as "consequence of the withdrawal of protection . . . [as promised] by the executive department of government."[93] Clayton advised his colleagues that Benson "will be utterly and absolutely ruined if some measure of redress is not passed this session." To facilitate matters, he suggested that the Treasury secretary be struck from the bill and that the secretary of State be inserted instead, inasmuch as the State department was custodian of relevant documents that the claims committee had been unable to procure.[94]

Private legislation of the sort designed to assist Benson traditionally evoked little notice; so long as no one objected, such matters were handled routinely and perfunctorily, typically being approved unanimously. Thus, when Senator James M. Mason of Virginia objected, saying that he was "sorry to interfere" but that he "must oppose the claim," the bill stalled. Mason explained that even though "it was hard upon this man to be misled by the Secretary of State," the senator was of the opinion "that no claim or obligation devolves upon this Government to relieve him," especially given the potential size of compensation—more than a million dollars. Consequently, the matter was set aside so that the appropriation bill might be taken up instead.[95]

The objection of a single legislator was usually obstacle enough to block any and all private legislation. Thus, Senate bill 42 might have immediately died had not Senator Clayton desired "to make one more appeal . . . for the sake of humanity [on behalf of] Alfred G. Benson, [whose affairs] are now in the hands of the sheriff. . . ." On March 3 Clayton proposed to amend the bill so that "nothing shall be allowed if, in the opinion of the Secretary of State, nothing is due," adding that the legislation "does not appropriate one dollar in money. It [merely] gives the man a tribunal in his last hour. . . ." Clayton then urged the Senate "to go on with this bill."[96]

Senator Mason again demurred, saying that in his opinion the amendment did not improve the legislation which would have the State department decide a case to which it was a party. Contending that the claim besmirched the memory of the late secretary of State, Mason asserted that Congress should adjudicate the matter—negatively. Senator John Slidell of Louisiana added that while he had studied the case carefully and had personally decided that Benson had "no claim on the United States at all," he was of the opinion that the matter should be referred to the recently created Court of Claims. Objecting that the court was not authorized to hear such matters, Senator George E. Badger of North Carolina suggested that Clayton's amendment be approved because it did not obligate the government financially on Benson's behalf but, rather, merely sought to ascertain the facts in the case, which the State department had failed to disclose. Clayton agreed with this interpretation, but Senator Richard Broadhead of Pennsylvania condemned both the amendment and the bill. The Senate consequently rejected Clayton's amendment by a vote of twenty-seven to eighteen, which effectively killed the measure. It was not considered again by the Thirty-third Congress.[97]

Senator Seward, who had remained uncharacteristically silent throughout the debate, nevertheless relentlessly pursued his constituent's interests in the next Congress, and in the next, in the process repeatedly reminding his colleagues of the importance of the valuable fertilizer to the economy of the United States, not that any of them could have easily forgotten. By the time Benson's first relief bill was defeated in 1855, several other American businessmen had followed him into controversy by seeking bird droppings on one of the Galápagos islands in the Pacific and on Aves island in the Caribbean—thereby creating other awkward diplomatic situations for the United States.

# 3

## Turtles and Birds: Cases of Mistaken Identities

Alfred G. Benson was not the only American businessman to catch whiff of profit potential in bird droppings. Well before his relief bill reached Congress, others had taken up the challenges of finding and importing feces from afar. Their efforts (likewise abetted by the U.S. government) led to an aborted diplomatic agreement with Ecuador to mine one of its Galápagos islands and to disputes with Venezuela over Aves island in the West Indies.

In 1854, as opportunistic entrepreneurs sniffed about the high seas for guano, the United States was a nation increasingly beset by opportunities and dilemmas. That year Commodore Matthew C. Perry opened Japan to American commerce. The issue of slavery in the territories came to a boil in Congress in the heated Kansas-Nebraska debates and to violence in "bleeding Kansas." Whigs (their party in shambles after the election of 1852) metamorphosed into either Know-Nothings or Republicans. U.S. diplomats meeting in Europe declared that, "by every law human and divine," Cuba should be American property.[1] And Franklin Pierce, the president of the United States, announced in his state-of-the-union address that "A new branch of commerce, important to the agricultural interest of the United States, has within a few years past been opened with Peru."[2]

However disastrous the so-called Guano War might have been for A. G. Benson, it had not lessened American appetite for the exotic fertilizer that promised to revive tired acreage. In 1853 Solon Robinson, editor of *The Plow* (as well as agent of the Barreda brothers), had published an essay in praise of Peruvian bird droppings, which he described as "the best . . . manure in the world, . . . not only the most concentrated—the most economical to the purchaser—but by its composition, . . . the best adapted to all the crops cultivated in this country. . . ."[3]

Such glowing, albeit self-serving endorsements greatly increased demand for the commodity. By the end of 1854 U.S. imports had risen to 175,849 tons annually (up from 50,000 tons) while retail prices had climbed to $53 a ton (up from $48) from 1852. Part of that price rise was attributed to a 10 percent increase in the South American government's severance tax, commencing in January 1854. Also contributing were escalating shipping costs, popularly ascribed to the uncertainty of loading in remote Peru, which was subject to the whims of dictatorial rule. Such did not dissuade the likes of American entrepreneur William Russell Grace who under contract with the Peruvians in 1854 began to ferry supplies to miners on the Chinca islands and to haul bird droppings back to the United States, commerce that underwrote the establishment of one of the globe's giant enterprises—W. R. Grace & Co.[4]

Unlike Grace, most Americans did not benefit from Peruvian policy. Higher prices squeezed farmers and perplexed politicians. Reacting to grumblings within its agrarian community, in February 1854 the Maryland legislature begged its congressional delegation "to urge upon the general government the necessity and propriety of making, as soon as possible, some arrangement, by treaty or otherwise, with the Peruvian government, by which the present monopoly in the sale of guano in this State and other States of the Union may be removed, and the agricultural interests of our country thereby be greatly promoted."[5] Maryland Senator Thomas Pratt asked and received unanimous consent of the upper chamber to refer his constituents' petition, along with a similar request from Louisiana, to the agriculture committee for study "to give the people of the country all the facts so as to enable them to understand the matter."[6]

That month the House of Representatives asked President Pierce "whether negotiations have been opened . . . with the government of Peru for the removal of restrictions . . . upon the exportation of guano," and, if so, what was the status of those talks?[7] William L. Marcy, Pierce's secretary of State, soon responded that he, like his predecessors commencing with John Clayton in 1850, had worked diligently to open Peru to free trade in guano; however, there had been no progress. As American envoy J. Randolph Clay had repeatedly reported from Lima, inasmuch as the Peruvian government was dependent upon its monopoly to finance affairs of state, it was not inclined to change either "the manner of disposing of the guano" or "the price at which it is sold." Peru steadfastly refused to consider either issue to be "subject-matter of negotiations with foreign powers."[8]

American farmers were hardly satisfied. In June 1854 "2,000 citizens of Delaware" complained that the price of the miraculous soil additive had climbed to $54 a ton, which they considered to be "an exorbitant sum." Furthermore, the commodity could only be obtained in limited quantities that were far too small to satisfy the agricultural needs of Delaware, much less those of the entire United States, even though (it was widely believed) the Chincas contained enough guano "to supply the world for more than twenty generations"—a gross exaggeration, as it turned out. Delawareans petitioned Congress to press Peru to cede one of its guano islands to the United States or, at the very least, to open its resources to freer exploitation.[9]

Without taking a position on "the acquisitions of territory in other quarters" (a deft reference to slavery in the territories and a most divisive issue in 1854 inasmuch as the Kansas-Nebraska Act was at that very moment before Congress), Delawareans contended that "the purchase of one of those islands would be to the people of the United States of more solid worth than that of . . . Cuba, and all of the Antilles besides." The Senate forthwith sent the memorial to President Pierce.[10]

No doubt anticipating angry voters in the fall, anxious House members promptly appointed a Select Committee on the Guano Trade to see what, if anything, might be done about the situation. On July 31 the committee reported that its investigations indicated that the government of Peru cleared between $17 and $20 a ton on its guano exports, a sum that committee members judged to be unfairly high; however, as envoy Randolph Clay in Lima insisted, the Peruvian government was unlikely to abandon its consignment system and even less likely to sell one of its treasured islands to the United States—or to anyone else.[11]

Therefore, some congressmen proposed that if Peru would not listen to reason, perhaps it would respond to economic pressure. The House's Select Committee wrote extraordinary legislation that would have continued to exempt Peruvian guano from U.S. import duties so long as it was offered for sale at less than $40 a ton; however, a tax of 4 percent would be assessed whenever marketed between $40 and $47 a ton, 10 percent between $47 and $50 a ton, and 60 percent whenever $50 or more a ton.[12] Fortunately, wiser heads ultimately prevailed, and the measure died without action.[13] It obviously made little sense to most legislators to tax the precious commodity and thereby further increase production costs for American farmers, the end users, who either would be compelled to bear the tariff burden or be priced out of the market entirely. Clearly, with worldwide demand for its guano far exceeding production, Peru would not suffer.

Ever-higher prices in the United States naturally made substitutes more attractive, and, in response to mounting demand during the 1850s, entrepreneurs commenced to look for alternatives. While some businessmen offered inferior bird droppings from African islands on a sellers' market, others looked for fresh feces in the Caribbean and the Pacific.[14]

About 1853 an unidentified Baltimore syndicate surreptitiously scraped what was claimed to be guano off of the uninhabited Western Triangle islands, which lie about one hundred miles northwest of the Yucatán peninsula in the Gulf of Mexico, and, for a time, sold it to gullible buyers as pure Peruvian. Although the stuff was described as "soft, powdery and generally similar in appearance to Peruvian . . . , it was actually quite different in composition."[15]

Like that found on most of the other guano islands subsequently discovered in the Caribbean sea and in the Pacific and Indian oceans, Triangles' material had actually undergone substantial leaching from rainfall that washed out most of the valuable nitrates and left behind less soluble (and less valuable) phosphates. Although initially sold at a premium price, inferior Triangles' fertilizer produced modest yields that, in addition to similar misrepresentations, led to Maryland's guano inspection law and to merchants slashing prices in half for "Mexican white" (as Triangles' guano became known) in order to reduce inventories. Worse, after clandestinely loading at the Triangles, two American ships became stranded by a storm along the nearby Mexican coast, thereby alerting local authorities to chicanery.[16]

After warning interlopers to keep off, Mexican president Antonio López de Santa Anna (no doubt dreaming of revenues similar to those enjoyed by Peru) conveyed exclusive rights to the Triangles to the Mexican Guano Company, a firm composed of friends and cronies and in which he probably held a personal interest; however, the islands proved to contain very modest amounts of so-called phosphatic guano, far too little volume to overcome heavily discounted prices. The islands also proved to be impossible to police. According to historian Richard Wines, for more than a decade "American merchants continued to help themselves to what guano they could find off the coast of Mexico."[17]

Publicity attending such frauds as representing Mexican white as pure Peruvian apparently altered an American soldier-of-fortune-cum-diplomat to alternative possibilities. In 1853 José Villamil, Ecuador's new chargé d'affaires in Washington, who was born and reared in New Orleans, wondered if the Galápagos (or Tortoise) archipelago (some two dozen large and small islands approximately 650 miles off Ecuador's coast) harbored any of the valuable soil additive. Villamil, who had fought with distinction in

Ecuador's war of independence, rising to the rank of general, later conceived the idea of colonizing the Galápagos, over which Ecuador had asserted sovereignty in 1832, but his scattered settlements did not prosper. Arriving in the United States during the height of "the guano mania" and five years before Charles Darwin was to call attention to the Galápagos as unique environmental laboratories of evolution, Villamil became aware of soaring fertilizer demand and presumed that at least some of the islands in which he retained an interest probably contained some precious feces.[18]

He hired Captain Julius de Brissot, a New Orleans mariner, to explore the Galápagos for guano, promising Brissot a share of the proceeds, if any. The captain returned to the United States during the spring of 1854 and reported to Villamil that he had found "eleven deposits, one of great size." He said he had buried evidence of claims at the best site, which he did not identify, and delivered samples which he claimed were "equal in quality" to the best of the Chincas. Apparently accepting Brissot's word without question, Villamil directed the captain to write Secretary of State Marcy to announce his (Brissot's) discovery and to ask the American government to recognize their claim. Meanwhile, Villamil set out for Ecuador "to protect his rights there."[19]

Secretary Marcy was less trustful. He sent a sample of guano allegedly taken from one of the Galápagos by Brissot to Harvard chemistry professor E. N. Horsford, who analyzed the stuff. He promptly reported that the specimen was indeed "on a par with the best average samples of Peruvian, and greatly superior to many varieties on the market."[20]

As Villamil traveled to South America Brissot retained Senator Judah P. Benjamin, a lawyer and prominent Louisiana sugar planter with an obvious personal interest in soil fertility, to represent him (Brissot) in all negotiations to make certain that he was not cheated. At Marcy's invitation, Benjamin and Brissot soon met with the secretary of State in Washington and convinced him that Brissot's discoveries offered the United States an excellent opportunity to obtain guano cheaply—perhaps for as little as two or three dollars a ton.[21]

Benjamin then announced that he was traveling to Ecuador on Brissot's account and, while there, would be willing to assist with negotiations. While not openly rejecting the powerful senator's help, Marcy merely instructed Philo White, the American chargé in Quito, to confirm Brissot's findings as well as his rights as discoverer. The American diplomat was also told to negotiate either a treaty with the Ecuadorians, by which the U.S. government would buy the guano island outright for no more than $3 million, or, in return for a direct but substantially smaller U.S. loan, an agreement by which

American companies would be allowed to mine the place at the most favorable prices possible, payable against the loan. If all else failed White was to secure terms no worse than those of any other nation.[22]

By the time Benjamin arrived in Quito in October 1854 American chargé White had broached the subject with Ecuador's foreign minister Marcos Espinel. No doubt anticipating revenues similar to those enjoyed by Peru in the Chincas, Espinel refused to open discussions until Benjamin had worked out a formal agreement regarding assignments of royalties between his client and Villamil, who had already successfully pressed his interest in the Galápagos with the Ecuadorian government. Meanwhile, as Benjamin sought "to iron out the difficulties,"[23] Peruvian president José María Urvina and Foreign Minister Espinel accompanied Matthew M. Game, the American consul at Guayaquil, on a personal inspection of the Galápagos, but they encountered nothing of value. Disturbed, White hired Emile Prats, a New Orleansian of Spanish descent who had accompanied Benjamin to Quito as aide and translator, to inspect the Galápagos further. Urvina even placed a revenue cutter at Prats's disposal, and Benjamin and Villamil went along to protect their respective interests, but they found no evidence of Brissot's reputed discoveries.[24]

Despite mounting questions as to the nature of Galápagos guano, Ecuador nevertheless signed a contract with Benjamin granting the "discoverers" one-fifth interest in any proceeds (one third to Brissot and two thirds to Villamil) and negotiated an agreement with envoy White, who had recently been promoted to U.S. minister to Ecuador. The proposal provided that in return for a $3 million loan from the U.S. government, American ships would be allowed to load in the Galápagos at a $1 per ton discount, the price being reduced merely for the duration of the loan. While far from being the hugely favorable terms originally envisioned by Secretary Marcy, even this modest concession (once the proposed treaty's terms became known in Quito) caused representatives of France, Great Britain, Peru, and Spain to protest loudly.[25]

Little matter. Senator Benjamin reported personally to President Pierce and Secretary Marcy upon his return to Washington in January 1855 that he was of the opinion there was no guano in the Galápagos and therefore no need for such a treaty with (or loan to) Ecuador. He apparently confided as much to his colleagues in the Senate who promptly asked to see Professor Horsford's report which had certified that Galápagos guano was as good as Chincan. Eventually it was surmised that Brissot, merely guessing that some of the islands of the archipelago which he had not actually seen probably contained valuable fertilizers, had lied about his find; evidently the samples that he had provided Villamil were actually from the Chincas, which accounted for their quality. While Pierce apparently agreed with Benjamin and consequently never sent the proposed treaty to the Senate for its advise and consent,[26] he viewed the meddling in the matter (especially by France and Great Britain) as proof that they were uniting "all over the world to block the advance of the United States."[27] It would not be the last time that those nations would square off over bird droppings.

Meanwhile, in the Caribbean other American entrepreneurs prospected for the exotic dung, leading to problems with Venezuela. During the spring of 1854 Philo S. Shelton, a Boston merchant and commodity speculator who was prominently involved in West Indian commerce, entered the guano trade by secretly mining Mexican white on Arenas key, off the northwest coast of Yucatán.[28] Shelton was said to be quite interested "in creating his own guano monopoly."[29] At the suggestion of James Wheeler, a business associate, Shelton outfitted the brig *John R. Dow* and directed Nathan P. Gibbs, its twenty-six-year-old captain, to sail tropical waters in search of other, better guano deposits. In April Gibbs came upon Aves (or Bird) island, an uninhabited, low-lying, desolate spit of sand approximately sixty-seven acres in size and situated 100 miles west of the great arc formed by the Lesser Antilles, or 350 miles north of the Venezuelan coast. The nesting site for countless sea birds, Aves island was littered with bird droppings, some of which Gibbs scooped up as samples.[30]

Specimen in hand, he sailed directly to Arenas key where Shelton employees clandestinely mined phosphatic guano. "In confidence"[31] Gibbs informed superintendent James Wheeler of his find on Aves, which he judged to be far superior to that of Arenas both in terms of quality and quantity. Wheeler, who had at least three merchant vessels and fifty laborers at his disposal, abruptly suspended operations and sent the ships (no doubt laden with Mexican white) back to Boston for refitting and for future operations on Aves. He and his workers then sailed with Gibbs for New Orleans where the men were released and where, before Wheeler boarded a fast steamer for Boston, Gibbs dispatched a letter to his employer outlining his discovery and staking his claim to a share.[32]

By the time Gibbs's slower vessel reached Boston, Wheeler had tried but failed to persuade Shelton and his partners, George R. Sampson and Lewis S. Tappan, prominent merchant-importers who operated a fleet of clipper ships as Sampson & Tappan, to give him (Wheeler)—rather than Gibbs—command of any venture at Aves and, of course, a share of the proceeds. Rebuffed, Wheeler solicited two Boston carpenters, John H. B. Lang and William W. Delano, who conducted business as Lang & Delano, to back an expedition to the island to gather guano. Intrigued, they agreed and outfitted the brigantine *Mahala H. Comery,* which sailed from Boston harbor on June 22 with the *John R. Dow* virtually riding its wake.[33]

Shelton and Sampson & Tappan had loaded Gibbs's two-masted schooner to the gunnels with cargo and supplies with which to occupy and mine the lonely and presumably unowned Caribbean island. In addition to lumber, nails, tools, and food, they put aboard two six-pound cannons, two dozen muskets, and twenty-seven pistols of assorted size, including two Colt .45 caliber revolvers (then the very latest in weaponry) just in case Gibbs and the twenty-eight mechanics and laborers he took with him should encounter trouble with the rival Lang & Delano crew. They almost did. Both *Dow* and *Comery* reached Aves almost simultaneously on July 15. As Gibbs later recalled, the vessels were within "sight of each other, . . . not an hour's difference in the time of our arrival."[34]

Circumstances made for an interesting scenario. Gibbs was under explicit orders from Shelton and associates to prevent the Lang group from taking any guano, "*by force,* if necessary."[35] Gibbs later said he did not believe that Wheeler and Lang & Delano held "any legal or rightful claim to any portion or share of the isle or the guano," and even though Gibbs's well-armed party outnumbered rivals by three to one, he decided to share the place "to avoid difficulty, and for the sake of peace, and as there was sufficient guano for all . . . , [leaving] the matter to be arranged and settled at home as the parties might deem advisable."[36] He and Wheeler went ashore and divided the place between them. Separate parties erected flagstaffs, each of them raising the Stars and Stripes before setting to work building necessary structures, such as houses and side-by-side wharves.[37]

Both labor gangs were soon digging away at the little island, and by one estimate, within five months they had stripped it of about 20 percent of its approximately fifty thousand tons of reserves. With his larger crew, Gibbs reportedly shipped the most, three fourths of the take, which was worth about $25 a ton on American docks—a price remarkably close to the value of its chemical content.[38] A relatively potent variety of phosphatic guano, it contained twice as much nitrogen and substantially more phosphate than most contemporary substitutes for Peruvian, such as Mexican white.[39] While Shelton and associates apparently shipped most of their output to Boston, Lang & Delano claimed that their "Cargoes are all imported into Baltimore, the [chief] guano market of the U.S., where they are sold to farmers of Maryland and the Southern States, and the article is rapidly taking precedence [over] the Peruvian owing to its somewhat reduced price. . . ."[40]

News of these American ventures quickly spread. In late July HMS *Devastation,* chasing pirates throughout the Caribbean, paused to investigate human presence on the little island, and, upon being informed by Gibbs and Wheeler of the work in process, its captain, Commander Algernon F. R. de Horsey, remarked that he thought the Americans had as much right to the place as anyone. Afterward a Danish vessel-of-war also called, and its skipper reportedly expressed similar views.[41]

The matter of sovereignty nevertheless greatly concerned carpenters Lane and Delano. In late August they wrote the U.S. State department, telling of their (but not Shelton and Sampson & Lane's) operations on Aves and asking "if we might have the right of possession of it, and if we can be supported in that right by our government, and if we can obtain the necessary documents authorizing us to retain possession?" Secretary Marcy responded on September 12 that while he thought the island was probably unclaimed, he declined to provide any documentation that would authorize private American occupation. He explained that although it "was incumbent" upon him "not to comment upon hypothetical cases, . . . if the authorities of any foreign government should attempt to prevent or interfere with you in removing guano from the Aves islands [*sic*], they will be expected to assign sufficient reason therefor."[42]

Actually, two nations (the Netherlands and Venezuela) eventually laid claims to the place. Dutch officials in The Hague apparently did not learn of American activities on the island before they had ended; however, Venezuelans unquestionably knew about Yankee occupation of the island in early November 1854. According to Charles Eames, the U.S. resident minister in Caracas, the South American government initially seemed perfectly indifferent to the mining operations—even though Venezuelan authorities mistakenly thought the place in question was not the Aves island in the middle of the Caribbean but, rather, "another [island] of the same name which lies very close to the Venezuelan coast and in the immediate vicinity of Curaçoa." Even so, the news "produced no movement by [the Venezuelan] government to disturb the Americans who were at work on distant Aves island . . . and probably would have produced none had not an opportunity presented itself for the government to realize a very considerable sum of money at once by its occupation."[43]

When American journalists reported that rival Boston syndicates were importing guano from Aves island, another group of businessmen (possibly confused as to which of the two places by that name was being mined) saw a chance to jump the claims. On behalf of himself and several associates from Philadelphia, J. F. D. Wallace visited Caracas in late November and offered Venezuelan president José Gregorio Monagas a $200,000 ninety-day note against royalties of $4 a ton for exclusive rights to all the guano extracted from the island during the ensuing fifteen years. Monagas (a corrupt oligarch who, with his brother José Tadeo, traded the presidency back and forth between them as though it were a family fief) apparently leapt at the opportunity and soon sent *General Falcón,* a gunboat under the command of Captain Manuel del Cotarro, to Aves island. It did not arrive until December 12—the delay perhaps occasioned by a fruitless search of the inshore island of the same name.[44]

On December 13 Cotarro ordered army Captain Domingo Díaz ashore with one cannon and ten armed soldiers. Díaz informed Gibbs and Charles H. Lang, John's brother who had replaced Wheeler as overseer in August, that he was taking possession of the island and its guano on behalf of his government which "had sold or leased, or was about to sell or lease, the isle to a Philadelphia company . . . [composed] of gentlemen of great influence and high in office in both countries. . . ." They had joined forces to make money on guano, "and . . . their influence was so powerful that it could not be resisted."[45]

Gibbs disputed Venezuelan claims with such vehemence that Díaz was taken aback. Asserting that even though he expected reinforcements within days, Díaz said he would nevertheless allow the Americans to continue to dig until the Philadelphia company took possession. He then scratched out two copies of a statement in Spanish, which none of the Americans could read, purportedly to prevent other Venezuelan warships from molesting Gibbs and Lang crews in the meantime, should Díaz not be present when they arrived. The document allegedly allowed the Americans to mine but not load guano, except for two vessels then awaiting cargo. Gibbs later claimed to have endorsed Díaz's document with considerable misgivings, and with good cause, for by doing so he and Lang, who also signed, unwittingly conceded Venezuelan title to the place.[46]

Leaving his soldiers to guard Aves, Díaz returned to his ship and sailed away (perhaps for further instructions) while the competing American crews returned to their labors. Two days later another Venezuelan warship, *Trece de Diciembre,* arrived. As it approached the island it raised the Venezuelan flag, as did soldiers ashore; they then exchanged cannon salutes, one of the soldiers on the island being mortally wounded in the process.[47]

The ship landed twenty additional troops, took the injured soldier on board, and sailed for St. Thomas in the Virgin islands for medical help. On December 30 it returned to find several new American vessels at anchor, awaiting cargo. Lang had obeyed Díaz and not attempted to ship phosphates; however, after leaving an underling in charge, he had promptly departed for Boston with news of Venezuelan action. Gibbs, on the other hand, had defiantly refused to concede Caracas's authority and continued to load those ships from his syndicate despite the presence of armed troops. The soldiers (so ill provisioned that they were quickly reduced to begging food from the miners) watched the proceedings without interfering. Angry at Gibbs's impertinence, on December 31 the commander of *Trece de Diciembre* ordered all Yankees off the island within twenty-four hours. Outnumbered and outgunned, Gibbs and the others submissively complied, which forced them to depart in such haste that they abandoned most of their property.[48]

Meanwhile, on December 21 Wallace had signed the proposed agreement with the Venezuelan government to mine Aves, authority he soon transferred to John Pickrell who, with others, organized the Philadelphia Guano Company, which was capitalized at $1 million. The new concern anticipated selling Avian feces in the United States at $25 to $40 a ton, wholesale, a sum sufficient over time to generate between $10 and $16 million in revenues. Venezuela promptly sold the firm's promissory note at a 50 percent discount to speculators in government paper who presented it for payment well before its due date. However ambitious and well financed the new guano enterprise might have been, it declined to redeem the draft early, and paperholders pressed the government of Venezuela to reclaim it. Instead, authorities canceled the Wallace contract and nationalized the island's guano.[49]

As would the Shelton and Lang syndicates, the Philadelphia Guano Company scrambled to repair damages with Venezuela by turning to the U.S. government for assistance. Secretary Marcy (eager to see at least some Americans gain access to cheap Venezuelan bird droppings) instructed envoy Eames to assist Pickrell in renegotiating an agreement that would not prejudice the Shelton and Lang cases. In September 1855, long before either Shelton or Lang would receive any satisfaction with respect to their claims, Pickrell signed a new contract with the South American government. It gave his firm access "to all the [guano] islands of the republic" for the next fifteen years and increased the government's share of the proceeds to $5 a ton.[50]

By then Venezuelan leaders were undoubtedly convinced that they would soon be rich from bird droppings, for American miners seemed to be everywhere. In June 1854 prospectors in the employ of Boston merchants John E. Gowen and Franklin Copeland had taken samples from the Monjes (or Monks) islands, three barren, uninhabited rocks that lie at the mouth of the Gulf of Venezuela in the Caribbean sea. "Upon analysis," according to a subsequent government study, "the guano proved to be exceptionally rich, and Gowen and Copeland sent men, machinery, and materials to the Islands, instructing their agents to take possession in the name of the United States, for the use and benefit of themselves."[51]

In August 1855 an armed Venezuelan vessel appeared at the islands and asked the Americans to leave, but they refused to go, whereupon the Venezuelans withdrew. In December a second warship arrived, landed a party of armed troops, seized the mining equipment, and expelled the work force. Informed that the islands lay within the concession awarded to the Philadelphia Guano Company, Gowen and Copeland eventually leased Monks from the American company for fifteen months. They also asked the U.S. State department for assistance in recovering from Venezuela $383,646, the alleged value of confiscated equipment, guano, and lost labor. However much guano the Boston businessmen may have removed from the islands over the years, they won a $20,000 award when their case was arbitrated in 1885 before the Venezuelan Claims Commission.[52]

Meanwhile, on behalf of himself and Sampson & Tappan, Philo Shelton had written Secretary Marcy on January 15, 1855, of the "outrage which seems to us unprecedented committed upon our rights by the government of Venezuela."[53] By month's end Shelton and his associates estimated their losses at $341,000, which included their half of the guano reserves, foregone freight receipts, and abandoned property on Aves.[54] Similar protests from Lang & Delano almost simultaneously reached the secretary's desk. Although they would not arrive at a precise figure for more than a year, the Boston carpenters eventually asserted they had suffered losses of $639,412.50. Most of that sum was the estimated value of reserves on the island—all of which they asserted they "owned outright," notwithstanding parallel claims of the rival Shelton group.[55]

Secretary Marcy promptly acknowledged Shelton's communications and assured him that his claims against Venezuela would be studied carefully. The diplomat sent copies of the businessman's letters to Charles Eames, the U.S. resident minister in Caracas, with instructions to investigate the affair. If he found that Venezuela had no legitimate claim of sovereignty over the island, Eames was to "present the case strongly and clearly to her government and give notice that this government expects our citizens will be indemnified for their losses, and hereafter allowed a free, unmolested access to, and a peaceable occupation of, that island."[56]

Eames soon reported to Washington that, despite Venezuela's claim to ownership of the obscure little place by right of succession from Spain (because it had allegedly been under the authority of the royal colonial *audiencia* that had been situated at Caracas), Aves was probably derelict and, hence, subject to exploitation by anyone. He also informed his superiors at the State department that he had learned from unofficial sources that Philadelphian J. F. D. Wallace's meddling in the matter had undoubtedly set off the Venezuelans. Nevertheless, the U.S. diplomat said that Foreign Minister Francisco Aranda contended that the American miners who had been kicked off Aves had acknowledged Venezuelan sovereignty in writing. Until that matter had been sufficiently explained Eames saw no way for the U.S. government to support American business claims for indemnity.[57]

Well before that occurred, the Netherlands had asserted its right to Aves, demanding in March 1856 that Venezuela forthwith renounce its seizure of the place and recognize Dutch authority. Holland claimed sovereignty because its citizens from San Sabá island in the Lesser Antilles had collected turtle eggs on Aves for more than a hundred years. Learning of the new claim, envoy Eames objected to any settlement that would deprive American citizens of their rights. Ignoring the United States, in 1857 Venezuela and the Netherlands agreed to submit the matter of ownership to binding arbitration by Queen Elizabeth II of Spain, who ruled ten years later that Aves rightfully belonged to Venezuela.[58]

Philo Shelton in the meantime had mounted a vigorous campaign in Washington to secure public assistance in his quest for compensation and, if possible, return of Aves. First, he hired his nephew, Henry Shelton Sanford, a thirty-two-year-old attorney who had previously served in the American diplomatic corps as legation secretary in St. Petersburg, Frankfurt, and Paris. Scion of a wealthy Connecticut family, Sanford was well connected politically. Shelton urged his nephew to contact John W. Forney, clerk of the House of Representatives, and Sidney Webster, Pierce's private secretary, for whatever assistance they might be able to render. The businessman even suggested that Sanford approach diplomat Charles Eames in Caracas to see if he was "workable."[59] Shelton also personally visited Secretary Marcy and President Pierce to enlist their support, and he wrote to New York senator William H. Seward as well as to newspaper editor Thurlow Weed, the senator's close friend and a reputed political kingmaker, asking them to speak with Marcy on his behalf.[60]

Having received no official news from Washington, in May 1855 Shelton once more wrote Secretary Marcy to reiterate his request for assistance. After recounting his group's claim to the guano on Aves, Shelton again denounced Venezuelan actions, asserting that its claim of sovereignty over the place was fallacious. He also suggested that President Pierce annex the island under the same authority that Thomas Jefferson had exercised in adding Louisiana to the commonwealth in 1803.[61]

Marcy soon replied that the Díaz document, in which Gibbs and Lang had explicitly acknowledged that the island belonged to Venezuela (a copy of which had actually been furnished by Shelton in February), "complicates the business" because there was no indication that it "was made under duress." The secretary also asked why Shelton had failed to acknowledge the Díaz document's existence in his original letter of January 15 that had solicited State department help.[62] Incensed by Marcy's "suspicions" that "do us great injustice," Shelton replied that he had not known of the "permit" at the time of his original letter; he again asked the government's help in his quest of "just redress."[63]

In the interim Lang & Delano had also pressed their case with the State department, with similar results. In June 1855 the carpenters hired Henry F. French, a New Hampshire attorney whose brother, Benjamin, was an assistant U.S. Senate secretary and a long-time friend of the president of the United States dating to Pierce's days as senator from New Hampshire. Henry French already represented Wheelright & Cobb, Boston merchants whose brig *Panola* had been turned away from Aves without cargo when the Venezuelans seized the place and who held that government responsible for demurrage (or loss of time) and forgone freight. If Lang & Delano's purpose in hiring French was to strengthen the firm's position politically, it seems to have been incredibly ill timed. President Pierce and Benjamin French were at odds about Know-Nothings in local elections—that very month ending their twenty-year friendship.[64]

John Lang and William Delano were similarly unsuccessful with James Wheeler, who had induced them to drop their hammers and saws and speculate with him in guano. Wheeler, who had originally jumped Shelton and Sampson & Tappan's ship over his share of Aves's bird droppings, climbed back aboard after Lang & Delano failed to include something for him in their claim with the government, especially when Shelton offered to buy Wheeler's interest.[65] By the spring of 1856 Wheeler asserted that he had suffered lost wages for "about six months' employment in a most disagreeable business, in a tropical climate on a desert isle." He was also bitter about being cheated out of what he contended was his fair share of profits for having suggested that Gibbs explore the island in the first place. Consequently, he was ill disposed toward everyone but Shelton, for whom he expressed "sympathy."[66]

Lang & Delano's attorney, Henry French, was equally unsuccessful in persuading Shelton and his associates of the wisdom of combining claims, a course of action that even Secretary Marcy suggested.[67] Shelton, who considered French to be "an ass,"[68] preferred that his nephew, lawyer Henry Sanford, handle his affairs separately. He did, ultimately becoming the attorney of record for all claimants in the Aves affair; however, well before that happened, he had contemplated suing both Domingo Díaz and the

Philadelphia Guano Company. Captain Díaz, reportedly in the United States to peddle guano on behalf of his government, was chased up and down the Atlantic coast by process servers who failed to catch and inform him of pending federal court action in New York that sought to recover damages of $350,000; without a defendant, the case was eventually dismissed. Furthermore, when Secretary Marcy refused to assure Sanford that a suit against Philadelphia Guano to recover the value of Aves droppings that had been sold in the United States would not preclude use of diplomatic channels, Sanford abandoned the tactic.[69]

Sanford simultaneously deluged the State department with documents supporting his clients' case, especially depositions by Nathan Gibbs, James Wheeler, and others to prove that the Díaz document had been obtained under duress and therefore should be disregarded. Finally satisfied, Secretary Marcy in December 1855 directed Charles Eames in Caracas to press American claims. By then Sanford had little confidence that Eames could be trusted to look after his clients' interests enthusiastically because, at Marcy's instructions, months before Eames had successfully renegotiated a new agreement between Venezuela and Philadelphia Guano that allowed the American company back on the island.[70]

Sanford probably said as much on December 20, 1855, when he met President Pierce at the White House. By letter to the chief executive four days later, the lawyer unquestionably threatened "to memorialize Congress" (that is, to exercise Shelton's First Amendment right to petition for a redress of his grievances), an action that Sanford predicted "might embarrass the executive." He added that he had persuaded his uncle to delay until Pierce had yet another opportunity to enforce Shelton's "claim against Venezuela for indemnity."[71] If intended as pressure, it had little effect because President Pierce did nothing; however, the State department continued its calm, deliberate discussions with Venezuelan officials through Charles Eames.[72]

Absent any other satisfaction, Philo Shelton finally petitioned Congress on April 29, 1856, on behalf of himself and others to confirm his rights to Aves island and to provide whatever remedy it deemed appropriate.[73] Included in his memorial to Congress was a proposed law to protect the rights of American citizens who might "discover and occupy derelict guano and other islands, keys, or rocks. . . ."[74] By then, the Senate had before it two other requests regarding guano islands, both filed on behalf of Alfred G. Benson.[75] To some legislators it surely must have seemed that the government of the United States was becoming mired in bird droppings.[76]

# 4

## Seward's Outhouse

By 1856 the Congress of the United States had delved into avian feces on no fewer than nine occasions.[1] House and Senate committees repeatedly studied the Peruvian guano monopoly but reluctantly concluded that nothing of significance could be done about the situation, short of war. Even so, commencing with the Twenty-eighth Congress (1843-45), members frequently introduced constituents' petitions that begged some sort of federal action that would bring the remarkable new fertilizer into the United States less expensively.[2]

The Thirty-fourth Congress (1855-57) was no exception. Early in its first session, Senator John R. Thompson of New Jersey presented to his colleagues "the memorial of R. S. Fields and others, citizens of the United States, praying the adoption of measures for the protection of American citizens engaged in the guano trade," which was referred to the Committee on Foreign Relations on January 21, 1856.[3] While the vast majority of such private appeals to Congress (including this one) effectively disappeared in the morass of the congressional committee system,[4] a few provided impetus for public legislation.

This was the significance of pleas for assistance by Alfred G. Benson and Philo S. Shelton. On March 10, 1856, Senator William H. Seward, who had introduced legislation to secure public relief for A. G. Benson in the previous Congress, reintroduced his constituent's memorial that sought to recover some or all of the million dollars the Brooklyn businessman claimed that he and his associates had lost in the Lobos affair. The matter was referred to the Committee on Claims whose chairman, Senator Richard Broadhead of Pennsylvania, had opposed and voted against the relief measure the year before. On behalf of his committee Broadhead again asked the Pierce administration to share with it relevant information that might illuminate both Benson's claim and government's role in the fiasco, all of which had been requested but not received by the previous (Thirty-third) Congress. Six weeks later Secretary William L. Marcy transmitted the tardy material, explaining that the delay was "owing to the large mass of documents which . . . had to be transcribed and of the papers in the Spanish language requiring translation. . . ."[5]

All told it aggregated seventy-five documents and enclosures (256 pages of printed matter), spanned the years 1852 through 1855, and contained the initial correspondence between James Jewett and Daniel Webster that had precipitated the affair—but not the version containing Webster's curious postscript requesting secrecy. Included were Benson's repeated appeals for help to President Fillmore and the State department, once the business venture had devolved into debacle, along with similar requests from Dana & Company of Boston. Documents detailed U.S.-Peruvian correspondence concerning the Lobos islands and demonstrated that the State department had worked diligently to salvage as much as possible for American entrepreneurs, but with limited effect. Also present was a list of ships charted by Benson that ultimately were turned away (or rechartered) by Peru, thereby somewhat substantiating his assertion of pecuniary losses.[6]

Over the course of the ensuing year the Senate's claims committee studied the information carefully and ultimately concluded that Benson

> is entitled to receive from the United States some adequate measure of redress and indemnification for the actual losses he suffered in the enterprise of obtaining guano from the Lobos islands, undertaken, as that enterprise unquestionably was, solely in consequence of assurances of protection given by the administration of President Fillmore. The suggestion of justice to [Benson] is further fortified by the suggestion of sound policy, that the enterprise of the American merchant should not be crippled by want of confidence in the disposition of this government to redeem all its pledges in good faith, and in a liberal spirit.[7]

By then chaired by Senator Benjamin F. Wade of Massachusetts, the committee also judged that if the agreement of November 17, 1852, between Washington and Lima to recharter American vessels to carry guano back to the United States had been "fairly carried out," Benson would have received "sufficient remuneration for his losses." This had not been the case inasmuch as the Brooklyn businessman, for all practical purposes, had been unjustifiably excluded from participation by the Peruvians, probably as punishment for having precipitated the mess.[8]

Therefore, on February 18, 1857, on behalf of the claims committee Wade recommended to the third session of the Thirty-fourth Congress the passage of Senate bill 606 "for the relief of Alfred G. Benson." It provided that the Treasury secretary be "authorized and directed to ascertain and pay" an amount equal to Benson's "actual damages and losses incurred in the enterprise. . . ."[9] For reasons not revealed by the public record, Benson's second relief bill failed to be considered by the upper chamber prior to adjournment on March 3. Thus, it too died, perhaps the victim of the lingering odor of scandal.

Boston businessman Philo Shelton was hardly more successful. On April 29, 1856, Senator Lafayette S. Foster of Connecticut formally presented the plea of Shelton and his associates for U.S. government support of their claim to Aves island in the Caribbean, which additionally sought an indemnity amounting to $341,000 for property confiscated by the Venezuelans in 1854. The petition was referred to the Committee on Foreign Relations.[10] The following day (well before committee members had the opportunity to study the matter) Senator Charles Sumner of Massachusetts offered "additional papers relating to the memorial"[11] that were likewise referred to the Foreign Relations committee. In August, apparently on behalf of the committee, Senator Seward (rapidly becoming an expert on the subject of guano) asked President Franklin Pierce to provide copies of his administration's correspondence with Venezuela, which were furnished the following January. Not long thereafter the Senate evidently decided that the matter was being adequately handled by the State department and dismissed Shelton's petition.[12]

By then another appeal involving Alfred G. Benson had reached the Senate, this one requesting governmental authorization for the private annexation of territory. On May 26, 1856, as the upper chamber was considering both Benson's and Shelton's memorials, Seward presented a petition on behalf of the American Guano Company that sought "title to certain [unspecified] guano islands lying in the Pacific ocean, acquired by discovery, purchase, and assignment." The petition further begged "legislative action by Congress . . . [to] recognize the acts of discovery and occupation, and [to] assert and maintain over the territory in question the jurisdiction of the United States." The request was referred to the Foreign Relations committee.[13] Trying to avoid claim jumpers while seeking official recognition of title, American Guano attempted to hide its discoveries, but to no avail. Rumors rampant in eastern American ports soon identified the mysterious places as Baker and Jarvis islands in the mid-Pacific.[14]

Baker (New Nantucket or Phoebe) island, a low-lying, uninhabited coral ring approximately one mile long and 1,500 yards wide, is situated about two thousand miles southwest of Honolulu and is loosely associated geographically with the Phoenix island group. Baker island was first sighted in 1832 by American whaler Michael Baker of South Dartmouth, Massachusetts, who, inasmuch as it was not on any of his charts, called it New Nantucket, marked its position on one of his map, and sailed on. Three years later and about 1,200 miles to the east, he encountered another, slightly larger, uninhabited island, shown variously on mariners' charts as Jarvis or Bunker island (and presently loosely related geographically to the Line islands). When he landed to search for birds' eggs, he discovered large quantities of guano, the value of which he claimed not to recognize at that time. He nevertheless "took possession of [the island] for his own account in the name of the United States."[15]

In 1839 the mariner was again in the vicinity of what eventually became known as Baker island, and a shipboard death took him and crewmen ashore to bury a seaman. While digging near the center of the island, in what once had been a shallow lagoon, they encountered what appeared to be "a most remarkable kind of soil, the dust of which so enveloped and choked the men that they were compelled to abandon the place first attempted and choose another nearer the shore, where it was not so dry."[16] Observing that the lagoon had been filled in to a depth of twenty feet or more with what appeared to be guano, Captain Baker later swore that he claimed the place, although his motive in doing so at that time is unclear.[17]

By the spring of 1855 the potential value of both islands was apparent. Asserting that these places contained "more than 200 million tons of ammoniated guano lying deposited fifteen to thirty feet deep,"[18] Captain Baker sold his rights to and interests in Baker and Jarvis islands for $25,000 to Captain Edward W. Turner, a Brooklyn-based mariner associated with A. G. Benson. Benson, Turner, and a half dozen others soon joined in partnership as the American Guano Company at a reported capitalization of $10 million.[19]

That fall, as Captain Turner sailed for the Pacific to inspect the islands personally and, thereby, to reinforce his association's claims, Benson wrote President Pierce on behalf of American Guano to request that the chief executive send a naval vessel to the as yet unidentified islands "to inspect, examine, and survey same, and take possession thereof, under the flag of the United States, as property of the undersigned." Pierce apparently thought enough of the prospect that he forwarded Benson's request to Secretary of the Navy James C. Dobbin with instructions to cooperate. On October 20, 1855, Dobbin ordered Commodore William Mervine at San Francisco, who commanded the U.S. Navy's Pacific squadron, to detach a vessel "at the earliest convenient opportunity" and, following the directions of "the bearer of this dispatch [who] will inform you of the precise locality," to sail for the guano islands. Mervine's command was to verify "the correctness of the information," to protect "our citizens rights," and otherwise to take "care of the interests of our country" with respect to this "extremely desirable" commodity.[20] Such assignments for the fleet were not at all unusual during the nineteenth century. As one naval authority has noted, "commerce in general provided a succession of stimuli for government-sponsored exploring and surveying expeditions."[21]

Thus, late in December twenty-two-year-old George W. Benson, Alfred's eldest son, hand delivered Secretary Dobbin's orders to Commodore Mervine[22] who, according to contemporary newspaper accounts, "took a lively interest in the enterprise," so much so that he personally commanded the two-vessel task force that arrived at Baker island with young Benson aboard his flagship on March 15, 1856. Mervine launched a whale boat under Lieutenant J. B. McCauley with instructions to land and gather guano samples, but the junior officer soon returned empty handed, reporting that "heavy" and "exceedingly irregular breakers" made it "dangerous to attempt to land at that time, although a good whale boat might do so at some other season." McCauley also observed that "there is no anchorage on the lee or southwest side of the island."[23]

Ignoring a hut that had been erected on the island by Captain Turner the previous December when he had landed to gather samples and to reinforce American Guano's claim to the place, Mervine abruptly sailed back to California without attempting to investigate the more remote Jarvis, and he unceremoniously deposited Benson ashore upon arrival in San Francisco. The commodore sent a copy of McCauley's report to Secretary Dobbin, Mervine superciliously adding that, because the island lay along the equator and hence was well within the rainy region of the Pacific, he was of the opinion that its guano was probably worthless anyway and therefore a waste of everyone's time.[24]

Well before Commodore Mervine's negative (and, as it turned out, incorrect) evaluation reached Washington, Senator Seward had introduced American Guano Company's petition to have its rights to Baker and Jarvis islands confirmed; moreover, he sought to simplify the process by which American entrepreneurs might claim global guano deposits under U.S. government aegis. His repeated efforts on behalf of Benson might easily be dismissed as merely constituent service (especially since Seward fails to mention the subjects of guano and guano islands in his voluminous published works), even if he and the Brooklyn businessman were known to have been on the opposite sides of some issues, such as the Compromise of 1850;

nevertheless, Seward and Benson were undoubtedly in total agreement about the resulting Guano Islands Act (1856) because it furthered Seward's objective of American commercial supremacy and promised Benson rich financial rewards. That the legislation also resulted in overseas possessions was almost coincidental.[25]

William Henry Seward (1801-1872), the senior senator from New York and an outspoken opponent of slavery, was also an unabashed champion of global commercial expansion, a philosophy that according to historian Ernest Paolino "did not ignore agricultural matters in [Seward's] concern for American supremacy in the world's marketplace."[26] An unsuccessful candidate for the Republican presidential nomination in 1856 and in 1860, Seward would serve as Abraham Lincoln's secretary of State. Wounded by a co-conspirator in the assassination plot that took the president's life, Seward recovered to serve President Andrew Johnson, steadfastly supporting the new chief executive against Radical Republicans who would have removed him from office and dealt more harshly with the defeated Confederacy. As Johnson's secretary of State, expansionistic Seward would be the chief architect of the purchase of Alaska from Russia in 1867, an action often derided by contemporary critics as "Seward's Icebox."[27] If so, surely the Guano Island's Act, which resulted in America's first overseas territorial acquisitions, was Seward's Outhouse.

On April 16, 1856, Senator Seward proposed legislation apparently based on the suggestion of Philo Shelton that had been attached to his contemporary memorial to Congress.[28] Seward's version, Senate bill 15, an act to protect the rights of American citizens who might "discover and occupy derelict guano and other islands, keys, or rocks, . . . and for maintaining such rights," provided that either a commissioned officer or a private citizen of the United States be vested with powers of eminent domain to take possession of such places not under the lawful jurisdiction of another nation, "unless expressly denied by the Executive or Congress of the United States. . . ."[29]

Furthermore, private citizens who might discover, claim, and file on such places by offering appropriate affidavits to the State department "shall have and possess . . . exclusive right of possession, ownership, and use of such island, key, or rock, and everything found thereon, until otherwise provided by law." Meanwhile, the president was "authorized to employ, when deemed necessary, the naval forces of the United States" to protect the rights of said American citizens. The bill would also have made guano islands subject to existing revenue regulations of the United States. Moreover, persons who might commit crimes thereon would be subject to U.S. law as though the offenses had been perpetrated on the high seas aboard nationally flagged merchant and naval vessels. The proposal was referred to the Foreign Relations committee where numerous objections were raised.[30]

On May 26 Seward offered a substitute, Senate bill 339, which was designed to address the reservations of some legislators concerning this extraordinary proposal. The new version struck out everything following the enacting clause and substituted instead provisions stating that whenever the government "should have received satisfactory information that any citizen or citizens of the United States have discovered a deposit of guano on any island, or other territory not within the lawful jurisdiction of any other Government," that, at the discretion of the president, it shall "be considered as appertaining to the United States for the use and behoof of the discoverer or discoverers, and his and their assigns, and shall be taken possession of in the name of the United States, with all necessary formalities."[31] Seward's "use of the word 'appertain,' " State department lawyers would eventually insist, was especially "deft, since it carries no precise meaning and lends itself readily to circumstances and the wishes of those using it."[32]

Seward's substitute required that for entrepreneurs to receive the protection of American law, they "be restrained from imposing onerous burdens on the consumers of guano. . . ." Bonds would be required to assure that the price of the commodity delivered to American vessels would not exceed $12 a ton; furthermore, the stuff would be imported freely into the United States as though transshipped from any domestic port. The provision in Senate bill 15 extending maritime law over guano islands was retained in S. 339; additionally, the president was authorized to use both "land and naval forces of the United States to protect the rights of the said discoverer or discoverers. . . ." The most significant change in Seward's substitute was "That nothing in this act . . . shall be construed obligatory on the United States to retain possession of said islands or territory . . . after the guano shall have been removed. . . ."[33]

Although Senator James M. Mason of Virginia offered to report the bill on behalf of the Foreign Relations committee as early as July 2, consideration of the legislation was twice postponed so that the chamber might take up instead the more pressing (albeit divisive) issue of Kansas statehood.[34] As consequence of that heated debate it was not until July 22 that Mason offered Senate bill 339 to his colleagues. They then convened as the Committee of the Whole, a parliamentary device designed to facilitate both discussion and revision of pending legislation. After consulting with Hamilton Fish, the junior senator from New York who had taken a keen interest in the subject, Mason offered yet another perfecting amendment designed "to make the bill large enough in its provisions to include any future discovery, if such there should be, of guano islands."[35]

Mason's amendment would strike out the bill's entire first section. In its place a substitute stipulated that whenever an American citizen should "discover a deposit of guano any island, rock, or key, not within the lawful jurisdiction of any other Government, nor occupied by the citizens of any other Government, and shall take peaceable possession thereof," the president, at his discretion, may consider it as "appertaining to the United States for the use and behoof of such discoverer or discoverers, or of their assigns, being citizens of the United States. . . ." The new section further required that claimants notify the State department "of discovery, occupation, and possession . . . as soon as practicable," providing precise location and supporting evidence. Mason also suggested that the maximum price of guano be reduced to $6 a ton *in situ,* for product of "the best quality," or $10 a ton when in tubs within reach of ship's tackle.[36]

Senator John M. Clayton of Delaware, who had been interested in bird droppings since his days as Zachary Taylor's secretary of State and involvement with the ill-fated Clayton-Tirado Treaty with Peru, took the opportunity to refute recent reports attributed to Commodore William Mervine that questioned the fertilizing value of Baker island guano. The senator pointed to published analyses of samples retrieved by Captain Edward Turner during his recent visit, which had been prepared by A. A. Hayes, "assayer to the State of Massachusetts," that assessed ammonia and phosphate contents at 11.5 and 73.2 percent, respectively. Clayton asserted that "These are very valuable fertilizers, [although] different from the Peruvian or Chinca island guano." As consequence, he said he was "decidedly in favor" of the proposed legislation as well as the perfecting amendment, which "was agreed to."[37]

Nevertheless, some legislators questioned the propriety of the proposal. Senator John P. Hale of New Hampshire remarked that he favored protecting the rights of American citizens at home and abroad but asked "why a special rule is endeavored to be inserted here, by way of this act of Congress, in relation to guano islands? ... the Government will undoubtedly enforce, at all times, the rights of discoverers of any of its citizens to any undiscovered land which they may discover." Senator Robert Toombs of Georgia inquired as to the logic of vesting in individuals exclusive rights to discoveries when international law insists that sovereignty accrues to a nation. He conceded that "it might be proper for the Government to make compensation to discoverers," but he questioned the wisdom of writing law whereby "the discovery should inure to the benefit of the individual discoverer."[38]

Hale and Toombs's qualms reflected ongoing debate in the United States since the earliest days of the republic—arguments that were keenly sharpened during the recent Jackson administration. What was the proper role of the public sector in the economy and, whenever the public sector does intervene in the marketplace, should commerce or agriculture be the principal beneficiary?[39] Seward and Fish, who represented emerging entrepreneurial interests, naturally sought to aid enterprise. Mason and Toombs, as well as Robert M. T. Hunter of Virginia and John Clayton of Maryland (all of whose states were major guano consumers and who were to take an active role in the ensuing debate), naturally sought to protect agrarian interests.

Senator Seward, silent until Hale and Toombs's queries, undoubtedly saw that the proposal stood in peril. Addressing his colleagues for the first time on the issue, he remarked that since he had introduced both the original bill and the substitute "perhaps it may be proper for me to explain the object which I had then in view, and which is carried out more effectively by the provisions of the bill . . . [as] amended by the Committee on Foreign Relations." He reminded the Senate that guano "is the best fertilizer that is available which is now known." It had become a "great article of commerce," a vital necessity to American farmers, "especially for worn out lands," but "exceeding expensive" because of the Peruvian monopoly. He observed that Peruvian guano, which exported for $30 a ton "at the Peruvian islands," cost $55 a ton in New York, $60 in Virginia, and $65 in Georgia, "and it is more especially in these southern states that the article is demanded."[40]

"The object of the bill, then," Seward stated, "is to favor and encourage certain American discoverers . . . to seek out, and to appropriate to the uses of the United States, under the authority of law, other deposits than those of the State of Peru." He asserted that this objective was practical because "more than one such island has been discovered by citizens of the United States," but legislation was necessary to assure them "that they shall be protected as discoverers, and have the benefit of their own exertions, and of the employment of their own capital, labor, and skill, while making the discoveries and extracting guano for the use of the people of the United States. . . ." Furthermore, he insisted that while benefits would undeniably accrue to discoverers and other entrepreneurs, cheaper fertilizer (which the enactment was designed to secure) would be "for the benefit of the whole people. . . . Everybody being at liberty to go and make the discovery, and everybody being at liberty to enjoy it, whoever may make it, . . . brings [gain] to all the people of the United States. . . ."[41]

Seward insisted that those who would engage in such enterprises deserved fair returns on their investments: for the dwellings necessary to house work crews of one hundred or so men "of the class usually employed in the whaling business, at from twenty to twenty-five dollars a month," for railroad tracks from remote deposits to wharves, which had to be built at substantial cost, and for the cost of obtaining "food, and water, and other supplies from distant islands or coasts." With maximum legislated prices of $6 a ton if individuals mined the material themselves, or $10 a ton if delivered to a vessel by an island's discoverer-developer, the senator believed that entrepreneurs would be assured of a fair return while providing fertilizer "at a saving of one-third or more" for American consumers.[42]

Seward said he understood the concerns of some of his colleagues.

> If there was any such thing as a prospect of dominion to be secured to the United States resulting from the discovery and occupation of these islands, it would be subject for some jealousy, but the bill is framed so as to embrace only those more ragged rocks, which are covered with this deposit in the ocean, which are fit for no dominion, or for anything else, except for the guano which is found upon them. There is no temptation for the abuse of authority by the establishment of colonies or any other form of permanent occupation there. . . . The bill itself [even] provides that whenever the Guano should be exhausted, or cease to be found on the islands, they should revert and relapse out of the jurisdiction of the United States [*sic*].[43]

He added that the proposal "gives no benefit to foreigners . . . [or] foreign nations. It gives no . . . privilege, or monopoly, to discoverers, being our own citizens, who are favored by it; but it is simply a measure of policy . . . with the direct purpose of benefit to our own citizens engaged in agriculture."[44]

Senator Hunter of Virginia expressed concern about "this matter of some importance. I do not know how far it may be inaugurating a new policy," he observed, "and one which may have consequences beyond the mere supply of guano to the agricultural interests of the country." He hoped that it was not the intent of the bill to grant the right of property to the discoverer. While Hunter was "willing that the discoverer be amply rewarded—well rewarded—for the addition he has made to the wealth of the country," he believed "that this bill proposes to do too much." He judged that six dollars a ton "would be an immense reward to give for the mere discovery of the island . . . [especially] in perpetuity. . . ." He asserted that "we should see that there is no chance of exposing . . . [American farmers] to a monopoly of our citizens, anything like that which they have now to suffer under a foreign Government." He preferred "that the grant should be made at the pleasure of Congress" and that "the reward" to discoverers should "be a percentage on the value of the guano." Finally, if prospectors were to enjoy the protection of the United States "they ought to be prohibited from selling it to any except citizens of the United States."[45]

Obviously eager to save the legislation, Senator Mason happily accepted Hunter's suggestions as friendly amendments to perfect the bill—feverishly scribbling down alterations even as the discussions continued.[46] Mason assured them that everyone has "the common object of enabling the people of the country to avail themselves of these new guano deposits if we can; if we differ on details, . . . it is only in the attempt to attain a common object." Nevertheless, it was necessary "to frame the bill so as not to deter the capitalists or enterprise of our country from taking hold of the thing."[47]

Mason also explained that the "accidental discovery of two small [Pacific] islands covered with guano," whose identities he did not disclose, had provided impetus for the legislation: "We had hoped to pass this bill into law in sufficient time to give this country benefit of discovery, . . . but if we fail to pass the law, the result will probably be that some new discoverers will be in possession before Congress shall meet again," even though President Pierce had sent "an armed ship of the United States . . . to enable the discovers to take possession. . . ." Mason contended that it was better to "run some risk of enabling the discoverers to make very large profits . . . than [to] run the counter-risk of losing the discovery altogether." This he very much feared, for "The material is much too valuable to escape the vigilant attention of the large commercial marine of other countries that is afloat on the ocean."[48]

Senator Toombs asked if he understood Mason to say that the islands in question "had already been taken possession of by an armed vessel of the United States?" Mason replied that "a ship has been sent . . . , but we have yet no information on its arrival." Toombs further inquired that if the U.S. Navy had so acted, would not "the title be as perfect in the United States as if you had passed a hundred acts of Congress, and the danger of losing it is no greater?" Mason conceded that might well be true, but he "presumed that the United States [government] will not embark in business as factors to obtain guano." Toombs agreed with Mason's assessment of probabilities; however, Toombs "presume[d] that the United States would let everybody go that wanted to take it." He did not believe the proposed legislation perfected title to the mysterious Pacific islands. Mason replied that Toombs had "misunderstood me to say that a public ship had been sent there to take possession. The discoverers have sent a ship to take possession on their own behalf." He explained that President Pierce had not given the U.S. Navy commander who had been dispatched to the scene authority to annex; rather, he was to go there and ascertain its value, coincidentally making certain that American citizens were not molested.[49]

Senator Hunter then offered an amendment to limit revenues received by discoverers of guano islands to an "amount of money . . . double . . . [that] expended by them at the time of the passage of the law," or, perhaps, to a profit of 10 percent. Furthermore, he would give Congress the option of buying out the discoverers to avoid the danger of a monopoly. Senator Seward objected that such language narrowed the legislation merely to include the two islands in the Pacific currently claimed by the American Guano Company when in fact many other places might well be found and exploited under the proposed law. Rather than "encumber the bill with such details," he thought it better to leave such matters to the discretion of Congress which would "undoubtedly have power . . . to regulate guano islands. . . ." He thought that "Congress is not likely to abuse that power." He also asserted that a 10 percent return on investment for an enterprise so "distant [and] hazardous . . . would be entirely inadequate." Senator Mason objected to the prospect of Congress buying out private developers and getting into the guano business. Hunter explained that he did not propose a public enterprise; instead, he wished to assure free and open access to any citizen who would go get guano and bring it back to American farmers, rather than "entrust the whole matter to a monopoly." His motion died for lack of second.[50]

Senator William P. Fessenden of Maine observed that the proposal "is something of a novel experiment, . . . a very new kind of legislation never known before." He said he was bothered by the prospect of granting monopolies and by the guaranteed price of $6 a ton to discoverers, which he like Hunter thought to be too high. Because he desired time to study the measure more thoroughly, he inquired if the bill would remain open for further change after the amendments currently proposed had presumably been approved by the Committee of the Whole. Seward replied affirmatively. Fessenden therefore suggested that they proceed to consider the changes currently before the body and, afterward, be provided printed copies of the amended legislation "so that we may have a little time to examine it."[51]

One by one Mason's amendments were considered. Except for the matter of price, which was purposely left blank to allow further scrutiny by the Senate, the Committee of the Whole approved each section. Again Senator Fessenden asked that sufficient time be provided to allow careful perusal of the legislation prior to final consideration, to which everyone agreed. The matter was placed on the calendar for July 24, two days later.[52]

When Senate bill 339 again came before the Committee of the Whole as scheduled, Mason predicted that it would require only five minutes of the upper chamber's time; however, he did not anticipate that Fessenden would offer substantive criticism and amendments. The senator from Maine objected to an implied monopoly in perpetuity that he believed the existing language provided, especially since the bill was being rushed through to benefit those who had already discovered deposits but who "do not wish to surrender that secret unless they can be compensated therefor by being allowed the exclusive right to . . . the guano. . . ." He also thought the price provisions in the legislation were twice as high as could be justified, especially if, according to some estimates, the Pacific islands contained as much as one hundred years' supply. He also argued that unless the law made it "incumbent on [discoverers of guano deposits] to deliver the article on shipboard, . . . there [likely] would not be facilities afforded for delivery."[53]

Thus, Fessenden proposed to strike "for the use and behoof of such discoverer or discoverers, or of their assigns, being citizens of the United States," and substitute instead

> That the said discoverer or discoverers, or his or their assigns, being citizens of the United States, may be allowed, at the pleasure of Congress, the exclusive right of occupying said islands, rocks, or keys, for the purpose of obtaining said guano, and of selling or delivering same to citizens of the United States, for the purpose of being used therein; and may be allowed to charge and receive for every ton thereof delivered alongside a vessel in proper tubs, within reach of a ship's tackle, a sum not exceeding five dollars per ton for the best quality.[54]

He explained that by striking "use and behoof" and substituting "exclusive right of . . . obtaining said guano," Congress would avoid the necessity of further legislation should it desire, after the guano had been removed and "the parties had been remunerated, . . . to throw [the places] open to the inhabitants of the United States generally," even if a later section of the legislation did not require the government to keep the islands once the guano was gone. Who could say what thc future might hold for such "appurtenances"?[55]

Mason admitted he had not contemplated such an eventuality, but he added he would not oppose that portion of the amendment. Seward was more cautious, wondering if "use and behoof" might not be retained if "to the extent herein mentioned, and no further" were appended. Fessenden thought not, for he did not wish to convey the idea "that these parties acquire any [other] rights in consequence of our Government taking possession." He believed that his wording better avoided such implications.[56]

As to the matter of price, Mason agreed with Fessenden that Congress should endeavor "to put the price of the guano to the consumer as low as possible," while at the same time providing "fair and liberal remuneration to the discoverers . . . and those who work it," but Mason "fear[ed] . . . that if we cut it too close . . . , we will dull the edge of enterprise . . . [and] frustrate the hopes we now have of getting additional supplies. . . ." While conceding that guano lay on the islands, free for the taking, he observed that the "greatest cost is the expense of getting it, and the expense of labor." He reminded his colleagues that the islands discovered by the American Guano Company were remote—"two thousand miles distant from the nearest habitable land, . . . [with] neither wood, nor water, nor vegetable products of any description," thereby implying enormous supply problems and expenses. Other discoveries were unlikely to be better situated.[57]

Moreover, "this work is to be done in that hot, unrelenting climate . . . [with] the most odious and disagreeable material that can be imagined." Mason asserted that no free "people of any portion of this country could be induced to leave the United States, and go to labor on that island, at twenty dollars a month, . . . when they could realize more at home. . . ." He pointed to the experience of Peru in the Chincas where that government had found it "impracticable to supply labor for those islands from adjacent coasts, and has resorted at last, as the whole world now seems to be resorting, Abolitionists and all, to the great hordes of China, for the unfortunate Coolies. . . ." Even they "have committed suicide, . . . throw[ing] themselves in the sea to avoid the lash of their taskmasters and the odious and detestable work. . . ." He predicted that labor costs on American guano islands "will far exceed the fictitious sums that were paid in California for labor, on the first realization of . . . gold there." Mason asserted that Fessenden was equating the delivery of guano with that of coal, "an utterly fallacious standard. . . ."[58]

Asserting that he was "as willing as anyone else to pay the price to accomplish the purpose," Fessenden inquired if Mason's committee had reliable data upon which it had based its proposed maximum prices of $6 and $10 per ton, depending upon whether someone mined the guano himself or took delivery aboard ship. Mason admitted that it had not, that the committee had merely extrapolated those sums from information furnished by those "who were interested in the work." Even so, Mason insisted that entrepreneurs had supplied what he considered to be very low estimates as to labor costs ($20 a month) which struck him as "highly chimerical." He believed that expenses would prove to be substantially greater, hence the prices set by his committee. Nevertheless, he expressed willingness to reduce maximum prices if such was the wish of the Senate.[59]

Seward was less conciliatory, especially if the price were to be lowered to $5 a ton, delivered dockside. As he commenced to address the issue of prices and profits, he was interrupted by Senator John B. Weller of California who expressed displeasure that the subject of bird droppings was occupying far more than the five minutes Mason had promised. Weller was "very anxious that the Senate go on with the internal improvements bills which were under discussion yesterday, or the Pacific railroad." Seward looked for guidance from Senator Solomon Foot of Vermont who chaired the Committee of the Whole. Before Foot could respond, Mason insisted that "This [issue] is one of great moment to the agricultural and planting States. I think we can be done with it in a few minutes. I know of no amendment but the one pending." Weller disagreed, saying "This subject is of much less importance than the Pacific railroad." Guano mattered merely "to one portion of the Union—to the worn-out lands of Virginia, Delaware, and Maryland." Mason bristled, retorting, "The Senator has not paid attention to the use of guano, or he would not make that remark." Weller replied, "I have paid as much attention to that as the Senator has to the Pacific railroad."[60]

Seward quickly resumed speaking, no doubt to allow tempers to cool. He stated that, according to the information he had been provided by those in a position to know, a stipulated price of $5 a ton, delivered alongside a ship, would result in a $2 loss, which obviously would not encourage entrepreneurs to provide the product. Moreover, he questioned Fessenden's assumption as to reserves on American Guano's Pacific islands. An accurate survey had not been conducted; consequently, there was no way of knowing for certain if there was "enough to supply the market for one hundred years, or whether the supply will be limited to five years."[61]

Senator Judah P. Benjamin of Louisiana, who had represented Julius de Brissot in Ecuador in 1854 concerning phantom Galápagos guano, remarked that inasmuch as he had "given some attention to [the subject] within the last two years" he thought he could provide particular insight into the matter. He observed that more than merely the droppings of sea birds might be classified loosely under the heading of guano; for instance, he would include "the remnants of sea-animals—of seals, sea-lions, and animals of that kind that die on shore"—all of which possessed fertilizing powers. Thus, he cautioned against writing the legislation too narrowly and thereby inadvertently failing to cover unforeseen properties.[62]

Then, noting that Fessenden had objected to "discrimination between the guano delivered on board the vessel by the discoverer and the guano as delivered by the men who go to seek it in its native bed," Benjamin suggested that such would inevitably be determined by the nature and location of deposits and of the shoreline from which the stuff would be shipped. "Of all these facts," he asserted, "we are [now] ignorant." Consequently, he thought a sound policy would retain two different rates in the legislation, but he agreed with Fessenden that maximum rates might well be paired back somewhat from the earlier proposal of $10 and $6 a ton, respectively; however, he insisted that the rate for the commodity delivered alongside a vessel for shipment should be higher than $5. He suggested that a $3-per-ton royalty paid to discoverers or their assigns, provided someone else mined it, would be fair remuneration, "then allow them one dollar a ton profit on the cost of delivering it, which would make four dollars for every ton they delivered clear profit. . . ." He projected that "the revenues of a company organized upon such a basis would amount to $1,000,000 per annum; and surely this is no niggardly reward for accidental discovery. . . ."[63]

Fessenden said he was not wedded to his figures and was willing to alter his amendment. In the spirit of compromise he therefore struck out $5 a ton and substituted $8 "to conform to what seems to be the more general impression" as to an equitable price. Benjamin then moved to alter the amendment further, inserting after "eight dollars a ton for the best quality" the phrase "or four dollars a ton in its native place of deposit."[64]

Those changes finally ended debate. Acting as the Committee of the Whole, the Senate voted first to accept the amendment to the amendment; second, to accept the amendment as amended; and third, to accept the amended substitute measure from the Committee on Foreign Relations. The Committee of the Whole then adjourned, and the Senate reconvened, whereupon the bill was reported from the Committee of the Whole, its title ("An act to authorize protection to be given to citizens of the United States who may discover deposits of guano") being read for the requisite third time. Senator Foot called the question, whereupon Senator Asa Biggs of North Carolina asked that the bill be read in its entirety as currently composed. "This bill has been so much amended," he complained, "that I do not exactly understand its provisions." The Senate's secretary therefore dutifully read the proposed legislation that afterward was passed on voice vote.[65]

Sent to the House of Representatives for its consideration, Senate bill 339 was returned on August 16, approved as written. Along with twenty-six other pieces of legislation that had originated in the upper chamber and likewise been endorsed by the House, it was transmitted to President Pierce, who signed all twenty-seven of them into law two days later. Twenty-three were private relief measures—including Senate resolution 24 "for the benefit of Susan Decatur, widow of Commodore Stephen Decatur, late of the U.S. Navy," who had been killed in a duel in 1820. Four measures were public legislation: fixing prices for government lands offered for sale near Greensburg, Louisiana; modifying the copyright law; requiring that foreign regulation of commerce be reported annually to Congress; and the Guano Islands Act.[66]

As Senator Hunter had predicted, the last enactment's impact was far reaching and its consequences largely unforeseen. For certain its first effect was to demonstrate conclusively that in the United States, flag follows enterprise.

# 5

## Pacific Appurtenances, 1856-1865

For a decade following passage of the Guano Islands Act, American entrepreneurs seemingly laid claim to every island, rock, or key around the globe that might possibly possess fertilizing agents. They were far from alone. Prospectors from rival nations likewise searched for and appropriated such resources as could be found, setting the stage for conflicts between countries over the most unlikely of prizes—bird droppings. Even so, well before the period was over much of the Central Pacific was known to some European geographers as "American Polynesia."

By 1856 much of the earth's fabled Seven Seas had been explored, publicly and privately. Commencing in the fifteenth century, Italian, Portuguese, and Spanish mariners began the modern epic of discovery. The likes of Vasco da Gama, Christopher Columbus, and Ferdinand Magellan greatly expanded maritime knowledge by opening such treasure-troves as Asia, the Americas, and the vast Pacific basin to European exploitation. They were soon followed by the French and the English, who sought shares of the spoils—enormous untapped resources of primitive peoples whose rights were ignored and cultures destroyed. Frenchmen mostly traced the path of explorer Jacques Cartier into North America during the sixteenth century, and of pirates Pierre d'Esnambuc and Urbain de Roissey into the West Indies during the seventeenth; not until Count Louis-Antoine de Bougainville's celebrated circumnavigation of the globe during the 1760s, which, among other things, visited the paradisiacal Society islands (including Tahiti), did France begin to exert claims in the Pacific. By then treks of English pirates such as Francis Drake across the globe's waters were centuries old, but detailed British knowledge of and claims in the South Seas stemmed mostly from the late-eighteenth-century voyages of Captain James Cook.[1]

Newly independent Americans were not far behind. Yankee traders had sailed the seas in search of profits since long before the Revolution and established themselves in such diverse settings as Africa, the Caribbean, and Europe. Commerce with the Orient began during the early days of the republic when the American merchant ship *Empress of China* sailed to Canton in 1784. New Englanders especially hauled African slaves about the West Indies, furs from the Pacific Northwest and ginseng to China where the root was revered for its reputed power to restore virility. Whalers, sealers, and missionaries soon followed, trolling for prey and souls, often mindless of the ecological and cultural devastation they left in their wakes. Complex conflicts with Great Britain between 1807 and 1815 that culminated in the War of 1812 greatly disrupted both trade and hunting patterns that were quickly re-established once hostilities ended, especially in the Pacific, Americans becoming an overpowering presence in Hawaii after 1820.[2]

They were everywhere—trading, hunting, exploring, proselytizing, fornicating; however, sailing the poorly charted Pacific during the early nineteenth century was very hazardous. Says historian Kenneth Bertrand, many Americans came "to grief on uncharted reefs and tiny atolls, even in daylight. For this reason New York and New England mariners were continually asking the government to provide them better charts."[3]

Prior to the 1830s and the establishment of the U.S. Navy's Depot of Charts and Instruments (later, Hydrographic Office), no American public agency systematically collected and disseminated maritime intelligence. In 1825 President John Quincy Adams recommended an expedition to chart the Pacific Northwest, which the United States claimed, but nothing of substance was attempted until 1828 when Jeremiah N. Reynolds, a popular lecturer who advocated public surveys of both Pacific and Antarctic waters, agitated Congress with petitions and memorials from like-minded citizens. That year the House of Representatives asked Samuel L. Southard, the secretary of the Navy, to send a single ship to explore the South Seas.[4]

Southard ordered Lieutenant Charles Wilkes to prepare for the mission; meanwhile, to assist Wilkes, Southard asked Reynolds to collect such maritime intelligence as was readily available among the merchant marine. Reynolds immediately traveled to "New London, Stonington, Newport, New Bedford, Edgartown, Nantucket, and other places" in New England, he later reported, "where information might be found of the Pacific Ocean and South Seas."[5] By talking with sailors and examining their charts and logs, he quickly compiled a list with locations (by latitude and longitude) of some 250 Pacific islands, rocks and keys, both phantom and real. Reynolds's list, which was published by Congress in 1835,[6] became the only tangible product of the proposed expedition because Andrew Jackson, the new president, had canceled the excursion as an economy measure. In the interim, Reynolds persuaded New England sealer Edmund Fanning to support a private expedition (1829-30). As Fanning hunted for seal skins along the Antarctic Circle, he also gathered natural history specimens and looked for many of the places on Reynolds's list, only a few of which had been located precisely.[7] Accurately fixed or not, real or imaginary, seventeen of the islands, rocks, or keys on Reynolds's list came to be claimed under the Guano Islands Act.[8]

Long before that happened, popular clamor for an official survey had intensified as maritime accidents increased in number. As a result, in 1836 Congress (led by Southard, now the junior senator from New Jersey and chairman of the Naval Affair committee) appropriated $300,000 with which to fund an official "United States Exploring Expedition" in the Pacific, the command of which was declined by a number of senior naval officers who apparently considered it to be either decidedly dangerous or a dead-end assignment. Secretary of the Navy Mahlon Dickerson finally selected Lieutenant Wilkes who had been detailed to conduct the aborted 1829 voyage and who, as chief of the Navy's new Charts and Instruments bureau, had recently completed similar work off the Georges Bank.[9]

Joined by assorted civilian scientists, the Wilkes Expedition (as the adventure became popularly known) departed Norfolk, Virginia, in August 1838 as a six-ship squadron of two sloops, one brig, one supply vessel, and two pilot boats. When the little flotilla returned to the East coast almost four years later it was minus four ships that had either been lost or abandoned as no longer seaworthy, thereby concluding a voyage of eighty-eight thousand miles at a cost of almost $1 million—about three times the original appropriation. In the process Wilkes obtained detailed information on some 280 Pacific islands, 13 of which were (at least temporarily) to become American appurtenances under the Guano Act.[10]

During the decade and a half that separated the Wilkes Expedition from passage of that legislation much more data concerning the globe's islands, rocks, and keys were collected by the U.S. Navy and made available to civilian mariners. For instance, Matthew Fontaine Maury, who headed the Navy's Charts and Instruments bureau after 1842, compiled a variety of maps that "revolutionized sailing and whaling," and his subsequent treatise, *Physical Geography of the Sea* (1850), actually initiated the scientific study of oceanography.[11]

At the direction of President Millard Fillmore and directly in support of American private enterprise, Commodore Matthew C. Perry in 1852 sailed toward Japan to open the Hermit Kingdom to western trade and commerce. The following year Commander Richard Ringgold undertook a three-year-long survey primarily of the North Pacific, an expedition complementary to Wilkes's mostly South Seas voyage.[12] Little wonder that Navy secretary James C. Dobbin could advise Commodore William Mervine in 1854, "The primary objects of the Government in maintaining a naval force in the Pacific Ocean have always been, and still are, the protection of our commerce and increasing the efficiency of our Navy. . . ."[13]

Meanwhile, sleek, fast Yankee clippers (as well as more ponderous whalers and sealers) in ever increasing numbers skimmed across placid and turbulent seas in pursuit of commerce and resources—all the while gathering more information, albeit hardly systematically, about dangerous atolls, islands, reefs, and rocks. Then, with U.S. acquisition of California and the subsequent discovery of gold, interest in the Pacific intensified, even as shipping tottered on the brink of an economic abyss.[14]

Commercial maritime prosperity in the United States, which had commenced during the middle 1840s, peaked in the following decade. For a time the U.S. merchant marine benefitted from widespread European crop failures, partial repeal of British corn laws, and America becoming "the granary of the world,"[15] as well as simultaneously increasing trade throughout the entire Pacific basin, including traffic with Oregon, California, Hawaii, and numerous Far Eastern ports, particularly in China and Australia. "The boom years of the clipper era were 1853-1854," says historian Raymond Rydell. "Then freight rates were highest, profits the heaviest, and most of the [speed] record passages took place."[16]

To capitalize on the situation, 270 clipper ships were launched from American shipyards during the era, 125 of those in 1853 alone. Designed for speed, clippers were substantially smaller and carried far less cargo than the lumbering freighters with which they competed. Furthermore, the new vessels required much more manpower per ton of cargo at a time when expanded employment opportunities ashore (along with abysmal working conditions at sea) caused labor shortages for shippers, thereby driving up wage rates. Where clipper ships had been relatively scarce and therefore could easily charge a premium for their rapid "express" service before 1850, overbuilding drove down freight bills just as the quantity of charter parties began to decline, coincidental with waning numbers of fortune seekers bound for California and other Pacific ports.[17] Furthermore, although clippers were exceptionally fast, they were very inefficient—as one contemporary mariner remarked, a "thousand-ton ship in capacity and a two thousand-ton ship to keep in repair."[18]

A glut of shipping capacity by 1856 meant that many Yankee clippers that had "driven at top speed to California, Melbourne or China, lay at their destination for weeks, only to be forced to sail for other ports with all or a considerable part of their original cargo intact," says maritime authority Carl Cutler. "Many of those fortunate enough to dispose of their merchandise frequently found it almost impossible to secure profitable charters, and drifted into the wretched coolie or guano trade."[19] Raymond Rydell adds that the owners of "once proud clippers . . . now availed themselves of any opportunity, however humble, to employ their vessels," such as ferrying bird droppings.[20]

Indeed, several of those shippers were in the very vanguard of the new endeavor, their filings under the Guano Act constituting the overwhelming majority of successful applications during the legislation's initial decade of existence. All told, between August 1856 and January 1863 (when the Lincoln administration unilaterally suspended the law by declining to process additional requests for title for the duration of the Civil War), the U.S. Department of State accepted ten separate bonds on fifty-nine islands, rocks, and keys in the Pacific and Caribbean.[21]

Of those early applicants Alfred G. Benson was by far the most active. He and his firms accounted for 85 percent of all filings before the Civil War. In fact, the first enterprise to benefit from passage of the Guano Act was his American Guano Company, whose memorial to Congress in the spring of 1856 regarding two remote Pacific islands (Baker and Jarvis) had prompted passage of the legislation. Fittingly, on October 28, 1856, the State department accepted American Guano's bonds on those places, thereby effectively conveying title to them even if, by then, their value as guano islands was widely questioned because of Commodore William Mervine's widely disseminated negative report based on his circumspect visit the previous spring.[22]

Perhaps to justify orders that had dispatched Mervine to the islands in the first place, as well as lame-duck President Franklin Pierce's endorsement of the Guano Act, Navy secretary Dobbin (just before leaving office in March 1857) ordered Mervine to send another warship to Baker and Jarvis to inspect them more thoroughly, to collect samples of their guano, if any, and, provided there was no evidence of conflicting claims, to take possession of them officially on behalf of the United States. By then wholly unimpressed with guano islands, in June Mervine detailed Commander C. H. Davis, skipper of USS *St. Mary,* to carry out the mission that was completed in October. After noting that Mervine had been correct in his assessment of the dangers of landing on both Baker and Jarvis (neither place offering safe harbor or bay), Davis nevertheless gathered samples, none of which particularly impressed him. Some of these he shipped to Washington and some he inexplicably shared with the French envoy to Hawaii who sent them to Paris for independent analysis.[23]

Upon receiving specimens from Commander Davis, Isaac Toucey (James Buchanan's Navy secretary) sent them to the Smithsonian Institution for analysis, work which was completed in May 1858. Chemist Joseph Henry reported that the samples from Baker and Jarvis islands were relatively devoid of nitrogenous matter, the most valuable fertilizing ingredient, containing on average merely 6.74 and 10.16 percent, respectively; however, they possessed an abundance of phosphates, Baker's samples averaging 65.4 and Jarvis's 71.6 percent.[24] On the strength of Henry's scientific evaluation, Boston newspapers were soon describing the stuff as "the richest ever brought to this market,"[25] claims quickly echoed by American Guano advertisements.[26]

By then, Alfred Benson (being hounded by creditors from his Lobos island debacle) apparently saw a way to recoup his losses. In the fall of 1856, shortly after passage of the Guano Act, he sent his second son, twenty-year-old Arthur W., to the Pacific to perfect claims to Jarvis and Baker islands and to retrieve a load of guano with which to test the market. It would also appear that Alfred secretly instructed Arthur to examine another nearby site, Howland island, about which the Bensons had recently learned. At Honolulu in December 1856 Arthur engaged Captain John Paty and his schooner *Liholiho* and, accompanied by guide Charles H. Judd (son of Alfred's acquaintance Dr. Gerrit P. Judd), sailed for the islands. Arriving first at Jarvis, on January 15 Arthur Benson's party scooped up ninety tons of what they presumed to be guano, raised the American flag, and, observing that the house previously erected for Benson's syndicate by Captain Edward W. Turner still stood, left nearby a notice of possession in the name of American Guano Company.[27]

Captain Paty then ferried young Benson and Judd some twelve hundred miles northwestward to Howland island, arriving at the low-lying, four hundred-acre expanse of coral outcrop on February 5. Rat-infested from a long-forgotten shipwreck, the place was wholly uninviting. Benson quickly gathered several samples of what appeared to be merely black sandy soil; however, under orders from his father to claim the place regardless of what he found, Benson had crewmen build a house. He then raised the American flag and, significantly, took possession not in the name of American Guano but, rather, for "Alfred G. Benson and associates."[28] Afterward, the party visited nearby brush-covered Baker island where they collected seventy-four bags of material and turned loose several pairs of rabbits, which, it was hoped, would multiply to become a source of food for future miners. Before departing, Arthur Benson reasserted American Guano's claim to the place.[29]

Returning to Honolulu in March, young Judd gave his father samples of Howland's "dirt" that the physician initially viewed as worthless. Having all but ceased the practice of medicine, Dr. Judd had recently become the Hawaiian agent for American Guano and routinely passed some of the material along to a chemist whose analysis disclosed the sample to be "very rich," containing 79.5 percent phosphate and 14 percent nitrates.[30] He promptly relayed this information to Alfred Benson in New York whose own chemist eventually confirmed the extraordinarily high phosphatic and (for American guano islands) nitrogen contents.[31]

While Dr. Judd began making arrangements to send his son Charles back to the islands with a crew of native laborers to begin mining, young Benson boarded a steamer for New York with four tons of Jarvis and Baker guano, leaving the balance of eighty-six tons (the first commercial load of phosphatic guano from American appurtenances to be offered for sale in the United States) to sail aboard a slower (and cheaper) freighter. By the time he reached New York on April 28 his father had resigned as president of American Guano, apparently abandoning his thirty thousand shares in that concern to creditors who held judgments against him; consequently, Arthur Benson delivered the cargo and reported the details of his expedition to Jarvis and Baker islands to the remaining association partners. Significantly, he omitted any mention of Howland island.[32]

Meanwhile, Alfred G. Benson had been very busy. He first learned about Howland (and that it might be more valuable than either Baker or Jarvis) when an associate, Captain William W. Taylor, had informed him that an acquaintance, George E. Netcher, knew of other "guano islands" in the Pacific. Netcher, a New England whaler, told Taylor that he had discovered Howland island in 1842, naming it after the lookout who first spotted it. Netcher also claimed to know about other such places that were excellent guano prospects.[33] After passage of the Guano Act Netcher and Taylor combined their knowledge about and interests in assorted Pacific places. They engaged Benson as "their agent for the sale of their rights and claims, and gave him power of attorney for that purpose." Benson, at that time "being embarrassed" by suits and judgments against him stemming from the Lobos affair, conveyed Netcher and Taylor's rights and claims (with their consent) to George W. Benson, Alfred's oldest son. Later, and again with the knowledge and consent of Netcher and Taylor, George Benson assigned those rights to Egbert Benson, a prominent New Yorker apparently unrelated to Alfred.[34]

On May 2, four days after his son's return from the Pacific, Alfred Benson advised the State department that as Netcher's agent he filed on Howland

and two others islands in the Pacific, Arthur's and Malden, under the Guano Act. As proof, he submitted affidavits signed by Netcher who claimed to have discovered guano on all of them while whaling in 1842.[35] Arthur's island, described by Netcher as a round coral formation thirty-five feet above sea level and about a mile and a half in diameter, which allegedly contained "a valuable deposit of Guano,"[36] turned out to be nonexistent. The only landfall in close proximity to its supposed location was Winslow reef, an oft-submerged coral outcrop some 190 miles southeast of Baker island. Perhaps, as diplomats later speculated, Benson "discovered the mistake, or fraud, and Arthur's island was never bonded."[37]

Malden (one of the Line islands and also known as Independence and as Tera Kupatea) was real enough. Originally discovered in 1825 by sailors aboard HMS *Blonde* under the command of Captain George Anson (Lord) Byron—the seventh baron, who succeeded to the title when his famous cousin, the poet, had died the year before—the island was named for one of Captain Byron's lieutenants who went ashore to explore. A low, triangular-shaped coral platform some thirty feet above sea level and approximately five miles long and four miles wide at its eastern end, Malden is situated four hundred miles southeast of Jarvis island and is covered with saltwater lagoons and scattered scrub vegetation. Early in the nineteenth century it lacked both fresh water and human habitation; however, pyramidal ruins and stone walkways leading to the sea suggest ongoing prehistoric occupation by Polynesian peoples. Malden island was of no particular interest to the British, and HMS *Blonde* sailed on. About 1848 an American whaler named Chapman, who was sailing out of Honolulu, reportedly landed on Malden and discovered a large quantity of guano, information that he apparently later shared with A. G. Benson's associate, Captain Netcher.[38]

Meanwhile, another American mariner had likewise stumbled upon Malden's treasure, information that he reportedly sold to Grice, Sumner & Company of Melbourne which began mining the island about 1868. Long before that activity commenced, A. G. Benson had posted bond on the place under the Guano Act and eventually secured U.S. government recognition of its title to the island; however, it is far from certain that his U.S. Guano Company ever exploited its claim. Rather, it would appear that whatever phosphates were removed from Malden by Americans before the end of the Civil War were swiped by a competitor.[39]

The reason rivals were able to filch feces from under Benson's nose was that he was intent upon claiming as many places as possible, far more than he could ever superintend even though he soon organized a corporation in which to house his growing list of properties—primarily to keep them out of the reach of his grasping creditors. First among Benson's new claims was Christmas (Kiritimati) island, situated 205 miles northeast of Jarvis. Christmas island in the Pacific is reputedly the world's largest atoll, that is, a ring-shaped coral island usually enclosing a lagoon. Thirty-two miles long and about 18 miles wide at its western end (with a land area estimated to be between 260 and 375 square miles), Christmas island is dominated by a large shallow lagoon at its western extreme. The atoll's terrain ranges from fifteen to forty feet above sea level and is pocked with many small, shallow lagoons, especially along its eastern axis. Its landscape is covered with luxuriant vegetation, including coconut groves. The big, shallow, western lagoon contains no harbor, and although several safe anchorages exist along the atoll's western coast, dangerous reefs (that eventually would impale numerous vessels) extend out to sea in every direction.[40]

Discovered by celebrated British explorer James Cook on Christmas Eve, 1777 (hence its name), the uninhabited Pacific atoll was well known by the mid-nineteenth century to mariners of many nations. Several came to be shipwrecked there, including the English whaler *Briton* in 1836, which was captained by George Benson (no relation to Alfred), who was marooned on the uninhabited atoll for eight months. Among those likewise acquainted with the place was New Haven whaler John Stetson who landed there in 1825. Claiming that the atoll contained much guano, on May 11, 1857, Stetson assigned his interest in it to Alfred Benson who immediately sent Jason L. Pendleton, one of his captains, to inspect it and to take possession in the name of the United States on behalf of Benson and his associates who soon incorporated as the United States Guano Company.[41]

Undoubtedly attractive to Benson's associates was a law enacted by the State of New York on April 15, 1857, "To authorize the formation of corporations for the purpose of mining, importing, and exporting Guano and other fertilizers."[42] Contemporary incorporation procedures in most jurisdictions of the United States were very complex—purposely designed to restrict the number and types of entities granted limited liability and other special privileges, such as perpetual existence. The New York law (designed to aid and assist firms engaged in the guano trade, obviously because legislators believed it to be in the state's interest to import cheap fertilizers) allowed five or more persons to incorporate for a period not exceeding thirty years simply by applying for charter with the secretary of state. New York incorporation vested firms with the right to buy and sell property in and out of the state.[43]

The relative ease of incorporation, as well as the right to hold alien property (such as guano islands that lay beyond New York's jurisdiction), along with individual shareholder liability being restricted to one's total investment in corporate stock, obviously appealed to businessmen engaged in the guano trade—including Alfred Benson's former partners in the American Guano Company who likewise incorporated under the new law on May 12, 1857. Benson's new associates and co-investors in U.S. Guano Company included his son, George W., as well as Egbert Benson, N. W. Burtis, F. B. Carpenter, George Hall, George Irving, Spencer Kirby, and N. B. La Bau (all of whom were portrayed by the contemporary press as prominent New York businessmen) along with captains Netcher, Pendleton, and Taylor; however, they did not finalize the paperwork required for their incorporation until November 25, 1858.[44]

By then A. G. Benson's third and final attempt to secure remuneration from the U.S. government over the Lobos affair (introduced in the Senate the previous March by Senator Seward) had died quietly in the Committee on Claims; therefore, Benson evidently believed that his best hope for financial recovery rested with his new enterprise. For certain, U.S. Guano immediately pressed the State department to recognize its claims to Arthur, Christmas, Howland, and Malden islands. The company posted the requisite bond on Howland on December 3, then filed formal declarations on Arthur, Christmas, and Malden on December 13. Two weeks later, U.S. Guano President Egbert Benson provided the State department with a bond for Malden but, perhaps significantly, not for Arthur. Acting for U.S. Guano, on January 11, 1859, George W. Benson also laid claim to two additional places in the South Pacific, Macauley island and nearby Goat key in the Kermadec group. The State department acknowledged receipt of the papers but never added Macauley island and Goat key to its official list of guano islands because the company neglected to post bond on them.[45]

In fact U.S. Guano did not offer the required surety for Christmas island for a full year, eventually posting that bond on December 30, 1859. Meanwhile, having been advised by the attorney general that additional documentation should be required of all applicants, diplomats demanded more paperwork, including additional affidavits regarding discovery and the quality of guano. Nevertheless, on August 21, 1860, the State department furnished U.S. Guano with a certificate formally recognizing its rights under the Guano Act to Howland island (a proclamation also published in the *New York Tribune*). Official action regarding Christmas and Malden islands appears to have been far more circumspect. Diplomats declined to recognize U.S. Guano's title to either place until the company had provided analyses of guano and proofs of occupation. U.S. Guano consequently submitted chemical reports and affidavits of visits by its representatives but could not document ongoing occupation.

Perhaps because of that flaw no certificate was ever granted for either place. Nevertheless, both Christmas and Malden islands were subsequently listed by the U.S. Department of the Treasury as American appurtenances owned by U.S. Guano.[46]

Alfred Benson was far from finished with filings on guano islands. Having succeeded Egbert Benson as president of U.S. Guano Company, Alfred posted bonds on February 8, 1860, on forty-six additional islands, rocks, and keys in the Pacific ocean, this being the ninth surety accepted by the State department under the law.[47] "To be on the safe side," Pacific islands chronicler Edwin H. Bryan has written, "the claimants . . . apparently listed every island in this region. . . ."[48] Of those places bonded by Benson's firm, only twenty-three actually existed. Furthermore, several were either inhabited or claimed by other governments and, hence, were legally unsuited to become appurtenances under the Guano Act. Additionally, three of the eligible islands (Enderbury, Phoenix, and Starbuck) had already been claimed by other American entrepreneurs under the same law and were eventually mined, but not by U.S. Guano. Finally, as of this writing only two of the forty-six sites that were claimed by Benson remain American territory (Palmyra and Swains islands), but neither of them was ever mined by U.S. Guano—or anyone else, for that matter.[49]

Much of "Benson's Monstrous Guano Empire,"[50] as historian Roy Nichols once pejoratively characterized what the State department simply labeled the "Number 9 Group," was covered by an affidavit dated February 12, 1859, and filed by Captain Taylor. According to a twentieth-century U.S. government investigation, Taylor "was probably influenced by his desire to sell his interest to the United States Guano Company and . . . he drew upon his imagination, and upon old, inaccurate charts, for many islands."[51] Benson was probably unaware that fully half of Taylor's "guano islands" were bogus; otherwise, the entrepreneur probably would have deleted them from the bond list (as he had nonexistent Arthur's island the year before) or, perhaps, he would not have posted bond (as with Macauley island and Goat key, neither of which contained guano). It made little sense to certify phantom feces, an action that might expose his company to equally fraudulent counterclaims.[52] Real or imaginary, Benson's empire in the Pacific, along with those of other American guano companies, were widely regarded for a time as U.S. property, or as "American Polynesia" as they were labeled on contemporary German maps.[53]

Benson was soon at odds with other entrepreneurs who claimed many of the same places. For instance, early in 1859 Dr. Judd (acting as agent of American Guano Company) sent his son Charles and a party of laborers to occupy Howland island, undoubtedly under the mistaken impression that

Arthur Benson had annexed the place and its valuable phosphates in 1857 on behalf of the syndicate for which the physician worked. Judd's action also no doubt stemmed from American Guano's early failure with Jarvis's product that had been shipped to the mainland the year before. The freighter *White Swallow* arrived in New York in September 1858 laden with twelve hundred tons of what shipper Charles Judd had assumed was guano and which his father had optimistically valued at $46 a ton.[54] Rather, it turned out to be mostly gypsum, "the greater part of which was far from being worth the expense of transportation." The company consequently sent a chemist to its digs on Jarvis to prevent a repetition of the error, "but it required a longer time for the reputation of the article in the market to recover from the ill effects of such a mistake."[55]

Aware of a very favorable analysis of Howland's phosphates, Dr. Judd undoubtedly believed that mining the island made business sense; however, like other central Pacific atolls, the place lacked safe anchorage. Drawing upon similar experiences with Baker and Jarvis, he had workers construct offshore moorings at Howland at considerable expense by using cables and chains. The phosphates were surfed to waiting ships in whaleboats manned by native Hawaiians or "Kanakas," who were described by one observer as "amphibious fellows, very skillful in their work, apt in choosing the favorable moment for passing breakers, and, in unlucky capsize, as much at home in the water as fishes."[56]

Such was the situation on June 25, 1859, when Jason Pendleton arrived at Howland aboard *Ivanhoe* with "laborers, food, water, [a] launch, hogshead barrels, bags, and other implements, apparatus and means necessary for" occupying and mining the place on behalf of U.S. Guano. Instead, they were met by armed men in the employ of American Guano who forbade them to land. Rather than shoot it out, Pendleton withdrew.[57]

When he returned to New York the next summer, Pendleton reported events to Benson who promptly protested to Secretary of State Lewis B. Cass. Reminding the diplomat that U.S. Guano held certificate of title to Howland, Benson requested that a naval vessel be sent to the island to evict American Guano employees, whom he characterized as thieves. Within the week Cass also received a letter from Caleb S. Marshall, president of American Guano, who, alerted to Benson's title to Howland by the *New York Tribune*'s reproduction of the State department's proclamation, asserted that U.S. Guano had obtained deed to the island fraudulently because Arthur Benson had been in American Guano's employ in 1857 when he had laid claim to the place. Marshall asked the secretary to nullify U.S. Guano's certificate and transfer ownership to American.[58]

After advising Benson that he had no authority to dispatch the U.S. Navy to settle business disputes, outgoing Secretary Cass asked Attorney General Jeremiah S. Black to render an opinion regarding Marshall's request for a revocation of U.S. Guano's title.[59] On four previous occasions Black had prepared official opinions regarding the Guano Act by outlining what the government should require of those persons or firms that filed for title to islands, rocks, or keys and by appraising American claims to Johnston atoll in the Pacific and Verd key and Sombrero island in the Caribbean.[60] Yet, in 1860 as he prepared to step down as head of James Buchanan's Justice department (ironically to assume leadership of the State department), Black set aside Cass's request and held it over for the new attorney general, Edwin M. Stanton, who never offered any advice whatsoever on the matter.

During the ensuing five years, Benson and Marshall besieged the State department with their conflicting views on Howland island, each of them repeatedly asking the government to sustain the claim of their respective company—but to no avail. Perhaps out of frustration in trying to deal with an unresponsive government, Alfred Benson dispatched a superior force that seized control of Howland island in September 1861, kicking American Guano miners off the property apparently without bloodshed.[61]

Even though the issues involved were clearly federal, dispossessed American Guano obtained an injunction in a New York state court (probably because both companies were incorporated in that jurisdiction) to restrain U.S. Guano from landing on, occupying, or removing guano from the atoll, or from interfering with American's activities there. U.S. Guano thereupon moved to have the injunction vacated by claiming exclusive title to the place under the Guano Act. On May 2, 1865, the Supreme Court of New York ruled that neither party "could obtain right to the exclusive possession by act of discovery, irrespective of the act of Congress. . . ." Apparently thinking that they were leaving the matter of ownership for the State department to determine, New York justices in effect held that both claimants' cases were tainted—U.S. Guano's by the Bensons' many machinations with respect to the island's possession and American's by its failure ever to file formally for title under the Guano Act. Yet, inasmuch as American had gone to the island while it was "in an unoccupied condition . . . and [had] expended money in erecting works and making improvements, and mining guano, . . . [it was] entitled to be protected in the enjoyment of such property, and in possession of the guano so mined." Nevertheless, it might not prevent U.S. Guano from similarly occupying and exploiting the place.[62]

Although it is unclear if either party to the litigation ever appealed the decision, C. S. Marshall of American Guano was hardly satisfied. On

October 18, 1865, he again asked the State department for what he considered to be justice—minimally regarded as revocation of U.S. Guano's title to Howland and recognition of American's claim. Secretary of State William Seward (who as senator from New York had been the chief architect of the Guano Act as well as Alfred Benson's most vocal champion regarding the Lobos affair) referred the matter to Attorney General James Speed for an opinion. Speed informed Seward two weeks later "you ought not . . . revoke the proclamation and issue a new one" in favor of American Guano. Speed thought that in all probability Benson had perpetrated a fraud by obtaining title to Howland island for himself, which he had transferred to U.S. Guano, but Speed believed that American Guano should be required to carry the burden of "the infidelity of its agent. . . . Having trusted Benson, the company should bear the losses consequent upon his conduct, and not be permitted to cast them upon persons who were ignorant of any trust or agency," namely the stockholders of U.S. Guano. In any case, the Guano Act vested no authority in any public functionary to revoke title once it had been issued.[63]

Thus forced to coexist, both American and U.S. Guano jointly exploited Howland's phosphates for a brief period. U.S. Guano soon sold its rights to and property on the island to Boston shipping merchants John Glidden and John M. S. Williams, who conducted business as Glidden & Williams. Operating a fleet of 150 ships, Glidden & Williams was eager to find cargo for return voyages from the Pacific and soon associated with like-minded New York merchants to organize Pacific Guano Company, a Massachusetts-based corporation that mined Howland island until 1878. American Guano apparently disposed of its assets on the island to British investors during the 1880s.[64]

Meanwhile, Alfred Benson's problems with business rivals were far from over. Before his U.S. Guano Company posted bonds on the giant Number 9 group that included several islands (Enderbury, Phoenix, and Starbuck) in the Phoenix group of the equatorial Central Pacific, Charles Augustus Williams of New London and Honolulu had filed on each of them, plus nearby McKeans island.[65] Scion of a prominent Connecticut whaling and sealing family, twenty-three-year-old C. A. Williams had moved to Hawaii about 1852 partially for health reasons and partially to find business for his family's numerous vessels, which, increasingly, were idled by the slump in maritime activity. For a time he operated freighters between Hawaii, California, and Puget Sound and chased sperm whales north of Hawaii for Williams and Haven of New London and for his own firm, C. A. Williams and Company. In 1859 Williams (by then partner in Williams and Haven) reportedly was aboard one of its whalers off McKeans (or McKean's) island (a low, circular atoll about three fourths of a mile in diameter in the Phoenix group), when the death of a sailor took him ashore as part of a burial party. There Williams discovered a layer of guano several feet thick. Aware of its value and of the Guano Act, he took possession of the island in the name of the United States. Intrigued by the implications of his discovery, Williams prospected other nearby islands—Birnie, Enderbury, Phoenix and Starbuck (which was shown on his charts as Barren island). At Phoenix he went ashore and left a declaration of annexation, but because of unfavorable seas he was unable to land on the others. Nevertheless, on March 14, 1859, Williams filed on all but Birnie. Not long afterward he (or his agents) discovered additional deposits on Canton (Mary), Hull, and Sydney islands in the Phoenix group, none of which he filed on but all of which he eventually mined briefly despite U.S. Guano's pretensions to title.[66]

In 1859 Williams organized the Phoenix Guano Company (a partnership between C. A. Williams and Company and Williams and Haven) to mine the islands and, in late December, posted bonds on Enderbury, McKeans, Phoenix, and Barren (Starbuck). By early 1860 the new company reportedly had a labor crew of thirty to forty men working McKeans island, which was estimated to contain upwards of one hundred thousand tons of "good quality" phosphatic guano.[67]

The first shipload of twelve hundred tons arrived at New Bedford aboard *White Swallow* in February 1860 and was advertised for sale under the trade name "Phoenix Guano," but eventually most of the stuff would find its primary market in southern states where fertilizers were in greatest demand. When the Civil War denied the company access to those ports and markets, it ignored Section 2 of the Guano Act that specifically restricted sales to the United States and shipped much of its McKeans island product directly to Europe where farmers initially rejected phosphatic guano because they preferred instead the nitrogenous Peruvian variety. Nevertheless, Phoenix Guano's relatively cheap price of £5 ($25) to £6 ($30) a ton inevitably found converts, and the company reportedly disposed of some seventy thousand tons, thereby generating revenues of about $2 million before expenses on European sales alone.[68]

Meanwhile, Alfred Benson sought to prevent Phoenix Guano from poaching on what he considered to be his firm's property. Having learned through newspaper accounts that the rival New London company had filed for title to Enderbury island, he wrote Secretary of State Lewis Cass on July 7, 1860, to protest. He pointed out that his firm had already posted bond on the island and, at that moment, had a work gang en route to the place. Benson requested that Cass ask President Buchanan to send "national forces to sustain [U.S.

Guano's] just and legal rights to this and other islands acquired by it in the Pacific ocean."[69] The State department apparently never answered Benson's letter, leaving the conflict to be thrashed out by private enterprise.[70]

Unaware of U.S. Guano's claims to either Enderbury or Starbuck island, Phoenix Guano had occupied Enderbury in late 1860 by sending its agent, John Griswold, and a party of fourteen Hawaiians to commence mining. A friend of the Williamses and the son of a prominent Connecticut shipbuilder, Griswold was on the island on January 5, 1861, when Benson's ship *Eagle* hove into view. Its captain, John Gunn, landed armed men and forcibly removed Griswold and his crew. Leaving two men and a cannon on the atoll, Gunn transported Griswold and the others to San Francisco where, despite their protests, they were set ashore and stranded. Phoenix Guano eventually gathered reinforcements and retook Enderbury island, all apparently without firing a shot. It also protested to the State department, demanding that U.S. Guano's certificate to Enderbury be canceled and that Phoenix Guano's claim to title be upheld. Again the State department failed to respond, once more leaving the matter to be reconciled between business rivals. Thus, as the bloody Civil War began in the United States, two Yankee guano companies also appeared ready to battle over an obscure Pacific atoll.[71]

Perhaps in retaliation for Benson's move against Phoenix Guano on Enderbury, Williams mined Malden from 1859 to 1861. Although it is far from certain that he was aware Benson's firm had laid claim to the place (even though the *New York Tribune* had published a list of guano islands on March 5, 1859, which reported Malden to be U.S. Guano Company property), Williams never filed for title to the island even though his firm removed a substantial quantity of what contemporary newspaper accounts described as "good guano."[72] Nor does it appear that Benson (undoubtedly busy overseeing his far-flung "Monstrous Guano Empire") knew of Phoenix Guano's poaching. For certain, when he later learned that the British were making off with Malden's phosphates, he objected strenuously to the State department—but to no avail.[73]

Contrary to the way diplomats dealt with fractious American businessmen who frequently squabbled over claims, the State department handled disputes over mining sites in the Pacific (and Caribbean) with much more aplomb whenever these involved U.S. citizens and other governments. A case in point is Johnston (Cornwallis, Morrison, Parker, or Ryan) atoll in the Pacific. Named for Captain Charles J. Johnston of HMS *Cornwallis* who first sighted it on December 14, 1807, Johnston island (originally about forty acres in size) is actually one of two bodies (along with Sand island, some ten acres) that are permanently above sea level and are surrounded by a low-lying coral ring some 8 miles long and 3 miles wide. Situated 717 miles west-southwest of Honolulu, the atoll complex was also reportedly seen in December 1852 by American mariner William H. Parker who said he noticed that the smaller body (Sand) was not designated on any of his charts; therefore, he named it Agnes (for his daughter), then sailed on.[74]

Following passage of the Guano Act, Parker filed notice of discovery with the State department, alleging that he had originally claimed Johnston atoll in 1852. He also associated himself with businessmen Robert G. Byxbee and Asa B. Stoddard and attorney R. F. Ryan, all of San Francisco, who agreed to bankroll an expedition to the atoll to verify Parker's claims of vast reserves of guano. They chartered and outfitted the schooner *Palestine,* which sailed early in 1858. It arrived at the atoll on March 19, and Captain W. R. Perriman led a party ashore on Johnston island, raised the American flag, and took possession of the entire atoll for the United States. After posting a notice to that effect, they loaded twelve hundred pounds of material as samples and sailed back to San Francisco where, on May 4, Parker formally filed for title. Following favorable analyses of samples that showed 17 percent ammonia and 69 percent phosphate, Byxbee, Parker, Ryan, and Stoddard joined with financial backers Louis Blanding, Cornelius S. Place, and William Thompson on June 8 by incorporating in California as the Pacific Guano Company to exploit Parker's discovery, which was estimated to aggregate one million tons.[75]

Pacific Guano then sent *Palestine* back to Johnston atoll for a load of guano, it arriving there on July 22. Those aboard ship discovered that during their absence the Hawaiian schooner *Kalama,* under the authority of one Samuel C. Allen, had visited Johnston island, torn down Parker's notice, and replaced it with another which asserted that both Johnston and Agnes (Sand) islands had been annexed by the Kingdom of Hawaii and their names changed to Cornwallis and Kalama, respectively. Not to be outdone, Captain Perriman removed the conflicting claim, rehoisted the American flag, and took on board another cargo of fertilizer. When he departed for California a few days later, he left two men on Johnston to guard the digs against Hawaiian interlopers. Well before he reached San Francisco, King Kamehameha IV on July 27 had formally attached the atoll to his kingdom,[76] only to renounce that action on October 16 when the Hawaiian minister of interior wrote Allen that "the government was embarrassed when it learned that the island . . . had already been annexed by the United States."[77]

About then Parker and his associates fell into dispute over undisclosed matters, and Parker sold his shares in Pacific Guano on November 6. Not long thereafter he went to Washington to press personally an independent claim to Johnston and Agnes (Sand) islands. Apparently learning of his activities, his erstwhile associates vehemently disputed his position, writing the State department to say that Parker had accepted then sold stock in the company in lieu of his interest in the atoll; furthermore, because his initial descriptions of the islands were at such variance with the facts, they very much doubted that he had actually seen either of them prior to his visit in 1858 aboard *Palestine*. Inasmuch as Pacific Guano had actually been in possession of the atoll since July 1858 and had regularly shipped its guano to the United States thereafter, they asked Secretary Cass to certify their ownership. Because they were unaware that the Hawaiian government had recently withdrawn its claim to the site, they also asked the State department to confirm U.S. jurisdiction under the Guano Act.[78]

Complicating matters was Parker's death in Washington on February 22, 1859—by his own hand, according to San Francisco newspaper accounts.[79] Secretary Cass eventually referred the dispute to Attorney General Black who rendered a four-part opinion on July 12: one, that Parker's visit and alleged annexation in 1852 had no validity under American law because it predated the discovery of guano; two, that the second visit by Parker and others aboard *Palestine* in March 1858 was no more valid because the Guano Act required "that the island shall be taken possession of and actually occupied, conditions which are not complied with by a mere symbolic possession or occupancy"; and three, that the "acts of the persons aboard the *Kalama*, however designed, were nothing more than empty ceremonies that could vest no jurisdiction over the islands in the Hawaiian government." Black concluded that "there is little room for doubt that the *Kalama* expedition was a sharp scheme of Americans, under cover of the Sandwich Islands' sovereignty, to lay claim to a discovery which they knew to be in course of prosecution under the flag of the United States."[80]

After noting that Pacific Guano had been in continuous occupation of Johnston and Agnes (Sand) islands since July 22, 1858, the date of *Palestine*'s second visit, Black was of the opinion that "Pacific Guano is the proper party to give the bond required by [the Guano] act, . . . without prejudice to any legal or equitable right Parker's representatives might have to share in the profits of the speculation. The nature and extent of those rights, if any exist, are proper for the determination of a judicial tribunal."[81] Accordingly, the State department accepted Pacific Guano's bond which was posted on September 6. Three months later, Secretary Cass deeded Johnston atoll (including both Johnston and Sand islands) to Pacific Guano of San Francisco.[82]

Because of the Guano Act, the ownership of two other places (French Frigates Shoals and Palmyra island) was debated briefly by citizens of Hawaii and the United States. Discovered and named by the French explorer

Jean F. La Pérouse in 1788, French Frigates Shoals is a crescent atoll 350 miles northwest of Niihau island in the Hawaiian chain. In 1859 Navy secretary Isaac Toucey informed the State department that J. M. Brooke, commander of USS *Fenimore Cooper,* had discovered twenty-five thousand tons of guano on French Frigates Shoals and claimed the place. Later that year George Baker of New York disputed Brooke's right to the Shoals. Baker contended that Brooke, as an officer of the government, could not legally own it; however, Baker said that as a private citizen he had taken possession of the place when recently shipwrecked there. The State department apparently failed to reply to either communication. Neither Brooke nor Baker ever offered bond nor was the place ever listed by the Treasury department as appertaining to the United States. After the annexation of Hawaii in 1898, Congress officially recognized the Shoals as part of Hawaii.[83]

Palmyra island (or Samarang atoll), approximately one thousand miles south of Honolulu, once consisted of about fifty islets surrounded by a deep, reef-encircled lagoon that offered mariners safe anchorage. The atoll was reportedly discovered in 1802 by an American seaman named Sawle, the skipper of *Palmyra.* Blessed with a "propitious climate," the low-lying, fertile islets were covered with coconut-palm, puhala, and koa trees[84] and were claimed under the Guano Act by Alfred Benson in 1859 on affidavit by William W. Taylor who said he had discovered bird droppings there many years earlier while sailing through the region. Listed as part of U.S. Guano's infamous Number 9 group, Palmyra was also visited and claimed that same year by Dr. G. P. Judd on behalf of American Guano, which neglected to file on it. In fact, according to the State department there is "no evidence . . . to indicate that either of these guano companies ever occupied Palmyra for the purpose of removing guano, or in fact for any other purpose."[85]

Naturalized Hawaiians Zenas Bent and J. Wilkinson settled on Palmyra about 1860 and, two years later, petitioned the Royal government of Hawaii to preempt the place, which was done by King Kamehameha IV on February 26, 1862. Afterward, until the atoll was officially annexed by the United States in 1898, Palmyra was more or less continuously occupied by citizens or corporations of Hawaii and was unofficially considered to be part of that territory, despite an attempt by Commander J. E. T. Nichols of HMS *Cormorant* to annex it for Great Britain in 1889.[86]

Several disputes with France and Great Britain over Pacific guano islands flared during the period and were not always easily reconciled. In 1856 the Peruvian government (ever in need of more money) appeared poised to cancel long-standing guano contracts with the French and British trading houses Montané and Gibbs in order to extort larger loans at more favorable terms, an action that was actually taken in 1860. Meanwhile, anxious lest they lose access to valuable Chinca reserves, the governments of France and Great Britain began to scour the globe for alternative sources.[87]

Thus, in 1858 Emperor Napoleon III awarded the trading house of Lockhart and Company of Le Havre mining rights on Bird (Reitorn) island in the Paumotu (Taumotu or Low) group, which is south of the Marquesa islands in the South Pacific and which France had claimed in 1844. For good measure the Emperor also gave Lockhart rights to Clipperton island (or L'île de Passion as the French then called it), which lay a thousand miles off the Pacific coast of Central America. Probably discovered by Ferdinand Magellan in 1520 and rediscovered by pirate John Clipperton about 1705, the island was sighted once more (but not claimed) by Frenchman Michel Bocage in 1711. In 1858 Napoleon dispatched French naval officer Lieutenant Victor Coat de Kervéguen aboard a Lockhart ship to annex Clipperton to the Second Empire; however, because of rough seas when the ship arrived off the American island in mid-November, Kervéguen was unable to go ashore to raise the tricolor. Little matter. Merchant marines who braved violent breakers and shark-infested waters retrieved samples that showed Clipperton's guano to be of poor quality—washed out by frequent tropical downpours. Nevertheless, Kervéguen proclaimed French authority over the atoll from shipboard, soon thereafter publishing an announcement of that action in a Honolulu newspaper.[88]

While France never attempted to exploit its claim, the Élysée Palace nevertheless officially notified Great Britain of its annexation of Clipperton. Interestingly, the French did not similarly inform either Mexico, off whose coast the island lay, or the United States, which, by the Monroe Doctrine in 1823, had declared American waters off limits to renewed European imperialism—a declaration extended to Hawaii by President John Tyler who warned the British and the French in 1842 against its annexation and reiterated in 1853 in regard to the Americas by President Franklin Pierce who vehemently objected to French and British meddling with regard to Galápagos guano. Unaware of a specious French claim to Clipperton, Phoenix Guano employee John Griswold landed there in 1861 to prospect for phosphates. Like Kervéguen, Griswold saw little of value on the remote atoll and quickly departed. Although Phoenix Guano never filed on the place under the Guano Act, after the Civil War other American entrepreneurs would claim it and mine the atoll for more than a decade—thereby initiating a three-way contest for title between France, Mexico, and the United States.[89]

Americans also filed unsuccessfully on two other Pacific islands, Madison and Bampton reef, that were also claimed by France and on one, Peak (Uracas), that was later annexed by Japan. In 1859 Commodore W. D. Porter asked the State department for a deed to Madison (Nukuhiva) in the Marquesas, which his father, Captain David Porter who commanded the American privateer *Essex,* had seized during the War of 1812, an action never recognized by the U.S. government. Diplomats rejected Commodore Porter's claim because his father's declaration had not involved the discovery of guano that the 1856 legislation was designed to encourage. Interestingly, their rejection made no mention either of French claims to the island (which dated to 1842) or to the island's sizable native population, both of which were well known to the department's functionaries.[90]

Saying that he had found guano, in January 1860 Rhode Islander Arthur F. White filed claim to Bampton reef (Parama island), which had been annexed by France in 1853 and which lay six hundred miles northwest of New Caledonia. In March 1860 one R. W. Cameron challenged White's claim, saying that the Rhode Islander had admitted to him that he had never set foot on the reef; Cameron asked for information regarding his own application for title to the place. Bureaucrats replied to both men, describing the proofs that were required: assays of samples, affidavits attesting occupation, and bond. Cameron never responded, but in 1871 White finally provided supporting evidence that the State department rejected. Noting that White obviously had not been in continuous occupation, as required by law, but, rather, had merely taken symbolic possession of the place, which Attorney General Black had observed in 1858 was insufficient, the department (apparently unaware of French claim to the place) rejected White's bond on the island. White pestered diplomats about Bampton as latc as 1896, without success; however, the State department's rejection had nothing to do with French assertions of sovereignty, a reason never mentioned by diplomats in their replies to White's numerous queries. Bampton was eventually mined under French lease by the Austral Guano Company of New Zealand.[91]

Late in 1859 Massachusetts mariner Frederick Crocker filed a notice of discovery with the State department on "Peak Island," which he described as three miles in circumference with an active volcano at its northwestern point. He said he had landed there on April 20, 1855, and, after discovering what he subsequently learned was "a valuable deposit of guano," had taken possession of the place in the name of the United States. Diplomats acknowledged receipt of Crocker's communication and advised him of the extent and types of documentation required before they could process his application, including evidence of peaceable occupation and proofs of quantity and quality of guano so that the department might set the amount of the required bond. Perhaps intimidated by the prerequisites, Crocker never responded, and "Peak" island (later surmised by diplomats to have been Uracas island, or Farrallon de Pajaros in the northern Marianas, a Spanish possession), was neither bonded nor ever listed by the Treasury department as an American appurtenance. Sold by Spain to Imperial Germany in 1899, the Marianas were seized at the outset of World War I by Japan, an action eventually sanctified by a League of Nation mandate.[92]

Few disputes with the British in the Pacific arose prior to the 1880s largely because many of the islands that later became subjects of conflicting claims were either misidentified or badly mislocated by American miners prior to 1865. U.S. Guano Company's "America island" is a case in point. Filed on by Alfred Benson by assignment from Captain William W. Taylor as part of the giant Number 9 group, America (said to be situated in the Central Pacific, north of Jarvis) quite likely was Fanning island, which had been discovered in 1798 by Connecticut whaler-sealer Edmund Fanning and then rediscovered and named America by a Captain Mather in 1814. A lush, low-lying tropical atoll some seventeen square miles in area and covered with breadfruit, coconuts, and pineapples, Fanning island once was inhabited by Polynesians from Tonga who left megalithic ruins. By the time Captain Fanning first saw the atoll, it had been abandoned for centuries.[93]

American missionaries from Hawaii occupied Fanning island in 1820, moving there with a handful of native neophytes, most of whom abandoned the place (and its spartan life-style) about 1822. In 1846 George Collie and Edward Lucett of Tahiti and Charles Burnett Wilson of Honolulu, all British subjects, moved to Fanning to manufacture coconut oil. Four years later adventurer Albert G. Osbun visited the island and found a Mr. Delia Williston, originally of Rhode Island, overseeing seventy Kanakas laborers from the Paumotu islands who were engaged in an enterprise that produced eighteen hundred barrels of oil annually that were worth $80 a barrel in Tahiti, sixteen hundred miles to the southeast.[94]

Briton John English apparently bought out Collie, Lucett, and Wilson about 1850 and took possession of Fanning island. He was joined seven years later by Scotsman William Greig. Eventually their settlement was augmented by immigrants from the Gilbert islands, one of whom Greig subsequently married. English, Greig, and the Polynesians cultivated coconuts on Fanning and nearby Washington island, seventy-five miles northwest, which likewise had been bonded under American law by the U.S. Guano Company in 1859; however, although residents of Fanning island eventually reportedly exported what has been described as "guano of an inferior quality,"[95] there is no evidence that any American firm ever attempted to occupy or mine either place. Greig's family was in occupation of both islands in 1888 when Great Britain formally annexed them, an action not opposed by the United States.[96]

Thus, while American citizens had laid claim to more than five dozen places in the Pacific under the Guano Islands Act, sparking relatively few clashes with international rivals, the same could not be said of contemporary activities in the Caribbean. There, efforts to exploit only a half dozen sites between 1856 and 1865 evoked direct conflicts with several nations over who would control valuable phosphate reserves.

# 6

## Caribbean Appurtenances, 1856-1865

Entrepreneurs also sniffed about seas close to home for bird droppings. By the end of the Civil War American prospectors had laid claims to several places in the Caribbean under the Guano Islands Act, and most of these came to be hotly disputed by other nations. That the United States government eventually chose to champion some of its citizen's filings (but not others) reveals much about nineteenth century American politics, public policy, and international relations.

First to seek title to islands, rocks, or keys in the Caribbean were John E. Gowen and Franklin Copeland, Boston merchants who had occupied and mined Monks island off the coast of Venezuela in 1854. Two years later they set their sights on Sombrero island, a twenty-foot-high coral bank approximately one mile long and a fifth of a mile wide and situated at the northwestern end of the Lesser Antilles (in the Angedaga Passage), amid what eventually became known as the British Virgin islands. On November 13, 1856, Gowen and Copeland filed an affidavit with the U.S. Department of State alleging that Captain Meltiah Jordan, Jr., in their employ and on a voyage of discovery, had found guano on Sombrero and retrieved a sample. Encouraged by what proved to be a valuable source of "rock guano," they subsequently sent a second vessel under Captain John Jordan who took peaceable possession of the place. Soon thereafter they had their attorney post bond on the island.[1]

Gowen and Copeland promptly sold their interest in the island to the New York firm of Wood & Grant, which commenced to mine the place about December 1.[2] Wood & Grant was soon claiming that "phosphatic guano, from Sombrero island, [in the] West Indies, [was] the richest deposit of phosphate of lime known to the world, containing about 80 per cent of bone phosphate of lime."[3] Citing a technicality upon the advice of Attorney

General Jeremiah S. Black, the State department declined to recognize Gowen and Copeland's bond as valid inasmuch as it had been signed by their lawyer without an attached power of attorney. Interestingly, even though Wood & Grant was notified of this defect, the New York firm made no effort to correct it; nevertheless, Wood & Grant continued to exploit the island's phosphates for the next several years, ultimately removing about fifty thousand tons for American and English markets.[4]

In November 1861 Ross W. Wood, erstwhile partner in Wood & Grant who had succeeded to sole control of Sombrero, reported to President Abraham Lincoln's secretary of State, William H. Seward, that Andrew C. Elliott of Baltimore, who, as a resident of New York three years earlier, had served as co-surety on the flawed Gowen and Copeland bond, now "threatened to take possession of Sombrero by force and make use of it for the Confederacy, or possibly the slave trade."[5] Wood said he had forty-five laborers on the island and, while acknowledging that the island "has never been proclaimed American territory," begged U.S. government protection.[6]

Intimately familiar with the Guano Act, Secretary Seward advised Wood not to worry. Seward was confident that Major General John A. Dix, stationed in Maryland to prevent that state from "going South," could deal effectively with Elliott. Somewhat less self-assuredly, Seward separately wrote Secretary of the Navy Gideon Welles of "the vital importance, at the present time, of the guano island of Sombrero, belonging to the United States, and the necessity of its protection by one of our armed vessels."[7]

As it turned out the threat to U.S. occupation of Sombrero was not Confederate but British. On March 18, 1863, HMS *Phaeton* arrived at the island and landed a party of armed sailors who ordered miners to haul down the Stars and Stripes; however, the ship's commander, a Captain Latham, "apparently admitted that the question of sovereignty was not settled and . . . permitted the American occupants to put up the flag again, at the same time claiming they had no right to do so."[8]

Ross Wood again wrote Secretary Seward. After noting that since the outset of the Civil War almost all of Sombrero's phosphates had been shipped to England and that he had no objection to continuing his operations under British aegis, Wood feared that he might be evicted from the island and lose his investment. He readily admitted that he did "not desire to occupy the Sombrero Key one day after ceasing shipments of guano, . . . [for] permanent occupation of the island by any power or person would be absurd," and he asked Seward to negotiate a fair settlement with the British.[9]

Secretary Seward referred the matter to Charles Francis Adams, son of the sixth president who served as U.S. minister to Great Britain, instructing him to discuss the matter with the British foreign secretary, John Russell. Seward directed Adams to say that while the U.S. government had yet to recognize Wood's title under the Guano Act, it was not prepared to acquiesce meekly to British assertions of ownership without knowing "upon what grounds the British government claims sovereignty over the Island of Sombrero. If no such claims exist, you will suggest that Captain Latham's proceedings seem to the President to deserve some censor. . . ."[10]

Responding to Minister Adams's note on the subject, Foreign Minister Russell directed her majesty's representative in the United States, Lord Lyons, to inform Secretary Seward that "Captain Latham's proceedings were not prompted by any desire to interfere with the commercial adventures of American citizens, but were adopted to assert the Queen's rights over an island regarded as a Dependency of the British Crown." Russell added that the British government was prepared to grant a five-year lease to the Americans to continue their operations on Sombrero. Although aware that such an arrangement was acceptable to the U.S. businessman involved, Seward declined the offer because "we are not prepared to acknowledge that the pretension of Great Britain to that sovereignty has any foundation. . . ." After consulting with Adams in London, Russell revised his response to observe "that the Government of the United States desires to reserve to themselves the right, if they should think fit hereafter to do so, of calling in question the title of Her Majesty to this island. . . ."[11]

Seward accepted the alteration and advised Wood that a lease had been arranged. Accordingly, the New York firm occupied and mined the island as late as 1893, all the while apparently continuing to ship phosphates primarily to Great Britain. Although the U.S. government had specifically reserved the right to do so, it never subsequently challenged British authority over Sombrero, even when on August 10, 1904, the uninhabited island was officially annexed to the colony of Leeward Islands (or British Virgin islands) by an order-in-council. Since the turn of the century, Great Britain has maintained a lighthouse on Sombrero island.[12]

About six months after Gowen and Copeland had initiated efforts to secure an American deed to Sombrero, Joseph Warren Fabens wrote the State department to say that he had discovered a large quantity of guano on an unidentified island in the Caribbean that he wished to exploit, and he asked for copies of records in the Sombrero island case which had been reported in the press.[13] Before diplomats could reply, he again queried the department regarding procedures for filing on several sites in the Caribbean: Bird rock, Great and Little Constable, Little Corn island, Man of War key, Roncador island, Swan islands, and West keys. Although other applicants had previously laid claim to islands, rocks, or keys under the Guano Act and even though the State department had already officially recognized American Guano Company's right to Baker and Jarvis islands in the Pacific, no one had ever asked diplomats about proper procedure; therefore, Secretary of State Lewis Cass referred the matter to Attorney General Black for an official opinion.[14]

Fabens, formerly the American commercial consul in Nicaragua, would have been better advised to have merely filed on the islands blindly because his letter (on behalf of himself and two associates) had the effect of flagging his application, thereby subjecting it to much more scrutiny than otherwise might have been the case. As a result, Fabens and his friends never secured formal governmental recognition of their rights to any of these places, even though they actively mined one of them for five years—the Swan islands, lying almost one hundred miles north of Honduras's Mosquito coast. Ironically, in the interim, other, less legally fastidious applicants secured American certificates of title to fifty-five islands, rocks, and keys around the globe with relative ease.[15]

Fabens's first complication was Attorney General Black's opinion of June 2, 1857, that set forth a seven-point procedure by which "the President shall be satisfied" that there is sufficient cause to consider "an island as an appurtenance of the United States": that an American citizen has discovered a guano deposit, that it is not within the lawful jurisdiction of another government, that the place is not occupied by citizens of another government, that the place is not otherwise being taken from any other government or people, that the discoverer takes and maintains peaceable possession in the name of the United States, that the discoverer promptly notifies the State department of these facts, and that appropriate notice is accompanied by both description and location.[16]

Once properly apprised of these points, at his discretion the president might proclaim a place to appertain to the United States and thereby allow the discoverer or his assigns to take guano under American aegis, provided bond had been posted to guarantee that the product would be sold exclusively to American citizens at a price not exceeding that stipulated by law. The attorney general noted that inasmuch as the Guano Act provided that "The discoverer will then hold the island 'at the pleasure of Congress,' " these requirements were obviously subject to revision by Congress. Moreover, although the law forbade the president to proclaim an island to be an American appurtenance prior to the completion of the foregoing conditions, Black observed, "The President is not bound, against his own conviction of public policy, to declare any particular island as appertaining to the United States."[17]

While awaiting word from Washington, Fabens and his associates, Charles Stearns (a prominent New York businessman) and Duff Green (journalist, politician, one-time member of President Andrew Jackson's "Kitchen Cabinet," and an industrial promoter then residing in Washington, D.C.), had organized the Atlantic & Pacific Guano Company under the favorable corporate laws of New York so as to aggregate the several island claims they proposed to exploit.[18] Advised in early June of Attorney General Black's procedural outline, Atlantic & Pacific's principals promptly proceeded to comply. On June 24 Assistant Secretary of State John Appleton reported to President James Buchanan that Fabens, Green, and Stearns had provided affidavits concerning the discovery, location, and description, and peaceable possession of the Swan islands, which were reportedly devoid of evidence of previous habitation. Appleton stated, "Since there is no reason to doubt the credibility of the affiants, the case seems to be sufficiently made out to bring it [the Swans] within the discretion of the President." Although neither law nor Attorney General Black's opinion stipulated such a requirement, Appleton added, "The *quantity* of guano does not appear [among the documents filed] and its quality is only referred to by Mr. Stearns, who says that . . . it [is] good."[19]

According to a subsequent State department study, "President Buchanan raised some [unspecified] objections to favorable action on the application. . . ."[20] As result, Secretary Cass rejected Atlantic & Pacific's request for title to the islands on June 29, 1857. He contended that the president "ought at least be satisfied that there is a sufficient quantity of Guano to justify . . . [the possible deployment of American] land and naval forces . . . , and that this is of good quality," evidence of which, Cass observed, had not been provided by the applicants.[21]

For Atlantic & Pacific Guano Company, the rejection was potentially catastrophic. At considerable expense it had already occupied and was mining the more valuable of its claims, Great and Little Swan islands—two low-lying dots of land about four square miles in area and situated ninety-eight miles off the coast of Honduras. Mid-Tertiary sedimentary formations that had risen from the seabed sometime after the Early Miocene epoch, the islands were densely covered by tropical vegetation and harbored huge colonies of sea birds (mostly gannets) when they were discovered during the seventeenth century by English pirate Henry Morgan who named them for fellow brigand Charles Swan. Officers of A & P envisioned Great Swan island eventually becoming a coaling station for ships plying Caribbean waters, especially American naval vessels. Meanwhile, by early 1858 the company was loading its vessels with guano bound for New York.[22]

Perhaps because of difficulties encountered in securing a deed to the Swans, Atlantic & Pacific abruptly abandoned all aspirations regarding Bird rock, Great and Little Constable, Little Corn island, Man of War key, Roncador island, and West keys—all of which had originally been listed by Fabens as places he and his associates intended to mine. These were never formally claimed by A & P; however, in an ongoing attempt to secure official government recognition of their title to the Swan islands, Fabens, Green, and Stearns continued to supply the State department with additional documentation, much of which was either misfiled or lost by bureaucrats. Diplomats later acknowledged that affidavits of workers on and visitors to the Swans simply disappeared[23]—no doubt adding to the businessmen's mounting frustration.

Seemingly more supportive was a U.S. Navy mission to the Swans in August 1858 led by Lieutenant George T. Sinclair to assay the guano on the islands. Visiting chemist Thomas Walker estimated that the islands contained three million tons of 69 percent pure rock phosphate.[24] Nevertheless, even this official governmental study that seemingly satisfied recently imposed quantity and quality requirements jarred neither diplomats nor president into action.

Little wonder that Fabens, Green, and Stearns explored alternatives. If they could not secure U.S. government recognition of their Caribbean operations, perhaps by backing the return of filibuster William Walker to Central America they could secure alternative title to the Swans. An American soldier-of-fortune, Walker had led a small band of men from California to participate in civil war in Nicaragua in 1855 and had risen in a tainted election the following year to president of the republic—an event that was warmly welcomed by proponents of Manifest Destiny in the United States who hoped that he would take control of all of Central America and attach it to the Colossus of the North; however, Washington refused to recognize Walker's regime, which weakened his grip on power and led to his ouster in 1857.[25]

Back in the United States, Walker found able champions in William and Jane Cazneau, an extraordinary husband-and-wife team of commercial promoters. William Leslie Cazneau, businessman in both the Republic and State of Texas, came to American prominence under the patronage of James Buchanan, whom Cazneau would eventually serve as "special agent" in the Dominican Republic during the 1850s. In 1856 Cazneau contracted with William Walker to furnish colonists in Nicaragua. Cazneau had also married Jane McManus in 1850. A journalist and liberated lady long before the term had gained currency,[26] "she influenced policy makers from Presidents to legation secretaries," one writer has observed.[27]

On the advice of Aaron Burr, twenty-five-year-old McManus had migrated to Mexican Texas from New York with her brother in 1832, where they hoped to recoup their family's dwindling fortune in a colonization scheme.[28] There she became acquainted with Mirabeau Buonaparte Lamar, the second president of the Republic of Texas, and they became "intimate friends, if not intimate."[29] During the Mexican War (1846-48), President James K. Polk and Secretary of State Buchanan sent her to Mexico as a secret peace envoy. Afterward she married Cazneau, and they participated in colonization efforts along the Río Grande, where she turned her writing skills to promotional tracts that extolled the virtues of life on the frontier but minimized hardships and dangers, such as intermittent Comanche raids.[30]

Among the Cazneaus' many financial interests may well have been stock in Atlantic & Pacific Guano Company. It is a fact that William Cazneau and Duff Green approached William Walker's lieutenant, Charles F. Henningsen, upon his arrival in New York in 1857 and promised "to rally public support and financing for Walker if he agreed to recognize and support their guano claims once he was restored to power in Nicaragua."[31] Jane Cazneau soon wrote to Secretary of State Jeremiah Black to insist that U.S. policy should support Walker's return, action that he undertook in December—an invasion thwarted by the U.S. Navy. Three years later Walker tried again, a misadventure that climaxed before a Honduran firing squad. By then the Cazneaus had moved on to other business endeavors, this time in the Dominican Republic,[32] apparently leaving their erstwhile associates in A & P Guano to their own devices.

Little matter. By then the company had substantially curtailed its operations on the Swans. Although depositions filed with the State department by businessmen still doggedly pursuing deed to the islands insisted that a dozen men mined the islands' phosphates as late as the spring of 1858, a year later "the Department . . . [was] informed by Lord Napier, the British Minister, that the superintendent of British Honduras had learned of the abandonment of American guano diggers on the Swan Islands. . . ." Because "there was no American Consul at Belize [City], the superintendent, on his own responsibility, had engaged a schooner and effected the rescue of these men, [who were] employed by the Atlantic and Pacific Guano Company. Reimbursement was suggested."[33]

The operation appears to have been totally abandoned by the time of the Civil War, perhaps because the company diverted resources to Aves island off the Lesser Antilles. About 1858 James Leeds, an agent of Atlantic & Pacific Guano, had rediscovered Aves and its guano, later swearing that at the time of his visit it was uninhabited and without sign of ownership. He claimed it for A & P and, in due course, reported his discovery to his bosses who (if aware of problems faced by Philo Shelton and Lang & Delano on that Caribbean island) were not deterred. A & P soon sent Samuel Fowler to take possession of the place and begin mining, but when he arrived on October 29 he found other Americans (apparently employees of Philadelphia Guano) already there, shoveling away. He nevertheless off-loaded supplies and equipment and began work, apparently without serious interference from Venezuelan concession holders. Then on January 23, 1859, a Dutch sloop of war, *Governor McIntosh,* arrived at Aves. Its commanding officer informed Fowler that the key's ownership was then in arbitration between his government and the Venezuelans, and he ordered the A & P crew (but not the rival group) off the island. Fowler and his men meekly departed.[34]

On March 1, 1860, Atlantic & Pacific's attorney, New Yorker Joseph S. Williams, filed a protest with the State department, asking diplomats to move against the Netherlands on behalf of A & P which asked $265,000 in compensation for lost property, including the guano. "Although no letter from [Secretary J. S. Black's] Department rejecting this claim has [ever] been found," says a twentieth century State department study, "there is little doubt it was rejected." For certain, when Williams renewed the claim with the Lincoln administration in 1861, diplomats summarily dismissed it by noting that there was no evidence in departmental files "that the Company has complied with the requirements of the Act of Congress in regard to the guano on Aves Island. . . ."[35]

By then, Atlantic & Pacific had much bigger problems. "Though opposed to secession, Green threw in his lot with the Confederacy."[36] His "going South" while his associates, Fabens of Massachusetts and Stearns of New York, remained Yankees, forced the liquidation of their firm. In October 1862 A & P sold its assets (principally its unrecognized claim to the Swan islands) for an undisclosed sum to George I. Crocker who, two days later, transferred the tainted property to the New York Guano Company.[37]

Interestingly, New York Guano was almost immediately successful where Atlantic & Pacific had failed—in securing official sanction of its claim to the Swan islands. Late in 1862 New York Guano began filing affidavits of discovery, location, description, quality, and quantity of guano, and occupation—all of them copies of documents previously supplied by A & P. New York Guano also posted a bond that was returned because it lacked "certificate of approval." This defect corrected, in late January 1863 New York Guano again mailed the required surety, redated December 30, 1862. On February 10, 1863, Secretary Seward wrote V. A. Baldwin of New York Guano to acknowledged receipt of all the information and to enclose a deed to the Swan islands that was embossed with the seal of the Department of State—the tenth such title issued by the U.S. government. The company was to retain control of the islands until 1870.[38]

It remains a mystery why the State department almost casually conveyed ownership to New York Guano, while having resolutely rejected Atlantic & Pacific's application—their filings being practically identical. Details of New York Guano's operations on the islands, if any, for the duration of the war are unknown.

America's third phosphate prospect in the Caribbean, Navassa island, became its only unqualified appurtenance in the basin under the Guano Act and, following Baker and Jarvis islands in the Pacific, its third permanent overseas possession—an acquisition not without ongoing controversy. Situated thirty-six miles west-southwest of Cape Dame Marie, Haiti and eighty-five miles east-northeast of Morant Point, Jamaica, at the time of the guano rush Navassa was austere and uninhabited, save for iguanas and sea birds.[39] Flat-topped (or "nava") and pear-shaped, the wooded island is an uplifted Eocene limestone block approximately two square miles in area. Its sheer, cave-pocked cliffs jut abruptly out of the Caribbean, peaking between 10 and 150 feet above sea level.[40] The place is completely unapproachable by ship, except along the southern shore, especially at Lulu bay, which is "a misnomer," according to one visitor, "as there is no bay whatsoever, the sea beating continuously against a 60-foot cliff, and gradually undercutting it."[41]

Perhaps sighted by Christoper Columbus in 1493, but more likely discovered in 1504 by Spanish explorers Diego Mendez and Bartholomew Fiesco, forbidding and largely uninviting Navassa island offered no attraction to *conquistadores* in quest of riches, and there is no evidence of any attempt at occupation prior to American exploitation during the nineteenth century. On July 1, 1857, Captain Peter Duncan of Baltimore purposely landed at Navassa to search for guano deposits.[42] He later declared that in addition to woody brush covering most of the island, he found "phosphatic guano varying in depth from one to six feet, and estimated in quantity at one million tons."[43]

On behalf of Duncan, mariner John L. Lewis took possession of the island in September, and approximately two months later, Duncan sold his interests in the place and its guano to Captain Edward O. Cooper, a Maryland mariner who was associated with his son, Edward Kernan Cooper, in a Baltimore mercantile house, which had a branch in Kingston, Jamaica. In December Duncan's attorney filed affidavits signed by Duncan and Lewis with the State department; these detailed discovery and occupation, a chemical analysis by Charles Bickel, Ph.D., showing its rock to contain 71 percent phosphate worth

$21.54 a ton, and Duncan's assignment to E. O. Cooper. Shortly thereafter diplomats formally acknowledged Cooper's interest in the island.[44]

Although the Coopers would not post bond on Navassa until September, as early as spring they had a crew of sixty laborers occupying and mining the place, and they shipped an estimated three thousand tons of phosphates to Baltimore over the ensuing six months.[45] Meanwhile, a former Jamaican business associate of E. O. Cooper, identified only as Ramos, had learned of the operation and traveled to Haiti to try to jump the claim in much the same way Philadelphia Guano Company had bumped rivals from Aves island in 1854—"a story which must have been familiar to all guano traders in the Caribbean."[46]

Ramos reportedly offered Henry Byron, the British consul general at Port-au-Prince, a share of the proceeds if Byron could secure an exclusive Haitian concession to the island. When Byron "inquired at the foreign office concerning Haiti's title to Navassa, he found the minister unaware of the existence of such a place and 'evidently in complete ignorance as to whether Navassa was Haytian territory or not'." Once Byron explained Ramos's scheme, historian Ludwell Lee Montague has written, "all doubt vanished from Haitian minds."[47]

The Coopers' men were digging away at Navassa's phosphates in the spring of 1858 when Emperor Soulouque of Haiti dispatched a two-ship flotilla to the island to order the Americans to cease operations. The commanding officer informed the miners that if they were willing to work for Ramos under Haitian authority they might continue operations, an offer rejected by the Coopers' supervisor. Somehow alerted that such might happen, E. K. Cooper had already written to Secretary of State Cass to request protection under the military powers clause of the Guano Act, and when informed that Haitians had in fact shut down his operation, Cooper protested vehemently. The following day he also furnished the State department several required affidavits that were missing from his application for title.[48]

The U.S. government was obviously eager to defend the Coopers' claim to Navassa even though their filing was far from perfected. Although Haiti had achieved independence from France in 1804 (the second nation in the Western Hemisphere, after the United States, to throw off the yoke of colonialism), it was not formally recognized as an independent nation by Washington until 1864. Until then, "Pro-slavery sentiment was strong enough in the nation and in Congress to prevent recognition of Haitian independence until after the Civil War [*sic*]," says diplomatic historian Charles F. Howland. "The southern representatives and their sympathizers were bitterly opposed to the recognition of negro republics, both because of their belief that this would acknowledge the equality of the black, and because after 1840 they thought to make the Caribbean an outpost slave colony."[49]

In late June, E. K. Cooper wrote President Buchanan describing the plight of his "eighty or ninety men upon the island" and "the damages I must necessarily suffer" unless the government protected him as the Guano Act promised.[50] Even though Attorney General Black a year earlier had noted with respect to the Swan islands that the law specifically forbade the president to declare a place to be an American appurtenance "before . . . prerequisites [such as positing bond] are complied with,"[51] Buchanan was evidently so eager to accede to the southern position with respect to Haiti that he directed Cass to have Secretary of the Navy Isaac Toucey dispatch "a competent force to the island and . . . order the officer in charge thereof to protect the citizens of the United States in removing guano therefrom against any interference from authorities of the government of Hayti, or of any other government." Cass added that the president hoped these objectives could be accomplished "not only without any effusion of blood, but without giving reasonable cause for offense in any quarter."[52]

The following day, Secretary Cass sent a copy of these instructions to E. K. Cooper who immediately replied that he was "profoundly thankful for the prompt attention." Cass wrote Cooper again on July 12, this time to remind him that he needed to post bond on Navassa island, as required by law, "so that you may enjoy the full benefits of the act." Cass said that a $100,000 bond should be furnished forthwith. Cooper promptly responded that because "the island is comparatively small, [and] the quantity of guano limited, . . . may I suggest this amount be reduced to fifty thousand dollars[?]" Cass replied that, under the circumstances, he had "no objection . . . to reducing the penalty of the bond. . . ." On September 2 Cooper forwarded the tardy surety, dated August 31, the third such guarantee accepted by the State department.[53]

Meanwhile, Commander T. Turner, skipper of USS *Saratoga,* had arrived at Navassa in early August to find that the Haitians had already withdrawn, leaving the Americans with orders not to mine the place. Turner assured a Mr. Frazier, the Coopers' supervisor, that he and his men were under the protection of the United States and that they might resume operations. Turner then sailed to Port-au-Prince and delivered a note to the Haitian foreign minister, the Duke of Tiburon, informing him that he, Turner, had been dispatched by his government to Navassa "to look after the interests of an American company . . . [and had been] directed by the President of the United States to afford them every necessary protection in the prosecution of their enterprise. . . ." Turner suggested "that the enlightened government of Hayti" should "revoke any orders" that violated "the rights of this company" under the Guano Act. Tiburon replied that "Navasa [*sic*] island . . . is part of the Haytian empire; that it was originally ceded to this government by the French. . . ." Turner responded that his orders were to protect the American company not to debate ownership, and he would obey orders. He further stated that he expected his "government would keep a cruiser there to protect [Americans] as long as they remained on the island," a threat sufficient to deter Haiti from further military action.[54]

Absence of diplomatic relations with the United States forced Haiti to employ B. C. Clark, its commercial agent in New York, to protest what it considered to be high-handed action by the Colossus of the North. In November Clark wrote Secretary Cass to say that the island in question had been passed by treaties from Spain to France to Haiti and that, informed of this, he was certain that the U.S. government, "consistent with the wisdom and justice of a great and generous nation," would bring to an end "the infringement on the rights of Hayti involved in the unauthorized occupancy of Navasa [*sic*] Island by citizens of the United States." Assistant Secretary Appleton promptly replied that an American citizen had "exhibited to this department proofs which were deemed sufficient that the island was derelict and abandoned, with guano of good quality, and having applied for the protection of this government in removing the guano therefrom, pursuant to the act of Congress of the 18th of August 1856, a copy of which is enclosed, [and] that application has been granted." Apparently in an attempt to soften the blow, Appleton added that "the act does not make it obligatory upon the government to retain permanent possession of the island," implying that once the guano was gone the United States would renounce its claim to the place.[55]

As Secretary Cass also explained, "The Government of the United States has determined to maintain the rights of its citizens to the Island of Navassa."[56] Afterward, as Haitian agent Clark attempted to argue the point, the State department simply "ceased to answer his letters."[57] It similarly ignored the protests of one J. H. Whitehurst who informed Secretary Cass during the summer of 1858 "that he had discovered guano on Navassa in 1855; that he had found the Island in the possession of Haiti; that he had entered into negotiations with the Haitian government in the winter of 1855-56 for a lease, but that this was not completed." He objected to the place being considered an American appurtenance under the Guano Act. As a State department study later noted, "no reply [to Whitehurst] . . . has been found."[58]

However supportive of the Coopers' claims to Navassa island the Buchanan administration might have been, E. K. Cooper fretted because he had not received a deed from the government, and late in 1858 he petitioned the second session of the Thirty-fifth Congress to recognize his family's right to the place by law. Maryland Senator Thomas G. Pratt introduced Senate bill 531 to achieve that end, but when the Foreign Relations committee sent the proposal to the State department for comment it was informed that Cooper "had already been admitted, by authority of the President, to all rights and privileges upon the island. . . . The committee therefore reported the bill back, with a recommendation that it not be passed, no further legislation being necessary. . . ."[59]

Still without documentation to that effect, in October 1859 Charles Gwinn, Cooper's attorney, wrote Secretary Cass stating that he believed the Guano Act required some formal action by the president. He suggested that on behalf of the government the Department of State should issue a certificate to Cooper through Duncan to recognize their successive rights to the island. Gwinn even enclosed a suggested draft, "which was corrected by someone in the Department and was subsequently used, not only with regard to Navassa but with regard to other islands also."[60] On December 8 Assistant Secretary Appleton informed Gwinn that because the attorney general was of the opinion there was no legal objection to such a procedure, a certificate acknowledging that "Edward K. Cooper is entitled . . . to guano on the said island" was enclosed therewith.

The Coopers mined Navassa island at least intermittently throughout the Civil War, reportedly shipping 1,635 tons of relatively high-grade phosphates to the mainland by 1864.[61] Because of the difficulty in recruiting workers, E. K. Cooper contracted with Maryland Governor Thomas Watkins Ligon to employ convict labor on the island, which was "above all known types of earthly punishment," one writer has asserted. "Desolation on the lonely islands [*sic*], boredom, untended illness and pyramiding resentments brought about reckless rebellion among prison laborers, and death was often concomitants of the cruel punishment. Tropical storms and hurricanes added to the prisoners' miseries, and following one severe storm forty of the unfortunates were found dead."[62]

Cooper may also have been involved with Antonio Pelletier, a sometime resident of New Orleans and, according to one government investigation, a notorious pirate and slaver. Pelletier appeared at Port-au-Prince in 1860 aboard the bark *William* and attempted to recruit "50 men and women (blacks, of course) to assist him in obtaining guano" on Navassa.[63] While Pelletier may well have been Cooper's agent, the Haitian government charged that he was actually bent on kidnaping its citizens with the intention of transporting them to New Orleans for sale on its auction blocks. Pelletier was arrested in Haiti, tried and convicted of slaving, and sentenced to death, a penalty that was reduced on appeal to five years.[64]

Perhaps because of ongoing labor difficulties, but more likely because he lacked the capital to exploit an island the size of Navassa (which contained phosphate reserves reestimated at 4.5 million tons), in 1864 Cooper traded his rights in the place for approximately $200,000 in common stock in Navassa Phosphate Company, a New York corporation bankrolled that year with $3 million by investors in Maryland, New York, Pennsylvania, and Rhode Island; John H. Fowler of Baltimore was elected its first president.[65] Much to its credit, the new company, which controlled the operation for much of the balance of the century, "worked the islands [*sic*] with paid labor instead of Maryland convict workers."[66] Nevertheless, Navassa was destined for infamy. In an era not known either for its humane working conditions or for progressive labor-management relations, a violent riot there in 1889 would call attention to it as a veritable Devil's island.[67]

E. K Cooper was not the only Marylander interested in the guano trade. For instance, Baltimore businessman William T. Kendall outfitted the brig *Fidelia* in November 1858 and placed it under the command of Captain Richard Daulby who was told to search the seas off Florida for likely prospects. Among the places Daulby examined was Verd key (or Cayo Verde), which is situated sixty miles west-southwest of Point Salina, Acklins island, the Bahamas. A narrow sliver of land two thirds of a mile long, seventy-two feet above sea level at its highest point, and covered with low sea-grape trees and prickly pears, Verd key is surrounded by rocks and reefs. Anchorage is tricky and landing very difficult.[68]

Daulby nevertheless ventured ashore. Poking about among the cactus he found no sign of human habitation but did discover substantial droppings, which had been deposited over the years by boobies and frigates. He directed his crew to erect a small shack out of ship's planking for shelter, then to commence loading guano, eighty tons of which his men eventually took on board as samples intended for delivery to Kendall.[69] They were still gathering cargo when a gale hit on November 22. The ship "parted her chains and went ashore—struck the reef and went down, and was totally lost."[70] The sailors made for nearby Ragged island in longboats but were rescued en route and taken to Havana, where they secured transportation to Baltimore and informed Kendall of the disaster.[71]

Far from discouraged, Kendall soon sent Daulby back to Verd key in command of the schooner *R. W. Troth,* which arrived there on January 20, 1859. The mariner later testified that the small shack that they had erected was still standing, undisturbed, and that they loaded another 130 tons of guano, which they transported back to Baltimore, arriving there in mid-March. Satisfied that the material was of commercial quality, Kendall again dispatched Daulby to Verd key for another load "and to take charge of the island." Once there, Daulby had the crew erect a more substantial dwelling. He also raised the American flag, and, on behalf of Kendall, claimed the island for the United States. While his crew was loading guano, HMS *Styx* arrived off the island and, to get the attention of those ashore, fired a shot. Daulby later swore that he raised and dipped his flag, whereupon *Styx* did likewise, then "went away."[72] When he departed for Baltimore in May, he left William L. Price behind in charge of a work gang of five men. Daulby instructed them to dig diligently while he was away hauling phosphates to Baltimore.[73]

Daulby landed the shipment in mid-June, and at month's end Kendall sent him back for more. Upon arriving at Verd key Daulby discovered the Union Jack flapping in the breeze above the island. Price came on board Daulby's ship and said that on June 8 an armed vessel under Theodore Farrington from Nassau in the Bahamas had landed at the island and informed Price that either he and his men would work for Farrington under British authority or Farrington would have them thrown into prison at Nassau. Price reluctantly agreed, and Farrington departed but not before stationing two armed men on the island. Soon after Daulby's arrival, Farrington returned and forbade the Americans from removing any of Kendall's property. Moreover, the Bahamian asked Daulby to transport a load of guano to Francis T. Montell, Farrington's agent in Baltimore, for $5 a ton freight, cash on delivery. His alternative being a return voyage with an empty cargo hold, Daulby accepted the offer with misgivings. Upon arrival in Baltimore, he delivered the cargo and attempted to collect the freight bill but instead was met by the sheriff with a writ of replevin that alleged that the guano had been stolen from British territory. The stuff was seized.[74]

Meanwhile, in May 1859 Kendall had formally filed on Verd key with the State department. In June he supplemented his application with additional documentation, including affidavits by Daulby and other employees attesting to the discovery of guano on the derelict key and its subsequent occupation. Assistant Secretary Appleton replied that the President has "deemed it his duty . . . to abstain from recognizing the privileges [that the Guano Act] . . . provides, unless he shall receive proof that the guano claimed to have been discovered is of a quality and in quantity such as would render it important in a national point of view."[75]

Within days Lord Lyons, the British minister to the United States, informed Secretary of State Cass that Verd key from which Americans were reportedly taking guano was Bahamian property as countless maps and charts published in the United States could readily attest. It had been leased to private individuals and might not be mined or visited without British permission. Cass replied that he would notify Kendall of the British claim, which the State department promptly did. By then aware of the situation, Kendall replied that Verd key was just as his documentation had described—derelict and perfectly suited, he thought, for exploitation under the Guano Act. He demanded that the U.S. government recognize his interest in the key and protect him from high-handed British interlopers.[76]

Secretary Cass referred the matter to Attorney General Black who was of the opinion that "The President of the United States has no right under the law to annex the island . . . or to put any American citizen in possession of it until the diplomatic question raised by the British Minister shall be finally settled, and not then, unless it be settled in our favor."[77] On March 19, 1860, the State department informed Kendall that "the President does not feel authorized, under the circumstances, to take any measures by which the said island would be considered as appertaining to the United States."[78] It apparently mattered little to Secretary Cass, Attorney General Black, or President Buchanan that circumstances surrounding Verd key were remarkably similar to those regarding Navassa, where the United States had cavalierly brushed aside Haitian claims.

Such did not escape Kendall's attention. Rebuffed by the administration, he petitioned Congress to redress his grievances, pointing to striking similarities of claims and counterclaims with respect to Navassa island and Verd key (except for the relative power of the nations involved) and asking for an indemnity of $105,604 to cover the value of the guano that his agent had discovered and then lost, as well as seized property.[79] Referred to the Senate's Committee on Foreign Relations, Kendall's plea was rejected because legislators agreed with the administration: that Verd key was long known to be part of the British Bahamian group. Hence, the committee saw "no reason to review the decision of the President."[80]

Meanwhile, although battered financially by the Verd key calamity, Kendall (obviously determined to remain active in the guano trade) had again dispatched Daulby aboard the brig *Delta* to prospect for other deposits. On March 19, 1860, Daulby sighted Alta Vela (or Alto Velo), a bell-shaped islet about three fourths of a mile long and one half mile wide and situated about twenty miles southwest of Point Beata, Dominican Republic. Daulby went ashore, found phosphates, claimed them under the Guano Act, loaded an undetermined quantity, and sent the ship home while he personally remained on the island with two men to work the place and to retain possession. Kendall informed the State department of these facts on May 14, adding emphatically that the uninhabited place lay outside the jurisdiction of any other government; he asked that he be officially recorded as its owner. On June 5 he wrote again and enclosed affidavits by Daulby and analyses that showed Alta Vela's guano was 66 percent pure phosphates. Kendall also asked that the department prescribe a suitable denomination for a bond so that he might complete his application.[81]

Assistant Secretary Appleton soon replied that his department was in receipt of a conflicting claim to Alta Vela which had been filed by Baltimoreans "Patterson and Murguiondo, through their agent Captain Kimball, also dated May 14, 1860. . . ." Appleton added that because of the counterclaim, because Kendall had not furnished information regarding the quantity of guano on the island, and because the Dominican Republic was likely to assert its jurisdiction over the place in question, the State department did not believe it advisable to suggest the appropriate value of a bond. Kendall quickly sent an analysis of the guano and, perhaps fixating on his recent problems regarding Verd key, stated emphatically that Alta Vela "was not within the jurisdiction of Haiti. . . ." He also asserted that Daulby had beaten Captain Kimball to the island by at least ten days. Despite Kendall's repeated attempts to secure U.S. government recognition of his claim to Alta Vela, the State department refused to alter its position.[82]

Baltimore businessmen Abram B. Patterson, a wholesale grocer, and Prudencio Murguiondo (sometimes spelled Murguiendo), the commercial consul of Uruguay who dabbled in imports and insurance, were neither novices with respect to guano islands nor uninformed as to State department policies and procedures. The previous July they had filed notice of discovery of guano on Monita island, a barren islet twelve hundred feet in diameter situated in the Mona passage (a sixty-one-mile-wide strait between Point Jiguero, Puerto Rico, and Cape Engaño, Haiti) and approximately three miles north of Mona island, a larger (six-mile-long, three-and-one-half-mile-wide) volcanic formation inhabited by wild cattle, goats, and swine and visited regularly by large flocks of sea birds. The State department promptly responded that it had previously been notified by the Spanish minister to the United States that both Monita and Mona belonged to Spain, they being dependencies of the Captaincy-General of Puerto Rico; indeed, American guano miners had been evicted from Monita in 1856, and Spanish authorities threatened prompt legal action against anyone who would mine their bird droppings without obtaining requisite permits from Puerto Rico. Apparently conceding the islets to Spain, Patterson and Murguiondo did not pursue the matter further.[83]

Rather, they looked elsewhere for fertilizers, and their quest eventually entwined with the impeachment of a president in a convoluted incident known to historians as the "Alta Vela affair."[84] Not long after failing to acquire title to Monita, Patterson and Murguiondo employed S. R. Kimball, master of the schooner *Boston,* to prospect other sites. According to an affidavit later filed by Kimball, he located phosphate deposits on Alta Vela on February 23, 1860, claimed it for his employers in the presence of witnesses, and left a note to that effect on the island. On March 23 (five days after Daulby had taken up residence on Alta Vela, or so he would later swear) Kimball returned and found the place to be uninhabited. He immediately began mining its phosphates. Precisely what (if anything) had happened to Daulby is unknown.[85]

On May 14 Patterson and Murguiondo notified the State department of Captain Kimball's discovery and enclosed a copy of a letter from the mariner outlining his find—a communiqué to which diplomats apparently never responded even though Assistant Secretary Appleton had promptly notified W. T. Kendall of Patterson and Murguiondo's counterclaim. While Kendall immediately supplied a variety of documents in support of his position, not until July 16 did Patterson and Murguiondo's attorney, George W. Barry (who apparently was unaware of Kendall's activity), provide affidavits from Kimball and others attesting to the discovery of guano on uninhabited Alta Vela; however, he gave no information regarding the quality or quantity of bird droppings—then or later. Nor was a bond either offered or provided for almost six years. Furthermore, the State department did not point out these inadequacies. In fact, diplomats failed to respond to Patterson and Murguiondo until December 1, at which time they merely acknowledged receipt of the information previously provided.[86] Why bureaucrats were so dilatory with respect to one claimant, while quick to reject the application of the other, is a question that has never been addressed.

Proceeding as though they believed a deed to Alta Vela would be forthcoming in due course, Patterson and Murguiondo occupied and mined the island from March 24 to October 24, 1860, their crews shipping 1,033 tons of phosphates to Baltimore where the commodity was reportedly worth $15 a ton, wholesale. By the end of September their digs had been visited on at least three occasions by naval vessels from Spain, Haiti, and the Dominican Republic, each of which peacefully sailed away upon being informed of the nature and nationality of the enterprise.[87]

The last visit, by the Dominican warship *Merced* in September, was occasioned by the request of its commanding officer for a sample of the guano, which was provided. Then on October 23 *Merced* returned with General Juan Evertz aboard. He went ashore, declared that the place was Dominican property, and told the dozen Americans then residing on the island to get off within twenty-four hours. When John A. Miller, manager for Patterson and Murguiondo, explained that it would be impossible to comply because they were without transportation, Evertz ordered fifty armed soldiers ashore who promptly destroyed the miners' camp, carted off selected pieces of equipment and two mules, and arrested the men who were forced aboard ship at gunpoint, hauled to Santo Domingo, and jailed. Captain Kimball soon arrived in that port aboard the schooner *Alice Mowe,* looking for his missing men, and he too was arrested. Eventually all the Americans were released to the resident U.S. commercial agent, Jonathan Elliott. He bade them be gone. They arrived in Baltimore on January 3.[88]

Outraged, Patterson and Murguiondo appealed to the State department for assistance in recovering Alta Vela, which, they contended, they were legally occupying under American law at the time of their eviction. They also asked for help in securing compensation for actual losses calculated to be $22,363.86. Secretary Jeremiah Black, who had recently moved from the Justice department to succeed Lewis Cass at State, replied on January 14 that the government would protect them in the enjoyment of any right they might have acquired under the Guano Act, but, inasmuch as the department had in fact warned another claimant (Kendall) in June of the possibility of Dominican sovereignty, he thought it best to ask his "special agent" in the Dominican Republic, William L. Cazneau, to ascertain the basis of Dominican claims.[89]

Obviously well acquainted with the guano trade from his involvement with Atlantic & Pacific Guano Company and the Swan islands off Honduras, Cazneau promptly talked with Dominican officials. He soon reported back to Washington that Dominicans contended "Altavela key . . . [was] within the line of the old Spanish colony, which now constitutes the territory of this republic." Cazneau observed that the island had been defined by Dominican law in 1855 as part of Azna Province, but, prior to the arrival of *Merced* in October, he could find no evidence that the republic had ever exercised authority over the place. Dominicans acknowledged that they were aware of Americans mining Alta Vela for some time before they had acted, and when asked why they had permitted foreigners to invest so heavily, "preparing it for extensive and profitable development, without warning them of the claim now put forth by their government," Cazneau said, "I was never able to obtain a lucid and satisfactory answer."[90]

Secretary Black, a Democrat, had departed the State department before Cazneau's report reached Washington. Ironically, William H. Seward, a Republican and principal architect of the Guano Islands Act, succeeded him as chief diplomat for the new president, Abraham Lincoln; however, Seward proved not to be a champion of his own legislation or a supporter of guano prospectors. On the other hand, Black became even more deeply immersed in bird droppings. Introduced by one of his relatives to Patterson and Murguiondo well before he had left office, promptly thereafter he became their legal counsel in all dealings with the government regarding Alta Vela.[91] Within weeks of his departure from the State department, private attorney Black wrote Secretary Seward to express the view that his clients, having submitted "evidence of their discovery and possession, . . . [were] entitled to be protected by the power of this government."[92]

In championing Patterson and Murguiondo's cause, Black conveniently ignored their glaringly incomplete filing, especially the absence of bond, which, as attorney general in 1857, he had insisted was absolutely necessary before a president could proclaim an island to be an American appurtenance, or defend it—an omission not corrected for five years when Black himself belatedly sent surety to the State department.[93] Furthermore, the separate opinion that "The President of the United States has no right under the law to annex the island . . . or to put any American citizen in possession of it until the diplomatic question" concerning sovereignty "shall be finally settled, and not then, unless it be settled in our favor,"[94] was wholly ignored by the very attorney general who had authored it. Rather, long before the shooting had started in the Civil War, Black was insisting that the Yankee government either compel the Dominicans to accede to U.S. claims to Alta Vela or risk implied weakness given "our domestic troubles."[95]

"By direction of the President," Secretary Seward ignored Black's repeated appeals because "the time was unpropitious to prosecute the claim of Patterson and Murguiondo, however just it might be." Not only were the southern states in rebellion, but, as far as the Lincoln administration was concerned, "Spain at the same time [was] waging a war of invasion and conquest against the republic of St. Domingo. . . ."[96] Black renewed his appeal on behalf of his clients each year throughout the Civil War, and, each year, Secretary Seward failed to reply.[97]

By 1867 circumstances had changed substantially, but, as far as Black was concerned, they had not improved. Although the Civil War was over and the Confederacy vanquished, Lincoln was dead and his successor, Andrew Johnson, was a weakling who deferred entirely to his secretary of State, William H. Seward, who openly desired to expand American interests in the Caribbean—but not through guano islands. For instance, Seward tried to buy the Virgin islands from the Danes in 1867, a purchase stymied when the islands were battered by earthquakes and storms, thereby raising substantive questions as to their real strategic value.[98]

More pertinent to the Alta Vela question, Seward (on behalf of the U.S. Navy) also tried to lease Samaná bay from the Dominicans who, once again, were free of Spanish control. When that failed, he had President Johnson hint in his 1868 state-of-the-union address at the island nation's outright annexation. "Under these circumstances," diplomatic historian Charles Tansill has written, "it was not likely that [Seward] would press upon the attention of the Dominican Government the claim of Messrs. Patterson and Murguiendo." In fact, Seward informed President Johnson "that while he was conducting [Samaná bay] negotiations during the first half of the year 1867 he had refused on the 'grounds of inexpediency' to support this claim to the island of Alta Vela."[99]

Although failing to respond directly to Black's repeated appeals on behalf of his clients, Seward did send Patterson and Murguiondo's case to the Bureau of Claims for evaluation. Observing the proximity of Alta Vela to both the Haitian and Dominican coasts, Examiner E. Peshine Smith concluded on June 17, 1867, that the place likely belongs to one or the other of them. "It is enough that *either* had it," he judged, "to make it improper for the government [of the United States] to support the claimant[s] in the demand for damages."[100]

Meanwhile, having had no response from Seward, Black wrote President Johnson to summarize the position of his clients and to ask that the U.S. Navy promptly restore their property. Rather than a reply to that communiqué, Black received instead notification of Examiner Smith's view that Patterson and Murguiondo's claim was insupportable and that President Johnson had accepted Smith's conclusion. Simultaneously Black learned from other sources that New Yorkers Henry Root and Thomas R. Webster (doing business at first as Webster & Co., then, later, as Alta Vela Guano Company) had leased the key from the Dominican government and, incorrectly, that Seward had blessed the new venture by advising the new tenants that the place unquestionably belonged to the Dominicans.[101]

Furious, Black again wrote President Johnson, praying that the chief executive was "wholly incapable of sanctioning, directly or indirectly, a naked robbery like this."[102] Vehemently attacked by radical reconstructionists in Congress for his conciliatory policies toward defeated Confederates, Johnson actually anticipated needing Black's considerable legal talents in an upcoming battle with the radicals, and, apparently as consequence, the president pressed Seward to revisit the Alta Vela matter. Accordingly, Seward directed Examiner Smith to study the case again. In a supplemental report dated September 19, 1867, Smith once more concluded that, by rule of proximity, the place in question belonged either to Haiti or the Dominican Republic; therefore, Patterson and Murguiondo had clearly failed to meet the test of claiming an island, rock, or key not under the lawful jurisdiction of another government, and their title should not be recognized nor should their claim for damages be supported.[103]

As diplomatic historian Charles Tansill has observed, Smith's opinions ignored three relevant precedents, all related to guano islands. First was Daniel Webster's assertion in 1852 during the Lobos affair that the ordinary jurisdiction of a state, by right of contiguity, extended merely three miles from a coast—of which it is "very possible that Smith was not aware. . . ."[104] Nevertheless, he almost certainly knew that Washington had pressured Venezuela to pay Philo Shelton and others $130,000 for their losses due to eviction from Aves in 1854. In fact, in 1863 (even as the Civil War raged at home) Secretary of the Navy Gideon Welles had dispatched Admiral Charles Wilkes aboard USS *Vanderbilt* to La Guayra, Venezuela, to collect Aves payments then in arrears, Wilkes forcing the Latin Americans virtually at gunpoint to agree to earmark customs duties to satisfy that obligation.[105] Moreover, the precedent of Navassa island, where the Buchanan administration had pointedly ignored proximity and, using naval power, vigorously defended Baltimore businessmen from Haiti (a parallel with Alta Vela continuously pointed to by Patterson and Murguiondo), according to Tansill, was "purposely overlooked in [Smith's] opinions. . . ."[106]

Black inferred that Seward had a personal reason for not defending American claim to Alta Vela. Seward's friend and political crony, journalist-lobbyist Thurlow Weed (who is sometimes credited with giving the secretary of State the idea of buying Alaska from the Russians), was alleged to have a financial interest in the new Dominican leaseholder, Webster & Co., an allegation Weed angrily denied.[107] Although no evidence of duplicity ever surfaced, Black readily believed the worst about Seward—"that he was sacrificing [Black's] clients not only for the sake of his diplomatic scheme to secure Samaná Bay [for the Navy] but also to line the pocket of his friend Weed."[108]

Securing a personal interview with President Johnson late in 1867, Black pressed his clients' case, threatening (if he did not receive satisfaction from the administration) to petition Congress where the chief executive faced enough problems, including the impending threat of impeachment. Johnson reportedly assured Black that he "would not support Seward in any dubious practices," but this failed to placate Patterson and Murguiondo. Although holding off on their memorial, they "put their claim before certain Republican Senators" who supported a resolution requesting from the administration "all correspondence relating to Alta Vela." On February 12, 1868, Seward "sent to President Johnson the file in the Department of State supposedly containing all the letters in question," which was sent on to Capitol Hill and published.[109]

One of Black's associates immediately charged that the file had been purged of damaging documents, especially correspondence that showed Thurlow Weed's involvement with Webster & Co. Black again wrote President Johnson to appeal to his "sense of justice" and to protest how Patterson and Murguiondo "are daily being robbed of their property by the company which holds possession of the island under the auspices of Mr. Seward. . . ."[110] Black enclosed a copy of his clients' proposed memorial to Congress (no doubt implying its imminent submission on Capitol Hill) as well as the draft of an order that Black asked Johnson to issue "placing the island of Alta Vela back in possession of the Baltimore claimants" to avoid the petition reaching Congress.[111]

By then the president's problems had multiplied. On February 24 the House of Representatives had approved articles of impeachment against him for having fired Secretary of War Edwin M. Stanton in violation of the Tenure in Office Act (1867). Desiring to employ eminent counsel for his defense, Johnson engaged Black as one of his attorneys for the forthcoming trial before the Senate, despite the vigorous opposition of Secretary Seward.[112]

Black's son and associate, Chauncey, soon secured endorsement of the Patterson and Murguiondo memorial from four of the seven Radical Republican House members who were to prosecute Johnson in the Senate, thereby implying that it would be "expedient" for Johnson—facing their wrath—"to favor the clients of Judge Black." When pointed pressure failed to produce desired results, Jeremiah Black presented the president with an ultimatum on March 14: order the Navy to restore Patterson and Murguiondo to the island, or he would withdraw from Johnson's defense team. Even though the embattled chief executive reportedly harbored severe reservations regarding Seward's handling of Alta Vela, he confided to Navy secretary Gideon Welles that, inasmuch as the issue of the island was then before Congress, he (Johnson) "was not inclined to make himself a party in the matter." Five days later Black carried out his threat and withdrew.[113]

As it turned out, Black's eloquence was superfluous, for Johnson survived trial in the Senate by a single vote. Patterson and Murguiondo's appeal to Congress (finally submitted in December) quietly died in the Senate's Foreign Relations committee, perhaps victim of legislator weariness with the subject. Unwilling to give up, in 1869 Black asked the Grant administration's State department to reconsider the matter, but it declined, allegedly because of the new president's interest in annexing the Dominican Republic.[114]

Many contemporary observers believed that Secretary Seward "had realized large dividends from his diplomacy." Especially was this true of

Seward's actions with respect to ratification of the Alaska Purchase Treaty—"activities which [reportedly] induced the House of Representatives to vote the purchase money only after some of its more important members had been bribed by funds from the Russian Minister." While these allegations were not confirmed by a subsequent investigation, diplomatic historian Charles Tansill asserts that "modern research has conclusively shown that if Seward was not personally corrupt he was none the less a bold and adroit liar."[115]

Perhaps William Seward's actions in the Alta Vela affair evidenced corrupt, even sinister statecraft, as Tansill has concluded; however, another interpretation is also possible. As previously mentioned, Patterson and Murguiondo's filing on Alta Vela was fatally flawed, falling far short of the standards imposed by none other than Jeremiah Black when he was attorney general. Even if the Dominican Republic had not asserted claim to the place, it is entirely likely that the Baltimore businessmen's application for title would have been rejected anyway by Seward's State department, if not by Black's which preceded it.

Then again, perhaps not. After all, the State department's oversight of American guano islands was consistently inconsistent.

# 7

## Shrinking Empire, 1866-1902

Interest in bird droppings intensified once more after the Civil War. Not only was the Guano Islands Act modified by Congress, but entrepreneurs also filed on many new places (and some old ones), increasing the number of official American appurtenances to sixty-six by 1884; however, over time the U.S. Department of State increasingly avoided the odious issue either by ignoring filings altogether or by declining to support claimants in disputes with other nations. Consequently, the number of guano islands officially recognized by Washington steadily decreased after 1884 until fewer than two dozen remained by the time the last complete application for title to yet another appurtenance was presented in 1902.

Ironically, even as American diplomats casually discarded national territory, the U.S. government unhesitatingly acquired other non-contiguous possessions, some large and some not. In 1867 the Johnson administration purchased Alaska from Imperial Russia for $7.2 million; also in 1867, at the direction of the Department of the Navy, which needed a coaling station, Commander William Reynolds (captain of USS *Lackawanna*) took possession of Midway island in the Pacific—both actions encouraged by the expansionistic author of the Guano Act, Secretary of State William H. Seward. In 1898 the Navy also seized Wake island in the Pacific for use as a cable station, and later that year by joint resolution Congress approved the annexation of Hawaii. Likewise in 1898, as a consequence of the Spanish-American War, the United States added Puerto Rico and Guam to the commonwealth, and, briefly, even the Philippines. The following year America acquired part of Samoa, dividing it with the Germans by treaty.[1]

Meanwhile, almost unnoticed by the public at large, American guano islands continued to exist—and, for a time, even to increase in number.

Furthermore, at the request of constituents, lawmakers repeatedly modified the Guano Act, mostly to suspend the prohibition against exports but also to extend filing privileges to widows and other heirs and assignees of discoverers. The first modification of the law was prompted by requests from American Guano Company, which, like other Yankee phosphate miners in the Pacific that were shut out of lucrative southern markets during the Civil War, begged legislative relief. Doubtlessly seeing the action as a wartime expedient, Congress consequently attached a rider to the 1862 tariff bill to suspend for one year that portion of the Guano Act which required "That no guano shall be taken from said island, rock, or key, except for the use of citizens of the United States, or of persons resident therein. . . ."[2]

This change in the law apparently alerted New York bondsmen William Russell and J. W. Delano, who saw an opportunity to jump a claim. They informed the State department that American Guano had been shipping phosphates illegally to Bordeaux and Hamburg for years. Declaring that they had no power to restrain the company, Russell and Delano asked to be relieved of their roles as sureties and asserted that, because the bond had been breached, American Guano should forfeit its rights under the Guano Act. Moreover, they asked that "they be appointed government agents to dispose of the guano for the benefit of the United States Treasury."[3]

Believing that the petition represented nothing more than "a business rivalry for control of the guano trade,"[4] diplomats nevertheless referred the matter to the U.S. Department of Justice for an opinion. Notwithstanding section 2 of the law, which specifically states that "any breach" shall be "deemed a forfeiture of all rights,"[5] Attorney General Edward Bates concurred with the State department, saying "that the mere breach of . . . bond is [not] sufficient reason for releasing its obligation. . . . It is my opinion that, by Constitution and law, the President has not any duty to perform in this case."[6]

The first suspension of the prohibition against guano exports expired in 1863, and, following a year's hiatus, Congress renewed it, this time for two years. Meanwhile, American Guano had continued to sell phosphates to Europe even though such was technically a violation of the law, an activity that evidently prompted Russell and Delano to reinstate their attempt at claim jumping. They argued with the State department that American Guano should relinquish Baker as well as other islands under its control because the company had allowed foreign ships to haul goods in contravention of Section 3 of the Guano Islands Act, which explicitly reserved such commerce to vessels of U.S. registry.[7]

Again diplomats referred the matter to the Justice department, and in 1866 Attorney General James Speed ruled that, having expressly suspended the section of the Guano Act which reserved products for the exclusive use of American residents and citizens, Congress by implication had likewise temporarily repealed the portion of the law which required the output of U.S. appurtenances to be carried exclusively by the merchant marine of the United States. With American Guano's title to Baker secure, the company mined the island intermittently for another two decades.[8]

After the Civil War, devastated and depressed southern agriculture offered scant market opportunities to those who mined guano, and American entrepreneurs became increasingly dependent upon Europe for their sales. Congress consequently renewed the suspension in 1867, 1872, 1878, and 1884 for periods ranging from one to ten years.[9] By the late 1880s guano companies were also experiencing ever-increasing competition from rock phosphate producers in the continental United States who suffered no similar restrictions on the exportation of their commodity; however, efforts in 1889 to suspend the guano export prohibition once more were effectively opposed by organized labor, which abhorred working conditions on guano islands such as Navassa in the Caribbean where a bloody riot that year resulted in deaths and in the prosecution of several workers for murder. Despite additional pleas for relief in 1891 by guano companies that claimed a reversion to an exclusive American market after 1889 had "operated disastrously upon all [guano] enterprises in which American citizens and capital are engaged,"[10] Congress thereafter declined to cooperate.[11]

The issue of dowager's rights under the Guano Act arose after the Civil War when Harriet E. Parker, who claimed to be the widow of William H. Parker (alleged discoverer of guano on Johnston island in the Pacific), petitioned Congress for relief. Even though Attorney General J. S. Black in 1859 had said William Parker's claim to the atoll was fatally flawed, Harriet Parker pursued title to the place through him, but her attorney said he could find no provision in the law by which she might file. Residing in Indiana, she solicited help from Representative William S. Holman who introduced legislation to allow her one year in which to perfect an application "to secure her interests . . . in the South [*sic*] Pacific islands called Johnston and Agnes [Sand] islands . . . as if the same had been done by William H. Parker, deceased. . . ." Passed without debate by the House of Representatives on April 2, 1870, the measure went to the Senate for its concurrence.[12]

The upper chamber scrutinized the proposal far more carefully. When the House bill was favorably reported without amendment by the Senate's Committee on Commerce in late April, members on the floor not only observed that the atoll was actually situated in the North Pacific but also questioned the need for a special relief bill. As the widow of the alleged discoverer of guano, did she not automatically inherit her late husband's rights, if any? The measure went back to committee.[13] While legislators checked geography and pondered entitlement, Parker solicited documentation from the State department to support her case. She also informed diplomats that she held one-half interest in her late husband's claim through inheritance from her son (and sole support) who had died in the Civil War and that she represented her daughter, Agnes (Parker) Burt, who held the balance. Furthermore, Parker asked for an outline of procedures by which she might post bond on Johnston and Agnes islands, asserting in passing that "the certificate to the Pacific Guano Company, signed by Secretary [Lewis] Cass, was a forgery. . . ."[14]

President U. S. Grant's secretary of State, Hamilton Fish, former junior senator from New York who in 1856 had assisted William Seward in securing passage of the Guano Act, curtly informed Parker that diplomats no longer delved into bird droppings. He said his department "must therefore decline to give advice, direction, or approval, in respect to the form, penalty or sureties in the proposed bond, and confines itself strictly to . . . [filing] papers which you deem material. . . ."[15]

Meanwhile, when the Senate's commerce committee again favorably reported the bill on June 14, this time with corrected geography, Senator George E. Spencer of Alabama disclosed that title to Johnston and Agnes islands was clouded by a California company, Pacific Guano, which had long since posted bond on the atoll, its deed having been obtained through William Parker's alleged original discovery. Senator Charles Sumner of Massachusetts consequently asked that the matter be sent back to committee for further study. Inasmuch as time in that session of Congress was growing short, Wisconsin Senator Timothy O. Howe suggested instead that as a compromise the bill be amended so that, subject to perfected proofs,[16] "no party entitled under this act is ever allowed to charge more for guano than one-half the prices in the act of August 18, 1856, . . . [and] that nothing in the act is to be construed to prejudice the rights or claims of any person claiming an interest . . . under any contract or agreement with Parker."[17] On June 15 the altered bill passed the upper chamber by a vote of twenty-eight to zero and was returned to the House for its reconsideration.[18]

A month later, Representative Ebon C. Ingersoll of Illinois asked unanimous consent to suspend the rules in order to approve the Senate's version with dispatch; however, Representative Aaron A. Sargent of California (by then alerted to the pending challenge to the rights of San Francisco's Pacific Guano Company) objected to the bill, saying "it is a fraud." He insisted that the proposal be reexamined by the House's Committee on Commerce. His opposition forced a vote to suspend the rules that failed sixty-three to sixty-one, a two-thirds majority being required.[19] When that session of Congress adjourned the following day without action on Harriet Parker's relief bill, the matter seemingly died.

Her petition resurfaced two years later when the Forty-second Congress voted again to suspend the prohibition against the exportation of American guano, this time for ten years. Attached to the House bill was a rider to amend the Guano Act in order "to extend to the widow, heirs, executors, or administrators of such discoverers, where such discoverer shall have died before perfecting proof," filing privileges under the law.[20]

Representative Sargent of California again objected. He said that William Parker "had sold for a valuable consideration all his interest in [Johnston and Agnes] islands to a guano company, which ever since has been in possession of them and working them, and which has invested a large amount of money. . . ." Sargent proposed to alter the bill by adding "That nothing herein contained shall be held to impair any rights of discovery, or any assignment by a discoverer heretofore recognized by the Government of the United States." Legislators approved the amendment and then both the ten-year suspension of the export prohibition and the limited rights of heirs by voice votes.[21] In late March the Senate similarly endorsed the measure without debate and sent it to President Grant who signed it into law on April 2, 1872.[22]

Armed with a revised statute, Parker renewed her effort to secure title to Johnston atoll by appealing to President Grant who called upon his Justice department for advice. On May 8, 1873, Solicitor General Samuel F. Phillips replied that "This whole question had been before . . . Attorney General Black in 1859, . . . [who] concluded . . . that [William Parker] never possessed any such rights in severalty, and that the Pacific Guano Company were [*sic*] entitled to claim the benefits of the act of 1856. . . ."[23] Furthermore, because Pacific Guano's title had been recognized and vested before 1872, the company was specifically "saved by the act of 1872," and "no person can now claim these islands through Mr. Parker." Phillips acknowledged that if Pacific Guano had subsequently abandoned the islands, as Harriet Parker asserted, they "are again subject to original proceedings before the Secretary of State. In any event, Mrs. Parker will be obliged to take possession and occupy [them] before she can be heard, . . . [whereupon] the question of forfeiture may be contested by those who pretend to adversary interests."[24]

Even so, she did not meekly abandon her prior claim to Johnston and Agnes islands, for she continued to file affidavits with the State department that alleged fraud by Pacific Guano. In 1873 diplomats advised her to seek redress in the courts. That having failed, Agnes Burt, Parker's daughter, attempted to renew her mother's claim in 1879, without success. Then, in 1879 one Melvina H. Parker, who said she was married to William Parker at the time of his death, asked the State department for deed to the islands. Diplomats similarly rejected her application; however, Melvina Parker's unsuccessful quest perhaps explains why Harriet Parker had so diligently pursued personal-relief legislation. Having apparently been divorced from William, she did not actually hold dowager's rights.[25]

Meanwhile, on Johnston and Agnes (or Sand) islands, Pacific Guano of San Francisco reportedly had removed phosphates intermittently after the Civil War. In 1885 the company asked the State department about the legality of transferring ownership of the atoll to a British corporation and was advised "that assignment of a guano grant to an alien owner would annul the relationship which the Government of the United States holds under the existing statute."[26] Evidently the sale never materialized, for the company reportedly remained in nominal control of the islands as late as 1892 when the British attempted to annex them, prompting the firm to request assistance from Washington. Even though the U.S. government declined to dispute the British move, Hawaii (which had apparently forgotten that it had renounced its claim to the atoll in 1858 in the face of an American challenge) did object, and the British "protectorate [was consequently] afterward withdrawn."[27] Following U.S. annexation of Hawaii in 1898, Johnston and Sand for a time came to be "regarded as part of [that] territory," but, according to the State department, "no record has been found . . . indicating when or how the Hawaiian Government took possession of these islands. . . ."[28]

U.S. diplomats sincerely desired to extricate themselves from the guano quagmire after the Civil War, as Secretary Fish had implied to Harriet Parker, but the odious appurtenances would not simply disappear. Indeed, many additional places were added to America's guano empire, albeit temporarily. Unequaled among post-war prospectors was James W. Jennett, a New York mariner active in the Caribbean and Gulf of Mexico. All told, he claimed two dozen tropical islands, far more than anyone since Alfred G. Benson, whose death in 1878[29] left Jennett unchallenged as America's foremost guanopreneur.

More obscure even than Benson, Jennett had sailed on an undisclosed mission prior to the Civil War—perhaps purposely searching for guano prospects, perhaps not. In any case, he later said that in April 1857 he discovered guano on the six (eleven, according to Jennett) islands that constitute Serraña bank (or keys), which are situated about three hundred miles southwest of Jamaica. Sometime thereafter he found other deposits throughout the Campeche bank in the Gulf of Mexico, northwest of the

Yucatán peninsula: specifically on Alacráns and Arcas islands and Triangle keys, none of which he immediately claimed under American law.[30] He later swore that in 1860 he occupied the most promising of these, the Serraña keys, but "when the War broke out," he said, "I abandoned them for a time. . . ."[31]

However Jennett might have been engaged during that conflict, afterward he returned to the pursuit of guano islands. He outfitted the schooner *Petrel* in 1866 and sailed into the Caribbean with the objective of "putting them under the American flag. . . ."[32] He scoured the basin between June 1866 and January 1867 for other likely prospects and located what he believed to be commercial quantities of bird droppings on such islands, rocks, and keys as Aves, Morant, Petrel (or Bajo Nuevo), Pedro, Quito Sueño, Rogues, Roncador, and Serranilla—all of them situated between Jamaica and the Central American mainland.[33]

Jennett occupied Serraña in September 1867 and commenced mining, using a half dozen Caribbean laborers. He shipped 260 tons of rock phosphate to New York aboard the schooner *Mary Mankin* in October and filed affidavits of discovery with the State department the following January, thereafter furnishing such supplementary documentation as diplomats demanded,[34] including the observation that the keys had a "splendid harbor" ideally suited to becoming a coaling station for the U.S. Navy, should the government be interested in buying it from him.[35] Ignoring the offer, Secretary Seward merely advised Jennett that the State department required a $50,000 bond on Serraña keys, which Jennett posted in August 1868.[36] No doubt encouraged by official recognition of his claim to Serraña, he also filed declarations of discovery on Aves, Arenas, Morant, Pedro, Petrel, Quito Sueño, Roncador, and Serranilla in 1869, applications that coincided with changes both in administrations and guano islands policy.[37]

In 1869 U.S. Grant succeeded the embattled Andrew Johnson as president, and, after a short hiatus, Grant appointed Hamilton Fish to replace the expansionistic William Seward as secretary of State. Circumspect and conservative, Fish earlier (when he was junior senator from New York) had helped Seward secure passage of the Guano Act (even to broaden its application), but, as secretary of State, Fish soon initiated a new hands-off procedure regarding American appurtenances. At his direction the State department became merely a caretaker for claims—a "depository of such papers as discoverers may choose to place in the files,"[38] as he explained to Harriet Parker. Diplomats thereafter did little beyond preserving information filed with the department and acknowledging that "this had been done."[39] As scholar Green Haywood Hackworth once analyzed the department's new policy, "There [was] no provision in the Guano Island Act requiring the

President to proclaim that the conditions of the Act have been complied with, and that a certain island or islands may be 'considered as appertaining to the United States.' "[40]

Following Secretary Fish's lead, departmental bureaucrats for a time thereafter steadfastly "declined to vouch for the legality of mortgages or assignments. . . ." Diplomats even came to contend that, notwithstanding the military powers clause of the Guano Act, "the Government does not grant protective rights to alleged discoverers of guano islands. . . ." Rather, its only role was "in the event of any of its citizens becoming embroiled in a controversy with citizens or subjects of a foreign Government with regard to ownership of a guano deposit, [at which time] it is to use its diplomatic interference to redress the wrongs inflicted upon its citizens should they not in any manner have transgressed the laws of a foreign nationality."[41] Therefore, as one critic of department policy has insisted, "Fish [arbitrarily] annulled to some extent the force of the [Guano] Act, and . . . [as a consequence] the United States abandoned as many islands as possible, Great Britain confiscating several of them."[42]

Abruptly and unilaterally altering procedures with respect to its handling of guano island applications about 1869, the State department failed to call public attention to this change in policy. Claimants consequently continued to file on islands, rocks and keys in the mistaken belief that, if they submitted enough paperwork, someday the government would officially recognize their title and issue proclamations to that effect. Rather, bureaucrats merely squirreled away such documents (some of which overlapped and conflicted), many of them inadvertently misplaced—lost![43]

Interestingly, as American diplomats became increasingly equivocal with respect to guano islands, officials with the U.S. Department of the Treasury became more conscientious about keeping track of these places since appurtenances were expressly exempted from import levies. Therefore, tax collectors compiled at least four rosters of American guano islands for use by customs agents and directed collectors to be especially vigilant to see that no foreign vessels be allowed to engage in this "coasting trade." The first, a printed list dated August 23, 1867, enumerated fifty-eight places (with locations) grouped together by the companies (or individuals) that claimed them, but in no discernible order. The second, printed and dated February 12, 1869, identified seventy-one place names alphabetically; it deleted such sites as Sombrero island (which by then had been surrendered to the British) but carried many duplicate entries such as Starbuck island (which had been filed on separately both as Barren and as Hero). The third, a typescript dated December 22, 1885, listed sixteen aggregations of guano islands grouped by the order of their bonds; it likewise contained many duplications. The fourth, a typescript dated September 16, 1893, reduced bonded groups to fourteen by deleting those places whose sovereignty by then had been conceded to other nations. Although it thereafter failed either to update the most recent list or to eliminate duplicate names and filings, by 1902 the Treasury department officially recorded bonds for sixty-six different islands, rocks, or keys around the globe.[44]

Jennett both benefited and suffered from these contradictory public policies—the State department's unilateral decision to renounce guano islands, on the one hand, and the Treasury department's scrupulous efforts to identify all appurtenances, on the other. Despite conflicting claims by Colombia, Great Britain, Honduras, Mexico, and Venezuela to many of the places he claimed (several of which, such as Venezuelan pretensions to Aves, were obviously known to American diplomats at the time of his filings), the mariner either was not informed of potential conflicts, or, even when notified, his applications (or those of his assignees) were almost routinely filed away by the State department—or were inadvertently listed by the Treasury department as bonded appurtenances, despite State's disapproval. In at least one instance (that of Booby key), the island did not exist but was nevertheless listed as a bonded appurtenance. Subsequent requests by Jennett in 1879 for deeds to Alacráns and Triangles resulted in the list of official American guano islands growing to sixteen bonded groups.[45]

In 1879 Jennett also filed on such Caribbean sites as Arcas key, Great island, and Gorda key, but he failed to post bonds for any of these; consequently, they were never listed by the Treasury department as American appurtenances.[46] Although he also offered an affidavit of discovery of guano on Rogues island (seventy-five miles north of Caracas, Venezuela) and claimed to have occupied and mined it for six months in 1869, neither he nor any of his numerous assignees ever posted bond on the place; hence, it likewise was never considered to be "under the protection and jurisdiction of the [U.S.] Government."[47]

While the U.S. government ultimately recognized the titles of other nations to all of Jennett's filings except Petrel and Serranilla bank,[48] many if not most of these places were in limbo for much of the balance of the nineteenth century. Several of them were also burdened by conflicting claims filed by other Americans. Either as sole operator or in association with others, Jennett purported to have mined Pedro, Petrel, Quito Sueño, Roncador, and Serraña islands between 1866 and 1885,[49] an assertion the State department found to be less than entirely credible. Diplomats later observed that there was "no evidence that any guano was ever removed from [Petrel] Key,"[50] and as to Quito Sueño, they declared that Jennett "lied" because "no one could live [there] from March to September . . . [as] almost all of it [is] completely under water."[51] While asserting that many of "his statements are not reliable," the State department nevertheless conceded that "he may really have taken guano off Serraña in 1867, and possibly at other times."[52]

Prior to his death about the turn of the century, James W. Jennett (once characterized by an American diplomat as a "worthless adventurer"[53]) repeatedly peddled his rights to various Gulf and Caribbean islands even though their titles were often clouded by the claims of other prospectors and their sovereignty contested by other nations. For undisclosed terms in 1869, he sold to one Thomas A. Mitchell the Serranilla keys, four tiny dots of land two hundred miles southwest of Jamaica; Morant keys, four islets forty miles southeast of Port Morant, Jamaica; and Arenas key, a six hundred by nine hundred foot reef situated one hundred miles off the northwestern point of Yucatán peninsula. Seven years later Mitchell conveyed them to John G. Wilson, who three years afterward transferred ownership to William L. Van Derlip, Charles D. Gilmore, and Howard A. Snow, principals for Caribbean Islands Guano Company of Washington, D.C. Answering a query from Van Derlip about these places (and the validity of Jennett's filings), the State department asserted that the United States "lays no claims to jurisdiction over [these] islands. . . ."[54] Nevertheless, when Van Derlip and associates offered bond in 1879, diplomats accepted it, and the islands were dutifully listed by the Treasury department as American appurtenances.[55]

Although it appears that Caribbean Islands Guano never mined any of these sites, its assignment derived from Jennett was still valid when, on August 1, 1877, Jennett again sold "all of his interests"[56] in the Morant keys to Prudencio de Murguiondo of Baltimore who, with Abram Patterson, had unsuccessfully attempted to occupy and mine Alta Vela before the Civil War. With Ward H. Lamon, a Washington, D.C., lawyer, Murguiondo organized Morant Guano Company in 1877 and sent the schooner *Eva* to the island for a load of phosphates. Murguiondo also filed for title under the Guano Act, an application ultimately rejected by the State department whose bureaucrats noted that the keys had been under British authority at least since 1862—a fact entirely overlooked by them two years later when they apparently inadvertently accepted Caribbean Islands Guano Company's bond on the same place. Meanwhile, Murguiondo and Lamon continued to exploit Morant until December 23, 1877, when HMS *Blanche* ordered their employees off. Protest though Murguiondo and Lamon did, the State department declined to intervene on their behalf.[57]

Even though he had already disposed of all his rights to Arenas key to Thomas A. Mitchell, in 1878 Jennett sold another quarter interest in the same place to Pascal A. Quinan, a Baltimore physician and sometime lecturer at the Washington University Medical School who eventually joined forces with Philadelphia businessman John G. Wallis who independently filed on the identical place two years later. Together they shipped several hundred tons of phosphates before Mexican authorities discovered their activities in 1881 and sent the gunboat *Libertad* to remove them.[58] Meanwhile, in 1878 Jennett had hawked another three-fourths interest in Arenas to one Michael Hooper. Twelve years later Jennett resold 100 percent of Arenas's guano to Jerome B. Graybill, Jennett's assorted assignments on the island by then aggregating 300 percent.[59]

In 1883 Jennett peddled his interests in Alacráns keys (Chica, Perez, and Pájaros islands), ninety miles north of Yucatán, to Edward Steel, that title passing eventually to South American Bird Guano Company, which apparently never exploited the keys. Seven years later Jennett resold rights to Chica island to Jerome B. Graybill and separately conveyed title to Perez island to one James H. Lancaster. That year Jennett also transferred the deed to Pájaros island to John H. Hall, who passed it on to Arthur Brash; Brash also obtained directly from Jennett the rights to nonexistent Placoa island, supposedly situated in the same group. Diplomats soon informed a no doubt chagrined Brash that "there was no record of any discovery of guano on these Islands by Jennett, and that they were not listed either under Alacráns or under their own names."[60] At the same time he purchased Placoa from Jennett, Brash also bought the title to the Western Triangles, which Jennett had transferred to Aves Guano Company ten years earlier.[61]

However commonplace Jennett's multiple conveyances throughout the Gulf, they were all vigorously contested by Mexico, which asserted that the most of these islands belonged to it. In 1894 the U.S. government consequently deleted Alacráns, Arenas, and the Triangles keys from its list of guano islands and formally recognized Mexican sovereignty over them.[62]

Indeed, uncontested ownership of Jennett's many properties was singularly lacking, as Aves Guano Company discovered. In addition to selling three of the six Serranilla keys to Thomas Mitchell in 1869 (license that passed to William Van Derlip's Caribbean Islands Guano Company during the ensuing decade), Jennett conveyed the other three keys to Aves Guano Company in 1880. Ten years later he resold all six of the Serranillas to Arthur Brash. In 1870 Jennett disposed of his clouded interest in Aves island to Stewart Newell, who transferred it to Aves Guano in 1880. Thus did that company come to possess two prospects that were claimed by other governments. In 1881, when Aves Guano asked the State department to award it title to Aves, U.S. diplomats informed the company that they had long recognized Venezuelan authority at that island—implying that the firm had been defrauded by Jennett. As mentioned, diplomats also eventually acknowledged Mexican sovereignty over the Triangle keys; nevertheless, they were mined intermittently by the American company. Not until 1893 did Colombia lay claim to the Serranillas, an assertion the U.S. government ignored even though there was little evidence that anyone, including Jennett and Aves Guano, had ever occupied or mined them under American law.[63]

As with many of his business deals, Jennett's involvement with Petrel (Bajo Nuevo), Quito Sueño, Roncador, and Serraña resembled legal labyrinths, and their ownership was eventually challenged by Colombia, Honduras, and Nicaragua. In 1868 Jennett posted bond on Serraña, three small rocks 240 miles east of Nicaragua's Mosquito coast. The following year he filed first on Quito Sueño, a coral bank 34 miles long and 8 miles wide lying seven to twenty fathoms under water with intermittent patches of dry land, and situated 40 miles northwest of Serraña; then on Roncador key, a three-million-square-foot coral platform about twelve feet above sea level and located 40 miles south of Serraña; and finally on Petrel, a five-by-fourteen-square-mile coral bank some 150 miles south of Jamaica. In two separate assignments in 1869 and in 1870, Jennett transferred all his rights to Pedro, Petrel, Quito Sueño, Roncador, and Serraña keys to Henrietta Stevens whom he subsequently married. As Henrietta Jennett, she leased Roncador and Quito Sueño back to her spouse in 1880 for ten years, and the following year she sold that claim (along with Petrel island) to the Petrel Guano Company, in which James Jennett was a partner.[64]

Jennett was "in charge of the partnership operations on the island of Roncados [*sic*]," the New York company's most valuable property, which produced upwards of one thousand tons of phosphate annually.[65] During the mid-1880s he quarreled with his associates and, according to them, began diverting shipments destined for New York and Philadelphia to Wilmington, Delaware. Jennett claimed that he had been abandoned by his partners who regularly failed to supply him and his men on the island, as promised; therefore, he had simply sailed to the first available market.[66] In any case, the Petrel partnership dissolved, and most of its interests eventually passed to Caribbean Guano Company, an Arizona corporation.[67]

Such did not prevent Jennett from reselling Pedro to Henry Dewey in 1881; or Petrel, Quito Sueño, and Roncador to J. H. Lancaster in 1890; and even Serraña to Arthur Brash in 1891.[68] Diplomats consequently could not figure out "from records in the State Department . . . who has the record title to guano on Serraña Keys," or any number of other places associated with the Jennetts because both "J. W. Jennett and his wife Henrietta [repeatedly] made assignments when they had no title. . . ."[69]

However tangled the titles to these properties, the U.S. government for a time declined to entertain conflicting claims by other governments. As previously noted, despite objections by both Honduras and Nicaragua, each of which asserted that Serraña keys belonged to it, officials in the State department had ruled in 1869 that Jennett (whom diplomats considered to be a consummate liar) was "entitled to the protection of the United States against the interference of any foreign government."[70] Secretary Seward did assure Nicaragua that while the U.S. government considered "it to be its duty to protect such citizens pursuant to the Act of Congress, . . . [it] does not contemplate the permanent occupation of any territory . . . after the guano referred to shall have been removed. . . ."[71] Honduran claim to Quito Sueño and Roncador was not advanced until 1928, that assertion being rejected by American diplomats who superciliously retorted that the islands "had been under the sovereignty and jurisdiction of the United States . . . since their discovery by Jennett. . . ."[72]

Meanwhile, officials in Bogotá (having just learned, or so they said, that Jennett was mining assorted islands, rocks, and keys in the Caribbean) in 1890 said that Quito Sueño, Roncador, and Serraña belonged to Colombia by right of succession from the Spanish colonial empire. Moreover, even had that not been the case, these places were not suitable for annexation under American law inasmuch as "old maps prove [that] the existence of guano on the keys was known at least before 1858 [*sic*], and [that] Jennett, therefore, . . . was not even the discoverer. . . ." American diplomats failed to respond for fear "an answer might prejudice the pending Costa Rica-Colombia boundary arbitration" because the U.S. government had a keen interest in which nation might end up in possession of the Isthmus of Panama.[73] Repeated protests by Colombia during the ensuing decades brought no resolution, until the United States finally surrendered its claims to the islands late in the twentieth century.[74]

Interestingly, however reluctant the U.S. government might have been to relinquish control of Caribbean appurtenances to sister American republics, it almost never disputed ownership with Great Britain once it became aware of English counterclaims, as with Morant keys. Similarly, Pedro keys (four islets composed of dead coral lying forty to fifty miles southwest of Jamaica) had been filed on by Jennett in 1869, and after he posted bond that year on Pedro, Petrel, Quito Sueño, and Roncador keys, he "was [also] given a certificate or proclamation signed by Secretary of State Fish and dated November 30, 1869, which recited that [one] James W. Jennett had complied with the provisions of the Act of August 18, 1856, [and] . . . was entitled . . . to all the privileges and advantages intended by that Act. . . ."[75]

It was the last such certificate ever issued by the State department. At the direction of Secretary Fish, diplomats thereafter declined to vouch for claimants. Rather, the department merely assumed the role of custodian for documents submitted to it by entrepreneurs seeking title under the Guano Act. In fact, diplomats tried to ignore the matter of appurtenances whenever possible. For instance, even though bureaucrats in 1878 became aware that the British had formally annexed the Pedro keys fifteen years earlier, they took no action to delete the place from the Treasury department's list of guano islands until 1884 when the British brig *Natalie* was detained at Norfolk, Virginia, in apparent violation of American navigation laws proscribing foreign-flagged vessels from hauling cargo between a U.S. appurtenance (Pedro) and a U.S. port. Diplomats advised federal revenuers that, despite the certificate on file, Pedro "is not now a guano island appertaining to the United States." Treasury officials consequently released *Natalie* and struck Pedro from its list of guano islands.[76]

While James W. Jennett was certainly the most active claimant in the Caribbean after the Civil War, he was not the only prospector to nose about that sea for guano islands. In 1879 his sometime associate, Dr. Pascal Quinan, filed on Arcas key, one hundred miles west of the Yucatán city of Campeche, the physician claiming that he had discovered guano there the year before. Upon learning of Quinan's action, Jennett protested to diplomats that the doctor's filing was fraudulent because he "had never been south of Cape Hatteras and had obtained all his information on Arcas key" from Jennett.[77] Neither claimant ever posted bond on the island, but Quinan and Philadelphian John Wallis reportedly mined it during the early 1880s, removing more than fifteen hundred tons of phosphates—without Mexican interference. Quinan repeatedly asked the U.S. government to recognize his claim and for permission to post bond, and, despite a favorable State department report that concluded there was "no protest from any other government," a subsequent internal study insisted, "there is no evidence that the Department took any action pursuant to this opinion."[78]

Arcas had been abandoned by 1893 when a Captain Alfred May queried the State department about filing procedures regarding it; however, following policy established by Hamilton Fish in 1870, diplomats simply did not respond. In 1899 the department requested that the American ambassador in Mexico City inquire "discreetly and unofficially" if that government owned the island. The reply was affirmative, and, thereafter, diplomats advised would-be miners that the "Arcas cays are claimed by Mexico. . . ."[79]

In 1882 Prudencio de Murguiondo claimed Vivario (or Vivorilla) keys, fifty miles northeast of Honduras's Laguna Caratasca, and presented assorted affidavits to the State department in support of his application for an American deed. Diplomats did not reply. Five years later, a Julius R. Schultz similarly filed documents supporting his request for title to the keys. Schultz said that he had actually been mining the place for two years under a Nicaraguan concession, but he feared he would soon lose it because his partner had murdered his wife—hence Schultz's filing under American law. Well before the State department had ignored Murguiondo's claim, diplomats (apparently anticipating American interest in the place, as well as being aware of Nicaraguan pretensions of sovereignty) had inquired of William Buchard, America's representative in Honduras, as to Vivorilla's status, and he replied that Honduras unquestionably owned it. Diplomats consequently advised Schultz's attorney that, while "Vivorilla key was claimed by both Nicaragua and Honduras . . . neither Government will likely attempt to dispossess him."[80]

In 1901 the State department received the last filing ever presented on a new Caribbean site—Calapatch (Avalo or Abalo key), a low-lying, three-mile-long reef in the Canarreos archipelago off the eastern tip of Cuba's Isle of Pines (present Isla de la Juventud). William A. Varty, a Kentuckian living in Havana, stated in an affidavit presented by his Washington attorney that he had landed on Calapatch on April 12 and found a large deposit of phosphatic guano. He said he took possession in the name of the United States, erected a sign reading NOTICE! NO TRESPASSING ON THIS KEY—W.A. VARTY, OWNER, and left an agent in occupation of the place until he could personally return and take up residence. Varty petitioned under the Guano Act for official recognition of his exclusive right to the island and its resources. Diplomats merely acknowledged receipt of Varty's lawyer's letter and its accompanying documents.[81]

Two years later Varty sold his interest in the island for $15,000 to Herbert J. Browne of Havana, who promptly submitted copies of the deed of conveyance and a bond in the amount of $50,000 to the State department. This evoked the following response: "The Department receives [these papers] and files [them] with the other papers in its archives relating to Calapatch Island merely as an office of record, without prejudice to any prior governmental or individual rights that may exist."[82] Diplomats dutifully forwarded the bond to the Treasury department, but Calapatch was never added to any list of American appurtenances probably because no list was compiled after 1893. Although Browne apparently did not personally mine the island he sold a one-fortieth interest for $2,500 to William H. Rohrer of Washington, D.C., who was empowered to remove its guano for one year. Rohrer appears to have been in the process of doing so when on July 11, 1904, the Cuban government ordered Browne to quit Calapatch by month's end.[83]

Through his attorney Browne asked the State department for help, noting that he and others had invested $20,000 in the key which, they contended, had never been occupied by Spain. Even if it had, the 1898 peace treaty with Spain had ceded the islands around Cuba to the United States, not to Cuba. Secretary of State John Hay asked H. G. Squires, the American minister to Cuba, to inquire by what grounds the government in Havana objected to Browne and Rohrer's enterprise and, in any case, to ask the Cubans to suspend their eviction order until the matter could be settled diplomatically. Squires soon replied that the Cubans (then in the process of negotiating a treaty with the United States over the Isle of Pines's jurisdiction) had agreed to allow the Americans to remain on the key but not to export any guano. Avalo (Calapatch), as well as other keys close by the Isle of Pines, they contended, belonged to Cuba both by right of proximity and historical occupation; indeed, in 1876 Spanish authorities had leased the place in question to guano miners, and as early as 1882 Prudencio de Murguiondo of Baltimore was importing and selling "Avalo Cuba Bird Guano" on the Maryland market. Browne's attorney soon urged Secretary Hay to insert into the Isle of Pines Treaty (signed that year but not ratified until 1925) a clause that would have guaranteed Americans the right to mine Calapatch under Cuban aegis, but the diplomat declined on the grounds that the matter was not germane.[84]

Moreover, the State department soon concluded that at the time of Varty's original filing the island was already within a foreign jurisdiction and, hence, was not suitable to become an American appurtenance. Cuba quickly confiscated Browne and Rohrer's property and in 1905 turned it over to one Reginald Schroeder who (operating with others as Avalo Improvement Company, a Delaware corporation) obtained the concession on the island.[85] It is not clear whether the company ever marketed Calapatch's phosphates in the United States.

There were comparatively few filings on Pacific islands after the Civil War; in fact, American guano companies throughout the basin actually disposed of several of their prospects to British operators who intensified their mining activities. In 1867 John Daggett, a Massachusetts mariner then living in Melbourne, Australia, wrote Secretary Seward asking "for a lease

. . . to work the guano on Ducer" (or Ducie) island, a twelve-foot-high, two-mile-square atoll some four hundred miles east of Pitcairn, the island made famous as the refuge of Fletcher Christian and fellow HMS *Bounty* mutineers. Seward advised Daggett of the stipulations and requirements for American recognition under the Guano Act, but the mariner never responded, neither filing affidavits nor posting bond. Discovered by Englishmen before the turn of the nineteenth century, Ducie was annexed by Great Britain in 1902 but was neither mined for phosphates nor ever considered to be an American appurtenance.[86]

Instructive of the change in U.S. government policy toward guano islands during Secretary Fish's stewardship of the State department was the case of the Huon islands, four small, low-lying atolls in the Cook islands of the central South Pacific. In 1877 Andrew C. Cushing's attorney and agent notified the State department that his client had occupied the Huons with the intent of removing their phosphates under the Guano Act, and he asked that they be placed under American jurisdiction. Secretary Fish replied that the application "must conform strictly with the essential requirements of the law in order to receive consideration." Cushing then asked that his attorney's previous letter be deemed his application under the law. He filed additional affidavits attesting to his occupation of the place, which he said was uninhabited and, according to the documents, not under the authority of any other government.[87] Filed therewith is a memorandum authored by Henry O'Connor, commissioner of claims, dated November 12, 1877: "The Department has already passed on the claim adversely, but nothing need be said to Mr. Cushing except a simple acknowledgment."[88]

"It is evident," an internal audit later noted, "that the State Department did not consider that Cushing had complied with all the requirements of the Guano Act," but it purposely did not advise him of perceived deficiencies. About then President Rutherford B. Hayes took office, and, at Commissioner O'Connor's suggestion, William M. Evarts, the new secretary of State, merely acknowledged the receipt of Cushing's paperwork. Perhaps unaware of the need to post bond, the miner did nothing else, perhaps thinking that his title had been perfected. Consequently, Huon never appeared on any Treasury list of guano islands. Little matter. If Cushing worked the Huons after 1877 there is no evidence of it. Moreover, they appear to have been French property, having been attached to New Caledonia in 1853. The islands were eventually mined after the turn of the century by the Austral Guano Company, Ltd., of Auckland, New Zealand, under a French concession.[89]

Huon was not the only nominal French claim that Americans tried to "high-grade," or steal, or so Paris later contended. In 1881 Frederick W.

Permien, a mariner from Oakland, California, investigated Clipperton island, which, in contravention of the Monroe Doctrine, had been annexed by France in 1858. Unaware of that specious French claim, Permien secured backing from San Francisco venture capitalists who, operating as Oceanic Phosphate Company, filed on the atoll under the Guano Act in 1892. Assistant Secretary of State Alvey Adee observed in reply that *Lippincott's Gazetteer of the World* (1883) reported Clipperton to be French property and that unless Oceanic could refute that allegation the department would decline to act on the application. The Californians did not respond, but they mined the place from 1893 to 1898 as though a deed had been registered. When Mexican authorities learned of American presence on the atoll (which they claimed and called Isla de Pasión), they sent a gunboat to dislodge them. Ironically, Oceanic had almost simultaneously sold its Clipperton island operation to the Pacific Islands Company, Ltd., of London. It soon acquired a Mexican concession to the atoll that lasted until 1915. After World War I, France was awarded sovereignty over Clipperton island as consequence of a controversial arbitration settlement that is still disputed by some in Mexico.[90]

The final claim under the Guano Act in the Pacific, or anywhere else, was shortly after the turn of the century on Marcus (Week's or Minami Tori Shima) island, a barren, triangular-shaped dot of land some 5 miles in area and situated 830 miles northeast of Guam. Andrew A. Rosehill had taken possession of Marcus island in the name of the United States in 1889 and employed a married couple to reside there for a year, but they left after eleven months when a passing ship presented the opportunity to depart the lonely little island. Meanwhile, Rosehill had filed on Marcus and was informed by William Q. Gresham, Grover Cleveland's secretary of State, that the prospector must comply with all requirements of the Guano Act and post bond before the president could consider his request for recognition under U.S. law.[91]

Whatever his immediate plans for developing the place, Rosehill instead went to work for the North Pacific Phosphate and Fertilizer Company in 1890 as assistant manager of its works on Laysan island in the Hawaiian chain, seven hundred miles northwest of Honolulu. Organized that year in Honolulu by George D. Freeth, C. N. Spenser, and G. W. Smith, North Pacific leased Laysan along with nearby Lisiansky island for twenty years from the king of Hawaii. North Pacific sold Laysan's phosphates primarily on the West coast of the United States until 1904 when, by then called Pacific Guano and Fertilizer, the company surrendered its lease to the island because reserves had been largely depleted by constant mining.[92]

Unemployed in 1902 and with California Senator George C. Perkins acting in his behalf, Rosehill refiled affidavits concerning discovery and occupation of Marcus as a derelict island. He submitted assays regarding the quantity and quality of its guano and posted bond in the amount of $50,000. On June 2 Rosehill's surety was accepted by the Treasury department, the seventeenth and final posting under the law,[93] "but as no list of guano islands was compiled by the Treasury Department after 1893," the State department later acknowledged, "Marcus Island does not appear on any of these lists of islands."[94]

Diplomats and tax collectors routinely accepted Rosehill's application and bond even though bureaucrats of both departments were unquestionably aware of a rival international claim to the place. On August 3, 1899, the Navy department had notified both State and Treasury departments that "Japan had seized Marcus Island a few weeks ago, thinking the island might be desirable for a cable station in case of the construction of a cable between Honolulu and Guam." The Japanese government learned of Rosehill's filing soon after he had posted bond and objected strenuously by promptly advising Washington that in 1898 "Minami Tori Shima" had been attached to its Bonin islands, seven hundred miles farther east, that it had been leased to a Japanese subject, a Mr. Midzutani (a fisherman and bird hunter, who employed forty or fifty people there), and that, "if the United States had authorized Rosehill's occupation of the island, this authorization should be revoked promptly in order to avoid unnecessary complications between the two governments."[95]

Abruptly deciding that the American claim was defective and that the Japanese "were entitled to the island," U.S. diplomats wrote Rosehill about the Chrysanthemum Throne's allegedly prior possession of the island. The Japanese government also sent the cruiser *Kasagi* to the island "to prevent any hostilities by the inhabitants upon the arrival of Captain Rosehill," who was said to be en route and unaware of the State department's letter. The warship preceded the American entrepreneur to the island and left an officer and fifteen armed marines with copies of American-Japanese correspondence on the subject, which were presented to Rosehill upon his arrival. He had no choice but to withdraw, and to ask Senator Perkins for more help. Assistant Secretary Adee curtly informed Perkins that "this government has not claimed title to, or asserted authority over, the Island. . . ." Diplomats more candidly admitted to President Theodore Roosevelt that "this Government finds itself embarrassed . . . by the fact that Captain Rosehill's claim under the Guano Act was not perfected by filing a bond until after Japan claimed sovereignty over the island."[96]

Rosehill's subsequent effort to secure U.S. government assistance vis-à-vis the Japanese was superciliously rejected by State department officials who informed him "that at the time of [his] discovery in 1889 the island was in the possession and occupation of Japan" (which is something the Japanese had never claimed) "and that, therefore, the Act of 1856 had not been complied with, so that, even if all [his] proceedings were in perfect form, [the department would be] unable to convey title either to the United States or to himself." Washington could be of no further service to him.[97]

With that, U.S. diplomats sought to close their guano islands files forever. They were apparently little disturbed that by then many American appurtenances had become British possessions. Good riddance. Some bureaucrats even contended that "The Guano Act should be repealed, since the demand for guano has largely disappeared. . . ."[98]

To the contrary, demand for raw phosphates had not diminished, as increased British mining of Pacific islands amply demonstrated. Indeed, as early as the 1860s Great Britain had authorized colonial governors to license firms to work unoccupied islands, and numerous contracts were let. In 1865 the Anglo-Australian Guano Company of Hobart, Tasmania, received Christmas island in the Pacific; in 1867 Grice, Sumner & Company of Melbourne got Malden; and in 1871 by license from colonial governors and through purchase from other firms, the London shipping concern of Houlder Brothers & Company acquired rights to Caroline, Christmas (in the Pacific), Flint, and Starbuck islands[99]—all of which were nominally owned by Alfred Benson's United States Guano Company.

Of these, Malden became the most valuable site by far, eventually being touted as containing the "world's most valuable guano deposit."[100] Grice, Sumner began mining the island about 1868 and was soon extracting fourteen hundred tons of high-grade phosphates annually. That news alerted A. G. Benson to poachers, and he protested vehemently to the State department. He demanded an indemnity from the U.S. government, which had failed to protect part of his fabled Number 9 group. Secretary Seward summarily rejected Benson's assertion by noting that the U.S. Guano Company had long since abandoned its rights to the atoll through its failure to occupy and mine it. Consequently, Malden passed peacefully to British possession, and its leaseholders extracted upwards of £100,000-worth of phosphates over the ensuing thirty years. Malden was eventually eclipsed in importance by Ocean and Nauru islands in the Gilberts, whose rich phosphate reserves were discovered at the turn of the century. In fact, mining on Malden ended so abruptly as consequence of these new, valuable discoveries that the British simply abandoned both their equipment and stores (canned goods, pharmaceuticals, and the like) to rust and rot in the tropical heat.[101]

Not all American appurtenances were acquired so easily by British interests. When Houlder Brother's representative, a Dr. Weston, arrived at

Christmas island on July 5, 1872, to inspect the place, he found a notice nailed to a board proclaiming that, merely days before, the place had been annexed to the United States by the commander of USS *Narragansett*. In fact the atoll was occupied by three employees of C. A. Williams's Phoenix Guano Company. Consequently, Weston discreetly withdrew, and Houlder Brothers & Company voluntarily surrendered its license to the atoll back to crown authorities. Nevertheless, the British firm continued to work other titular American territory, especially Flint island where its "enterprising employee, John T. Arundel"[102] (no doubt looking forward to the day when the phosphates would be gone) planted coconut palms even as mining progressed.[103]

About 1874 Arundel left the Houlder Brothers and organized his own firm, John T. Arundel & Co. He simultaneously acquired the right to Vostok from the British colonial office. Unable to land on the atoll because of heavy seas when he soon thereafter sought to inspect the place, he apparently never occupied or mined it. No matter. There were far better prospects elsewhere. By the mid-1880s, he held British leases on such untended American appurtenances as Birnie, Canton, Enderbury, Flint, Gardner, Hull, McKeans, Phoenix, and Sydney. Although all of these places had been claimed by U.S. Guano Company, none of them had ever been worked by Benson's firm; however, rival Phoenix Guano, which had counterclaimed several of them, had mined Enderbury (1862-77), McKeans (1859-70), and Phoenix (1860-71). When Arundel arrived on Enderbury about 1886 he found a horse and a mule that had been left behind by Americans when they had departed nine years before. The Englishmen promptly caught the animals and yoked them to rail cars that had likewise been abandoned.[104]

Sometime during the period Arundel reportedly purchased Phoenix Guano Company's titles to Enderbury, McKeans, Phoenix, and Starbuck islands in the Phoenix group and may also have acquired claims to Baker, Howland, and Jarvis from American Guano Company. Baker, which had been mined continuously from 1859 to 1878 by American Guano, served as the Englishman's headquarters in the Central Pacific from 1886 to 1891 during which time he removed thousands of tons of phosphates that had been rejected as inferior by Americans. Rat-infested Howland, extensively worked by American Guano, Pacific Guano of Massachusetts, and U.S. Guano, was likewise exploited by Arundel during the 1880s, but Jarvis was not because it had apparently been picked clean by American Guano. Reportedly at Arundel's request, Great Britain annexed the Phoenix islands in two separate orders-in-council in 1889 and 1893, actions that specifically mentioned Jarvis but neither Baker nor Howland; however, after the turn of the century the British laid claim to all three. Probably not at Arundel's request were Great Britain's appropriation of Nassau in the Pacific in 1888; the claiming of Clarence (Nukufetau), Duke of York (Atafu), Humphrey (Manihiki), Palmyra, and Rierson (Rakahanga) in 1889; and the annexation of the Dangerous (Pukapuka, Motukoe, and Motukavata) islands in 1892—all remnants of Alfred Benson's gigantic Number 9 Group, none of which had ever been worked.[105]

Meanwhile, having heard that C. A. Williams had left Christmas island in the Pacific, Henderson, McFarlane & Company of London and Auckland asked the British foreign office to investigate. It consequently queried the U.S. State department whose functionaries replied that they had not been notified that U.S. Guano had abandoned its claims to the place; therefore, American diplomats "still considered [that company] to be entitled to the protection guaranteed by the laws of the United States."[106]

Nevertheless finding Christmas to be uninhabited in 1882, Henderson, McFarlane occupied the island, and six years later Sir William Wiseman (aboard HMS *Caroline*) formally annexed it to Great Britain, along with nearby Fanning in the Line islands and Penrhyn (Tongareva), a lonely but inhabited atoll south of the equator—all formerly claimed by Benson's U.S. Guano Company. Henderson, McFarlane reportedly never mined Christmas. Instead, the company established a copra operation that was acquired after the turn of the century by Pacific Plantations, Ltd., which was owned by the soap-magnate Lever brothers. Unlike Christmas island, which had been worked by American guano companies, none of the others was ever mined. Fanning, along with nearby Washington island, had been occupied about 1846 by British subjects who manufactured coconut oil. Penrhyn (Tongareva), long inhabited by Polynesians from Manihiki, had traded for years with Englishmen from the Cook islands, 750 miles farther south, and in 1888 the British annexed Penrhyn (Tongareva) and made it a protectorate—an act too late to shelter its people from slavers who, kidnaping unwary natives throughout the Pacific to work in Peruvian guano mines, had all but depopulated the island.[107]

In 1897 Henderson, McFarlane & Company merged their phosphate- and coconut-producing properties in the Gilbert, Line, Marshall, and Samoan islands with John T. Arundel's similar operations situated primarily in the Fiji, Line and Phoenix groups to create the Pacific Islands Company, Ltd., of London and Auckland. The "idea underlying the [new] company," a financial reporter for *The Times* of London observed, was "the fusion of large firms trading in the Pacific, in order to avoid unnecessary competition and to conduct business with greater economy."[108] No doubt both parties to the merger anticipated a substantial reduction in mining and a greater reliance on coconut production in the near future because, by the middle 1890s, "All the known phosphate deposits in the Central Pacific had been worked out. . . ."[109]

That business strategy became unnecessary because Pacific Islands employee Albert F. Ellis discovered "the greatest high-grade phosphate deposits in the world"[110] in 1899 when he happened to notice that a rock used as doorstop in the firm's Sydney laboratory was remarkably similar to rich phosphates he had seen on Baker island when he had lived there in the late 1880s. Analysis of the stone from equatorial Nauru island, situated at the western edge of the Gilberts, showed it to be of phenomenal quality; however, inhabited Nauru recently had been conceded to the Germans when a tripartite agreement signed in Berlin in 1899 had split Samoa between the United States and Germany, Britain being compensated elsewhere. Yet, inhabited Ocean (Banaba) island, Nauru's nearest neighbor and outside that agreement, was conceivably well within the British sphere of influence. Consequently, Ocean island was promptly prospected and found to be almost as rich in phosphates, and it was abruptly annexed by Great Britain and leased to Pacific Islands Company, which soon restructured as Pacific Phosphate Company, Ltd. It sold its coconut plantations to Lever brothers to raise capital with which to commence mining. Six years later Pacific Phosphate signed an agreement with Jaluit-Gesellshaft, which held a ninety-four-year lease from the Imperial German government on Nauru, to acquire that island as well. During World War I Great Britain confiscated Nauru island and its phosphates, and in 1920 the British government purchased the assets of Pacific Phosphate and other private interests in the Pacific, combining them into the British Phosphate Board, an imperial monopoly.[111]

It had been "somewhat humiliating" for Englishmen on Baker and Howland during the 1880s, "having to clean up after the American company had taken the cream, and to work places in the adjacent Phoenix Group which they had rejected," Albert Ellis later remarked. Nevertheless, he said "we more than evened up . . . when we found the enormous high-grade phosphate deposits on Ocean Island and Nauru, which [the Americans] had missed. . . ."[112]

While it is undeniably true that Nauru and Ocean proved to be more valuable than all American guano islands combined, both places were inhabited and, therefore, legally unsuitable for exploitation under U.S. law. Such considerations in no way constrained the British.

# 8

## Peddling It: The Aroma of Profit

The possibility of financial gain lured many Americans into the search for guano islands. Assorted businessmen (whalers and merchants mostly) scoured the seas for derelict sites covered with valuable bird droppings that promised to enrich both farmers' fields and entrepreneurial pocketbooks; however, many of those who prospected under the Guano Islands Act often did not understand either the object of their quest and its many manifestations, or the risks involved—puzzlements that similarly perplexed peddlers and purchasers. The aroma of profit often proved to be a very elusive fragrance.

By the middle of the nineteenth century empirical evidence suggested that effective fertilizers contained nitrogen (N) to speed plant growth, phosphorus (P) to stimulate early root development, and potassium (K) to foster maturation. Eventually phosphorus in particular came to be seen as a key element for life on earth because of its central role in plant photosynthesis and animal metabolism,[1] but, at the outset of the great guano rush, these roles and relationships were not clearly understood. Furthermore, prospectors were not always able to easily identify the naturally occurring compounds that contained one or more of these elements—especially the nitrogenous and phosphatic material contained in so-called guanos.

Although the word guano had originally referred exclusively to the dried excrement of sea birds, popular usage soon made it generic, expanding its definition to encompass a variety of animal remains, mineral deposits of dubious biological origin, and even a number of synthetic products purposely blended by chemists. As Senator Judah P. Benjamin had predicted during debates over the enactment of the Guano Islands Act, both the feces and the carcasses of seals, turtles, and walruses (which sometimes defecated ashore) as well as that of bats (whose droppings often piled up high in arid caves) came to be mined globally during the nineteenth century. All of them were commonly labeled "guano" when sold as fertilizers.[2]

Peruvian guano, especially from the arid Chinca islands, was not only the first important fertilizer of its type but the standard by which all others came to be judged. In a class by itself, it was the peculiar product of species and climate. Among vertebrates, only birds and mammals have the complex nervous and physiological systems necessary to produce feces suitable for use as fertilizer; however, bird physiology produces semi-solid urine in which the principal nitrogenous compound is uric acid, a stable and insoluble substance. Mammals on the other hand pass liquid urine, principally in the form of the nitrogenous compound urea, which is an unstable and soluble substance particularly prone to rapid evaporation. For eons sea birds such as albatrosses, gannets, gulls, frigates, pelicans, penguins, petrels, shearwaters, terns, and especially cormorants in immense numbers feasted from a brimming sea and deposited their chemically rich droppings on arid islands off the Pacific coast of South America. These served as rookeries for countless seafowl whose nitrogen-laden feces over time compacted into white-to-brown layers, which ranged in consistency from powder on top to solidified, rock-hard matter a hundred or more feet deep.[3]

Globally, other isolated albeit wetter islands (similarly visited by enormous numbers of assorted sea birds and other defecating animals) produced decidedly different results. Humidity reduced the uric acid (and hence nitrogen) content of their droppings, and almost any amount of rainfall washed away much of the rest. Guano from the virtually rain-free but relatively humid Lobos islands, for example, was substantially less potent than that of the far drier, neighboring Chincas, and heavy precipitation common to other places caught up in the great guano rush quickly leached nitrogen from feces and also prevented droppings from accumulating to any great depth. With rainfall approaching two hundred inches annually in some tropical climes favored by sea birds, the chemistry of the excrement that remained was markedly altered. Moreover, insoluble phosphates were percolated downward through porous coral limestone, typical of island formation, which changed the rock chemically.[4]

Complicating matters is an oceanic environment in which only some phosphatic deposits are of direct biological origin. Many are clearly an admixture of fecal and assorted decayed matter from a variety of animal sources, either having accumulated on or been leached into limestone and other host matter through the process of precipitation. Others are clearly geological in origin. Phosphorus, the tenth most abundant element in the earth's upper crust, commonly saturates sea water and is removed by marine organisms through life processes. The chemical element tends to concentrate about shallow coral reefs especially in areas subject to the effects of upwelling (in trade-wind belts and at the edge of land masses); whenever reefs are subsequently exposed either by tectonic uplift or by falling sea level, phosphates settle out as deposits, typically converting soft pockets of coral into calcium phosphate, which is surrounded by harder, more impervious portions of limestone. Navassa island in the Caribbean and Nauru and Ocean islands in the Pacific are especially characteristic of this process. Jarvis island, with three distinct layers of phosphate deposits separated by coral gravels, is likely the product of both geological and biological processes.[5]

So-called soluble guanos, typical of South American islands, contained relatively large amounts of nitrogenous matter but differed enormously both in appearance and composition. Many varieties, especially those from Peru and Bolivia (which were similar in potency) ranged from white powder to brown rock, much of the latter being a yellowish friable material easily adaptable to agriculture.[6]

"Insoluble (leached or phosphatic) guanos," typical of U.S. appurtenances, were also markedly dissimilar in appearance. In the Caribbean, they ranged from white enamel, rock-hard substances (hence the term "rock guano") common to Monks and Rogues islands; opaque, snow-white crystalline masses (actually classed as mineral and named Monite) on Mona; light-colored (blue, green, pink, yellow, and white) phosphatic powders containing lumps of solidified material on Sombrero; brownish granular aggregations on Aves, Morant, and Pedro; pockets of brown, gray, and red matter packed tightly into spaces between hard limestone on Navassa; and major and minor variations in color and density elsewhere.[7]

Central Pacific islands such as Baker, Christmas, Howland, Jarvis, McKeans, Malden, Starbuck, and Phoenix typically possessed shallow saltwater lagoons that were often filled partially or wholly by yellowish bogs consisting of a phosphatic crust ranging from an inch to a foot thick, with a brownish congeal below. Beneath everything was either a phosphatic limestone base (the product of soluble substances having percolated downward to alter the coral foundation chemically) or gypsum produced by the evaporation of the central lagoon. Invariably, the moist mess produced the pungent scent of hydrogen sulfide by the simultaneous decomposition of guano and gypsum.[8]

Marine phosphorites (such as those common to Christmas island in the Indian ocean, Nauru and Ocean islands in the Pacific, and even ancient seabed deposits in Florida, South Carolina, and Tennessee) ranged from the mineral apatite (variously colored nodules of calcium fluoride phosphate, $Ca_5F(PO_4)_3$, with chlorine, hydroxyl, or carbonate sometimes replacing fluoride in the formula) to sequences of black shale, phosphatic shale, and phosphorite laid on the sea bed; deposits of blue, brown, and white river pebbles consisting of phosphatic limestone; and hard-rock deposits that were the results of successive layers of dissolved phosphates having filled cavities. Marine phosphorites found a ready market in the United States. Often mislabeled as "rock guano," they were commonly treated with sulfuric acid to create either ingredients for assorted blended fertilizers that usually claimed to be guano, or they were marketed as Superphosphate.[9]

Regardless of origin, all so-called guanos contained some nitrogenous matter, especially ammonia ($NH_3$), and phosphates (usually phosphorus pentoxide, $P_2O_5$, and phosphoric acid, $H_3PO_4$), as well as alkaline salts (especially aluminum, calcium, and magnesium), sulfate of lime (gypsum), assorted other organic matter, and silica (sand). The precise mix of these elements and compounds gave guano both its potency as plant nutrient and profit potential as a commodity.[10]

Chemical variations among competing fertilizers inevitably led to outlandish advertising claims. In its *Report of Experiments with American Guano* (1860) from Baker and Jarvis islands, American Guano Company insisted that its product was just as powerful as Peruvian and only about two-thirds as expensive—assertions seemingly verified by testimonials from more than a dozen farmers. Rival Phoenix Guano Company was equally adamant that its phosphates from McKeans island were second to none—contentions backed by certificates from scores of planters that were proudly reproduced in one of its advertising tracts.[11]

Little wonder that farmers needed scientific assistance in sorting out the truth. Although he was not the first to do so, J. C. Nesbit, an English agricultural chemist, analyzed the value of ingredients in guanos and published the results of his study in 1860. In it he offered a simple formula by which anyone who knew the constituents in a sack of fertilizer could calculate its worth per ton: pure nitrogen, £74 ($370 U.S.); ammonia, £60 ($300); phosphorus pentoxide, £8 ($40); phosphoric acid, £24 ($120); alkaline salts, £1 ($5); gypsum, £1 ($5); and other organic matter, £1 ($5). Sand, some of which was commonly found in commercial guanos, was agriculturally worthless.[12]

Dried bird droppings derived entirely from the Chinca's nearly ideal environment produced guano composed on average of 50 percent organic matter, 22 percent phosphorus pentoxide, 17 percent ammonia, 6 percent assorted alkaline salts, 3 percent phosphoric acid, and 2 percent silica (sand).

By Nesbit's formula these constituents yielded a value of £13 5s ($66.25) per ton. All other guanos were worth less because they had undergone substantial alteration, rainfall having leached out much of the powerful uric acid, reduced the other nitrogenous content, and even washed away some of the valuable phosphates.[13]

As consequence of his chemical analyses, Nesbit grouped other guanos into two inferior categories. Class II material had been moderately depleted of nitrogenous substances and therefore was somewhat less potent (and valuable) than Chincan: Ichaboe island off Africa, £9 1s ($45.25) a ton; the Peruvian Lobos islands, £9 7s ($46.75); Bolivian guano in general, £7 4s ($36); Chilean guano in general, £7 4s ($36); and the Patos islands off Mexico's Baja California, £6 4s ($31). Class III substances, into which he relegated all American guanos, had been largely depleted of nitrogenous material, and their fertilizing properties were provided primarily by the soluble and insoluble phosphates that remained. Baker island guano, with an extraordinarily high residue of insoluble phosphates (78 percent), was valued at £7 12s ($38) a ton, but other products sometimes mined by Americans and analyzed by Nesbit were far less precious. These included Aves island stuff, which was worth £2 8s ($12); Jarvis island, £3 10s ($17.50); Navassa island, £5 1s ($25.25); Pedro key, £4 ($20); Sombrero island, £6 1s ($30.25); Swan islands, £2 17s ($14.25); and assorted Mexican guano, such as that on Alacráns island, £2 9s ($11.25).[14]

Inferior though they may have been, insoluble guanos and rock phosphates of assorted origins competed vigorously with pure Peruvian bird droppings for the farmer's fertilizer dollar. Although there is no clear evidence of an organized guano commodity market in the United States—all of the stuff apparently being sold on spot markets or consigned to jobbers—the sudden availability of an array of relatively cheap substitutes (many of which were touted as equal in potency to Peruvian) greatly disrupted business, perhaps even contributing to an appreciable decline in the importation of prized South American guano. An anonymous journalist in New Bedford, Massachusetts, reported in 1858 that the South American commerce, which once "employed several hundred . . . large ships, seems to be entirely fading out. There is stated to be a two or three year stock now on hand for all the markets where it has been sold. . . ." Only thirteen vessels were said to be loading at the Chincas, seven of them American, the others British and French, down from 180 the year before. Four of the American vessels awaiting cargo were reportedly bound for England, one to France, and two to the United States.[15]

From a high of 175,849 tons entering the United States during the fiscal year ending June 30, 1855, South American guano imports dropped to 75,197 tons in 1858, and to 70,813 tons in 1860, before collapsing to 2,568 tons in 1863—that tumble undoubtedly caused by the loss of Southern markets during the Civil War. Although demand recovered somewhat with peace, peaking at 76,770 tons in 1867, it again declined to 13,329 tons by 1869.[16] Numerous reports by then indicated that Peruvian supplies, especially from the Chincas, had been greatly depleted and bordered on exhaustion—a situation that was exacerbated by periodic climatic vagaries in the Pacific called "El Niño," an upwelling of warm-water currents that, among other things, supports fewer fish and, hence, seafowl.[17]

Shrinking South American supplies seemingly provided entrepreneurs in the United States with a competitive advantage; however, miners on American guano islands often had no idea what to dig up and ship back to Baltimore, Boston, New York, and other major fertilizer markets. Consequently, during the early years of the trade, inferior phosphates and even some virtually worthless matter frequently filled cargo holds of ships before businessmen reluctantly concluded that resident geologists were expensive but necessary employees. For instance, American Guano Company hired J. D. Hague to inspect its claims in the Pacific between 1859 and 1861, "and to search for others like them. . . ."[18]

Similarly, New Yorker Ross W. Wood hired Alexis A. Julien to reside at and oversee mining on Sombrero from 1860 through 1864, a relatively safe billet during the Civil War; afterward, Julien joined the faculty of what then was Columbia College in New York City. Companies without the resources to employ resident geologists had samples from shipments regularly assayed by specialists,[19] but such after-the-fact analyses, as North Pacific Phosphate and Fertilizer Company of Hawaii discovered late in the era, often led to nearly worthless dirt being mined and hauled great distances at enormous expense. Better to engage an expert, even at the princely salary of $10,000 a year plus 2 percent of profits, as North Pacific Phosphate did at the turn of the century.[20]

Differences in the potency of phosphates typically provided by American guano islands prompted purveyors in the United States to offer "blended guanos"—a technique actually developed early on to assist farmers who, unfamiliar with powerful Peruvian fertilizer, frequently spread far too much of nitrogen-rich pure guano on growing plants and "burned" them in the process. To reduce this effect, G. F. Ober & Sons of Baltimore as early as 1856 had added phosphates to Chincan droppings, thereby successfully introducing mixed, blended, or "manipulated" fertilizers to the American market. More commonly, weaker "American guano" required fortification with nitrogen and potassium. William Davidson and John Kettlewell, Baltimore partners who had been grinding and selling acidified bone and oyster shells on the fertilizer market since 1832, dissolved their joint operation and, about the time of the guano rush, independently strengthened rock phosphate from the West Indies and Mexico by adding acidified bone. Dr. P. S. Chappell and his brother Thomas, who had been engaged in the fertilizer business in Baltimore since 1846, performed alchemy on assorted apatites with refuse from sugar refineries and bone fragments from local button manufacturers.[21]

Others added everything from fish scrap to petroleum refining by-products. Menhaden, an inedible fish common to American Atlantic and Gulf waters, had been used by Algonquin Indians since prehistoric times to fertilize corn, a technique they taught to early colonials. As early as 1844 Boston chemist Charles T. Jackson suggested that menhaden might serve as an inexpensive substitute for Peruvian guano, which, he observed, was nothing more than fish that had passed through the digestive system of birds. Not until 1850 did anyone invest in the idea. The first menhaden oil and fertilizer works belonged to D. D. Wells, which he established on Long Island, New York. His "fish guano" was a revolting dark and foul admixture, and the resulting stench led neighbors to secure an injunction that forced him to move to a remoter region. Area farmers nevertheless savored Wells's prices, $15 a ton for raw scrap or $23 to $30 a ton, cured. Over the next two decades, fish guano plants sprouted all along the Atlantic seaboard.[22]

While Wells and his numerous competitors thus began to offer a relatively inexpensive alternative to Peruvian guano, other innovative entrepreneurs added fish scrap to the phosphate-rich products of American appurtenances. At considerable risk during the Civil War the Pacific Guano Company of Massachusetts, which somehow "came into possession and control of the celebrated 'Howland Island,'"[23] hauled its phosphates back to Spectacle island in Boston's harbor where it was dried in the vats of an abandoned salt works—the company losing two ships at sea to Confederate raiders in the process. Sluggish sales caused Pacific Guano to increase the nitrogen content of its product with menhaden oil and scrap. To do so more efficiently, directors moved the firm's entire operation to Woods Hole on Cape Cod and began acquiring refuse from area fishermen. In 1864 the company introduced "Soluble Pacific Guano" and solicited distributors throughout the country, among them John S. Reese & Co. of Baltimore. John Reese, who for years had sold John Kettlewell's manipulated Mexican guano, asked Dr. Gustav A. Liebig, an analytical chemist and the son of fertilizer pioneer Justus von Liebig, to analyze the new product.[24]

The results were so startling that Reese & Co. promptly dropped Kettlewell and became Soluble Pacific Guano's most aggressive agent. At its own expense Reese & Co. soon published advertisements touting "at a fair price . . . the best cargo of guano that ever came to Baltimore. . . ."[25] In 1865 Reese and other middlemen sold 7,540 two-hundred-pound sacks (754 tons) of Soluble Pacific Guano at $5 a sack, or $50 a short ton,[26] mostly throughout the Chesapeake bay region including war-ravaged Virginia where dozens of farmers readily attested to the new fertilizer's powerful effects. One of them, Thomas R. Joynes of Onancock, Virginia, said he had scientifically compared Soluble Pacific Guano and pure Peruvian by applying them to potatoes, cotton and garden vegetable, "and in every instance, thus far, the appearance is in favor of [Soluble] Pacific Guano, in color and growth."[27]

Such testimonials undoubtedly fostered even greater demand. Pacific Guano Company more than quadrupled its sales the following year. By 1870 it was marketing more than thirty-five thousand tons of Soluble Pacific Guano annually, a level of output that quickly depleted Howland of its ready reserves, and the company abandoned the island that year—having scraped its surface clean of some forty-three thousand tons of phosphates.[28]

Had Pacific Guano not meanwhile moved to acquire alternative sources, it might well have been forced out of business. Having foreseen supply problems, during the middle 1860s the company began acquiring rock phosphate in the Caribbean, most notably from Navassa island (owned by Navassa Phosphate Company of New York) and from the Swan islands (property of New York Guano Company). Neither source was completely satisfactory. Navassa's high aluminum content presented peculiar refining problems, and, although Pacific Guano eventually bragged about (and even bought outright) the "vast deposits of high grade guano"[29] on the Swans, it too had to be specially treated to be useful. While it is unclear how much phosphate from Navassa island came to be blended in the manufacture of Soluble Pacific Guano, only two shiploads of raw materials for the highly successful product originated on the Swans between 1866 and 1869.[30]

Little matter. American guano island phosphates were no longer critical to the company because about 1867 it had acquired a large portion of the rock phosphate beds that lay along the Ashley river near Charleston, South Carolina. These rich deposits (consisting of pure phosphate nodules ranging in size from peas to boulders that weighed thousands of pounds, mixed with the remains of extinct animals) overlay marl beds (clays, carbonate of calcium, magnesium, and remnants of shells) which were also valuable as ingredients in fertilizers. The Ashley river site had been exploited intermittently since 1859; however, not until Pacific Guano (along with ten other firms) began working these beds after the Civil War did they become significant commercially. Pacific Guano, the largest early operator in the area, erected a refinery at Charleston and also acquired Chisolm's island, midway between Charleston and Savannah, which was also rich in phosphate nodules.[31]

Although Pacific Guano thus had largely solved its supply problem with domestic phosphate sources, it did not entirely abandon guano islands. In 1870 John M. S. Williams, a principal in the shipping firm of Glidden & Williams of Boston as well as a stockholder in Pacific Guano, purchased the Swans islands outright from New York Guano for an undisclosed sum. He then apparently leased them to Pacific Guano, which began mining their phosphate beds with as many as three hundred laborers; however, with far superior raw materials available in relatively close by South Carolina, the Swans only occasionally provided phosphates for the manufacture of Soluble Pacific Guano. To recover his investment, Williams promoted the Swans as a site for a lighthouse and as a coaling station for the U.S. Navy, undoubtedly hoping to sell or lease the islands to the government. He tried other uses (notably tobacco production) in an attempt to wrest value from the tropical site.[32]

Even though the Swans were reportedly considered to be "a white elephant,"[33] Pacific Guano bought them from Williams in 1882 and retained ownership until 1895 when, in bankruptcy because of fierce competition in the fertilizer business, the company's creditors sold them to businessman Warren K. Blodgett of Boston. Connecticut-based American Agricultural Chemical Company acquired the balance of Pacific Guano's assets and moved most of its production to Maine.[34]

By then numerous rival enterprises had found many other ways to fortify phosphatic guano, thereby greatly intensifying competition. Foremost among innovators was R. W. L. Rasin, a Ph.D. chemist who had overseen the processing of product from Aves and Monks islands for Philadelphia Guano Company since 1854. Hired away two years later by E. K. Cooper of Baltimore, Rasin was immediately confronted with the task of making Navassa island's phosphates, which were laced with aluminum salts, less alkaline, and thus more potent. Reportedly at the suggestion of a Yale chemist, he began experimenting with local slaughterhouse refuse—blood, bone, offal, and waste water that contained high concentrations of animal urine and, hence, ammonia. The results were most promising. Infused with capital when Cooper's operation reorganized as Navassa Phosphate Company, Rasin began buying carloads of cheap and abundant packinghouse tankage from Chicago, especially from Armour & Company, which, until then, had routinely dumped such unwanted by-products into the city's sewers. After refining the meatpacker's mess, Rasin added it to acid-treated Navassa phosphates.[35]

During the early 1870s Rasin's concoction competed vigorously with Soluble Pacific Guano as well as numerous other fortified phosphatic fertilizers, many of which were processed in Baltimore, a city that had proudly touted itself as America's guano capital since the early days of Peruvian imports. Baltimore's large chemical industry (especially its steady output of sulfuric acid, which was necessary to treat both raw rock phosphate and phosphatic guano) complemented a budding fertilizer industry that included the manufacture of Superphosphate, guano's chief competitor during the nineteenth century.[36]

P. S. Chappell's Chemical Works in the city concocted not one but four of its own brands ("Champion Super-Phosphate," "Cotton King Super-Phosphate," "Pendleton's Guano Compound," and "Empire Guano") as well as other formulae that it (like most other manufacturers) blended on order for assorted clients who sold the special creations under their own trade names. Joshua Horner mixed Peruvian guano, bone dust, concentrated animal matter, and muriate of potash into what he called "Maryland Super Phosphate" and sold it for $50 a ton, retail. Isaac Reynolds & Sons made "Chesapeake Guano" that, it was claimed, was "an ammoniated soluble phosphate containing all the properties of bone and Peruvian guano." Maryland Fertilizing and Manufacturing Company produced what it named "Cotton Food & Ammoniated Phosphate." Other independent guano manipulators then known to be operating in the city included Lazaretto Guano Company, Patapsco Guano Company, and Standard Guano Company, each of which synthesized products for themselves and for others.[37]

Added to these firms was Chemical Fertilizer Works, which Rasin and Cooper founded in 1872 after leaving Navassa Phosphate Company. Purchasing raw phosphate stock from numerous Caribbean guano islands and packinghouse tankage from the Midwest, they relied upon Rasin's chemical knowledge and engineering talent to capture much of the trade. Not long afterward, Charles Victor Mapes began experimenting with specialized formulae for particular crops: citrus, corn, cotton, grapes, potatoes, and assorted fruit trees. In 1877 he incorporated his enterprise as Mapes Formula & Peruvian Guano Company.[38]

By then the output of all U.S. fertilizer manufacturers approached $20 million annually, about half that production having originated as American guano island phosphates. With business mergers and acquisitions increasing during the latter half of the nineteenth century, many firms marketed products under a variety of trade names. One corporation in New York state registered more than a thousand brands of mixed fertilizers, with seventy different names for a single formula. The state imposed order in the marketplace by levying a hefty tax on each registered trade name, which reduced the number of brands by one half.[39]

The multiplication of brands greatly complicated matters for farmers, as one contemporary observer noted, and made the trade "particularly liable to fraud."[40] However, it does not necessarily follow that, as historian Roy Nichols has contended, "The guano business was apt to be a dirty one . . . ,"[41] or at least any more prone to chicanery than other contemporary American enterprises. Throughout the nineteenth century the U.S. economy was replete with ruthless entrepreneurs and offensive business practices—from the likes of Daniel Drew and Jim Fisk whose market manipulations and bribery of public officials were notorious, to "robber barons" such as John D. Rockefeller and Andrew Carnegie who ruthlessly crushed competitors, to meatpackers such as Philip D. Armour and Gustavus Swift who (investigations eventually disclosed) routinely adulterated food products. They and innumerable other unscrupulous businessmen with nefarious schemes prompted assorted state and federal oversights,[42] not unlike that of the State of Maryland in 1846 (as previously noted) to regulate the sale of guano within its jurisdiction;[43] however, the effectiveness of Maryland's inspection laws in preventing product tampering is unclear. It would appear that the widespread availability of substitute fertilizers (at least as much as increased public oversight) discouraged fraud.

Key to intensified national and even international fertilizer competition was the discovery of huge rock phosphate deposits in the United States, first in South Carolina, then in Florida, followed before the turn of the twentieth century by other large finds in Arkansas, Idaho, Kentucky, Montana, Tennessee, Utah, and Wyoming—total reserves eventually aggregating trillions of tons. Having led the way in exploiting these deposits, Pacific Guano Company was quickly dwarfed by other, better capitalized firms, especially by Coosaw Mining Company, which soon came to hold exclusive rights to most of South Carolina's best deposits, as well as by those operators who flocked to Florida during the 1880s to dig even richer deposits of hard rock, land pebble, river pebble, and soft rock phosphates. Among them were the Marion Phosphate and the Dunnellon Phosphate companies that shipped as much product to Hamburg, Liverpool, and London as to Baltimore, Boston, and New York.[44]

Increased availability of resources naturally attracted additional fertilizer producers. In 1859 the United States contained 47 fertilizer mixing plants; in 1869, 126; in 1879, 364; in 1889, 390; and in 1899, 422. Some of the new participants were likely market entrants. Others were not. Armour & Company, which had been selling packinghouse tankage to Baltimore firms since 1868, began studying alternatives by the late 1880s. Offered potash from Germany and able to purchase phosphates inexpensively from South Carolina, Florida, and Tennessee, Armour experimented with its own blends of bone, blood, and other unwanted by-products; however, success came serendipitously when a vat of sulfuric acid used to transform insoluble rock phosphate into phosphoric acid was inadvertently left in the open during a rainstorm. Rather than throw away the diluted acid, workers used it anyway and produced "an excellent article" that became the basis of Armour brand fertilizers, which were first marketed in 1893. In conjunction with their meatpacking plants, Armour (and arch rival Swift & Company) soon operated fertilizer facilities throughout the United States[45]—incredibly foul-smelling establishments that meatpacking critic Upton Sinclair compared unfavorably with Dante's inferno.[46]

A seemingly less likely participant in the fertilizer trade was Standard Oil Company, which allegedly "worked an [American guano] Island on a very large scale and at a great profit, mixing [guano] with the refuse that comes from the refining of oil. . . ."[47] If indeed Standard Oil ever mined an American appurtenance, neither direct evidence nor circumstantial corroboration has been found. In any case, the company did eventually manufacture fertilizers from petrochemical by-products that, as with meatpackers' tankage, proved to be a very valuable use of otherwise unwanted residues. Much more predictable was the eventual foray into the field by W. R. Grace & Company. In 1954 it acquired the Davidson Chemical Corporation of Baltimore, an early participant in phosphate refining. By that act Grace in effect returned to its origin, figuratively coming full circle from its days of hauling guano from Peru a century before.[48]

Increased competition inevitably led to overproduction, especially of South Carolina and Florida rock phosphate, which was mined with cheap (black and convict) labor. Overproduction in turn caused what one authority has called "price demoralization." South Carolina rock phosphate, 57 to 67 percent pure, that sold for $14 a ton 1867, was being undercut by the mid-1880s with 70 percent pure tricalcium phosphate from Florida that brought merely $6 a ton.[49] American guano island phosphate, restricted by law to a minimum of $4 and a maximum of $8 a ton, wholesale,[50] simply could not compete—especially when the cost of transportation was added.[51]

As domestic rock phosphate production dramatically rose (12,262 tons in 1868; 65,241 tons in 1870; 211,377 tons in 1888; 510,499 tons in 1890;

941,368 tons in 1893; 1,038,551 tons in 1895; 1,491,216 tons in 1900; and 1,947,190 tons in 1905[52]) guano island output, which had never been great, stagnated, then ceased altogether:

| | | | |
|---|---|---|---|
| 1869 | 15,622 tons | 1884 | 9,333 tons |
| 1870 | 17,068 | 1885 | 12,100 |
| 1871 | 14,154 | 1886 | 5,770 |
| 1872 | 4,209 | 1887 | 8,226 |
| 1873 | 11,014 | 1888 | 5,765 |
| 1874 | 6,877 | 1889 | 10,439 |
| 1875 | 7,269 | 1890 | 1,176 |
| 1876 | 14,785 | 1891 | 15,857 |
| 1877 | 6,060 | 1892 | 4,288 |
| 1878 | 17,930 | 1893 | 4,376 |
| 1879 | 8,733 | 1894 | 5,137 |
| 1880 | 12,795 | 1895 | 8,082 |
| 1881 | 16,883 | 1896 | 6,929 |
| 1882 | 15,249 | 1897 | 5,310 |
| 1883 | 7,873 | 1898 | 4,562 |
| | | Total | 283,871 tons[53] |

No shipment from American appurtenances officially passed through any U.S. port after 1898. Consequently, in 1906 Secretary of Commerce and Labor V. H. Metcalf directed customs collectors to discontinue rendering quarterly reports on the commodity.[54]

Fierce competition in Florida phosphates naturally led to further shakeout and consolidation, the fertilizer business as a consequence coming to be dominated by those firms already engaged in Superphosphate production. Relying primarily upon nitrate of soda imports from Bolivia, Chile, and Peru and potash from Germany, American firms increasingly became fertilizer mixers by blending native rock phosphates with cheap foreign nitrates and potassium to formulate nutritious plant foods. German overproduction about the turn of the century led to the creation of a cartel (Kali Syndikat, G.m.b.H.) to control European potash output and price, which was countered in the United States by the merger of many northern and southern fertilizer mixers into the American Agricultural Chemical Company and the Virginia-Carolina Chemical Company, respectively. About 1908 financier J. P. Morgan tried to combine those and other leading firms (including Royster Guano Co. of Baltimore, Armour Fertilizer Works, and Swift & Company's fertilizer subsidiaries) into a gigantic trust to be called the United States Fertilizer Company, but the majors balked. Morgan's efforts eventually resulted in the creation of International Agricultural Chemical Corporation, which was composed primarily of Tennessee phosphate mines and the Buffalo Fertilizer Company.[55]

By the time of World War I mixed fertilizers had so captured the American market that relatively little guano entered the United States from Peru, or anywhere else. Both Antony Gibbs & Company and W. R. Grace & Company (both long associated with the South American guano trade) by then concentrated instead on acquiring and transporting nitrate of soda (especially from Chile) to buyers (fertilizer mixers and explosives manufacturers) in Europe and North America. Similarly surpassed as a supplier of fertilizer ingredients before the turn of the century even by steel slag (a by-product from smelting and a cheap source of 15 to 19 percent pure phosphoric acid), American appurtenances likewise no longer contributed to the productive process.[56]

Nevertheless, for a time the word "guano" continued to be a valuable trade term, and many of the new giants in fertilizer manufacturing retained one or more subsidiaries that employed the term (if not the chemistry). By 1913, according to the Federal Trade Commission, which monitored such matters, the nation's seven largest manufacturers (and their subsidiaries) were: Virginia-Carolina Chemical Co. (which included Commercial Guano Company, Savannah and Columbus, Georgia, among its subsidiaries); American Agricultural Chemical Co. (Chicopee Guano Co., New York; Dixie Guano Co., Spartanburg, South Carolina; Lazaretto Guano Co., Baltimore; Pacific Guano Co., a Maine corporation; Palmetto Guano Co., Columbus, South Carolina; Pocomoke Guano Co., Norfolk, Virginia; Zell Guano Co., Baltimore); International Agricultural Chemical Corporation (Charsworth Guano Co., Charsworth, Georgia; Fletcher Guano Co., Columbus, Georgia; Home Mixture Guano Co., Columbus, South Carolina; Rainbow Guano Co., Montgomery, Alabama; Vance Guano Co., Henderson, North Carolina); Armour Fertilizer Works; Baugh & Sons Co.; F. S. Royster Guano Co.; and Swift & Co. Together they accounted for 46 percent of the nation's acid phosphate production, none of which (despite numerous corporate names) had originated on guano islands, American or otherwise.[57]

The estimated four hundred thousand tons of rock guano that entered the U.S. marketplace from American appurtenances during the nineteenth century[58] had undeniably stimulated fertilizer manufacturing and enhanced agricultural productivity, thereby augmenting the national economy. By contrast, the profitability of the great guano rush is far less certain.

The expectations of profit that had propelled eager American prospectors about the seven seas in pursuit of bird droppings may well have been elusory for most of them. While many early participants undoubtedly hoped to realize a return of $20 a ton or more from the trade (the amount of monopoly profits, it was frequently alleged, that Peru enjoyed from exploiting its Chinca islands[59]), there is no persuasive evidence that any of those who were prominently involved in the guano trade—especially as miners—became wealthy as a result of their digs.

Anticipating maximum yields proved to be unrealistic because all of the islands exploited by Americans under the Guano Act were uniformly leached clean of the valuable nitrogenous matter that sustained the highest prices. Of course such facts did not prevent entrepreneurs from claiming as much profit as possible when seeking remuneration from the public purse for ventures gone awry. Alfred Benson suggested that Congress should pay him upwards of $3 million in recompense for two hundred thousand tons of Lobos island guano that he claimed he had been prepared to sell in the United States at $35 a ton, for a profit of $15 a ton after expenses.[60]

In 1855 Philo Shelton said his prospect on Aves island was worth $12.50 a ton, and he consequently asked Congress to pay him $341,000 for losses directly and indirectly related to having been kicked off the island by the Venezuelan government. John Lang and William Delano, likewise expelled from Aves by authorities in Caracas, were more conservative in their estimation of prices, they anticipating merely $10 a ton profit; however, they doubled Shelton's guess as to the amount of guano involved and petitioned the U.S. government for $639,412.50 in compensation.[61]

William Kendall alleged he had forgone a $10 per ton return on his discovery of 10,000 tons of guano on Verd key that had been confiscated by the British in 1859. Baltimore businessmen Abram Patterson and Prudencio Murguiondo produced documents showing they had averaged $8.32 a ton profit on eight shipments totaling 1,074.5 tons during their seven months' occupation of Alta Vela, before being evicted in 1860 by the Dominican Republic; however, by estimating that the island contained upward of

100,000 tons of the commodity, they asserted that they had lost approximately $850,000, including $22,000 in actual capital outlays.[62]

Some promoters were overly optimistic when touting mining prospects. Organizers of Caribbean Guano Company, who sought to raise $5 million with which to work Roncador, Pedro, Petrel, and Quito Sueño islands in the West Indies about the turn of the century, asserted that these islands and keys contained

> upward of 2,000,000 tons of Bird Guano . . . worth $30 a ton, [after] allowing $5 a ton for excavating, loading, and freight to American ports, there will be a net profit of $50,000,000—sufficient to pay 30% dividends for 30 years, on the total capital of the Company."[63]

Dr. Pascal Quinan provided a far more conservative (and undoubtedly realistic) appraisal of the value of rock phosphates from American appurtenances in general in 1880 when he estimated that Arcas key's 150,000 tons of product represented a potential profit of $1 a ton.[64]

Perhaps it is true as writer T. Courtenay Whedbee has asserted that E. K. Cooper "made a fortune"[65] from Navassa's guano, but Cooper's riches more likely flowed from R. W. L. Rasin's special blend of cheap island phosphates and packinghouse tankage. In any case, Navassa Phosphate Company was hardly an unqualified success. Blessed with very large reserves (approximately 4.5 million tons of phosphates) and with relatively inexpensive mining costs (estimated at no more than $1 a ton in 1866), the company's expenses nevertheless steadily climbed thereafter as it increased its investment in the Caribbean island. While data are incomplete, it seems apparent that rising labor and transportation costs, coupled with increased competition from domestic American rock phosphate production, doomed the operation. By 1887 it was in receivership.[66]

Alfred G. Benson, by all accounts America's leading guanopreneur, was far less successful than his "monstrous guano empire"[67] might have implied. According to the *New York Times* Benson "never fully recovered"[68] from the Lobos fiasco. He died in relative poverty. And if James Jennett made money on guano islands, it was probably (as the U.S. State department once unabashedly asserted) from bilking buyers of his island prospects.[69]

C. A. Williams's Phoenix Guano Company appears to have been the most financially successful of all the American guano operations. It reportedly sold upwards of seventy thousand tons of phosphates from its Pacific island mines mostly on "the European market [which] absorbed all that could be shipped," thereby generating revenues of between $1.75 and $2.1 million; however, its actual rate of profit (the return on investment) is not known.[70]

The most detailed records extant on a guano island mining operation are those of North Pacific Phosphate and Fertilizer Company (Pacific Guano and Fertilizer Company after 1896) on Laysan island, and they do not reveal inordinate profits. By selling its product for $30 to $35 a ton in Hawaii, on the West coast of the United States, and in Europe between 1891 and 1899, the company realized annual returns of between 5 and 10 percent on an investment in excess of $250,000. Sales thereafter steadily declined as cheaper sources of rock phosphate became increasingly available worldwide.[71]

If guano mining profits were not spectacular, part of the reason for mediocre returns undoubtedly revolved around the unusual risks such enterprises faced. Courtenay Whedbee asserts, "The guano trade was a messy business and hated by many who were engaged in it." One Baltimore importer was sued for damages by a merchant who alleged that his "valuable cargo of coffee [was ruined when stored] in the same warehouse with a shipment of guano."[72] Cargo vessels were similarly contaminated, the foul odor of guano (especially ammonia-rich feces from Peru) eventually permeating every nook and cranny of a ship and forcing owners either to bear the expense of fumigation afterward, or condemning vessels forever to the guano trade.[73] Toxic vapors sometimes overwhelmed sailors at sea, perhaps to the extent (an English physician once speculated) that some ships were actually lost because their crews were rendered incapable of manning them. For certain "the effects of the vapours upon the iron materials of the ships was remarkable for the rapid development of rust; 'it eat them through,' to quote the sailors' term, chain cables, anchors, and bolts of the timbers. . . ."[74]

At least one vessel, the British bark *Ann,* is known to have sunk as a direct consequence of its cargo of bird droppings. A new ship carrying the prized commodity from African Ichaboe to England in 1845, it grounded on an Atlantic sand bank. While washing about on the incoming tide, *Ann* shipped sea water that splashed into the cargo hold and onto the dry, phosphorus-laden commodity—precipitating a flash of combustion. Smoke billowing out of the hold caused all hands to abandon ship just as a violent explosion blew the stern completely off the vessel. Fortunately, no one was injured, but *Ann* went down. It was merely one of two ships engaged in the guano trade lost that year by the same owner.[75]

Far more commonplace was the destruction of vessels at guano islands as they attempted to off-load supplies or to take on cargo. Baker island in the Pacific (almost entirely surrounded by a protruding reef) was especially dangerous. No fewer than a dozen ships wrecked there between 1860 and 1871, another five being severely damaged. Most of those that were lost, such as *Lady Washington* out of Boston in 1864, were reportedly driven ashore by tropical storms and impaled on reefs. Some, as with *Mary L. Sutton* (also from Boston) that went aground on the island in 1865, were adequately insured, that vessel carrying $70,000 in coverage; however, many apparently were not, and their owners recovered little more than salvage, which rarely exceeded $200. One ship, *Robin Hood* out of San Francisco, is said to have been the victim of arson. Disgruntled seamen allegedly set fire to the vessel after it had taken on more than a thousand tons of the island's phosphates; loyal crew members and workers ashore saved some stores and the ship's rigging by chopping down the masts. Human danger was also very real. At least three persons lost their lives at Baker island in these incidents, mostly the victims of drowning.[76]

Other American appurtenances were not much safer. Between 1863 and 1869 at least fourteen vessels came to grief at Howland island because of severe weather and dangerous reefs. Pacific Guano Company of Boston, which reportedly had thirty-three ships regularly hauling phosphates from the island to its Woods Hole facility, lost four ships at the atoll—twice as many as to the more celebrated cause of Confederate raiders during the Civil War. Disasters struck America's guano fleet in the Pacific with regularity (at Clipperton, Enderbury, Jarvis, Johnston, McKeans, Malden, and Starbuck islands), resulting in enormous property loss and even some deaths.[77] Claims mounted, as when *Silver Star* out of Boston in 1861 went aground at Jarvis while loading phosphates. Described by journalists as "a fine clipper of 1195 tons" and insured for about $50,000, it was a total loss that underwriters (Equitable, Alliance, and Neptune insurance companies) made good.[78]

Underwriters invariably dumped risky policies at the first opportunity, as when insurance for North Pacific Phosphate's ship *Mary E. Foster* was abruptly canceled in 1891, the vessel then being overdue from Laysan and its term of coverage having expired.[79] Other insurers expressly prohibited cargo ships protected by their policies "from all guano islands, except the Chincas,"[80] which possessed an especially safe harbor.

In 1868, when two freighters returning from Navassa in the Caribbean with loads of phosphates were lost at sea, Albany City Insurance Company of New York and Narragansett Fire and Marine Insurance Company of Boston, respective insurers, refused to pay claims submitted by the vessels' owner, David Whiton of Boston, because the ships had been specifically proscribed from American guano islands. Whiton brought suits in Massachusetts state court to recover damages, he asserting that his crafts carried rock phosphates, not guano, and, hence, had not violated any stipulated prohibition. The question posed to the jury by the combined cases "was not whether the material was scientifically and chemically a guano, but whether it was commonly and commercially known as guano, and whether the island of Navassa was called and known in commerce, trade, navigation, and the business of marine insurance, as a guano island. . . ."[81]

Both sides called experts who respectively swore that what was being mined on Navassa was either rock phosphate or guano, depending upon which interest they represented. Insurance companies offered numerous public documents as proof of their contention that Navassa was a forbidden port: copies of the Guano Islands Act; Secretary of State Lewis Cass's 1858 letter to Navy secretary Isaac Toucey, asking the squadron to protect E. K. Cooper's digs on the island from Haitian interference; and other official correspondence from assorted printed public documents indicating that the U.S. government considered the place to be an American appurtenance—all of which were excluded by the judge as inadmissible because they were not originals.[82]

The jury consequently found for Whiton whereupon the insurers appealed to the Massachusetts Supreme Court. Ruling that the trial judge had erred by excluding "appropriate evidence of the action of the national government"; that the preponderance of admissible evidence tended to show (regardless of the precise chemical nature of the substance being mined) that "Navassa was commonly called and known as a guano island"; and therefore, that for legal purposes "the deposit on Navassa was guano," the state's high court overturned the decision.[83] The U.S. Supreme Court declined to review the case, and rock phosphate from American appurtenances consequently came to be legally defined as guano, whatever its actual chemical composition or geological origin.

By 1900 it was also mostly gone, having been removed by legions of generally nameless workers whose lives and labor on guano islands have been mostly forgotten.

# 9

## Shoveling It: Life and Labor on Guano Islands

No nineteenth-century job—not the mind-numbing repetition of assembly lines then steadily taking over America's industrial production; not the choking dust of coal mines, even with attendant claustrophobic confinement; not gandy-dancing on remote railroads; not forced isolation of lumbering in faraway woods with outrageously priced goods and services in company towns; not the slashing, razor-sharp knives and gut-wrenching stench of butchery in meatpacking; nor even mucking about in the filth of meatpackers' fertilizer works—was as difficult, dangerous, or demeaning as shoveling either feces or phosphates on guano islands. Worst conditions of all were in Peru where workers (many of them literally kidnaped into slavery) routinely resorted to suicide as their only means of escape. Most American guano mining operations were unquestionably more humane, but none was pleasant.

The Chincas (three perpendicular volcanic promontories approximately one square mile each, ranging from one hundred to three hundred feet in elevation and lying fifteen miles off the port of Pisco, Peru) were the most dreadful guano islands of them all. People in Pisco could even smell them. Tropical heat, high humidity, and yet virtually no rainfall made the Chincas a hell on earth. Thick, seasonal fogs that shrouded them mostly at night metamorphosed outer layers of bird droppings into a greasy paste, which baked during the day into hard crust that only picks and shovels could penetrate. Provided with no more than two meals daily (usually a cup of maize and four unripe bananas), grass mats for beds, and reed huts for dwellings, men (a few free Peruvian native laborers, but mostly indentured coolies, kidnaped Pacific islanders, convicts, army deserters, and a handful of black slaves) labored twenty or more hours a day, six days a week, to fill quotas of four to five tons each, for which they were paid three reales (about a third of a peso), two of which were withheld for meals.[1]

Workers dug trenches sixty to one hundred feet deep or more (literally down to bedrock) to chisel out large and small chunks of aggregated feces, which were hauled by wheelbarrow loads to the edge of a precipice. In good weather, ships moored close inshore in deep water (practically touching cliffside rocks that were almost masthead high) to await cargo that workers ashore slid through canvas chutes directly into cargo holds. Billowing clouds of thick, ammonia-laden dust belched skyward with each dump, enveloping vessels and rendering respiration of anyone nearby almost impossible. Ships' crews typically retreated high into the rigging to escape as much of the odious, airborne powder as possible, while "trimmers" (guano workers assigned to cargo holds) struggled to level the mess. To protect themselves from dust and ammonia vapors, most trimmers wore improvised oakum respirators (loose hemp or jute fiber masks plastered together with tar) that they tied across their mouths and nostrils. Even then they could remain below deck no more than twenty minutes at a time. Often, as they clambered up on deck, gasping for air (naked, wet with perspiration, and covered with feces), they suffered nosebleeds and even temporary blindness. While they recuperated, other trimmers ventured below, two work crews thus alternating to load seven hundred or eight hundred tons in no more than three days, in fair weather. Whenever rough seas prevented inshore moorings the stuff had to be ferried in two hundred pounds sacks by launches to vessels waiting offshore—a far more laborious, time-consuming, and expensive undertaking.[2]

Occupational ailments abounded among miners and trimmers even in such widely separated places as the Peruvian Chincas and African Ichaboe, the same maladies occasionally even afflicting sailors who hauled guano and, more rarely, farmers who sprinkled it on their crops. Respiratory problems (asphyxiation from ammonia vapors, coughing or spitting up blood, "embarrassed breathing," and fainting spells) were widely reported among miners. Gastrointestinal complaints (abdominal cramps, diarrhea, dysentery, fever, malaise, nausea, vomiting), although not diagnosed by contemporary physicians, doubtlessly included histoplasmosis and shigellosis, both diseases borne of feces likely ingested inadvertently by workers. Swollen limbs (especially legs), purpura (subcutaneous eruption of blood vessels characterized by purple skin blotches), and scurvy (bleeding gums, loosened teeth, and mouth ulcers), probably the consequences of inadequate diet, were commonplace.[3]

Injury and death were omnipresent dangers. Trenches caved in, burying miners alive on the Chincas, on Ichaboe, and probably elsewhere. Those who did not work diligently enough to satisfy overseers were set upon by vicious, half-starved dogs employed to instill fear. Other workers were whipped, two dozen lashes with cat-o'-nine-tails being minimal punishment, which invariably left victims breathless and incapable of vigorous labor. Under the best of circumstances, their hands cracked open from constantly wielding picks and shovels, from pushing heavy wheelbarrows, and from mucking about in cargo holds—sores, ulcers, and other open wounds frequently infecting but rarely healing. On the Chincas, those no longer capable of using their hands were yoked to wheelbarrows, like mules, to haul heavy loads cliffside. Those weakened by sickness, corporal punishment, and/or diseases and infections (and therefore unable to stand) were reduced to working on their hands and knees, picking small stones from the guano before it was dumped into the chutes that emptied into cargo holds. Rather than endure more, some laborers ended their lives with headlong plunges down the chutes. Cemeteries on both the Chincas and Ichaboe reportedly overflowed with the rotting corpses of those who failed to survive and who had been buried in graves too shallow to protect remains from scavenging dogs, human bones consequently being liberally scattered about.[4]

Such abominable working conditions made recruiting free labor virtually impossible, especially in Peru, which also required a large labor force for the multitude of cotton, sugar, and cochineal plantations situated along the verdant river valleys of the coastal strip. The nation's relatively small population (about two million persons in 1850) was insufficient to furnish enough manpower for all needs, especially since the typical peasant farmer (usually a native inhabitant of the highlands) abhorred working on lowland plantations and on guano islands—except in the winter, when he reportedly returned "home as soon as he has got together ten or twenty dollars."[5]

African slaves, theoretically emancipated by José de San Martín during the revolution in 1821, actually were not liberated in Peru until 1854, five years after the British Navy had effectively interdicted traffic between Africa and South America; however, blacks (free or slave) constituted a tiny percentage of Peru's total population,[6] far too small to suffice even had they been inclined to work on plantations or on guano islands. Most were not. According to one authority of the period, "they were not very industrious." In all fairness, neither was the typical mestizo nor white proletarian in Peru eager "to work with his hands,"[7] especially in such a demeaning and disgusting endeavor as shoveling bird shit.

"In these circumstances," as historian Watt Stewart has written, "it was necessary to look abroad for the fulfillment of [Peru's] labor needs."[8] Following independence the country sought to encourage immigration from Europe, but, given low wages and limited opportunities for newcomers to acquire land, the effort came to naught. In 1847 Peru's lawmakers would have authorized capitalists or landholders to "introduce foreigners" by offering four tons of tax-free guano for each colonist recruited, but the bill failed of passage. Two years later (principally at the urging of Domingo Elías, a prominent politico, merchant, and plantation owner) legislators enacted statutes to encourage the immigration of Chinese "colonists" by paying a bounty of 30 pesos for each person between the ages of ten and forty who was "introduced" by recruiters, incidentally giving Elías and his associates a four-year monopoly on recruiting for much of the country.[9]

Thus commenced what Stewart has aptly termed "Chinese bondage in Peru."[10] Prostrate from opium wars and divided into spheres of European influence, China was unable to protect her citizens from Occidentals who seduced them to emigrate. Poor, illiterate Chinese peasants—especially at Macao after the British Passenger Act (1855) drove the "coolie trade" from Hong Kong—were easily duped by foreigners who promised them better lives, often in the gold fields of California, once indentures of four to five years had been satisfied. Others were simply kidnaped, chained together in the holds of ships that were little different from African slavers. Mostly under the pretext of legitimate labor contracts, countless vessels flying the flags of Great Britain, France, Portugal, Spain, and the United States hauled an estimated three-quarters of a million Chinese to Australia, Brazil, Cuba, Hawaii, Peru, Tahiti, and the United States between 1849 and 1881. Clipper ships owned by the Boston firm of Sampson & Tappan (sometime American guano miners, as on Aves island in 1854) were prominent among them even though the partners were simultaneously actively involved in the abolitionist movement, an hypocrisy noted by the *New York Herald* in 1859.[11]

Much money was to be made hauling coolies to Cuba or Peru, four times as much as carrying ticketed passengers to California; however, if the poor souls discovered what was in store for them, they sometimes mutinied. In 1852, when Chinese, crowded aboard the American clipper *Robert Browne,* suffered the indignity of having their queues (pigtails) shorn, which under Chinese custom and law meant they could never return home, they realized what was happening to them; they rebelled, killed the captain, took control of the ship, and sought refuge at Patchusan in the Ryukyu archipelago. British and American gunboats soon landed marines, captured survivors, and hauled them back to China for trial, Secretary of State Daniel Webster foremost among those demanding western justice.[12]

Most coolies discovered too late that they were not destined for California's gold fields but, rather, for virtual slavery in Cuban cane fields or for Peru's plantations and guano islands, from which few ever returned. By 1875 between 90,000 and 150,000 Chinese had been landed in Peru; another 10,000 or so are estimated to have died en route. Four fifths of the survivors found relatively easy lives on coastal plantations, but the rest were doomed to the Chincas. Countless numbers of them preferred suicide: overdoses of opium, hanging, slashing their own throats, and even headlong dives off hundred-foot cliffs onto the rocks below became commonplace escapes. Outcries in Peru as well as abroad led to the abrogation of the "Chinese Law" in 1856. Nevertheless, traffic in Asians continued for the next several years, albeit at a somewhat diminished pace. English entrepreneurs building a railroad between Lima and Chorrillos imported hundreds of coolies as laborers under special licenses, and large Peruvian landowners easily obtained thousands more, both legally and not.[13]

As the number of Chinese nationals available to labor on Peruvian guano islands diminished, opportunists provided alternative manpower. The nineteenth-century Pacific basin was awash in people eager to make money through "blackbirding," an euphemism for enticing dark-skinned islanders (Melanesians and Polynesians) to work for European and even American entrepreneurs. "Labor recruiters" had originated during the 1840s with the trade in sandalwood, the fragrant timber then very much in demand in Europe. Commercial quantities of sandalwood required substantial labor, which at first was provided by islanders who happily traded valuable logs for white man's trinkets, but, eventually, European desire to regularize the supply of the wood led Englishmen to establish sandalwood stations on large islands such as Espíritu Santo in the New Hebrides and to recruit natives to work on them. When migrant labor shortages developed, some mariners resorted to kidnaping islanders, whom they sold to the highest bidder. In time blackbirding spread and furnished laborers (willing and not) for coconut, cotton, and pineapple plantations, and for mining operations on Peruvian guano islands as well as phosphate digs throughout the Pacific.[14]

Unsavory characters such as William Henry (Bully) Hayes, an American pirate, sailed into tropical paradises like the Fiji islands intent upon filling their holds with human cargo. Recruiters often promised naïve natives wages as high as £18 ($90 U.S.) for three years' service, at the end of which, it was solemnly promised, they would be returned home. Many recruits were never seen again. If offers of money were rebuffed, blackbirders frequently resorted to western material culture (inexpensive cutlery, gaudy patterned dry goods, cheap gin) to entice islanders below deck on the pretense of bartering; instead, they were seized and taken captive. Some unwary souls were literally plucked from their canoes as they paddled alongside labor schooners. Others were lured aboard with promises of sexual adventures with girls and young women similarly kidnaped elsewhere.[15]

During the late 1850s blackbirders plundered the South and Central Pacific, virtually depopulating some islands by enslaving men, women, and children who were hauled to distant markets, particularly in Peru. Many died of diseases en route. Others were killed when they rebelled against their captors. Those who survived transit were auctioned off under the pretext of recovering transportation costs. Then, in 1862, two separate events helped bring the Peruvian traffic to an end. A mass raid on Easter island, some twenty-four hundred miles off the coast of Chile, subdued all able-bodied men, about one third of the island's 3,000-person population—including Chief Kaimakoi, Crown Prince Maurata, and all the priests who could read the hieroglyphs on the island's unique statuary. They were carried off to Peru where they were condemned to the guano islands. An estimated nine hundred of them died very quickly. A similar blackbirding expedition that year to mid-Pacific Penrhyn (Tongareva) island brought another 280 hapless men, women, and children to Lima. These events evoked the outrage of a French cleric on Tahiti who goaded his government to protest vehemently, an outcry echoed by the British. An embarrassed Peruvian government quickly agreed to repatriate the survivors. While en route home, 85 of an estimated 100 Easter islanders died of some civilized scourge (smallpox according to some accounts, measles, or even tuberculosis by others); those who lived infected their fellows ashore, spawning an epidemic that decimated the island's remaining population. Many Tongarevans similarly succumbed to disease before they could be returned home; others were reportedly dumped on the first convenient island.[16]

Peruvian blackbird traffic disappeared within a year, in part because islanders were obviously unfit for forced labor on plantations or guano islands. To their good fortune Melanesians and Polynesians thus found little ongoing demand among those who otherwise might have been willing to bid for their services and, thereby, further encourage the slavers. Loud protestations especially by Great Britain, France, and the United States (provoked by their missionaries throughout the Pacific) also greatly embarrassed the Peruvian government, which formally banned the "immigration" of Pacific islander "colonists" in 1863; however, by then, Peru had an alternative source of labor at its disposal. In 1861 the coolie trade had been revived under pressure from plantation owners and guano exporters.[17]

For the next dozen years unwitting Chinese peasants were again conscripted to live and die on the Chincas despite a short-lived Spanish intervention commencing in 1863—designed not to end the despicable coolie trade but, rather, to seize Peru's guano islands as a first step toward reestablishing Madrid's colonial possessions in Latin America. Although the U.S. Congress in 1864 forbade Americans to participate in coolie commerce, a score or more U.S.-flagged vessels continued to ferry Asians to and fro as late as 1877, at a when time W. R. Grace was regularly hauling unemployed Chinese from California to Peru. Neither was Great Britain especially eager to abandon the lucrative traffic, particularly with respect to the recruitment of coolies within the Empire even though official British policy abhorred slavery. Only after Peru and China had negotiated a treaty in 1874 to end the traffic did the British government take firm steps to prevent its citizens from engaging in the trade—and then only after the number of Orientals in Australia had increased to a level sufficient to frighten local residents.[18]

Reluctant to deal with coolie traffic though the British government may have been, it took the lead in putting an end to blackbirding. By the mid-nineteenth century both French and British enterprises relied heavily upon illicit trade in natives to supply their growing labor requirements throughout the Pacific basin. French naval vessels regularly furnished human cargoes for Tahitian and New Caledonian plantations, while British kidnappers were feared throughout New Guinea, the New Hebrides, the Ellice, Gilberts, Lines, Solomons, and other island groups. In answer to vociferous outcries especially among missionary groups, Parliament passed the Pacific Islanders Protection (or Kidnaping) Act in 1872 to forbid the transportation of natives except in licensed ships; four years later Parliament empowered her majesty's navy to enforce that law even in areas technically outside British jurisdiction, which was the first practical step toward eliminating this commerce in human beings. While the worst abuses of "labor recruiters" (the outright kidnaping of Melanesians and Polynesians) consequently diminished, employment practices bordering on indentured servitude, reinforced by late-coming imperialists (both the Germans and the Japanese), survived in one form or another throughout the Pacific as late as World War II.[19]

There is no evidence that coolies were employed on any U.S. guano island; however, both Melanesian and Polynesian workers were commonplace on American appurtenances throughout the Pacific, albeit as contract laborers—a technicality that may well have been lost on the workers. The principal Yankee phosphate firms in the basin (American Guano, Pacific Guano of California, Pacific Guano of Massachusetts, Phoenix Guano, and United States Guano) employed mostly native Hawaiians, known as

"Kanakas" (meaning "people" in Hawaiian), a term that came to be applied widely to South Seas islanders, especially Polynesians. On Baker, Jarvis, and Howland islands,[20] American businessmen came to greatly value these "amphibious fellows": "Sometimes, when high surf made the reef quite impassable for boats, it was an easy task and good sport for one of these Kanakas to swim from the shore to a ship at the mooring and return, carrying messages in a bottle tied about him."[21]

Life on islands, rocks, and keys typically mined by Americans was difficult even for Kanakas. During much of the year places such as Baker, Clipperton, Howland, Jarvis, and Johnston in the Pacific (as well as Navassa in the Caribbean) received scant rainfall, amounts wholly inadequate to support large-scale human habitation. Consequently, residents collected such rainfall as occurred, typically during nighttime showers in the dry season or during heavy squalls commonplace throughout the rainy season. They also employed diverse company-furnished distillation apparatuses to extract drinking water directly from the sea when supplies were short, but much if not most potable water had to be hauled in a considerable expense by cargo vessels. Food was also a problem. Many firms introduced rabbits and even sheep and goats to the islands to augment natural supplies, which typically consisted of eggs, birds, fish, and, more rarely (as on the Phoenix islands), coconuts.[22]

Island overseers occasionally took along their families. Such was obviously the case on Howland (at least toward the end of its occupancy) because Joseph Spencer, his wife, and three children were removed (as well as thirty-four Kanaka employees) by Pacific Guano of Massachusetts when it abandoned those digs in 1878. When Andrew Rosehill claimed Marcus in the western Pacific in 1889 he hired a husband and wife team to live there, symbolically to maintain his possession.[23]

Common laborers rarely enjoyed female companionship. Historian William Lane Harris says of Aves island in the Caribbean, which was jointly mined by rival American firms in 1854,

> At times there could have been as many as 100 men working the island. The island was visited several times by the wives of the men who came out on the ships. It seems that some of the vessels even had stewardesses. At least one family with children came to the island but it is not known if the women and children stayed on the island for any length of time.[24]

The Swan islands off Honduras reportedly were intermittently inhabited by families[25] rather than merely by solitary and (presumably) frustrated heterosexual men. Even so, Atlantic & Pacific Guano Company, which mined the Swans, is said to have "treated labourers so badly that they all had to quit."[26]

Some American operations demonstrated concern for the welfare of their workers. North Pacific Phosphate and Fertilizer Company instructed its overseers on Laysan in 1890, "You will of course seek to maintain good discipline among your men, at the same time treating them with kindness."[27] Even alleged swindler James Jennett thoughtfully provided for the comfort of Caribbean islanders in his employ. Among the list of provisions—navy bread (hardtack), flour, corn meal, potatoes, peas, salt pork, molasses, vinegar, coffee, tea, peppers, matches, tobacco, blankets, mattresses, and fishing gear—with which he supplied workers on Rogues was also five gallons of Jamaican rum.[28]

Nevertheless, many laborers found living and working conditions under American auspices to be appalling. In 1859 Hanuu, a Kanaka from Oahu, Hawaii, and twenty-five of his fellows who had shoveled phosphates for almost eight months on Enderbury, McKeans, and Phoenix islands, sued C. A. Williams (and others doing business as Phoenix Guano Company), demanding significantly greater compensation than the $10 per month for which workers had contracted. Alleging that the firm had promised to provide them with "wholesome and sufficient food and drink and with proper lodging," the Kanakas claimed that they had instead "been subjected to great hardship and privation. . . ." Therefore they asked for an additional $400 each. Williams and his associates countered by offering as evidence the original contract signed by each of the claimants (with an "X" to denote illiteracy) by which the company had promised only to "provide board and lodging . . . [and] passage from Honolulu to the Phoenix islands and back to Honolulu. . . ."[29] The court agreed with Williams and dismissed the case. When similarly sued by an unhappy laborer in 1868, Williams defended himself by saying that the agreement was the same as had been in general use since 1859 and that employees clearly knew its terms. The court agreed, once more finding for Williams.[30]

Labor crews nevertheless had ample cause for complaint, their lives and labor on desolate, isolated guano islands being uniformly unpleasant and dangerous. Phosphates on Baker island (which is as dry as a desert much of the year) were in the form of a fine powder that filled the air whenever disturbed—swirling about the diggers, attaching to sweaty bodies like cement, and choking them as they tried to breathe. Howland was literally overrun with rats. Survivors of some long-forgotten shipwreck, the pests constituted both a great annoyance and an added burden for human habitation. Rodents contaminated food stores, bit unwary workers, and otherwise made nuisances of themselves, not the least of which was their relentless scavenging on birds' eggs, which imperiled long-term phosphate supplies. Some Kanakas were employed solely to kill the vermin in a vain attempt at controlling their numbers, upwards of four thousand rodents being exterminated daily—without any noticeable effect. Although rats had also infested Jarvis by 1858 (no doubt escaping ashore from visiting ships), they never became the pests they were on Howland.[31]

Clipperton island, approximately seven hundred miles southwest of Acapulco, swarmed with land crabs that made human habitation of the isolated atoll precarious at best. Oceanic Phosphate Company of San Francisco, which mined the place between 1893 and 1898, mostly with mainland immigrant labor, was forced to elevate all of its wooden structures above ground, setting them on posts to prevent the crustaceans from moving in with the men and attacking them in their sleep. The company even had to sheathe the wooden pilings with sheet metal to keep the crabs from devouring the buildings splinter by splinter. Worse, workers were frequently marooned on the remote island, left there far longer than the firm had promised. Supplies sometimes ran critically low. One poor caretaker languished alone for almost six months, Oceanic Phosphate refusing to retrieve him unless he agreed to pay his own passage home.[32]

Regardless of the island involved, the work was arduous and perilous. Rock phosphate mining (whether on isolated islands, rocks, or keys, or on the mainland) was labor intensive—hard work that consisted mostly of pick-and-shovel toil. On most American guano islands, men scooped up phosphates, piled them onto trams, hauled the stuff to the sea, and loaded it aboard small boats that were often paddled through heavy breakers toward vessels waiting in relatively safe, deep water. Small boats sometimes swamped in the surf, or capsized, dumping men and cargo into shark-infested seas. Ocean-going vessels, usually moored to buoys or to lines leading out from shore, were in constant danger of coming to grief on the reefs should the wind abruptly shift or, as was always possible in tropical climes, a storm suddenly blow up out of a clear blue sky.[33]

American appurtenances were neither enumerated in any official nineteenth-century census of the United States nor included in any compilation of national health statistics; therefore, nothing but anecdotal detail remains from which to infer morbidity and mortality among workers. However commonplace death might have been due to disease, privation, and accidents on these appurtenances, there is scant evidence of such calamities. Two employees of Phoenix Guano, having awaited relief for nine months and reduced to eating wormy bread for more than three months, were reportedly near death from scurvy on Enderbury island in 1861 when a new crew finally arrived with supplies. A man identified only as Carstens, "a faithful servant of the Company," was somehow killed in 1894 while working on Laysan, but the circumstances of his death are unknown. Pacific Guano and Fertilizer Company gave his daughter $250 in compensation.[34]

In 1891 Columbian Guano and Phosphate Company, an American corporation allegedly pilfering Roncador's phosphates which Petrel Guano Company claimed belonged to it, hired a dozen Jamaicans to mine the island clandestinely, but seven of them abruptly left in a boat while the other five disappeared. Some time later two corpses were found on the island by a turtle fisherman who reported his grisly discovery to Honduran authorities, thereby initiating an investigation that led to a successful lawsuit by Petrel to recover its property. Apparently no official determination was ever made regarding either the remains or the workers' disappearances.[35]

Once, forty convict laborers were said to have been found dead after a hurricane battered Navassa island in the Caribbean, but the largest number of deaths ever associated with an American guano operation supposedly occurred at the end of the nineteenth century on Clipperton island. One hundred Japanese reportedly perished from drinking contaminated lagoon water, but no corroboration (even of the employment of such a large number of Asians on the island) has been found.[36]

The most infamous American appurtenance of them all unquestionably was Navassa in the Caribbean. By the end of the nineteenth century it had become notorious as a veritable corporate "Devil's island."

# 10

## Navassa Island

Navassa, still an American possession despite ongoing Haitian claims to the contrary, was mined longer and more extensively than any other island, rock, or key that ever appertained to the United States. It was the site of a violent labor disturbance late in the nineteenth century, an event that caused the United States Supreme Court to review the constitutionality of the Guano Islands Act.

Claimed by Americans in 1857 and worked ceaselessly by the Navassa Phosphate Company after 1864, Navassa island's ownership was again challenged by Haiti in 1872 when that government (citing American abandonment of Alta Vela and Key Verd as precedents) formally presented diplomats in Washington with documentary evidence that Navassa had been discovered by Christopher Columbus in 1493 and had been included in the treaty of 1697, by which Spain ceded the western part of the island of Hispaniola to Paris, as well as the Ordinance of 1825, by which French king Charles X recognized the independence of Haiti. Secretary of State Hamilton Fish rejected Haitian assertions of ownership, noting that "Not one instance is given of actual occupation of the Island previous to its possession and occupation by citizens of the United States in 1857, . . . [nor is any] instance given in which Haiti has ever attempted to enforce any of its revenue laws in Navassa." Observing that the United States had deferred to others with respect to Alta Vela and Key Verd because both were substantially closer to adjacent islands (which was not precisely correct), and because, unlike Navassa, both had been specifically named in the territorial laws of claimant governments, Fish rejected Haitian pretensions to the island, as well as a similar assertion the following year.[1]

At no time during these diplomatic exchanges was work on Navassa interrupted. Its phosphates were regularly extracted between 1857 and 1898 and shipped mostly to the United States, which was no easy task. Pear-shaped (with its stem pointing northwestward), the two-square-mile island rises abruptly out of deep water, its vertical limestone cliffs looming 10 to 150 feet above sea level. Almost completely encircled by a submerged (2 to 36 meters deep) reef, it lacks both sheltered harbor and safe landing places. The island's surface is divided into two flat terraces: a tilted, narrow (150- to 900-foot-wide) ring that is composed principally of limestone pocked with deposits of mostly gray phosphates, and a huge upper plateau (called "the mountain" by miners) that looms 35 to 105 feet above the lower terrace and contains mostly less valuable red phosphates, likewise encased in host limestone. The whole island structure is honeycombed with caves and crevices, many of which are packed full of phosphates.[2]

With a semi-arid climate, the island's lack of a "protracted rainy season [naturally] favored the preservation of phosphate deposits."[3] It also produced a thin soil that supported merely stunted timber (wild fig, mastic, palm, pigeon plum, and coral sumac or poisonwood trees) and desert vegetation (prickly pear cactus and century plants).[4]

Human habitation was consequently quite difficult. Occupied by crews working for E. O. and E. K. Cooper of Baltimore in 1857, Navassa had to be sustained entirely with supplies from the mainland, and, at considerable expense, the businessmen constructed two separate harbor facilities, both adjacent to the lower terrace. The first was situated along the northwestern coast, at a place called "Brownstone" (so named for a rich outcrop of phosphates on the upper terrace), the second being a mile south at a small notch in the island's nearly vertical face, known as Lulu bay. Neither harbor was ideal because of submerged reefs, jutting cliffs, and sometimes turbulent seas. Ships usually stood offshore a quarter of a mile or more, supplies and cargo being laboriously ferried to and fro by lighters. By 1889 reserves of hard phosphates had been exhausted above Brownstone harbor, which was closed, and mining on the mountain moved southeastward to a point above a tram, which transported material to Lulu bay for processing and shipment.[5]

The Coopers established Navassa's lone settlement near Lulu bay and called it Lulutown, which at first was merely a collection of rough-hewn rock hovels barely capable of sheltering a dozen workers during seasonal tropical downpours. After acquiring the island in 1864, Navassa Phosphate reportedly invested $50,000 in numerous improvements. The settlement, looming sixty feet above sea level, by 1889 had grown to include two dozen buildings constructed mostly of native limestone: the superintendent's house (a two-story dwelling), officers' quarters (called "the Blazing Rag"), the night watchman's house ("the White Elephant"), several small, earthen-floor quarters for the men (known collectively as "the Barracks"), a cook house, a blacksmith shop, a commissary (or company store), a chapel, an infirmary, a jail ("the Reformatory"), a long covered shed (the "Drying House"), a warehouse for phosphates, and an unknown number of privies situated strategically over excavated crevices. In addition to a cistern to collect and hold rainwater, Navassa Phosphate also added a boiler with which to distill salt water from the sea and a narrow-gauge railroad (or tramway) over which to haul phosphates.[6]

The arduous nature of life on the island undoubtedly explains why the Coopers contracted with the State of Maryland at any early date to employ convict labor, mostly whites and rarely in excess of forty persons. Prisoners were said to have rebelled against inhumane living and working conditions, and the Coopers' overseers once reportedly shot several inmates to retain control.[7] After the Coopers merged their interests with other investors to create Navassa Phosphate Company, the new operation ceased using convict labor and began relying instead upon recently freed American slaves and other African-Americans for manpower. By 1866 the firm regularly employed as many as 180 blacks (mostly as laborers) and 30 whites (all of whom were either officers or mechanics) on the island.[8]

Between the end of the Civil War and 1889, when Navassa island was shaken by a bloody riot, blacks living in the Chesapeake bay region (and much of the United States, for that matter) faced limited opportunities for gainful employment. Poverty was widespread. According to one study, during the 1880s "Negro farm laborers in the South [averaged earning] . . . about fifty cents a day,"[9] when they could obtain such seasonal work. Another historian of the era has written that while urban African-American males enjoyed "a much more diverse occupational structure than rural blacks, . . . [they] shared a common and depressed economic status."[10] "There were few employment opportunities for blacks in the southern cities," say Peter N. Carroll and David W. Noble. "Slaves and free blacks had been artisans and craftsmen . . . before 1865. But between Emancipation and 1900, they were systematically driven from those jobs by hostile whites."[11]

Circumstances were no better in border states. For instance, Baltimore (a city of four hundred thousand persons by 1889), from which Navassa Phosphate recruited most of its labor force, contained an estimated seventy-seven thousand African-American residents, a tiny percentage of whom were either professionals (attorneys, clerics, physicians, teachers) or affluent entrepreneurs, a score of whom, collectively, were estimated to be worth a half million dollars (butchers, caterers, coal dealers, grocers, morticians, oystermen, produce jobbers). The vast majority of Baltimore's black businessmen were hardly so well off; most were small shopkeepers who dealt "mostly with the colored people and the poorer whites." Furthermore, only a small minority of the city's blacks could be classified as skilled labor (brick-makers, carpenters, painters, printer-typesetters, ship-caulkers). The overwhelming majority were either semi-skilled (hod-carriers, oyster-shuckers) or day laborers of one sort or another.[12] With such limited economic opportunities, many African-Americans "placed their hopes largely in mining," W. H. Harris has observed, "where more blacks were employed than in any other southern industry."[13]

Navassa Phosphate had little difficulty finding workers for its Caribbean mine despite a labor contract whose stipulations were quite severe, even for that era. In return for $8 a month (plus bunk, board, and transportation to and from Baltimore), usually accompanied by a $10 advance against wages, employees agreed to work "either on shore or in boats . . . [as] directed . . . by . . . Navassa Phosphate Company, or its agents, and for as many months as the said . . . Company may desire, but not exceeding fifteen from the time of arrival at Navassa Island, until discharged therefrom, at which time their wages are to commence and cease." Accumulated earnings were due upon return to Baltimore, unless workers "fail to obey the orders and instructions of said Navassa Phosphate Company, or its agents, or refuse at any time to labor, [whereupon] they shall forfeit all claim for wages and compensation which shall be due them." Should employees be unable to work at any time because of illness or injury, they were required to pay the company fifty cents a day for board, their wages being suspended until they resumed work. In any case, fifty cents per month were deducted from wages for medicine and medical attention. Furthermore, if, upon arrival at Navassa, recruits were judged "not competent to perform the duties as stated herein, they [were] to pay their own passage back to the United States. . . ."[14]

While the vast majority of the 139 African-Americans residing on Navassa in 1889 apparently were first-time employees, several had been there repeatedly—one of them later claiming to have resided on the island off and on for a total of fourteen years.[15] Therefore, both Navassa and its living and working conditions must have been relatively well known throughout Baltimore's black community.

Despite financial problems that forced Navassa Phosphate into receivership in 1887, it continued to mine the island with a full complement of workers. Digging that had commenced near the settlement in 1857 progressed steadily eastward, workers extracting gray phosphates along the flank of "the mountain" mostly. About 1864 they also began laying narrow-gauge railroad track around the southeastern rim of the island as they chipped away. By 1889 the tramway's tracks aggregated 1.75 miles, most of that distance stretching from near Arnold's bay along the island's eastern rim (the farthest point of excavation) to Lulu bay. The men also dug a deep trench near Lulu bay northeastward thirteen hundred feet or so into the side of the mountain to tap the more valuable gray phosphates underneath the red and laid track into the slit. Miners atop the plateau dumped material through a two hundred-foot-long canvas chute into hopper cars sitting on the siding.[16]

The work was exhausting. Commencing with a whistle that blew between 6:00 and 7:00 A.M., six days a week, men dug at the island's riches, prepared them for shipment, and loaded them aboard vessels standing off shore.[17] Eighty-five percent of both gray and red phosphates on Navassa occur as pockets of "soft earth" in cavities or fissures that are rarely more than twelve to fifteen feet wide and ten to twenty feet deep, surrounded by hard, barren limestone. When dry, the stuff easily yielded to picks and shovels, but, even after a brief shower, it coagulated into "a sticky mess, difficult to dig, handle and transport."[18]

Whatever its character, by 1889 each worker averaged handling one and one-half tons of product daily. Typically a single man in a deep crevice dug at phosphates all day long; periodically he filled a cylindrical can with phosphates. Another worker at ground level lifted the can by rope and poured its contents into a wheelbarrow that someone else pushed to growing piles of product that were dumped either beside the canvas chute atop the mountain or next to the tram on the lower plateau. Whichever, laborers continuously raked the stuff, spreading it out to speed drying. A few days of exposure to air reduced the moisture content substantially, provided it did not rain. Eventually work gangs shoveled the somewhat aerated matter into twelve-foot-long, four-foot-wide hopper cars capable of holding fifty cubic feet of material, which weighed between one and one-half and two tons.[19]

The other 15 percent of the island's phosphates (likewise located in cavities and fissures) was rock hard. Occasionally this material consisted of "un-decomposed lumps within the body of the softer earthy phosphates"; however, more often than not it was firmly attached to the limestone walls of individual pockets. As one visiting geologist described the process, "The phosphate rock is readily extracted from a series of contiguous pockets, though at a considerable discomfort sometimes to the laborer, who frequently has an opening only large enough to squeeze his body into, affording scarcely room enough to scrape or dig out the material," mostly using five-pound sledge hammers and 15-inch-long "striking bars." Sometimes even those tools could not pry the stuff loose, forcing workers to dynamite it out. Rarely could a single man chiseling in rock-hard phosphates produce more than two thirds of a ton daily.[20]

Hard phosphates were likewise moved by rail, which was no simple process. Although the tram ran mostly along the lower terrace, the tracks were inclined upward all the way from the settlement to the end of the line; therefore, cars "would come down the grade thirty or forty miles an hour if not braked."[21] Runaways and wrecks were constant dangers, and no one volunteered to work the line in part because (once horses and mules were removed from the island about 1870 as an economy measure) cars unloaded at Lulu bay had to be pushed uphill back to the end of the line by hand, a treacherous task. Walking barefoot to minimize the chance of slipping, the men danced along sun-baked, one-and-one-half-inch-wide iron rails in constant "danger of falling on the rocks [between the tracks] and injuring themselves."[22]

At the settlement men shoveled phosphates into piles sixty feet long and ten feet high, usually under a covered roof to protect product from rain. The sides of the Drying House were open to expose the material to breezes that, along with morning and afternoon sunshine, facilitated drying. Aerated phosphates formed a coarse granular powder, which was eventually moved to an enclosed warehouse where it was segregated by value (or color, gray and red) and stored for shipment.[23]

Workers delivered phosphates by rail car to the wharf (a platform forty-seven feet above sea level) whenever transport vessels arrived, which was irregular. From the wharf, they shoveled material into canvas chutes that funneled it to any one of seven company lighters (or cargo barges) stationed below—powder-dry phosphates spewing forth like great clouds of dust, which enveloped everything. Manned by as many as five laborers each, a lighter held about four tons of material that were ferried to ships anchored a quarter to a half mile off shore in safe, deep water. With favorable wind and weather a lighter could handle seventy-five tons in a ten-hour day, a pace (considering constant currents and swells) that could rarely be maintained for more than two days running by the same crew.[24]

Hard labor and dangerous working conditions were far from the workers' only grievances. Even though the company released chickens and goats on the island to forage for themselves in the hope they would eventually supplement staples from the mainland, food was of poor quality (mostly "rotten salt pork and beef," as some of the men later bitterly complained[25]) and seldom in sufficient quantity to satisfy those engaged in vigorous manual labor. Workers could augment furnished fare with provisions bought on credit at the company store (open Saturday evenings when crews were released from the week's work), but prices were high—five cents a pound for flour that cost a penny in Baltimore. Candy, canned goods, and tobacco all reportedly sold for exorbitant prices. In fact unhappy workers eventually accused the company of price gouging: $2.50 for a shirt that retailed for thirty-five cents in Baltimore, $1.50 for fifty-cent overalls, $4 for $2 shoes. Furthermore, Navassa Phosphate provided laborers no mattresses to soften the earthen floors of their Barracks; however, thin mats could be rented at the commissary for $4 each, about twice their mainland price, new. As many as 72 of the 139 blacks on the island were said to be so deeply in debt to the company store that advances likely would absorb all wages due, if not exceed them. Those who owed money would not be allowed to return home until they had worked off their debts. White storekeeper-bookkeeper Thomas N. Foster rendered accounts quarterly, the next statements being due September 30, 1889.[26]

Many men were also angry over the increasing use of corporal punishment for petty offenses. Blacks later charged that white "officers were accustomed, for any offense or violation of the rules, to trice them up by rope tied to their wrists, with the arms outstretched above their heads, and to fasten them in that position, with their toes only touching the ground. . . ."[27] Tricing reportedly lasted for as long as six hours in a blazing sun.[28] Such cruel discipline was of dubious legality; in 1886, when Pacific Guano Company of Massachusetts had asked Secretary of State Thomas F. Bayard if its manager on the Swans "might be invested with the power to preserve order on the islands," the diplomat replied that Attorney General A. H. Garland was of the opinion that the executive department of government did not have the authority "either to prescribe additional laws or to empower others to do so."[29]

However questionable it might have been for corporate rules to carry the weight of statutes, on Navassa island there was no mechanism for appeal. Only the superintendent, George W. Tipton, was authorized to punish workers, and by all accounts he was a fair man—never subsequently accused of capricious justice. He also held eleven white subordinates in check, reportedly forbidding them even to curse the men. Then on September 4, when Tipton died of some unreported malady and was replaced by Dr. Charles D. Smith, conditions abruptly changed. Forty-one-year-old Smith, an 1882 graduate of the Baltimore College of Physicians and Surgeons, allegedly had a drinking problem. Whatever his credentials, he had arrived the previous June to take charge of the island's hospital— a facility that was far from humane under his supervision, some of the men would eventually allege.[30]

With Smith as superintendent, discipline disintegrated. Alcohol, absolutely forbidden by the company (and a prohibition rigorously enforced by

Tipton), quickly appeared. Charles Davenport, a thirty-one-year-old black baker from Washington, D.C., openly brewed beer in the cookhouse, and both blacks and whites reportedly bought rum from sailors aboard the Jamaican sloop *Dom Pedro,* which called regularly. Whites later claimed that blacks became sullen and less cooperative, supposedly because of moonshine as well as mounting debts at the company store. Blacks said whites (including Smith) became increasingly abusive, routinely cursing them. James ("Mac") Mahon, the white "car boss" who was hated by all the blacks, for no apparent reason doubled to two weeks each man's turn on the hopper cars, the hardest and most dangerous of all duties.[31]

Then, about September 12 Mahon also "triced up . . . a [black] man named Smallwood" with whom Mahon "had some words. . . ." Smallwood, just out of the hospital, was promptly released by Dr. Smith, but the moment the physician's back was turned, Mahon "triced [Smallwood] up again."[32] Obviously uneasy, Charles Wesley Roby, the white, thirty-five-year-old "superintendent of mines," commenced carrying a pistol.[33]

According to some eyewitnesses, simmering anger boiled over into conspiracy. William ("Richmond Shorty") James, a twenty-two-year-old black from Baltimore, later testified in court that he was approached the day after Smallwood's tricing by eight men—Edmund ("Blueball") Francis, Henry Johnson (also known as Thomas Welch), Albert Jones, Henry Jones, George S. Key, James Phillips, James Robinson, and Edward Woodfork—who told him they intended to kill all the white officers the next day, beginning with Roby, whose gun they wanted. William James, who later said that he had heard rumors for more than a week that a plot was afoot, was told to crush Mahon's skull with a shovel, which James said he refused to do. He claimed to be willing to go out on strike but would not murder anyone. Richard ("Slim") Ellis, a twenty-three-year-old West Indian who had been on Navassa island since January, later testified that he too was approached on the evening of the thirteenth and asked to help kill Roby. Rather than become involved, Ellis said he faked illness and persuaded Dr. Smith to check him into the hospital, which may not have been very difficult if, as alleged, the physician was stumbling drunk at the time.[34]

Most of those identified by James and Ellis as conspirators later insisted that no such meetings ever took place; what transpired on Saturday, September 14, 1889, was a spontaneous uprising—a riot. According to Edmund Francis, who had been on Navassa for nine months, when he arrived at the digs about 8:00 A.M. in September 14, mining superintendent Roby was either drunk or hung over and in a foul mood. Roby cursed Francis for being late, telling him to dig, or "The next grave I measure out will be yours."[35] Francis later claimed that he reacted reflexively, striking Roby on the side of the head with a cutting bar, and rendering him unconscious with a single blow—the officer's pistol mysteriously disappearing in the fracas. Samuel Marsh, Roby's thirty-year-old assistant who had been on the island for about eight months, ordered his superior loaded aboard a hopper car and directed that all hands proceed to Dr. Smith's residence for "an investigation"; however, Marsh inexplicably remained behind at the digs.[36]

As the car rumbled down the track—Roby propped up in a sitting position for all to see, lifeless and bleeding profusely—a score or more of black miners walked along behind, toward Lulu bay, gathering more workers as they went. By some accounts several of them suggested that now was the time to stand up to the bosses, to demand better treatment. By other reports, some called for revolution—for murder. Al ("Texas Shorty") Jones, reportedly yelled, "Now is our time. Kill the white [sons-of-bitches]!"[37]

Work ceased all about the island, and upwards of one hundred men gathered outside the gate to the superintendent's house. Dr. Smith was absent, hunting pigeons that morning on the mountain with a borrowed fowling piece. He was searched out about 11:00 A.M. by Alfred Brown, a forty-five-year-old laborer who had spent three tours on the island. The black man informed Smith that Roby was injured but said nothing of the circumstances. As the physician hurried toward Lulu bay, he was met by Thomas Foster, the forty-year-old bookkeeper, who claimed that Roby was dead, murdered by mutineers, and that his body had been taken to the officers' quarters. Upon arriving at the Blazing Rag, Smith instead found the man to be semi-conscious; Roby did not know how he had been hurt.[38]

Dr. Smith ran to collect his instruments from his nearby quarters (the superintendent's cottage) where he found a crowd of angry men at the gate awaiting him. Still armed with a shotgun, he confronted them and asked who had struck Roby, but no one answered. Instead, Tom Henderson, one of the laborers, complained of living and working conditions.[39] He told the physician, "Stop cursing us, stop working us to death, stop Mr. Roby from threatening us at the mines, and give us suitable food."[40] As he later testified in court, Smith replied, "Go to work, you black [bastard], or I'll blow your brains out." James Henry ("Snow") Robinson, a twenty-five-year-old laborer who had arrived in March, held a club in his hand, but finally backed away, saying, "Come, boys, let's go."[41]

As the crowd melted away, most of the men retreating to the Barracks, Smith returned to the Blazing Rag to treat Roby. There, as he bandaged the injured man's head, he instructed those officers present (Joseph N. Fales, a white, thirty-eight-year-old otherwise unidentified twenty-year employee of

Navassa Phosphate; Henry A. Jones, a fifty-three-year-old carpenter and wheelwright; and the hated car-boss, James Mahon) to gather up all the firearms and go to his quarters. Smith also sent Henry Jones, a nineteen-year-old black laborer from Baltimore, to the mines to fetch Sam Marsh, Roby's assistant, and John O'Rourke, the pile boss. As those summoned supervisors hurried toward the superintendent's house, they were confronted by several men led by Al Jones, James Henry Robinson, Ed ("the Devil") Smith, and Edward Woodfork. According to O'Rourke's later testimony, they threatened to kill Marsh who panicked and fled up the mountain. O'Rourke begged for his associate's life and easily dissuaded the men from violence. As the disgruntled workers moved on toward Lulu bay, O'Rourke ran after Marsh, eventually overtaking him. Together, they again made for the settlement.[42]

When they arrived at the superintendent's house, all was quiet. Dr. Smith directed O'Rourke to blow the whistle to see if the men would return to work, but no one budged from the Barracks. Obviously anxious about the situation, Smith gathered more arms and ammunition and distributed them; expecting a siege, some of the white officers took up stations at windows on both floors. Then, pistol in hand, Smith set out for the Barracks to confront the workers, and several white officers—all armed—trailed along behind.[43] As they walked, Smith allegedly remarked to his companions, "I will kill six or seven of these niggers, and that will settle it."[44] Believing that they were about to be attacked, blacks scattered when they saw the whites approaching, but Smith called to them, asking that they meet at his house to talk.[45]

Most of the island's work force promptly gathered outside the superintendent's gate, and Smith confronted them. He asked if they were willing to return to work. Several said they were. When the physician pointedly asked James Phillips, a twenty-two-year-old black from Greensboro, North Carolina, if he would work, Sam Marsh spoke up, mistakenly identifying Phillips as the man who had struck Roby. Marsh also said he thought Phillips had Roby's gun. Smith ordered Henry A. Jones, the carpenter, to arrest Phillips. When Jones dutifully stepped forward, his pistol drawn, Phillips— conjecturing that he might as well die then and there— grabbed Jones's wrist. As they grappled for control of the gun, several men in the crowd yelled, "Kill them! Kill them!" Smith pulled his pistol and fired two shots into the air. At that moment Thomas Fales ran from the house and shot Phillips in the face, freeing Jones from the black man's grip.[46] The whites retreated into the house, with Jones hysterically yelling "Upstairs! Upstairs!" and firing two shots back toward the crowd as he fled. Phillips, merely grazed by Fales's bullet, was carried off to the hospital.[47]

Taking refuge outside the house behind nearby hopper cars, workers began pelting the structure with rocks. Someone yelled: "Kill the [sons-of-bitches]! We've got them now! Give us Mac! We want Mac. We'll kill the [son-of-a- bitch]!"[48] Unarmed, Dr. Smith stepped out onto the balcony to try to reason with what had quickly devolved into an angry mob. He asked that the officers be allowed to leave the island on an English brig that was lying at anchor off Lulu bay, but his request was met with derision and more demands for the surrender of James Mahon. Charles H. Smith, also known as John Ward, a thirty-one-year-old black who had been to Navassa five times, had apparently come into possession of Roby's pistol and, resting it on a car for better aim, fired two shots at the physician who scampered back inside unscathed.[49]

In a momentary display of defiance, Mahon strolled out on the porch, whereupon someone in the crowd screamed, "You're the [bastard] we want." Shaken, Mahon retreated. Roby, having recovered enough by then to function, boldly marched out onto the balcony and fired two shots in the general direction of the mob, apparently hitting no one.[50]

Rather than become involved in impending bloodshed, some of the blacks headed either for the Barracks or the mountain while others escalated the conflict. Several of the latter group menacingly sharpened knives and axes on grindstones within plain sight of those trapped inside. Young Henry Jones, whom Smith had sent after Marsh and O'Rourke earlier in the day, reportedly threatened Henry Johnson (Thomas Welch) with an axe, promising to split his skull open if he did not promptly reveal where, at Marsh's orders, he had hidden dynamite. Johnson (Welch) complied. Moses ("Dakota") Williams, a twenty-two-year-old mixed blood Indian, and Alfred Brown recovered the explosives and, along with Johnson (Welch), commenced throwing lit sticks against the superintendent's house. The uncontained detonations did little more than rattle windows and unnerve occupants; however, about 3:00 P.M., when those inside the house observed rioters affixing a fuse to a fifty-pound can of blasting powder, most of them fled rather than chance being blown up. At that moment it started to rain, wetting the fuse and rendering the bomb impotent.[51]

White officers nevertheless scattered. John O'Rourke jumped out of a second-story window and fled to the blacksmith shop, whose doors were closed and barred. O'Rourke begged its white occupant, John Jacobson, to open up and let him in, but Jacobson refused. By then a dozen blacks had surrounded the building, and young Henry Jones ordered O'Rourke to surrender his gun, which he did when William ("Preacher") Henderson (also known as Henson) promised the pile boss he would not be hurt.[52]

Dr. Smith had similarly run from his house when its destruction seemed imminent, throwing away one of two pistols he carried as he ran toward the

Reformatory. Inside, he looked through the jail's barred window and saw Thomas Foster, the bookkeeper, crouched defensively behind a rock on which he rested a rifle. Someone yelled at him, "Drop your gun, you [son-of-a-bitch]," to which Foster replied, "Come and get it." At that moment, as Smith eventually testified, he saw a rock strike Foster in the head, causing the man to reel out of his line of vision.[53]

According to other witnesses, Foster had been knocked senseless by Caesar Fisher, after which young Henry Jones chopped the helpless man in the abdomen and back with an axe, mortally wounding him. The next thing Dr. Smith saw was Charles H. Smith (alias John Ward, who had already taken two shots at the physician) in possession of Foster's rifle. As he entered the Reformatory, Smith (Ward) demanded the doctor's remaining gun. It was immediately surrendered. Preacher Henderson told Dr. Smith to go to the White Elephant, the watchman's quarters, where other white officers had taken refuge. Henderson said he would try to protect them.[54]

Roby, his head still bandaged, had likewise run for his life but was surrounded by the mob within twenty feet of the superintendent's house. Charles H. Smith (John Ward) demanded at gunpoint that Roby surrender his pistol, which he did. As he gave up the gun Roby said, "John Ward, I've never harmed you." The remark apparently disarmed Smith, who lowered his pistol and bid Roby to be on his way. As he departed he saw Edward ("the Devil") Smith "raise a broadaxe to cut Marsh, [but] John Morris, one of the colored men, pointed a shotgun at Smith and threatened to blow his brains out if he did not drop the axe, . . . [an] action [that temporarily] . . . saved Marsh's life." Together, Roby and Marsh fled to the White Elephant, which Roby shared with night watchman H. Nelson Vail.[55]

Carpenter Henry A. Jones arrived almost simultaneously. En route he had observed William Shea, the wharf boss, running for his life. As Jones later testified, "I saw Stephen Peters [a twenty-eight-year-old black man from Salisbury, Maryland, who had been to Navassa repeatedly] with a gun at his shoulder aiming at Mr. Shea, about 15 feet ahead of him. Peters fired and Mr. Shea fell in a rock hole about 30 or 40 feet from the cliff."[56] Like Joseph Fales, already at the White Elephant, Jones meekly surrendered his gun to blacks who had surrounded the cabin; then he, Marsh, and Roby submissively went indoors to await an unknown fate. Already there were Nelson Vail, the nineteen-year-old night watchman, pile-boss John O'Rourke, and car-boss James Mahon, who had likewise been disarmed. Terrified, Mahon was hiding under a bed. They were soon joined by Dr. Smith. Afterward, for a time, things seemed calmer, the relative quiet occasionally punctuated by angry shouts to send out Mahon.[57]

About 5:00 P.M. the officers were called to by Preacher Henderson who promised them food. As most of the whites paraded outside, single file, mob members James Tasker (or Tascar) and George S. Key pushed past them, rushing inside to search for Mahon. Roby (lying on his cot, under which Mahon cowered) said to Tasker, "Jim, let him alone. Let him stay there." Tasker replied, "No. That is the man we want." He dragged Mahon, kicking and screaming, out from under the bed. Once standing, the car boss bolted out the door with Key (armed with a pistol) close behind. As Mahon reached one of many nearby holes from which phosphate had been extracted, Key shot at him, striking the fleeing man in the side of the head. Mahon cried out and fell (or jumped, according to differing accounts) into the cavity. Key then calmly walked to the edge of the hole, aimed point blank at Mahon, and pulled the trigger, shooting the car boss in the center of the back and through the heart.[58]

When Mahon had run from the White Elephant, Sam Marsh and Joe Fales apparently lost their nerve and likewise scampered away. Several strikers immediately set out in pursuit. Edward Smith, who had previously threatened Marsh with an axe, several witnesses later testified, was among those who took off after the assistant mine boss, this time with a rock, eventually crushing his skull. Young Henry Jones, who had hacked Thomas Foster with an axe, reportedly chased after Fales, who was eventually found dead—his left arm completely severed above the elbow, and his left leg chopped almost in two, just below the knee.[59]

Henry A. Jones, John O'Rourke, C. W. Roby, Dr. Smith, and Nelson Vail remained where they were, inaction that probably saved their lives—along with the timely intervention of Preacher Henderson who pleaded for calm. About then Charles Davenport, the baker, sent for Dr. Smith; having helped carry mortally wounded Thomas Foster to the hospital, Davenport said the man desperately needed medical attention. The mob let the physician go, and along the way Smith stopped to examine Mahon. He was dead. Blacks standing around the body asked Smith if they should throw his remains into the sea, but the physician insisted that they carry the body back to the White Elephant. At the clinic Dr. Smith found Foster with "a gaping wound in the stomach, . . . [and upon turning] him over on his side, found a wound in his back, cutting through his ribs and exposing his lung."[60] Smith administered morphine and sewed up the wounds. The dying man asked Dr. Smith to see that his mother in Baltimore got his bank book.[61]

By then the violence was spent. As most blacks and whites retreated to their respective quarters, Dr. Smith resumed the practice of medicine by treating assorted injuries. Sam Marsh, incoherent from concussion, was carried to the hospital by several blacks. Numerous other workers arrived, many suffering gunshot wounds—most commonly in their feet. After Foster died, Davenport (the baker) supervised the collection of bodies. He had Foster's remains removed from the hospital and carried to the superintendent's house, where he was laid out on the dining room table. His corpse was soon joined by those of Fales and Mahon. Shea's body was never found.[62]

According to some witnesses, the blacks met that evening at the Barracks, with James Robinson presiding. Ringleaders allegedly threatened to kill any among them who would talk of what had transpired. Significantly, no one apparently suggested that the only way they might escape justice would be to murder the surviving whites who surely would talk if permitted to live. Neither was the company store looted, even though—under the circumstances—none of the whites was in a position to prevent it.[63]

An odd calm set in. The next day, Sunday, September 15, Dr. Smith met with Preacher Henderson and Charles Davenport, the baker. Smith said that all but life-sustaining work should cease; he also said that everyone must return to the mainland, preferably in a U.S. Navy vessel. He proposed to send a message to the captain of the British brig, still lying off Lulu bay, and request that he take a letter outlining events to the American consul at Kingston, Jamaica. Henderson read both the note and the letter and did not object to the dispatches. That day, Henry A. Jones, the carpenter, built coffins for Fales, Foster, and Mahon, who were buried before dark. For the next five days men on both sides of the battle line idled away the time.[64]

On Friday, September 20, HMS *Forward* dropped anchor offshore. As no U.S. naval vessel was available, the American consul in Jamaica had asked the British to respond.[65] *Forward*'s captain and two officers came ashore in a gig, and the commander informed the blacks that if they harmed any more of the whites, he would send sailors ashore and "clean them up."[66]

Marsh, suffering greatly from concussion, was taken aboard the warship, which was better equipped to deal with his head injury. Delirious, he got up from his sickbed, wandered up on deck, and fell overboard. Rescued, he was again confined to a hospital bed, where he soon died. He was buried at sea. On September 28 the British commander decided the best thing to do was to remove all the surviving whites, along with three blacks (Charles Davenport, William Henderson, and Albert Sanders), all of whom had been threatened with retribution for protecting whites. They were transported to Kingston where the American consul arranged passage to Baltimore.[67]

Meanwhile on October 4, USS *Galena*, flagship of Rear Admiral Bancroft Gherardi's North Atlantic squadron and skippered by Commander G. W.

Sumner, arrived at the island. Gherardi sent ashore a five-man board of inquiry, headed by Lieutenant H. P. Huse, the admiral's aide. With them was a detachment of U.S. Marines under Lieutenant George T. Bates to establish and maintain order, if necessary, but all was quite peaceful. Over the ensuing week, the board interviewed numerous witnesses, some of whom were taken aboard *Galena* to repeat their stories to Admiral Gherardi. They described privation and cruelty leading to the riot as well as the ensuing bloodshed. In the end, sailors arrested and took on board the six blacks whom the admiral believed to be ringleaders: James Johnson, Henry Jones, George S. Key, and Amos Lee (all suspected of murder) and Albert Jones and James Phillips (who were suspected of mutiny and assault with intent to kill). Three others—Robert Downes (or Downs), William James, and George Ward—were also taken aboard and placed in protective custody as material witnesses. Another 124 blacks (many of whom were thought likely to be guilty either of murder or complicity) were loaded aboard the brigs *Romance* and *Alice,* which had recently arrived and were anchored off Lulu bay awaiting phosphates. The freighters were commandeered by Gherardi because *Galena,* a small wooden corvette, was incapable of carrying everyone.[68]

News of the flotilla's approach caused Thomas G. Hayes, U.S. district attorney for (and a former mayor of) Baltimore, to intercept *Galena* off the coast of Virginia. "Attorney Haynes practically held court on board ship," says legal scholar Henry J. McGuinn, "and selected eighteen of the men as leaders of the riot." These names he eventually presented to a grand jury for indictment.[69] When *Galena* docked at Baltimore October 27, Admiral Gherardi turned his prisoners over to Deputy U.S. Marshal J. C. Le Grand Cole who was àccompanied by Charles Roby, who identified the men. When *Alice* and *Romance* likewise anchored offshore five days later, tugboats were sent to meet them; Cole, Roby, and U.S. Court Commissioner G. Morris Bond were on board—Roby to identify the miscreants, Cole to arrest them, and magistrate Bond to certify that all was done properly. As the press had advertised well both their alleged crimes and their impending arrival, on both occasions curious crowds gathered dockside to watch barefoot blacks in leg chains parade to Baltimore's city jail.[70]

On Wednesday, November 6, a federal grand jury was impaneled by the U.S. Circuit Court in Baltimore to hear evidence of the riot, and on Thursday, November 14, that grand jury returned five separate indictments against the eighteen blacks Hayes had identified: first, that George S. Key had shot James Mahon and that the others aided and abetted in that murder; second, that Caesar Fisher and Henry Jones had killed Thomas M. Foster with a stone and an axe, the others being accessories; third, that Henry Jones had murdered Joseph Fales with an axe, the others being accessories; fourth, that Edward Smith (alias "the Devil") had killed Samuel Marsh with a stone, the others being accessories; and fifth, that Charles H. ("Pompey") Davis, Stephen Peters, and Charles H. Smith (alias John Ward) had murdered William T. Shea in an unknown manner, the others being accessories. In December, as trials on these allegations proceeded, twenty-five others were also charged with rioting.[71]

Between Tuesday, November 19, 1889, and Saturday, February 15, 1890, five separate trials were conducted in Baltimore's U.S. Circuit Court which, prior to enactment of the Circuit Court of Appeals (Evarts) Act of 1891, was the court of general jurisdiction (federal district courts at that time being quite limited in scope). As then was standard practice, the Navassa cases were presided over by two jurists, Thomas J. Morris, federal judge for the District of Maryland, and Hugh Lennox Bond, a U.S. Supreme Court justice who, like all his colleagues on the high court, rode circuit—his being the Fourth Circuit, or the state of Maryland. The first trial, that of George S. Key for the murder of James Mahon as well as others for complicity in that act, attracted such curious throngs that the courtroom was packed to overflowing for all ten sessions over a two-week period, forcing Judge Morris to order that once spectator pews were filled to capacity the doors be closed and guarded by U.S. marshals.[72]

The Order of Galilean Fishermen (a black fraternal organization headquartered in Baltimore) and the Brotherhood of Liberty (a militant black organization founded in Baltimore after the Civil War to seek justice for African-Americans otherwise denied equal protection under the law) hired six lawyers (three whites and three blacks) to defend the men. At a preliminary hearing African-American attorney E. J. Waring asserted that U.S. title to Navassa island was specious. Arguing therefore that the government had no jurisdiction in the matter, he asked that the charges against Key and the others be dismissed; however, U.S. District Attorney Hayes, who personally prosecuted the cases, countered that the Guano Act had specifically vested jurisdictional authority in the executive branch of government, a line of reasoning accepted by judges Bond and Morris. Another defense objection, by white attorney Archibald Stirling (a former U.S. district attorney), that the government had improperly joined separate felonies in the same indictments, was similarly overruled by the court. Bond and Morris ordered the trial against Key to proceed. Jury selection produced an all-white male panel.[73]

Government witnesses included all but one of the surviving whites from Navassa and twenty-one blacks. John Jacobson, the white blacksmith who had barricaded himself in his shop at the outset of the affair, had apparently claimed to have seen nothing. In any case, Navassa Phosphate immediately sent him back to the island, perhaps, as was later alleged, purposely beyond reach of a defense subpoena. The others (Henry A. Jones, John O'Rourke, Charles Roby, Dr. Smith, Nelson Vail) all testified as to events, especially Mahon's death. Each of them denied that blacks had any cause whatsoever for dissatisfaction, much less for murder.[74]

Of the black witnesses called by the prosecution, William ("Richmond Shorty") James and Robert Downes were reportedly the most effective. According to a journalist covering the trial, James recounted in "a fluent, straightforward way"[75] being approached by conspirators before the riot; of seeing Charles Roby's bloody head; of participating in the violence merely by throwing rocks against the superintendent's house; of seeing Caesar Fisher hit Foster with a rock and Henry Jones chop him with a broadaxe; of later seeing Jones, axe in hand, chasing Fales; of seeing Shea running for his life with C. H. Davis, Stephen Peters, and Charles H. Smith in hot pursuit; and of hearing numerous people say that Key shot Mahon twice. Downes testified that he saw Edmund Francis strike Roby repeatedly with a five pound sledgehammer and James Phillips hit him with a cutting bar; that he saw Fisher and Jones murder Foster; that he saw Jones chop off Fales's arm and leg; and that he saw Key shoot Mahon. Although rigorously cross-examined by the defense, neither man's story wavered. Nineteen other witness generally corroborated their testimony, including Francis's alleged attack of Roby with a sledgehammer.[76]

The defense called sixteen witnesses (all blacks), eleven of whom were defendants. Generally they described the living and working conditions that had led to the events of September 14. Edward Woodfork said most of the officers had been drinking heavily for days. Some witnesses, such as Edmund Francis, refuted specific elements of prosecution testimony; he readily admitted hitting Roby but said it was merely once, with a cutting bar. Others, such as James Johnson, acknowledged participation in the riot by throwing rocks and dynamite, but only under threat and duress by others— particularly William James, one of the government's star witnesses. Stephen Peters denied he had anything to do with Shea's death. C. H. Davis admitted chasing Shea and throwing stones at him, but he said that when he cut his foot on a sharp rock, he stopped and went to the Barracks where he remained for the rest of the day; Davis insisted that the last time he saw Shea, the man was alive and running like a rabbit. None of the other principals—Key, Fisher, Edward Smith, or C. H. Smith (John Ward)—took the stand at the first trial.[77]

In rebuttal, the government called William James, who denied that he had forced James Johnson to do anything, and Charles Roby, who swore there was never any liquor on the island, much less that he and the others officers were intoxicated as several defense witnesses had claimed. Perhaps significantly, John O'Rourke (so drunk the day he was scheduled to testify before the grand jury that he was tossed into jail for contempt of court) was not asked to testify on this point. In his summation to the jury, prosecutor Hayes argued that living and working conditions on the island were immaterial. The defendants had rioted (mutinied) and murdered, for which there was no mitigation.[78]

Each of the six defense attorneys spoke, the most incisive summation reportedly offered by Joseph A. Davis, an African-American. Denying the government had presented credible evidence of a conspiracy, he made light of one alleged motive—indebtedness to the company store, documentation for which had not been offered. If such were truly a cause, why had the commissary escaped looting? He assured the jury that Edmund Francis had struck Roby reflexively and in self-defense after Roby had threatened him; furthermore, the single blow was obviously delivered with a cutting bar and not with a sledgehammer, and certainly not repeatedly as one government witness had claimed, or else Roby surely would be dead. Indeed, by his own testimony Roby was soon well enough to fire shots at the mob. Attorney Davis asked why the government had not called the blacksmith Jacobson to testify and why, instead, the man had been hustled back to Navassa with a fresh labor crew, out of reach of the defense. Davis insisted the government's evidence had proven that the riot was spontaneous, provoked by Dr. Smith's threats to shoot the men if they did not go back to work and inflamed by the abortive attempt to arrest Phillips. Seventeen of the defendants deserved outright verdicts of not guilty, Davis argued, and, Key, who had shot Mahon in "a sudden paroxysm of passion," was guilty of no more than manslaughter.[79]

Following two days of deliberation, the jury found Key guilty of murdering Mahon and Moses ("Dakota") Williams not guilty of complicity. The jury was unable to reach verdicts with respect to the other sixteen defendants—some men on the jury (according to newspaper accounts) holding out for murder convictions against all of them. The most significant of these defendants was James Tasker (Tascar) who, unrefuted testimony had shown, had pulled Mahon from under the bed before Key shot him. Nine jurors reportedly favored his conviction for manslaughter while three voted him guilty of murder. Eventually, the government would seek and secure a separate indictment against Tasker for manslaughter. Although Key's sentencing was deferred until after the conclusion of the other cases, with a quivering voice (according to a journalist present) he announced he would appeal his conviction.[80]

Proceedings against Caesar Fisher and Henry Jones for the murder of Thomas Foster as well as against the others for complicity in his death (likewise before judges Bond and Morris) commenced December 13. With far less public interest (and journalistic coverage) than that attending the first trial, the case progressed rapidly and concluded ten days later. Most of the same witnesses were heard, and they described many of the same events, including the assertion that Fisher and Jones had killed Foster with a rock and an axe. Young Henry Jones (who had not testified at the previous trial) took the stand this time in his own defense and admitted he had hacked the bookkeeper but, he claimed, only in self-defense after Foster, dazed by a rock thrown by Fisher, had pulled a razor from his pocket and threatened to cut him. Jones also stated that William James, a prosecution witness, had told him that he, James, had killed Joseph Fales, for which Jones likewise stood accused.[81]

A jury of twelve white men was not persuaded, and it declared Jones guilty of murder and Fisher and seven others guilty of manslaughter. Two were found not guilty, and the jury deadlocked with respect to the remaining seven. Again, sentencing was held in abeyance until all of the proceedings against the defendants had been concluded.[82] Apparently satisfied with one first-degree murder conviction against Jones, the government never prosecuted him for Fales's death.

The third trial began February 10, 1890, and it combined the fourth and fifth indictments—of Edward ("the Devil") Smith for the murder of Samuel Marsh with a stone (the others being accessories) and of C. H. Davis, Stephen Peters, and C. H. Smith for the murder of William Shea in an unknown manner (and the others for complicity). After merely one and one-half days of testimony these matters were in the hands of the jury which reportedly had much difficulty in sorting out the facts in order "to agree upon a verdict in regard to each of the prisoners."[83]

After being locked up overnight, the jury found Edward Smith guilty of murder in the first degree in the death of Marsh, and C. H. Davis, Caesar Fisher, Edmund Francis, Alfred Jones, Henry Jones, Amos Lee, Stephen Peters, James Phillips, James H. Robinson, and C. H. Smith guilty of manslaughter. The jury declared George S. Key, James Tasker, Moses Williams, Norman Wooster, and Edward Woodfork to be not guilty. In the death of William Shea, all defendants were found not guilty. Reportedly the absence of a corpse had substantially weakened the prosecution's case. The fact that all the defendants except Tasker, Williams, Woodfork, and Wooster by then had been convicted at least of something likely also persuaded the jury to find for the defendants in the last and most difficult murder case.[84]

Two other trials transpired. In the first, twenty-three of the twenty-five men charged with rioting were convicted. In the second, James Tasker (Tascar), Edward Woodfork, and Norman Wooster, who had benefited by hung juries in one or more of the earlier proceedings, pleaded guilty to manslaughter. All told by February 15, 1890, three had been convicted of murder, fourteen of manslaughter, and twenty-three of rioting. Only Moses Williams had been exonerated in each and every proceeding, except the last one. Prior to it, the government had asked that any and all charges pending against him be dismissed, a request granted by the court.[85]

On February 20, "in a spectacle never before witnessed [in Baltimore's U.S. Circuit] Court," forty men stood before "Judges Bond and Morris [who] sat together, each taking part in passing the sentences in which justice was meted out to the doomed men." Henry Jones, George S. Key, and Edward Smith, each convicted of murder, were sentenced to hang on March 28 in Baltimore's city jail. According to news reports Judge Bond took the liberty of advising the men "'to repent and seek God that He may have mercy on you' . . . The three doomed men turned away nonchalantly and resumed their seats."[86]

Of the fourteen men who had been convicted of manslaughter, C. H. Davis, Caesar Fisher, Edmund Francis, Alfred Jones, Stephen Peters, James Phillips, J. H. Robinson, and James Tasker (Tascar) were each sentenced to ten years in prison at hard labor; James Johnson, C. H. Smith (John Ward), Edward Woodfork, and Norman Wooster to five years each; and Alfred Brown and Amos Lee to two years each, all sentences to be served in a New York state penitentiary because the federal government at that time did not maintain prisons but, rather, contracted with states to house its inmates. Twenty-three others convicted of rioting received terms ranging from six months to two years in Maryland's House of Correction.[87]

The executions of Jones, Key, and Smith were stayed pending appeal, which, as provided by law, reached the U.S. Supreme Court on a writ of error during the summer of 1890. Attorneys for the convicted men argued some ten points, mostly relating to U.S. authority over Navassa island, the constitutionality of the Guano Act, and the jurisdiction of American courts in the matter. Responding point by point for the government was U.S. Attorney General W. H. H. Miller. In November the court unanimously agreed with Miller that the acquisition of territory was a political not judicial question; that the Constitution empowered Congress to enact the Guano Act; that Congress had the authority to extend criminal jurisdiction over such appurtenances; and that Navassa island had been lawfully acquired and held under the legislation. Therefore, finding no error either in law or proceedings, the court upheld the conviction and sustained the judgments. The men should die.[88]

Resentenced, Jones, Key, and Smith each filed for executive clemency, actions that further stayed the execution of sentences. Meanwhile, members of the Brotherhood of Liberty circulated petitions throughout Baltimore in support of clemency, which garnered both black and white signatures; however, these pleas might well have fallen on deaf ears had not a letter from Fred Carter (a black man from Washington, D.C.) reached President Benjamin Harrison about the same time the clemency requests and citizens' petitions arrived at the oval office. Carter protested he was being held on Navassa longer than the fifteen months for which he had contracted. Having arrived on the West Indian island in September 1889, he claimed when he asked to be returned to the United States in January 1891 the officer in charge had refused to let him go. Carter said he had been virtually reduced to slavery. He begged the president to rescue him.[89]

Harrison sent Carter's letter to Secretary of the Navy Benjamin F. Tracy, saying in a cover note that, "In view of the evidence developed in the trial of the Navasa [*sic*] rioters, I am inclined to believe that there is something worthy of investigation in this poor man's complaint. I do not intend that any system of slavery shall be maintained on that island." He directed Tracy to have Admiral Gherardi "make a thorough inquiry. . . ."[90]

Like Commodore Mervine before him, Gherardi apparently considered one visit to a guano island adequate, and rather than go himself he ordered Commander Horace Elmer, captain of USS *Kearsarge* (the steam sloop that had sunk the Confederate raider *Alabama* during the Civil War), to proceed to the island to investigate Carter's situation, to report directly to the secretary of the Navy, and to send a copy of that report to the White House.[91] Elmer immediately steamed for Navassa, arriving April 29, whereupon he personally commenced "an investigation of Fred Carter . . . as well as the whole situation there. . . ." Elmer quickly concluded that the "statements of Carter to the President . . . are entirely correct." F. M. Everett, the new superintendent of the phosphate works, explained that Carter had not been allowed to leave because no Navassa Phosphate ship had visited the island since February and because company officials in Baltimore had decreed that dismissed workers were not to be allowed to book return passage on any other vessel, unless they paid their own way. Elmer offered to take Carter (and any other workers whose time had expired) to Key West, remarking also that he thought the company was liable for their passage on to Baltimore. Everett agreed to let him go.[92]

Before *Kearsarge* could get underway with Carter aboard the next day, Commander Elmer received a frantic message from Everett that another riot had almost erupted overnight and that an insurrection seemed imminent.

Approximately 140 of the 189 laborers on the island refused to go to work and threatened to kill those who might. Commander Elmer promptly appointed a three-man board of inquiry, headed by his executive officer, and directed it to go ashore to investigate.[93]

The board interviewed three company officials and eleven men, five of whom were strikers. The officials (superintendent Everett, storekeeper B. F. Berry, and physician G. A. Haefner) contended that some of the men were simply using *Kearsarge*'s visit to attract attention. Everett identified eight laborers whom he accused of being ringleaders, and he asked that they be arrested for mutiny and turned over the proper authorities for prosecution.[94]

Eleven workers (strikers and nonparticipants alike) told a far different story, much of which the board found to be credible. The "majority of laborers" were "discontent and unwilling to work," the naval officers judged, because of "misrepresentations made to them . . . as to the character of the island and on account of poor food, . . . [and] cruel punishments," which included being "placed in stocks with their hands ironed and triced up to keep them standing upon their feet." Workers claimed they had been told in Baltimore that if they were dissatisfied with Navassa they might leave after six months upon forfeiture of $20, rather than be forced to remain for the full fifteen-month contractual term; however, once on the island, no one was ever permitted to leave after six months, and, sometimes, as in the case of Fred Carter, not even after a full term of employment had been completed.[95]

The board of inquiry observed that "the discipline maintained on the island seemed to be that of a convict establishment, without its comforts and cleanliness. . . ." Consequently, riots were bound to occur, and reoccur, one being very likely to break out "in the absence of a man-of-war, unless some means is taken to redress grievances. . . ." Investigators suggested that, ultimately, the island be placed "under [direct] Government supervision to prevent misunderstandings and misrepresentations. . . ." Meanwhile, they recommended when *Kearsarge* departed for either Florida or Jamaica (to report the matter to Washington and seek further instructions), that to maintain order on the island either ringleaders be taken on board or a Marine detachment should be left on the island while the ship was away.[96] Superintendent Everett quickly seconded the suggestion, saying he feared for his and other lives if Marines were not put ashore.[97]

Accepting most of his board's recommendations, Elmer sent ashore First Lieutenant G. T. Bates (who, ironically, had helped arrest Navassa rioters in 1889) with a detachment of twenty-two Marines to police the place until *Kearsarge* returned.[98] He also took on board storekeeper B. F. Berry, whom Elmer planned to send to Baltimore to persuade Navassa Phosphate of the desperate need to remove several of the men. While en route to Port Antonio, Jamaica, the captain composed a report for Secretary Tracy and President Harrison. In it he confirmed Carter's complaint, described the situation he had found on the island, explained his actions, and recommended that "a Commissioner or Representative of the United States [be permanently stationed] on this island with power to redress grievances and administer the law. In the present anomalous condition of affairs," Elmer observed, "trouble such as exists now is certain to occur at frequent intervals, and in the absence of a Man of War, riot and bloodshed would probably ensue as did happen two years ago."[99]

By telegraphic dispatch from Jamaica, Elmer asked the Navy department for guidance. Washington soon wired its reply in code: "Preserve peace at [the] island. No [other] instructions can be given until [receipt of] your report."[100] By return cipher, he informed the Navy department that he had sent the report to Secretary Tracy by the steamer *Ethelwold* on May 6, the same day he had put Berry aboard ship bound for Baltimore.[101]

When *Kearsarge* steamed back to Navassa, arriving May 8, all was quiet. Those individuals "well disposed" toward work, some 77 men, continued their labors without interference, while 111 strikers remained idle. Commander Elmer was appalled by their filthy living conditions, and he divided them into labor parties and, refuse to work or not, required them clean their quarters, which were then inspected daily by Lt. Bates. On May 9 the Atlas Line steamer *Athos* arrived, bringing much needed supplies before sailing on to other Caribbean ports; three days later, its sister vessel, *Alvo,* called at the island, but when the superintendent asked its captain to take 25 of the most militant men aboard and carry them home, he declined, refusing even to wait long enough to take mail bound for the mainland, an action Elmer considered "not only discourteous, but inexcusable. . . ."[102]

Later that same day, "Lieutenant Bates found it necessary to arrest [William Harrison, a laborer] for attempting to excite the others to create a disturbance."[103] The next day, Bates also arrested John Hall, another black, for insubordination. Both men were taken aboard the warship in irons and jailed in the brig. The superintendent hoped to send the men home aboard the company's bark *Adirondack,* which was expected to call on the fourteenth, but it failed to appear as scheduled.[104]

Needing supplies and desiring further instructions, on May 15 Commander Elmer ordered *Kearsarge* back to Jamaica, leaving Bates and his Marines on Navassa to keep the peace. At Port Antonio, Elmer learned that officers of Navassa Phosphate had assured Secretary Tracy that *Albemarle* had been dispatched to the island and should arrive within eighteen days to retrieve "mutinous strikers." Company officials asked that, even if they had been accorded passage home before it arrived, *Kearsarge* should remain on station to protect the firm's property until *Albemarle* dropped anchor.[105]

Accordingly, *Kearsarge* returned to Navassa to await the company's vessel,[106] but when it still had not arrived by May 30, Commander Elmer steamed back to Jamaica for more supplies and mail. There he found another message: "Remain at Navassa until dissatisfied men are embarked."[107] He dutifully returned to the island to await the tardy *Albemarle,* which did not hove into view until June 15. It took five days for it to discharge cargo, take aboard Fred Carter and about twenty-five disgruntled workers (including the two men in *Kearsarge*'s brig), and set course for Baltimore. That done, Elmer recalled Bates and his Marines, who had passed seven weeks ashore, and set course for Key West for supplies, reportedly leaving seventy-four men working peacefully on the island.[108]

By then the latest troubles at Navassa were public knowledge. On May 14 the *New York Times* had announced the existence of "Slaves under our flag" in an article telling of Carter's letter to Harrison, the latest strike at the island, Navy and Marine Corps intervention, and details of the labor contract, which, it judged, "bears hard upon laborers."[109] These allegations were denounced the following day by Thomas M. Lanahan, Navassa Phosphate's attorney, who characterized the strikers as unruly "young negroes . . . who would be discontented anywhere. . . ." He asserted the company's employees had never been harshly treated: "The only punishment inflicted upon them is confinement." Lanahan remarked that both judges Bond and Morris, who had tried the Navassa riot cases, had privately confided to him that, in their opinions, workers there "were treated as well as laborers anywhere are treated."[110]

President Harrison did not agree. Having received applications for executive clemency for Henry Jones, George Key, and Edward Smith almost simultaneously with the receipt of Fred Carter's letter, the chief executive paid particular attention to Commander Elmer's report regarding conditions on Navassa, which judged "that the fault does not seem to lie with the Superintendent, but with the company. . . ."[111] Harrison observed that workers on Navassa island

> were American citizens, under contracts to perform labor upon specified terms, within American territory, removed from an opportunity to appeal to any court or public officer for redress of any injury or the enforcement of any civil rights. Their employers were, in fact, their masters. The bosses placed over them imposed fines and penalties without any semblance of trials. These penalties extended to imprisonment, and even to the cruel practice of tricing men up for

> a refusal to work. Escape was impossible, and the state of things generally such as might make men reckless and desperate.[112]

Acknowledging that the guilt of Jones, Key, and Smith had been "satisfactorily established" in a court of law, that their "crime was a grave one, but [that there were mitigating] antecedents and incidents,"[113] Harrison therefore commuted their sentences to life in prison, to be served at the Kings County Penitentiary, Brooklyn, New York.[114]

President Harrison's concern with living and working conditions on American guano islands was so pronounced that, in his 1891 state-of-the-union message to Congress, he recommended

> legislation that shall place labor contracts upon this and other islands having the relation that Navassa has to the United States under the supervision of a court commissioner, and that shall provide at the expense of the owners an officer to reside upon the island, with power to judge and adjust disputes and to enforce a just and humane treatment of the employees. It is inexcusable that American laborers should be left within our own jurisdiction without access to any Government officer or tribunal for their protection and the redress of their wrongs.[115]

Although Congress failed to act, after 1892 the resident manager on Navassa island assumed the title "governor" instead of "superintendent," perhaps to imply official status and, hence, legal authority over laborers.[116]

Over the ensuing years Navassa Phosphate Company sought to deflect public criticism of its employment practices. In 1891, in the wake of President Harrison's rebuke, it revised its labor contract by deleting the provision whereby those who might refuse to work stood to lose all accumulated wages and replacing it with a stipulation to the effect that the wages of those idled for whatever reason would be suspended until they returned to duty. However questionable the assumption of political authority by a corporate entity (according to the 1886 opinion of Attorney General A. H. Garland), the new contract nonetheless included a paragraph that spelled out the power of a superintendent and/or assistant superintendent—"the same authority and control in the discipline and government of the undersigned that a Captain of a ship at sea has over his crew and enforced discipline in like manner."[117]

Adverse publicity apparently made it increasingly difficult for Navassa Phosphate to recruit laborers, and, by one report, the firm considered hiring blacks from the Bahamas; however, the company's notorious reputation raised the possibility that the British government would insist upon inspection rights to protect its citizens, an extraterritorial privilege the U.S. government was not prepared to permit. According to another report, Navassa Phosphate began employing Austro-Hungarian immigrants who were probably ignorant of working conditions on the island.[118]

Whatever the actual source of its subsequent workforce, Navassa Phosphate mined the island continuously until May 7, 1898, when, at the outset of hostilities in the Spanish-American War, President William McKinley ordered all inhabitants removed by the U.S. Navy. Shortly thereafter, Haitians raided the place, stripping it of everything movable that the company had left behind. Responding to an official American protest, the Haitian government arrested the thieves, seized such stolen property as could be recovered, and surrendered it to the American consul who sold it at auction and turned the proceeds over to the company.[119]

By then vigorous competition from phosphate mines within the continental United States had rendered the operation on Navassa island wholly unprofitable, and the company never resumed digging. Still in receivership in September 1900, Navassa Phosphate's assets were sold at auction by order of the New York Supreme Court, an action requested by the state's attorney general to pay creditors. The island brought a single bid of $25,000 ($750 down and the balance on time) from John B. F. Jefferson and Wyatt Owen, both of Baltimore; however, in July 1901 the court set the sale aside when a minority stockholder, Horatio King of Brooklyn, filed an injunction to stop title transfer on the grounds that action to dissolve the company had been fraudulent because assets, he contended, were worth at least $500,000.[120]

Meanwhile, the previous October Jefferson and Owen had dispatched a four-man work crew to the island, apparently to prepare it for full-scale operations, and the Atlas Steamship Line, which delivered the men and supplies, agreed to take them off again for $110 when so requested by the partners. Jefferson was soon persuaded that Navassa would never be profitable; therefore, he sold his rights in the venture to Owen for $1,000 and, to absolve himself of contractual obligation to the workers, sent a check for $110 to Atlas and asked it to retrieve the workers, an order Owen immediately countermanded unless Jefferson also agreed to pay one half their outstanding wages, which he declined to do. Atlas (contending that it had a contract with the Jefferson-Owen partnership, which no longer existed) returned Jefferson's check and refused to act rather than become embroiled in the dispute.[121]

Consequently, workers on Navassa were practically marooned. Except for small amounts of provisions dropped off by a British warship that they happened to hail, and, occasionally, supplies from other passing vessels, the men were forced to live off the island—hunting its goats and even cats, which had been introduced years before to control an ever increasing number of rats. According to a letter posted by a passing ship from superintendent James A. Woodward to his wife, they were in desperate straits by the spring of 1901: "We are short of provisions and all of my ammunition is gone." He added, "I wrote to the President of the United States last week telling him of how Owen is acting and asking him to bring us home."[122]

Mrs. Woodward also asked the State department to send a naval vessel to rescue her husband, who she said was starving. The Navy promptly dispatched USS *Mayflower*; however, its commander soon reported that the men were all well and had refused to leave—perhaps out of fear of losing accumulated wages if they abandoned the place. Sailors consequently gave them some provisions and departed. Alerted by reporters, Jefferson hired the steamer *Alps,* which departed New York on May 18 to pick up the men, with or without Owen's approval.[123]

When this last Navassa work crew reportedly reached the mainland about June 12, 1901, for all practical purposes the great guano rush in the United States ended. No island, rock, or key claimed under the Guano Act was subsequently worked by Americans, although several of them—rediscovered by the U.S. government—were later occupied and exploited for other purposes.

Ironically, about then, American guano islands (most of which had long since been abandoned by mining companies) received considerable attention because of the precedent they offered for insular territories, such as those recently acquired as result of the Spanish-American War. In the March 1900 issue of the *Yale Law Journal,* Paul R. Shipman of New Jersey argued that the wording of the Thirteenth Amendment to the Constitution did not absolutely forbid slavery in such new territories,[124] a view that was vehemently rejected by the editors of the *New York Sun* who pointed specifically to American guano islands as places "subject to our jurisdiction when the Thirteenth Amendment was adopted, and under the specific provision of that amendment neither slavery nor involuntary servitude, except as a punishment for crime, could Constitutionally exist in them."[125]

The following year the U.S. Supreme Court agreed with the *Sun,* ruling in *Downes* v. *Bidwell* (regarding Puerto Rico as an American "territorial appurtenance") that "Places subject to the jurisdiction of the United States, but which are not incorporated into it, and hence are not within the United States in the completest sense of those words, are recognized by the provisions of U.S. Const[itution's] 13th Amend[ment], prohibiting slavery within the United States 'or any place subject to their jurisdiction.' "[126] If those African-Americans who had labored on Navassa island were aware of this decision, they probably questioned its reality.

# 11

## Guano Happens

Between 1856 and 1903, American entrepreneurs laid claim to ninety-four islands, rocks, and keys around the globe under authority of the Guano Islands Act. Of these places, sixty-six (mostly in the Caribbean sea and Pacific ocean) were at least temporarily recognized by the U.S. Department of State to be American appurtenances, but fewer than two dozen of them were ever mined. Today, nine erstwhile guano islands continue to be U.S. possessions.

Through the encouragement of entrepreneurs to find remote deposits of feces and phosphates, politicians set the course of the United States toward overseas expansion—not the acquisition of a glorious collection of exotic lands, but, rather, a handful of isolated islands, rock, and keys that diplomats disowned at first opportunity, only to have many of those bird-splattered places rediscovered and reclaimed early in the twentieth century when public officials found other uses for them. Throughout it all, the government in Washington practiced what one historian has disparagingly labeled "guano diplomacy."[1] Mostly, though, American policy reflected the entwining of public and private interests—not the myth of *laissez faire* but, rather, the reality of the political economy that historically has been the essence of the United States.

By the turn of the twentieth century, as the mining of American appurtenances ended, the State department had abandoned title to more than two thirds of the nation's original guano empire and seemingly stood poised to forsake much of the rest. There were exceptions. American claims to Monita in the Caribbean (which diplomats had rejected under the Guano Act because Spaniards said the place belonged to them) were revived in 1898 when the United States acquired Puerto Rico as a prize in the Spanish-American War.

Commencing in 1903 and in return for a royalty of forty cents per ton, the territorial government of Puerto Rico leased Mona and Monita islands to the Mona Island Phosphate Company, a Louisiana corporation, but the extent of its operation on the islands, if any, is unknown. Sovereignty over French Frigates Shoals and Palmyra, both claimed under U.S law but never mined by American businessmen, was effectively challenged by the royal government of Hawaii; however, these islands unquestionably passed to U.S. control upon annexation of Hawaii in 1898.[2]

Nevertheless, at the end of the nineteenth century the State department did not want more appurtenances. Diplomats declined a request from Treasury officials in 1894 to verify a list of U.S. guano islands. To comply would be "to pass upon the rights of a large number of private parties" which W. Q. Graham, Grover Cleveland's secretary of State, "preferred not to do unless the actions of the parties themselves renders this action necessary."[3] A similar invitation from Treasury's Bureau of Navigation in 1899 caused Third Assistant Secretary of State Thomas W. Cridler to inform customs officials that, confidentially, he (and presumably many other careerists in the department) had "not much sympathy with the questions involved." He explained that "since Mr. Hamilton Fish's time [as secretary of State, 1869-77] very little, if anything, has been done beyond filing of papers in the Department and acknowledging that this has been done."[4]

Not surprisingly, about then, whenever queried about the status of American appurtenances, denizens of "Foggy Bottom" (a derisive term for the State department and its Washington-based bureaucrats, derived from peculiar climatic conditions along the nearby Potomac river) increasingly referred public officials and private citizens alike to Section 5578 of the revised statutes which provided that nothing in the law obliged the government to retain possession of those places once the guano had been removed. Accordingly, and apparently without explicit White House authorization, diplomats therefore unilaterally began renouncing American claims. "The United States possesses no sovereign or territorial rights over guano islands," State department legal affairs officer S. Y. Smith asserted in a memorandum to Assistant Secretary of State A. A. Adee in 1904. "It simply protects American citizens who discover guano on an island, or their assigns, in the prosecution of their enterprise which extends only to appropriation and disposal of guano."[5]

Global strategic considerations soon caused diplomats to rethink the matter, first in the Caribbean. In 1907 the Isthmian Canal Commission wished to place a navigational light on Navassa island to serve traffic to and from the Panama Canal, which was then under construction. It consequently asked the State department about the political status of the place, long since abandoned by miners. Then acting as secretary of State, Adee replied that

> it cannot be claimed that this or other guano islands 'belong' to the United States, . . . [and therefore] there is no present authority to erect a light-house. . . . Nevertheless, it would appear that internationally speaking this Government is in a position to assert full authority over Navassa Island should such action be deemed desirable. . . .[6]

Although Adee did not think that any other "government could reasonably object to such an assertion," he did believe that some specific legislative action by Congress would be necessary. Even so, presidential authority to use military force to protect guano islands might constitute sufficient authorization with which "to proceed at once to the erection of a light-house thereon with funds which are entirely under the control of the War Department. . . ."[7]

Even though questions were subsequently raised in the House of Representatives as to how the United States had come into possession of the island in the first place, in 1913 Congress appropriated $125,000 with which to erect a lighthouse on Navassa.[8] News of American intentions led the government at Port-au-Prince to protest, terming the project an "invasion of the sovereign rights of the Republic of Haiti on the island." Citing the U.S. government's most recent review of Haitian claims to the place (in 1873 by Hamilton Fish), Secretary of State Robert Lansing likewise rejected Haiti's renewed assertions of ownership and reiterated the American position: Navassa belonged to the United States, now and forever.[9] To emphasize the point, on January 17, 1916, President Woodrow Wilson (specifically citing the Guano Act as the authority by which "Navassa is now under the sole and exclusive jurisdiction of the United States and out of the jurisdiction of any other Government") proclaimed it to be U.S. territory and reserved it for lighthouse purposes.[10]

Construction (which had actually begun in January 1915) required twenty-one months. The lighthouse tower (situated near the highest point on the island and built of reinforced concrete by Cuban and Jamaican laborers) loomed 157 feet above the limestone base and 395 above sea level, thereby becoming the tallest beacon then in existence. The walls of its massive base were six feet thick, sufficient to survive even the most powerful hurricane and even severe earthquakes. Complementary structures included keepers' quarters and a three-seat outhouse strategically situated over a deep crater that had been gouged out of the limestone by phosphate miners. When

Navassa's forty-seven thousand candlepower light switched on for the first time on October 21, 1917, it was visible in fair weather over an area of twenty-two hundred square miles.[11] U.S. Commissioner of Lighthouses George R. Putnam called it to be "the most important lighthouse built by the United States in the last quarter century."[12]

It was also one of the most problematical. Difficult to supply, its keepers and their families were often forced to forage—to live off the island's eggs, birds, fish, and goats. Work was also monotonous, and life lonely. As early as 1923 the superintendent of lighthouses recommended automating the facility, which he calculated could save the government $8,500 annually, but the proposal was rejected by Putnam supposedly because the keeper's coincidental weather observations were too valuable to shipping to be suspended; however, mounting supply costs mandated automation in 1929, but not before a laborer who was working to install an acetylene gas pipeline from Lulu bay to the tower was killed when one of the old mining cars (pressed into service to haul equipment) ran wild, crashed, and crushed him.[13]

Mechanized ever since, the Navassa light has continued to illuminate surrounding waters, albeit with interruptions. Demands by the Haitian Chamber of Deputies in 1934 that the island be "returned," as well as assertions in the Haitian constitution of 1935 that Navassa belonged to that republic, were superciliously ignored by the U.S. government. Under supervision of the U.S. Coast Guard after 1939, the light was vandalized in 1947 by Haitian thieves, who (at American insistence) were arrested and punished by authorities at Port-au-Prince. In 1966 the light was converted to electricity and has since been updated to solar power. Vandalized again in 1980 (its classic glass lens smashed), the light was repaired with a modern 250 millimeter hard plastic optical piece. Visited annually by a U.S. Coast Guard crew that services its equipment, Navassa island is "off limits" to all but those who have secured permission to visit from the Coast Guard's Miami office. In recent years ham radio operators (with U.S. government approval) have occasionally raised antennas there for the sport of "DXing," or long-distance transmission. Haiti continues to dispute American ownership.[14]

Navigational lights on appurtenances elsewhere in the Caribbean have likewise embroiled the United States in controversy. Quito Sueño, Roncador, and Serraña (sold by Petrel Guano Company to Caribbean Guano Company in 1911) were apparently never exploited by their new owner. In any case, President Wilson reiterated U.S. sovereignty over all three in 1919 (his authority derived from the Guano Act) and reserved them for lighthouses, an action that evoked protests from Colombia, which also claimed them. Responding that it considered the islands, rocks, and keys in question to be

United States property, Washington proceeded to erect beacons anyway: on a forty-five foot white concrete tower on Quito Sueño, on a fifty-two foot red pyramidal skeleton tower on Roncador, and on a seventy-two foot red pyramidal skeleton tower on Serraña—the light from each visible for eleven to twelve nautical miles and maintained by the Panama Canal Company. In 1928 the United States and Colombia exchanged notes regarding these places whereby the two countries acknowledged their conflicting claims and agreed to respect the other's property on and possible rights thereto without prejudice, especially U.S. navigational lights and fishing by Colombians. Washington also promised not to grant any additional guano permits on the three islands until the dispute over sovereignty had been reconciled.[15]

Honduras, which also claimed Roncador and Quito Sueño, was not a party to this agreement and objected, but the State department (referring to diplomatic exchanges with Honduras in 1869 about the islands) said that it had not changed its mind: these places belong to the United States by virtue of James Jennett's filings under the Guano Act. In 1932, when the State department revisited the entire issue of American appurtenances in a 976-page report, diplomats concluded that Roncador had been derelict when claimed and occupied by Jennett and that the United States had legally assumed ownership under the Guano Act, an action reinforced by the erection of a navigational light. Even though it was only intermittently exploited under that law, Serraña was similarly acquired by the United States through Jennett's claims (diplomats asserted) because its only occupation had been by American citizens under the Guano Act and, later, as site for a U.S.-erected navigational beacon. Acknowledging that Quito Sueño (usually underwater) was uninhabitable, and therefore probably never actually occupied by Jennett (contrary to his assertions), American diplomats nevertheless believed that no country had a superior claim to the place—especially since the erection of its light in 1920.[16] At no time in its correspondence with either Colombia or Honduras did the State department mention that it considered Jennett's frequent filings to have been fraudulent.

There the matter rested until 1972. In the interest of improved relations, the Nixon administration negotiated a treaty with Colombia by which the United States renounced its rights to Roncador, Quito Sueño, and Serraña. Because Quito Sueño was not permanently above water, American diplomats had belatedly decided it was not properly subject to the exercise of sovereignty; nevertheless (without seeking to prejudice the claims of other states, such as Honduras), Washington transferred ownership of and responsibility for lights on all three islands to Colombia, provided that fishing privileges of American citizens about these places would not be restricted. Ratified by

Colombia in 1974, the treaty was not approved by the U.S. Senate until 1981, entering into force on September 17.[17]

Some disputes over Caribbean guano islands have been far more protracted, at times actually taking on the aura of spy novels. Having anticipated the construction of a canal across Central America, perhaps through Nicaragua, in 1896 the U.S. Light-House Board secured permission from Warren K. Blodgett of Boston to erect a navigational beacon at the west end of Great Swan island, Blodgett being eager to improve the Swans for possible future sale. According to a private opinion issued by Judson Harmon, President Cleveland's attorney general, the islands unquestionably had been an American appurtenance since 1863 and, as such, were a suitable site for a navigational aid, which was soon authorized by Congress.[18]

Thus began an odd odyssey for these islands. Great Swan and Little Swan (aggregating about four square miles of lush tropical vegetation some ninety-eight miles off the east coast of Honduras) had been claimed and exploited by a succession of Americans since 1857. Blodgett acquired title in bankruptcy proceedings in 1896. Five years later he sold them to Albion Chemical & Export Company of Baltimore, which proposed to mine the Swans once more; however, by 1904 the company was insolvent, and its directors ordered them abandoned. Alonzo Adams, Albion's agent on the islands, dutifully departed on February 5 but returned the following day to claim them for himself. Although Adams filed incomplete affidavits in 1904 with the U.S. State department under the Guano Act, he never attempted to mine the Swans; rather, he farmed the large island (raising fruit, coconuts, and tobacco) and remained in residence there with his wife and two children until 1916. Meanwhile, in 1908 he had leased space on Great Swan to Wireless Telegraph Company (a subsidiary of United Fruit Company), which broadcast weather warnings and other maritime notices to United's banana fleet that operated throughout Central America. Later that year Adams also sold the balance of his rights to the Swan Island Commercial Company (a Maine corporation doing business in Massachusetts), which planned further agricultural development. The company inquired of the State department as to procedures for filing under the Guano Act; however, it never offered a bond.[19]

The switch from mining to farming raised questions concerning the Swans' sovereignty. In response to a query from the Department of Commerce and Labor in 1909, American diplomats advised against granting coastwise clearance to a schooner from the islands because the Guano Act contemplated abandonment of islands no longer being mined. However many questions the State department might have had about their status as lawful appurtenances, the Swans nevertheless effectively remained under American aegis, their facilities being continuously utilized by U.S. corporations and government agencies for another half century. The U.S. Weather Bureau established an observation station on Great island in 1914 and staffed it with U.S. Navy personnel for more than a decade. Throughout the 1920s the islands were reportedly home to a score or more: a caretaker and his family, ten black laborers (citizens of the British West Indies), and eight American meteorologists and radio operators.[20]

Perhaps because of questions concerning the legality of coasting trade with the Swans, United Fruit began hauling Swan Commercial's produce back to the mainland with its own commodities. Ultimately, not even that made the islands a financial success, for about 1921 Swan Commercial relinquished its rights back to Adams's heirs. About then, one M. Ellis, head of the Anti-Blue Law League, proposed to establish a new Monte Carlo on the Swans (with himself as king), but nothing came of the scheme.[21]

Continuous occupation in no way resolved the issue of sovereignty. When the U.S. Navy became interested in establishing a coaling station on Great island in 1918 and consequently asked the Department of Justice for a legal opinion as to the islands' status, Acting Attorney General John W. Davis opined that "The United States has never acquired sovereignty of any kind or to any extent over the Swan islands by reason of the Guano Islands Act"; however, he did assume that the U.S. government "might assert its sovereignty over the Swans Islands by appropriate action [because] no other country has any proper claim to these islands."[22]

Doubtlessly seeing an opening in that view, the government of Honduras in 1921 asserted that the Swans belonged to it, claiming title by right of succession from the Spanish empire; however, American diplomats promptly rejected that argument. While conceding that the Swans had indeed lain within the historical empire, they observed that the islands had never been occupied by Spain or, later, by Honduras; hence, the Swans were derelict (or *terra nullis* in diplomatic jargon) at the time of American occupation in 1857, under whose control they had since unquestionably remained.[23]

Confused by the contrary views expressed by Attorneys General Harmon in 1896 and Davis in 1918, Secretary of State Charles Evans Hughes in 1924 asked Attorney General John G. Sargent to reexamine American claims of sovereignty over the Swans.[24] The next year Sargent declared Davis to have erred because he was unaware of Secretary W. H. Seward's February 11, 1863, proclamation on behalf of New York Guano Company that had recognized the Swans as American appurtenances. "It is my opinion, therefore, that the dominion of the United States was extended over the Swan Islands," Sargent said, "and that the sovereignty of the United States attached to said islands as of that date." Had Davis known of the 1863 certificate, Sargent added, he undoubtedly would have ruled likewise.[25]

As an internal State department investigation later observed, "before 1925 no unequivocal assertion of complete sovereignty was made . . . [with respect to any guano island. In fact,] there were a number of denials of sovereignty." Diplomats acknowledged that they had repeatedly advised other agencies of the U.S. government that American jurisdiction was limited: in 1873 they told the Justice department that, in their opinion, once abandoned, guano islands were "open again to discovery, possession, etc."; that year they also notified the postmaster general that the United States "possesses no sovereign or territorial rights over the islands"; in 1904 they counseled the Commerce and Labor department that the United States exercised jurisdiction "solely for the purpose of extracting guano"; in 1917 they informed the Department of the Navy that "this Government has taken no steps to extend its own sovereignty" over guano islands and that it "would require an act of Congress to make the Swan islands legally a part of the United States." Indeed, prior to Sargent's statement, diplomats admitted that their department harbored "a wavering uncertainty—an uncertainty which characterized the attitude of this government with respect to all guano islands. . . . After that opinion sovereignty was [aggressively] claimed," not only with respect to the Swans, but elsewhere as well.[26]

Although abandoned by the U.S. Weather Bureau in 1927, the Swans were nevertheless occupied privately by Donald E. Glidden, a Cayman islander employed as caretaker by Alonzo Adams's heirs. Learning that the weather station had closed, Honduras soon reportedly planned to seize the disputed islands but was warned off by the U.S. government. During the 1930s the Honduran government repeatedly protested the American position. Consequently, Assistant Secretary of State Sumner Welles suggested that the issue should be arbitrated. While accepting the concept of arbitration in principle, President Franklin Roosevelt asserted that the islands held little economic significance and therefore were a trivial matter; nevertheless, he believed that Honduras's claims were weak, and, in the interest of hemispheric solidarity, it should accede to U.S. ownership. Thus, nothing came of Welles's advice, and in 1940 the State department again rejected the Central American republic's pretensions.[27] As far as American diplomats were concerned the islands "remain in the exclusive possession" of the United States.[28]

In 1946 the U.S. Department of Agriculture leased eight acres of Great Swan island from the Swan Island Trustees of Boston (Alonzo Adams's heirs) for $200 a year for use as an international livestock quarantine station for the control of hoof-and-mouth disease. The USDA operated the facility until 1949 when it was closed for economic reasons. The government's lease was transferred to the Civil Aeronautics Administration (present Federal Aviation Administration), which constructed a small airfield and placed an aviation beacon and a weather station on the island. In 1952 and again in 1962 the U.S. government and the Swan Island Trustees revised their agreement whereby Washington gained unspecified additional use of the islands in return for higher payments that eventually rose to $900 annually.[29]

As it turned out, some of that unspecified additional use was by the Central Intelligence Agency, which was trying to topple Fidel Castro from power in Cuba. In 1960 the Gibraltar Steamship Corporation of New York (a CIA front) improved the existing runway and placed an ostensibly commercial radio station on Great Swan island, a fifty-kilowatt amplitude modulating (AM) broadcast beacon powerful enough to reach much of Central America, including the western tip of Cuba. Honduras immediately protested what it termed the violation of its sovereign rights on the islands, a position rejected by the U.S. State department. At the United Nations Castro soon denounced what he called the seizure of Honduran territory, claiming that the *Yanquis* were training troops there for an invasion of Cuba, assertions that American diplomats categorically denied.[30]

Inflamed by contemporary news reports of an official U.S. census count on the Swans—which turned up six U.S. citizens (employees of the FAA) and twenty-two Cayman islanders (sixteen men, including Donald Glidden, caretaker, and six women "laborers"), but which somehow missed counting another twenty "Radio Swan" operators and engineers (all reportedly employees of the CIA)—a dozen armed Honduran university students boated to the islands in April 1960 to assert their nation's sovereignty. They were routed by a single worker, weather bureau cook John Hamilton who warned them they had better leave their weapons in the boat. They did. After peacefully raising the Honduran flag (on an American-provided flagpole) and asserting their nation's claims, they were entertained by CIA station chief Horton Heath. Following lunch, the Hondurans lowered and folded their flag, then departed.[31]

Meanwhile, Radio Swan had begun broadcasting taped programs of "Radio Free Cuba" that featured Miss Pepita Riera, a Cuban exile better known as "Havana Rose," who denounced Castro as a dictator and agitated daily for his overthrow. Then, in the early morning hours of April 17, 1961, Radio Swan beamed coded messages to the Cuban underground to alert partisans that American-trained Cuban exiles were headed for the Bay of

Pigs where they would begin liberating the island. The clandestine base (which reportedly also served as command and control center for the doomed operation) never broadcast news that the landing was an unmitigated disaster, nor did it immediately discontinue operations. Restyled as "Radio America" after 1962 and supposedly operated by Vanguard Service Corporation of Miami, it remained on the air as late as 1963, broadcasting anti-Castro messages throughout the western Caribbean and occasionally entertaining visitors.[32]

In 1962 Prince S. Crowell, a septuagenarian Bostonian whose father had been a chemist for Pacific Guano Company and who wished to see the island where his father once resided, secured permission from Sumner Smith, patriarch of the Adams Trustees, to visit the Swans. Smith actually arranged for the CIA to fly Crowell and his wife, Ethel, to Great island aboard a company DC-3, which regularly supplied the clandestine base from Florida. The Crowells, who were billeted in the station chief's house, puttered about the islands for days (Donald Glidden acting as their guide) before flying back to the mainland—all the while wholly unaware that they were visiting a top-secret CIA facility.[33]

Eventually Radio America went off the air, and sometime after 1963 the CIA ostensibly abandoned the Swans. In 1969 President Richard Nixon directed the State department to settle the long-standing dispute with Honduras over the islands. Hewson A. Ryan, American ambassador to Honduras, and Ramón E. Cruz, the republic's president, worked out an accord whereby the United States would acknowledge Honduran sovereignty over the Swans without totally abandoning its property. The agreement provided that the two nations would establish and maintain cooperative meteorological and telecommunications facilities on the islands, with Honduras assuming sole responsibility for the Swans' radio air navigational beacon. Ratified by respective legislatures in 1972, the treaty entered force on September 1.[34]

Despite U.S. recognition of Honduran sovereignty, CIA involvement with the islands resumed about 1987 when the agency "built a new supply center on [Great] Swan island, . . . [which became] a busy arms transshipment center" for American-supported "contras" in Nicaragua. The CIA reportedly employed 130 Nicaraguans on the Swans to off-load supplies brought in by freighters from Texas and Florida and to place it aboard planes bound for the mainland. Air drops continued until February 29, 1988, when Congress cut off funding for the project. With tons of cargo remaining on the island, matériel was diverted to the contras' base at San Andrés, Honduras, where, theoretically, it was stored for future use that would not be in violation of American law. The only reported Honduran challenge to American utilization of the islands came when a Honduran army officer visited the Swans and tried to seize a dozen lethal Redeye anti-aircraft missiles (costing $20,000 each), which had been earmarked for contras in Nicaragua. The CIA commander on the Swans warned the Honduran officer through an interpreter in no uncertain terms: "Keep your hands off. These missiles are U.S. government property." He did.[35] The current involvement of American spies (if any) with the strategically placed islands is unknown.

Meanwhile in Boston, Alonzo Adams's heirs were outraged by what they considered to be the Nixon administration's arrogant, unilateral forfeiture of their property. Adding insult to injury, the U.S. government even demanded the return of all the rent it had paid Swan Island Trustees over the years. With Donald Glidden still in residence on Great Swan, in 1970 Sumner Smith filed suit against the U.S. government in federal district court in Boston, seeking damages; among other things, Smith claimed Washington had failed even to make all of the lease payments for which it had contracted. Attorneys for the U.S. Department of Justice countered that under the Guano Act private property rights were severely limited, a view the U.S. Supreme Court had upheld in *Duncan* v. *Navassa Phosphate Company* (1891) when it ruled that miners merely held licenses (and not an estate in or a title) to an island, rock, or key. Furthermore, government lawyers observed that Alonzo Adams was not the discoverer of Swans' guano; that his title had never been recognized by the State department; and, therefore, that his heirs had no right to lease the place to the USDA and subsequent government agencies. In 1971 the parties to *Smith* v. *U.S.* agreed to the dismissal of the complaint without prejudice. In effect Smith recognized Washington's right to dispose of the islands, and the U.S. government abandoned all efforts to recover lease payments.[36]

The status of two other islands in the Caribbean, Petrel and Serranilla (both claimed by James Jennett under the Guano Act), is uncertain, both of them having fallen into diplomatic limbo. According to a 1932 State department study, Petrel (an oval coral bank composed of two reefs, the larger of which is five feet high and fifteen hundred square yards in area) was unquestionably recognized as an American appurtenances after the Civil War; however, diplomats say there is "no evidence that any guano was ever removed from the Key, . . . [nor any] record of any statement made or position taken by the State Department with regard to Petrel Island since the issuance of the certificate to Jennett in 1869." Although observing that Great Britain had never claimed Petrel as part of Jamaica, they also noted in 1933, "It may be that, should the United States revive its claim, the Government of Colombia would contest it, on grounds similar to those alleged in the

Colombia claim to Roncador and Quito Sueño." Nevertheless, State department officials believed that conflict was unlikely, for "it is reasonable to assume that the United States has now lost by abandonment whatever interest it may once have had in and to Petrel Island."[37] Contemporary maps often show Petrel as belonging to Colombia, but, the United States has never formally conceded its sovereignty to any other nation.[38]

Serranilla (a coral bank composed of three small, sand-and-coral keys scattered across 480 square miles of otherwise empty Caribbean sea and centered about 220 miles north northeast of the mainland at Cabo Gracías á Dios, Honduras) was claimed both by Jennett (in 1869) and Pascal Quinan (in 1882), conflicting interests that the State department never officially reconciled; however, diplomats did eventually assert that one of Jennett's assigns (William Van Derlip) was the lawful holder of the American concession. Not included on any Treasury list of bonded guano islands until 1893, thereafter Serranilla was consistently designated as American property, but it was never subsequently formally annexed as were neighboring Quito Sueño, Roncador, and Serraña in 1919.[39]

Besides the United States, only Colombia appears ever to have harbored aspiration toward owning Serranilla—perhaps mistakenly. Although the island was not mentioned in 1893 in Colombia's blanket claims in the Caribbean (by which that government first asserted sovereignty over Quito Sueño, Serraña, and Roncador), when the Latin American republic later protested the pending erection of lights on those islands by the United States, it referred to Serranilla (for which no light had ever been proposed) rather than Serraña. In responding to Colombia, officials in Washington also initially incorrectly identified Serranilla instead of Serraña as the islet in question. According to the State department, "The error was finally perceived, although no mention is made of it, and Serraña, not Serranilla, was included in the Treaty [*sic*] of April 10, 1928, between the United States and Colombia" by which each agreed to respect the rights of the other at those places.[40] Although the United States does not currently assert claim to Serranilla, according to a State department spokesman it "reserves a right . . . to make [such] a claim. . . ."[41]

Strategic considerations in the Pacific early in the twentieth century likewise caused the U.S. government to reassess its position regarding American appurtenances, even to embrace some places it had heretofore largely ignored. James D. Hague, the geologist who had inspected American Guano Company's claims throughout the Central Pacific and surveyed other possible digs in the basin about the time of the Civil War, wrote to Secretary of State John Hay in 1900 to suggest that U.S. claims to Baker and Jarvis islands were equal to those of the British, who, he understood, had abandoned those places. "Whatever may be said of other islands, now or formerly claimed by American citizens, under the Act of 1856, these two, Jarvis and Baker, seem to be indisputably American possessions," Hague asserted. "Whether these two islands still have any value for guano deposits, I am unable to say; but I think either of them quite as likely as Strong's Island (Ualan) to become desirable for a [transoceanic telegraphic] cable station," a possibility then under discussion.[42]

Although American officials did not immediately follow up on Hague's suggestion that certain guano islands had special commercial and strategic value, other events over the succeeding years forced forgotten appurtenances back into national consciousness. During World War I, as diplomats commenced to formulate global strategy, the State department's Far Eastern Desk began "to develop a policy to protect American interests" in the Pacific. "Japan," says political scientist Werner Levi, "though an ally, was suspect and believed to be in the war for purposes of territorial expansion," the prize being scattered German islands that could have military potential and, thereby, threaten American communications with far eastern possessions such as the Philippines. In surveying the basin, diplomats looked principally to islands north of the equator and considered "those in British hands as reasonably safe from the standpoint of American interests."[43]

Levi observes that other places posed large question marks:

> No one department or bureau in the American government had jurisdiction over outlying American possessions at that time or took care of American interests in the vast regions of the Pacific. The administration of the various possessions was scattered among the War, Navy, Interior, and Treasury departments, without any coordination. Nobody knew exactly what territorial claims the United States had in the Pacific or over which islands it was entitled to exercise jurisdiction. Obviously, the elaboration of a proper policy for the region was greatly hampered by such uncertainty and maladministration.[44]

With the approval of Secretary of State Robert Lansing, about 1917 the department's Far Eastern Desk undertook a study embracing the whole Pacific, "especially with a view to establishing American ownership of certain islands. . . ." Diplomats judged that "Although most islands were clearly under the jurisdiction of several of the Western powers, many others, heretofore unimportant but gaining significance in the radio and air age, were of doubtful and possibly American ownership. . . ."[45]

Eager to prevent strategic locations in the Pacific from falling into the hands of potentially unfriendly foreign powers (especially the Japanese), some American diplomats agitated to reassert and/or to solidify U.S. claims to numerous one-time guano islands—especially Baker, Christmas, Howland, Jarvis, Johnston, Marcus, Palmyra, and Washington (Prospect or New York), and perhaps even Clipperton, Easter, and the Galápagos. These places had value, diplomats argued, as naval bases and as stepping-stones for trans-Pacific aviation; however, the U.S. Navy's General Board thought otherwise. With the exception of Christmas island, which might be developed as a submarine base, most of the rest (naval strategists contended) were either useless or indefensible as naval facilities and, therefore, represented substantially more cost than benefit. Moreover, sailors considered neither Clipperton nor Easter island vital to the defense of the North American mainland, whereas the Galápagos had potential military value and, hence, they thought the United States should not renounce any possible interests (if any) in them.[46] In a separate exercise the Navy nevertheless dutifully located each and every American guano island claim in the Pacific, often in the process pointing out their limitations as habitable places.[47]

Pledged to a war policy of "no material gain," President Wilson ultimately forbade the State department to pursue either claims to nominal American guano islands or to German possessions in the Pacific.[48] There the matter seemingly rested until the 1930s; however, it was not entirely forgotten. After the war, as the Department of the Interior's General Land Office struggled to determine definitively which guano islands still appertained to the United States and which did not so that it might issue a correct map depicting American territorial and insular possessions,[49] it asked the State department for help that Foggy Bottom declined to give—as it had in 1894 when the Treasury department had similarly begged assistance. Quoting the reasons for the earlier refusal (which "would require passing on the rights of a large number of private persons") Secretary Hughes, while noting that he was unaware of any current mining activity on any of the islands, significantly added, "I do not feel, however, that under the circumstances I should be justified either in directing that the list of Guano Islands be revised or in making a positive declaration regarding the ownership of the islands, since I might prejudice not only the present but possibly the future rights of American citizens to remove guano from them."[50]

However unlikely that American entrepreneurs might search out fresh feces (given vast reserves of cheap rock phosphates within the continental United States), it is evident that diplomats were no longer willing to casually abandon all claims to guano islands. In fact they were increasingly eager even to embrace places that had been claimed but never mined under the Guano Act. For example, Swains island (approximately two hundred miles north of Pago Pago, Samoa), was one of the forty-six places filed on (under the name of Quiros island) in 1860 as part of the giant Number 9 group of Alfred G. Benson's U.S. Guano Company, but, according to the State department, "there is no evidence that guano was ever taken from the island or that it was ever occupied under the Guano Act. . . ."[51] Nevertheless, it became a U.S. territory during the 1920s, its formal acquisition justified, in part, by that legislation.

A lush tropical atoll approximately six miles in circumference and about twenty feet above sea level, Swains (or Quiros) island was discovered in 1606 by Spanish explorer Pedro Fernandez de Quirós and named Isla de Gente Hermosa for the beautiful women who inhabited the place they called "Olosega." Except for a brackish lagoon at its center, the island was covered with sandalwood trees and coconut palms. It and its people remained mostly undisturbed until the nineteenth century principally because Quirós's location of the place was substantially in error. Sometime before 1840 a New England whaler named Swain also sighted it, and he shared that information with numerous people, including members of Charles Wilkes's exploring expedition who visited in 1841 but who, because of a dangerous barrier reef, did not venture ashore. From a vantage of more than a mile off shore American sailors failed to observe any sign of human habitation. The expedition accurately fixed the location, named it for Swain (by which it has since been known), and sailed on.[52]

Sometime afterward an English sea captain named Turnbull also happened upon the place, which he immodestly named for himself and claimed (but never occupied) for Great Britain. He eventually traded his rights to an American whaler, Eli H. Jennings of Long Island, New York, reputedly for a bottle of gin. Meanwhile, a Frenchman named Bullock had taken up residence on the island to work its copra, hiring the natives with western trinkets. When Jennings moved to the island with his Samoan bride in 1856 Bullock happened to be away hawking coconut oil. Jennings took up peaceable residence among the natives and immediately set out to convert them to Christianity. When Bullock returned and discovered his cohabitants, he abandoned the atoll rather than share it (and presumably its native women) with another westerner, especially a religious zealot.[53] According to the U.S. State department, "From 1856 until 1909, 'King Jennings' and his family reigned supreme upon Swains island, paying no taxes and submitting to no outside control or regulation."[54] By judiciously maintaining a coconut plantation on what by all accounts is a veritable tropical paradise, both the Jenningses and the islands' natives prospered and intermarried.[55]

In 1909 the resident commissioner for the Gilbert islands visited Swains and, ignoring the American flag that the Jenningses regularly flew above the settlement, collected approximately $85 in taxes on behalf of the British government. Eli Jennings, Jr. (who had inherited title to the island from his parents), filed claim against Great Britain to recover the money. Asserting that Swains was American property, he also asked the U.S. consul at Apia, British Samoa, for assistance.[56] The consul referred the matter to Washington, where diplomats were in a quandary as to "whether Swains Island was ever in fact discovered and occupied with the sanction of the United States and whether the United States has ever actually ever exercised jurisdiction over the island."[57] Little matter. Before Foggy Bottom could decide, the British High Commissioner for the Western Pacific informed the American consul at Apia that Jennings's taxes would be refunded because "the British government recognized Quiros island as an American possession where the American flag had been flown continuously for fifty years. . . ."[58]

Quandary or no, Secretary Hughes recommended to President Calvin Coolidge in 1924 that he seek congressional action to extend American sovereignty over Swains island formally. Hughes explained,

> The fact that the island is included in the list of guano islands appertaining to the United States and has since 1856 been continuously in the possession of the Jennings family, who have always regarded themselves as American citizens, and that American jurisdiction over the island has been recognized by Great Britain, the only other country which might be in a position to dispute an American claim thereto, would seem to place upon this Government the responsibility of either extending its sovereignty over Swains Island and assuming obligations which such a course would necessarily entail, or of disclaiming the exercise of any control or jurisdiction over the island and the inhabitants thereof.[59]

Accordingly, Coolidge asked Congress to regularize Swains's status, which legislators did in 1925 by officially annexing the atoll and attaching it to American Samoa. On May 13 Lieutenant Commander C. D. Edgar, captain of USS *Ontario,* visited Swains under Navy orders, raised the American flag, read a proclamation of sovereignty, informed the island's approximately one hundred residents that they were officially U.S. citizens, and fired a twenty-one gun salute as celebration.[60]

Perhaps emboldened by the Swains island experience, some diplomats continued to believe that several other nominal American guano islands were strategically valuable and that U.S. claims to those places were as valid as any. In 1932 the department's Office of Legal Adviser undertook an exhaustive study of the "Sovereignty of Islands Claimed under the Guano Act and of the Northwestern Hawaiian islands, Midway and Wake," which was completed the following year. While the resulting 976-page treatise conceded that many American titles were flawed beyond redemption and that the vast majority of islands, rocks, and keys that had been filed on under the Guano Act, probably belonged to Colombia, Cuba, Ecuador, Great Britain, France, Japan, Mexico, and/or Venezuela, other places were clearly U.S. property. The study contended that American claims to Navassa, Petrel, Quito Sueño, Serraña, Serranilla, and the Swans in the Caribbean were equal or superior to those of any other nation, and although the situation in the Pacific was far more muddled, unequivocal American sovereignty reigned over five erstwhile guano islands (French Frigates Shoals, Johnston atoll, Kingman reef, Palmyra, and Swains) and strong cases could be made for four others (Baker, Jarvis, Howland, and Starbuck), all of which were believed to be counterclaimed by Great Britain.[61]

Having offered a strong case for American ownership of more than a dozen places because of the Guano Act, diplomats then called for its repeal "since the demand for guano has largely disappeared, and since the provisions of the Act have created opportunities for fraud and dishonest speculation with which the State Department has been wholly unable to cope."[62] The plea fell on deaf ears both in the White House and on Capitol Hill, for, as of this writing, the measure remains U.S. law.[63]

The department's assertion of American ownership of several islands, rocks, and keys in the Pacific proved to be largely correct. Some (such as French Frigates Shoals, Johnston atoll, Palmyra, and Swains) had already been absorbed into the United States through direct or indirect acts of annexation, but the rest clearly required some formal action, if not concessions on the part of Great Britain. An exception was Kingman reef, which had been claimed only by Americans. Discovered in 1798 by New England whaler-sealer Edmund Fanning and called Dangers rock, Kingman reef is a small (eleven-hundred-square-foot), low-lying (five- to six- foot-high), triangular-shaped atoll situated approximately 920 miles south of Honolulu and 35 miles north of Palmyra. Sighted again in 1853 by mariner W. E. Kingman, master of the *Shooting Star* out of Boston who warned sailors of its presence and potential danger in a letter to the *Honolulu Friend,* the reef consequently became popularly known for him.[64]

Claimed (as Dangers rock) in 1860 by A. G. Benson's U.S. Guano Company, Kingman reef was bonded as part of the infamous Number 9 group; however, as the State department later observed, it is "practically certain that no guano was ever removed from it, at least by claimants under the Guano Act."[65] No one else seems to have been interested in the place until 1922 when Lorrin A. Thurston annexed it on behalf of the United States in the name of his employer, Palmyra Copra Company, which wished to use it as a fishing base. Before departing the atoll, Thurston left documents in a glass jar to proclaim his firm's ownership. Palmyra Copra later informed the State department of his action. Assistant Secretary A. A. Adee acknowledged receipt of the information on behalf of the government but expressed neither approval nor disapproval of Thurston and Palmyra Copra's actions.[66]

In their study of "Sovereignty of Islands Claimed under the Guano Act," State department lawyers had concluded in 1933 that while "the United States had no valid claim to Kingman Reef arising under the Guano Act,... [it had] an inchoate right to the reef, possibly because of discovery by Captain Kingman, . . . and possibly because of the formal possession taken by the Island of the Palmyra Copra Company. . . ."[67] Whatever the legal justification, President Franklin Roosevelt placed Kingman reef (along with Johnston atoll and Wake island) under the control and jurisdiction of the U.S. Navy by executive order on December 29, 1934, thereby formally asserting American sovereignty over the reef.[68]

Unlike many of his predecessors, President Roosevelt happily embraced guano islands, especially those that might become valuable airdromes sites for trans-Pacific air routes. Cases in point were Baker, Howland, and Jarvis islands. Picked clean of phosphates and abandoned by English businessman John T. Arundel about 1891, these Central Pacific atolls might still have been claimed by the British Phosphate Commission (successor to Arundel's interests) had that enterprise not acquired far better prospects at Nauru and Ocean island in the Pacific and at Christmas island in the Indian ocean. Therefore, the British did not object when on October 14, 1935, the U.S. State department announced that it was annexing Baker, Howland, and Jarvis. Chagrined, two days later American diplomats amended their announcement to say that no annexation was necessary since the United States already owned those places by authority of the Guano Act; the islands had merely been reclaimed by Washington. Even so, to reinforce American assertions of sovereignty over these places, the Commerce department's Bureau of Air Commerce recruited Hawaiian schoolboys to reside on each of the atolls—lest the British try to reoccupy them before the matter was forever settled. On May 13, 1936, Roosevelt placed these islands under the jurisdiction of the Interior department's Division of Territories and Island Possessions, which promptly established weather facilities on each of them to assist commercial flight.[69]

The British resolutely resisted similar moves by the United States to reassert authority over Canton, Christmas in the Pacific, Enderbury, Hull, Phoenix, and Sydney islands. When President Roosevelt signed an executive order on March 3, 1938, that placed Canton and Enderbury under the Interior department, the British objected. His majesty's government notified the State department that it took exception to American claims. Whitehall even sent a warship to raise the Union Jack on Canton, and the British officially reoccupied Christmas, just in case. Although the U.S. Interior department subsequently erected a navigational light on Canton, it did not press the issue by manning it; however, Pan-American Airways proceeded to construct an airfield there. On August 11, 1938, the two governments agreed to joint occupation of Canton and Enderbury for fifty years, subject to renewal; by this understanding both nations would be permitted to establish commercial aviation facilities on the islands. Other places that were disputed between the powers were not specifically mentioned in the agreement; nevertheless, in 1940 Congress placed Canton and Enderbury (along with Baker, Howland, Jarvis, Johnston atoll, Kingman, and Palmyra, as well as Midway and Wake islands) under the jurisdiction of the U.S. District Court in Honolulu.[70]

About then the United States commenced to consolidate its gains by erecting lighthouses on several of the Central Pacific islands that it had recently reclaimed and, no doubt to promote trans-Pacific aviation, by constructing an air strip on Howland island for use by celebrated aviatrix Amelia Earhart in her famed-but-doomed 'round-the-world jaunt in 1937. She disappeared on July 2 while en route to the island from New Guinea.[71]

Far less publicized was contemporary construction at Canton, Johnston atoll, and Palmyra island to provide the U.S. Navy with facilities for flying boat patrols, both to screen waters west of Hawaii and, eventually, to serve commercial aviation. Of these places Palmyra was the most perplexing in terms of public policy, for the U.S. government actually tried to steal it from its owners of record. A lush, coconut-covered atoll composed of some fifty-two small islets lying one thousand miles south of Honolulu, Palmyra (claimed but apparently never mined by both American and Hawaiian guano companies) was acquired in 1885 by Pacific Navigation Company, a Hawaiian corporation, which apparently raised coconuts and hunted sea slugs (biche de mer) that are considered delicacies by the Chinese. Although the record is far from complete, Pacific Navigation appears to have abandoned the atoll about 1887.[72]

Around the turn of the century it "nearly became the property of a group of Chicago ladies, man-haters, who [reportedly] wanted to retire to this lonely spot in the mid-Pacific. . . ."[73] Rather, in 1911 Hawaiian Judge Henry

E. Cooper purchased rights to the place from the successors to Pacific Navigation. Cooper formally filed for and received title to the atoll in fee simple from the Land Court of the Territory of Hawaii. Occasionally thereafter residing on the tropical paradise, he harvested its coconuts. In 1922 he sold to Leslie and Ellen Fullard-Leo of Hawaii all but two of the atoll's islets, which, following his death in 1929, passed to his heirs. Operating as Palmyra Copra Company, the Fullard-Leo's farmed their fifty islets for the next several years, in the process also laying claim to Kingman reef.[74]

Anticipating its use as a military facility, the U.S. Navy began bargaining with all owners of record in 1938 to "lease the land—negotiations which were proceeding amicably and satisfactorily to [all] parties when, for the first time, it appears to have occurred to somebody in the government service that ownership was in the United States."[75] Consequently claiming that the place was not properly subject to private ownership, bureaucrats instigated proceedings in federal district court in Honolulu in 1939 to acquire title. The Fullard-Leos and the Cooper heirs resisted, and they ultimately prevailed, thereby acquiring uncontested title—but not until well after World War II. Meanwhile, the U.S. Navy had occupied the island and turned it into a seaplane base. The military also built a runway that was used by the U.S. Air Force as late as 1961.[76]

Of all America's Pacific guano island bastions, Johnston atoll became the most important by far—both in the short and long runs. Having created a wildlife preserve under the auspices of the Agriculture department by President Coolidge in 1926, the atoll (along with Kingman reef) was transferred to the U.S. Navy in 1934 by President Roosevelt; in February 1941 he designated the seas about Kingman, Johnston, Midway, Palmyra, and Wake islands to be naval defensive areas and their airspace to be naval reservations, actions that effectively closed the region to all but those persons expressly permitted to enter by the Navy department. About then Navy secretary Claude A. Swanson proclaimed Johnston atoll to be a "Category A" facility, thereby giving its defense top priority. Congress soon appropriated $1.2 million for construction.[77]

Work to transform the former phosphate digs into a military base had actually begun in 1939 with the objective of providing facilities to support a squadron of seaplanes. Civilian contractors cut a hole in the atoll's barrier reef, which surrounded Johnston and Sand islets, to provide an adequate runway for seaplanes as well as easier access for ships. Workers dredged the lagoon and erected creature comforts on Sand—barracks for four hundred men, a mess hall, an underground hospital, water tanks and desalinization equipment, power and radio stations, and a laundry. They also enlarged the land mass of Johnston island with fill from lagoon dredging to provide an area sufficient for an airstrip. Once finished, the island had grown from about 40 to 160 acres. Those additions were actually completed by Navy Seabees because eight days after the Japanese attacked Pearl Harbor, they commenced shelling Johnston and Sand from a submarine that surfaced offshore, thereby forcing the government to remove and replace civilians construction workers. By war's end, the tiny base (serving as an important refueling station for submarines and air transports) housed 13 amphibians, 76 land planes, 70 officers, and 1,118 enlisted personnel.[78]

Other American appurtenances were also attacked, with some effect. Although the seaplane base at Palmyra was never threatened, the Japanese bombed the lighthouse at Howland on December 8, 1941, partially destroying it and killing two civilian residents. The attack caused the Interior department to abandon the Central Pacific (especially Baker, Howland, and Jarvis islands) for the duration of the war. The Japanese also shelled Pan-Am's facilities at Canton, doing minimal damage; nevertheless, civilians were evacuated and air service discontinued. U.S. armed forces took control of the island and its facilities for the duration.[79]

United States occupation of Clipperton island during the war demonstrates that not all public policy was purely in pursuit of the war effort. Claimed in 1892 by Oceanic Phosphate of San Francisco, the atoll (seven hundred miles southwest of Acapulco) was sold to Englishman J. T. Arundel in 1898 after the State department declined to recognize it as an American appurtenance. Mined intermittently under a Mexican contract as late as World War I, it was the site of harrowing melodrama about then when a handful of women and children were terrorized by a madman-rapist. Afterward, Clipperton was awarded by arbitration to France, which has never occupied it. During the late 1930s, when an Australian aviator sought to develop the atoll as an airdrome, President Roosevelt became concerned that it was about to fall into the hands of the British and thereby would afford them the advantage of a postwar air route across the Pacific. Consequently, in 1944 he ordered the U.S. Navy to seize the place. For more than a year a small weather station on the atoll was one of the military's most closely guarded secrets but least valuable bases. When word of American action finally leaked, the French became furious, but this did not prevent Roosevelt from laying plans to acquire the atoll permanently after the war, a course of action he was actively pursuing at the time of his death in 1945. His passing, along with the end of the conflict, terminated official American interest in and occupation of Clipperton island.[80]

The war's end also caused the U.S. government to reassess the value of its guano islands once more, especially those in the Pacific. By then technology had so advanced aviation that the stepping-stones which remote appurtenances offered trans-Pacific commercial flights were no longer vital; nevertheless, there were other potential uses. In 1946 the United States asked Great Britain to relinquish claims to Christmas and Canton islands in the Pacific, as well as to Funafuti (Ellice) island, all of which naval strategists considered important to American defense; however, the British politely declined to accommodate the Americans, insisting that London's interests in these places was at least as critical as Washington's.[81]

Abandoned by the Lever brothers about 1908, Christmas island in the Pacific had been purchased by Father Emmanuel Rougier—a one-time Roman Catholic priest dwelling on Tahiti whose actual calling was far more secular, and entrepreneurial. He operated the island as a copra plantation from Tahiti until his death in 1932; afterward, his heirs ran it until the copra market collapsed, about 1939. Occupied during the war by as many as ten thousand American troops who turned it into an important air base, the island was abandoned again after the bombing of Hiroshima—notwithstanding U.S. efforts to secure its title. About then the British Colonial Office purchased from Rougier's heirs their rights to Christmas island for £50,000, and, perhaps to emphasize their contention that it was British property, used it as site for a hydrogen-bomb test, "Operation Grapple," in 1957. Malden island, four hundred miles to the south and also once claimed as an American guano island, served as instrumentation island for the test. Having been abandoned by the British Phosphate early in the century, Malden's stores of canned goods and pharmaceuticals still littered the landscape when scientists arrived in the mid-1950s to set up apparatuses to measure the bomb's power.[82]

Canton, jointly administered by Great Britain and the United States since 1938, came under exclusive American jurisdiction (with British permission) in 1965 so that the Department of Defense might install a tracking station for the U.S. Air Force's Pacific Missile Range. Obsolete by 1979, the station was closed, an action that undoubtedly led Washington to reconsider its position with respect to other such places in the Pacific.[83]

Inasmuch as joint-occupation accords with the British were scheduled either for expiration or renewal within the next decade, the Carter administration found the moment propitious to divest the United States of unwanted appurtenances and to acquire goodwill with emerging Pacific nations then being granted independence by the British. In a series of three agreements, Washington consequently disposed of most of its remaining Pacific guano empire, only eight of which (Canton, Enderbury, Hull, McKeans, Malden, Phoenix, Starbuck, and Sydney) had ever been occupied and mined under American law. In 1979, by treaty with Tuvalu (the former Ellice islands), the United States relinquished claims to Nakufetau (filed on as Duke of Clarence island) as well as Funafuti, which, although never claimed as a guano island, had been briefly coveted by American military planners after World War II. Also that year, by treaty with the Republic of Kiribati (former Gilbert islands), the United States surrendered title to Birnie, Canton, Caroline, Christmas (Kiritimati), Enderbury, Flint, Gardner (Nikumaroro), Hull (Orona), McKeans, Malden, Phoenix (Rawaki), Starbuck, Sydney (Manra) and Vostok; however, the United States retained the right of joint utilization of the facilities it had constructed on Canton. And in 1980, by treaty with the Cook islands, the United States gave up interests in Danger (Pukapuka), Humphrey (Manihiki), Penrhyn (Tongareva) and Rierson (Rakahanga) islands.[84]

Of the seventy places in the Pacific that had been claimed under the Guano Act, merely eight remain American territory as of this writing. French Frigate Shoals and Swains island, filed on under the legislation but never exploited, have been officially incorporated into Hawaii and American Samoa, respectively. The other six (like Navassa island in the Caribbean) are "unincorporated territories of the United States."[85]

Abandoned during World War II, Baker, Howland, and Jarvis continue to be uninhabited. The lighthouse at Howland was reconstructed during the late 1940s, automated, and dedicated to the memory of Amelia Earhart; the airstrip is no longer serviceable. Otherwise, the three lonely little guano islands again have become rookeries for some twenty species of sea birds and, in the case of Howland, home to tens of thousands of rats. Administrative authority for all three places was transferred to the U.S. Fish and Wildlife Service in June 1974, and they became animal refuges. Closed to public access, they may be visited legally only by permit from the Service's Honolulu office. Uninhabited Kingman reef, thirty-five miles northwest of Palmyra, continues to be administered by the U.S. Navy, which has never maintained any facilities there.[86]

Although incontrovertibly reverting to private ownership and control in 1961 when it was abandoned by the military, Palmyra's legal status was muddled somewhat that year when President John Kennedy by executive order vested its administration in the Interior department, an action apparently never disputed by its owners. In 1974 the usually uninhabited atoll was the setting for the especially grisly murder of a San Diego couple, Mac and Muff Graham, who were sailing across the Pacific and who innocently put in at the lush atoll where they were killed for their yacht by a marooned mariner, Buck Walker. Walker and his girlfriend, Stephanie Stearns, were soon arrested in Honolulu aboard the Graham's boat, which was recognized as stolen, but because no corpse was initially found on Palmyra they were only prosecuted for and convicted of theft. In 1981 one of the bodies was discovered, and the resulting trial of Stearns for murder became the basis of a best-selling book by lawyer Vincent Bugliosi, *And the Sea Will Tell,* as well as a television mini-series (on CBS) in 1991.[87]

Meanwhile, in 1979 the U.S. government had announced that it was considering the purchase of Palmyra for use as a nuclear waste dump, but the South Pacific Forum (a coalition of thirteen nations led by Australia and New Zealand) vehemently opposed the idea. Furthermore, the atoll's owners refused to sell it to the government for that purpose, and the proposal was shelved. Its value perhaps enhanced by notoriety, Palmyra was offered for private sale in 1988, and two years later Peter Savio of Honolulu leased it for seventy-five years, an agreement that includes an option to purchase the place for $36 million. Savio's Palmyra Development Corporation reportedly plans to promote the remote spot as a residential and recreational spa.[88]

Finally, Johnston atoll remains among the nation's most closely guarded military reservations. Unauthorized civilians are not allowed to visit. Although the atoll "lost some of its strategic value . . . after World War II . . . with the advent of long-range land planes,"[89] its role and mission have since evolved significantly. In 1948 the Navy transferred its administration to the U.S. Air Force, which contemplated using the isolated site as a command center for nuclear testing in the region.[90] Ten years later it was placed under control of a joint Defense department task force "for use as launch site and support base for atmospheric nuclear testing operations," a role that demanded more land surface. Additional dredging and filling in 1964 created two new islands (dubbed North and East), bringing the atoll's aggregate land area to 625 acres.[91]

In 1970 the facility was transferred back to the Air Force, which, the following year, leased forty-one acres to the U.S. Army for use as depot for chemical weapons formerly held on Okinawa. About then the Air Force also began stockpiling the defoliant Agent Orange on Johnston atoll. In 1977 those stocks were incinerated in place. Meanwhile, in 1973, the Air Force had transferred administrative control of and responsibility for the atoll to the U.S. Defense department's Defense Nuclear Agency, which has primary responsibility for matters concerning nuclear weapons, nuclear weapons systems acquisition, and nuclear weapons effects. Anticipating the future resumption of atmospheric nuclear-weapons testing, the agency erected facilities on the atoll at a cost of approximately $1 billion to monitor weapons' tests in the Pacific and to house requisite personnel, then mothballed them.[92] In keeping with Defense department policy, DNA will "neither confirm nor deny the presence or absence of nuclear weapons" on the atoll; however, because federal law requires that nuclear waste be stored only at approved sites (which does not include any of the four islands that constitute the atoll's complex), a spokesperson for DNA asserts categorically, "There are no nuclear wastes stored on or about Johnston atoll."[93]

In 1983 Congress authorized the Army to create the "Johnston Atoll Chemical Agent Disposal System," which originally contemplated destroying only the chemical munitions used in M-55 rockets. By the time construction commenced in 1985, the complex housed "13,000 tons of active and obsolete chemical weapons, including two nerve agents, stored in underground bunkers,"[94] with more matériel slated to be moved to the site because Congress had ordered the destruction of all the nation's chemical weapons, a task originally scheduled for completion by 1997. Operation of the first of nine incinerators, which was expected to cost $3.8 billion and which was scheduled for full-scale use in 1989, was delayed for more than a year by the enlarged scope of the task and was further complicated by the end of the cold war. With tensions easing in Europe in 1990, the U.S. Army retired an estimated one hundred thousand artillery shells containing sarin and VX nerve gases and shipped them to the atoll for disposal.[95]

The complex's notoriety as "the toxic waste disposal center of the world" greatly distressed the South Pacific Forum. Member nations again objected to American plans to use the Pacific basin as "an experimental area."[96] Their protests led President George Bush to assure the Forum in October 1990 that the munitions stored at and en route to the complex would be "destroyed safely . . . and that, once the destruction is completed, we have no plans to use Johnston atoll for any other chemical munitions purpose or as a hazardous waste disposal site."[97]

Many Americans were equally unhappy with the use of the atoll. On September 27, 1990, Senator Daniel K. Inouye of Hawaii introduced legislation "To prohibit the Secretary of Defense from transporting chemical munitions to Johnston Atoll for the demilitarization or storage of such munitions," but the proposal died in the Senate Armed Services committee.[98]

The facility, operated for the U.S. government by Raytheon Services of Nevada, housed 1,010 civilian and 319 military personnel in October 1990. As of this writing detoxification and incineration continues on the atoll, albeit at a diminished pace caused by repeated mechanical breakdowns that reportedly reduced the plant's operating time by one half by mid-1992. The facility had also recorded twenty-two accidents, but none of them resulted in injury.[99]

It is ironic that a humble guano island that once provided bird droppings (in some ways the most dangerous of fertilizers) to enhance America's agricultural productivity now houses some of the nation's deadliest chemical munitions—a use of these appurtenances that framers of the Guano Islands Act could never have anticipated. As the Law of Unforeseen Consequences insists, no event ever really ends, nor, once committed, can it ever be contained.

Indeed, public actions often have wholly unexpected ramifications, both good and bad. For instance, the Guano Act—its constitutionality upheld by the U.S. Supreme Court in *Jones* v. *U.S.* (1890)—provided President Harry Truman with the legal basis to order that "the natural resources of the subsoil and sea bed of the continental shelf beneath the high seas but contiguous to the coasts of the United States [are] declared . . . by proclamation to appertain to the United States and to be subject to its jurisdiction and control. . . ."[100]

The great guano rush is an important albeit generally overlooked chapter of American history. As the first commercial fertilizer to achieve widespread use in the United States, guano educated farmers about scientific agricultural techniques, augmented their productivity, and increased their incomes. It also helped to politicize them. Their repeated calls for public action that would afford them cheaper fertilizers were an early step toward the transformation of individual farmers into a distinct political pressure group, the agrarian sector, and helped lead to the creation of the U.S. Department of Agriculture in 1862 as the first advocacy agency within the federal government.[101]

The interplay of supply, demand, and price often impacts on politics in the United States; however, seemingly minor events such as the great guano rush are often ignored by economists and historians, even when such events offer particular insight into the national experience. Historically, since the outset of this nation's existence under the Constitution, public aid and assistance to private enterprise have been daily occurrences, at all levels of government—even if the public sector frequently behaves inconsistently with respect to the forces it consequently sets into motion.[102] To be certain, governments in the United States (local, state, and federal) are usually prodded into action by special interests that beg preferential assistance, but the fact remains, the public sector is very responsive to those pleadings—which is hardly evidence of *laissez faire* that most Americans mistakenly associate with U.S. economic policy.

In the case of the great guano rush, the Congress of the United States deputized each and every American citizen to claim territory for the commonwealth, an act that has no parallel in history. Even Great Britain (which authorized crown monopolies such as the East India Company to raise armies and even to legislate for indigenous populations) never granted such extraordinary power as territorial aggrandizement to individual private citizens.[103] Moreover, phosphate companies that mined islands under the aegis of the empire needed explicit crown permits to operate. Nor did the French allow individuals to claim or exploit these resources. When claiming guano islands, Napoleon III sent commissioned officers to annex territory officially to the Second Empire.[104] Yet, the experience of American appurtenances points to a spirit of governmentally assisted individualism, even in entrepreneurship, which continues to permeate the national psyche—even if it is not fully recognized or appreciated.

This entwining of public and private interests in the United States has woven a colorful fabric, one that often allows the bright and shining examples of entrepreneurial successes to overwhelm the more muted hues of public assistance without which such economic gains often would have been impossible. Consequently, meaningful chapters in history such as the great guano rush are often overlooked, even ignored, especially when they fail to fit preconceived notions of the national experience. As a result, instructive episodes with implications for agricultural, business, diplomatic, economic, labor, legal, and political history have been all but forgotten.

# APPENDICES

## Guano Islands Act(s)

34th Congress, 1st Session. Chapter 164—*An act to authorize protection to be given to citizens of the United States who may discover deposits of guano.*

[Sec. 1]. *Be it enacted by the Senate and House of Representatives of the United States in Congress assembled,* That when any citizen or citizens of the United States may have discovered, or shall hereafter discover, a deposit of guano on any island, rock, or key not within the lawful jurisdiction of any other government, and not occupied by the citizens of any other government, and shall take peaceable possession thereof, and occupy the same, said island, rock, or key may, at the discretion of the President of the United States, be considered as appertaining to the United States: *Provided, however,* That notice be given by such discover or discoverers, as soon as practicable, to the State Department of the United States, of such discovery, occupation, and possession, verified by affidavit, describing said island, rock, or key, and the latitude and longitude thereof, as near as may be, and showing that such possession was taken in the name of the United States, and that satisfactory evidence be furnished to the State Department that such island, rock, or key was not, at the time of discovery thereof, or of the taking possession and occupation thereof by the claimants, in the possession or occupation of any other government or of the citizens of any other government.

Sec. 2. *And be it further enacted,* That the said discoverers or discoverers, or his or their assigns, being citizens of the United States, may be allowed, at the pleasure of Congress, the exclusive right of occupying said island, rock, or keys, for the purpose of obtaining said guano, and of selling and delivering the same to citizens of the United States, for the purpose of being used therein, and may be allowed to charge and receive for every ton thereof delivered alongside a vessel, in proper tubs, within reach of a ship's tackle, a sum not exceeding eight dollars per ton for the best quality, or four dollars per ton in its native place of deposit: *Provided, however,* That no guano shall be taken from said island, rock, or key, except for the use of citizens of the United States, or of persons resident therein, as aforesaid. *And further provided, also,* That said discoverer or discoverers, or his or their assigns, shall first enter into bonds, with such penalties or securities as may be required by the President, to deliver the said guano to citizens of the United States, for the purpose of being used therein, and to none others, and at the price aforesaid, and to provide all necessary facilities for that purpose within a time to be fixed in said bond. And any breach of the provisions thereof shall be taken and deemed a forfeiture of all rights accruing under and by virtue of this act.

Sec. 3. *And be it further enacted,* That the introduction of guano from such islands, rocks, or keys, shall be regulated as in the coasting trade between different parts of the United States, and the same laws shall govern vessels concerned therein.

Sec. 4. *And be it further enacted,* That nothing in this act contained shall be construed obligatory on the United States to retain possession of the islands, rock, or keys, as aforesaid, after the guano shall have been removed from the same.

Sec. 5. *And be it further enacted,* That the President of the United States is hereby authorized, at his discretion, to employ the land and naval forces of the United States to protect the rights of said discover or discoverers or assigns, as aforesaid.

Sec. 6. *And be it further enacted,* That until otherwise provided by law, all acts done, and offenses or crimes committed, on every such island, rock, or key, by persons who may land thereon, or in the waters adjacent thereto, shall be held and deemed to have been committed on the high seas, on board a merchant ship, or vessel belonging to the United States, and be punished according to the laws of the United States relating to such ships or vessels and offenses on the high seas; which laws, for the purposes of aforesaid, are hereby extended to and over such islands, rocks, or keys.

APPROVED, [and signed into law by Franklin Pierce], August 18, 1856.[1]

## Revisions

By 1860, seven decades of national legislation had resulted in sixteen volumes of public enactments that, according to the New York *Times,* were "confused, contradictory, and uncertain." Massachusetts senator Charles Sumner consequently urged his colleagues to revise and condense these, an idea endorsed by Abraham Lincoln in his first state-of-the-union message. Civil War delayed the task until 1866, when Congress appointed a three-man commission headed by Caleb Cushing (former Massachusetts congressman, envoy to China, and Franklin Pierce's attorney general) and directed it "to select from the entire body of the statutes all those where are of a 'general and permanent' character; to arrange them in a convenient order of subjects, to revise and condense the language in which they are expressed, ... and submit them to Congress for enactment, if approved."[2]

Among those statutes deemed "general and permanent" by the commissioners was the Guano Islands Act, whose six sections were recast into eight, one being added to protect the rights of widows, other heirs, and/or assignees should discoverers die before perfecting title.[3] In 1926, Congress further codified existing U.S. statutes to purge "the general and permanent laws ... [of those that] are inconsistent, redundant, and obsolete."[4] Now in its eleventh edition, Title 48, Chapter 8, of the U.S. *Code, containing the general and permanent laws of the United States in* force on January 3, 1989 (1989), is devoted to the Guano Islands Act. A five year suspension of the prohibition against the exportation of American guano, included in the *Revised statutes* (1873), was deemed superfluous in 1926 and omitted from the U.S. *Code.*[5]

U.S. *Revised statutes* (1873), Title 72, Sec. 5570-5578; and U.S. *Code* (1989), Title 48, Chapter 8, Sec. 1411-1418:

@5570. (@1411.) Whenever any citizen of the United States discovers a deposit of guano on any island, rock, or key, not within the lawful jurisdiction of any other government, and not occupied by the citizens of any other government, and takes peaceable possession thereof, and occupies same, such island, rock, or key may, at the discretion of the President, be considered as appertaining to the United States.

@5571. (@1412.) The discoverer shall, as soon as practicable, give notice, verified by affidavit, to the Department of State, of such discovery, occupation, and possession, describing the island, rock, or key, and the latitude and longitude thereof, as near as may be, and showing that such possession was taken in the name of the United States; and shall furnish satisfactory evidence to the State Department that such island, rock, or key was not, at the time of discovery thereof, or of the taking of possession and occupation thereof by the claimants, in the possession or occupation of any other government or of the citizens of any other government, before the same shall be considered as appertaining to the United States.

@5572. (@1413.) If the discoverer dies before perfecting proof of discovery or fully complying with the provisions of the preceding section (of section 1412) his widow, heir, executor, or administrator, shall be entitled to the benefits of such discovery, upon complying with the provisions of this chapter. Nothing herein shall be held to impair any rights of discovery or any assignment by a discoverer recognized prior to April 2, 1872, by the United States.

@5573. (@1414.) The discover, or his assigns, being citizens of the United States, may be allowed, at the pleasure of Congress, the exclusive right of occupying such island, rock, or key, for the purpose of obtaining guano, and of selling and delivering same to citizens of the United States, to be used therein, and may be allowed to charge and receive for every ton thereof delivered alongside a vessel, in proper tubs, within reach of a ship's tackle, a sum not exceeding $8 per ton for the best quality, or $4 for every ton taken while in its native place of deposit.

@5574. (@1415.) No guano shall be taken from any island, rock, or key (mentioned in section 1411 of this title), except for the use of the citizens of the United States or of persons resident therein. The discoverers, or his widow, heir, executor, administrator, or assigns, shall enter into bond, in such penalty and with such sureties as may be required by the President, to deliver the guano to citizens of the United States, for the purpose of being used therein, and to none others, and at the price prescribed, and to provide all necessary facilities for that purpose within a time to be fixed in the bond; and any breach of the provisions shall be deemed a forfeiture of all rights accruing under and by virtue of this title. This section shall, however, be suspended in relation to all persons who have complied with the provisions of this Title, for five years from and after the fourteenth day of July, eighteen hundred and seventy-two.[6]

@5575. (@1416.) The introduction of guano from such islands, rocks, or keys shall be regulated as in the coasting trade between different parts of the United States, and the same laws shall govern vessels concerned therein.

@5576. (@1417.) All acts done, and offenses or crimes committed, on such rock, or key (mentioned in section 1411) of this Title, by persons who may land thereon, or in the waters adjacent thereto, shall be deemed committed on board a merchant ship or vessel belonging to the United States; and shall be punished according to the laws of the United States relating to such ships or vessels and offenses on the high seas, which laws for the purpose aforesaid are extended over such islands, rocks, or keys.

@5577. (@ 1418.) The president is authorized, at his discretion, to employ the land and naval forces of the United States to protect the rights of the discoverer or of his widow, heir, executor, administrator, or assigns.

@5578. (@1419.) Nothing in this Title [chapter] shall be construed as obliging the United States to retain possession of said islands, rocks, or keys, after the guano shall have been removed from the same.

## Places Claimed and/or Acquired under the U.S. Guano Islands Act

**(Name of island, rock, or key appearing in all capital letters denotes acquisition under U.S. Guano Islands Act)**

| islands, rocks, and keys (*denotes mining) | alleged location | discoverer or claimant, and filing date | bond number and date | disposition |
|---|---|---|---|---|
| Alacrans island* | 22°24'N<br>89°42'N | James Jennett<br>Sept. 13, 1879 | No. 16<br>June 21, 1884 | conceded to Mexico1894 |
| Alta Vela island* | 17°28'N<br>71°38'W | Patterson & Murguiondo<br>May 14, 1860 | none | conceded to the Dominican Republic 1867 |
| Alta Vela island* | 17°28'N<br>71°38'W | W.T. Kendall<br>May 14, 1860 | none | conceded to the Dominican Republic 1867 |
| America (Fanning?) island | 3°40'N<br>159°28'W | U.S. Guano Co.<br>Feb. 12, 1859 | No. 9<br>Feb. 8, 1860 | Fanning island annexed by Great Britain, 1888 |
| Anne's island | 9°49'N<br>151°15W | U.S. Guano Co.<br>Feb. 12, 1859 | No. 9<br>Feb. 8, 1860 | nonexistent |
| Arcas key* | 20°13'N<br>91°58'W | Pascal A. Quinan<br>May 14, 1879 | none | conceded to Mexico, 1899 |
| Arcas key* | 20°13'N<br>91°58'W | James Jennett<br>Sept. 3, 1879 | none | conceded to Mexico, 1899 |
| Arcas key* | 20°13'N<br>91°58'W | Alfred May<br>March 10, 1898 | none | conceded to Mexico, 1899 |
| Arenas keys* | 22°24'N<br>91°25'N | James Jennett<br>May 24, 1869 | Nos. 13 and 15<br>Sept. 8, 1879 and Oct. 18, 1880 | conceded to Mexico, 1894 |
| Aves (Bird) island* | 15°40'N<br>63°37'W | Atlantic & Pacific Guano Co.,<br>Mar. 1, 1860 | none | conceded to Venezuela, 1855 |
| Aves (Bird) island* | 15°40'N<br>63°37'W | James Jennett<br>May 20, 1869 | No. 14<br>Sept. 13, 1880 | conceded to Venezuela, 1855 |
| BAKER (Nantucket) ISLAND* | 0°15'N<br>176°30'W | American Guano Co.<br>Aug. 30, 1856 | No. 1<br>Oct. 28, 1856 | unorganized U.S. territory |
| Barber's island | 8°54'N<br>178°W | U.S. Guano Co.<br>Feb. 12, 1859 | No. 9<br>Feb. 8, 1860 | nonexistent |
| Barren (Starbuck) island* | 5°40'S<br>155°55'W | Phoenix Guano Co.<br>March 14, 1859 | No. 6<br>Dec. 27, 1859 | transferred to the Republic of Kiribati by treaty (1979) |

| islands, rocks, and keys (*denotes mining) | alleged location | discoverer or claimant, and filing date | bond number and date | disposition |
|---|---|---|---|---|
| Bauman's island | 11°48'S 154°10'W | U.S. Guano Co. Feb. 12, 1859 | No. 9 Feb. 8, 1860 | nonexistent |
| Birnies island | 3°35'S 171°39'W | U.S. Guano Co. Feb. 12, 1859 | No. 9 Feb. 8, 1860 | transferred to the Republic of Kiribati by treaty (1979) |
| Boobie (Bobby) key | 14°14'N 80°30'W | James Jennett June 30, 1866 | none | nonexistent |
| Calapatch (Alvalo) island* | 21°34'N 82°10'W | William A. Varty April 12, 1901 | none | conceded to Cuba, 1905 |
| Caroline island | 9°54'S 150°07'W | U.S. Guano Co. Feb. 12, 1859 | No. 9 Feb. 8, 1860 | transferred to the Republic of Kiribati by treaty (1979) |
| Canton (Mary, Abariringa) island* | 2°53'S 172°W | U.S. Guano Co. Feb. 12, 1859 | No. 9 Feb. 8, 1860 | transferred to the Republic of Kiribati by treaty (1979) |
| Christmas (Kiritimati) atoll | 1°58'N 157°10'W | U.S. Guano Co. Dec. 13, 1858 | No. 7 Dec. 29, 1859 | transferred to the Republic of Kiribati by treaty (1979) |
| Clarence, Duke of, island | 9°07'S 171°40'W | U.S. Guano Co. Feb. 12, 1859 | No. 9 Feb. 8, 1860 | transferred to the Republic of Tuvalu by treaty (1979) |
| Clipperton island (atoll)* | 10°18'N 109°13'W | Oceanic Phosphate Co., July 30, 1892 | none | conceded to France, 1893 |
| Constable island | 4°52'N 51°50'W | J.W. Fabens May 19, 1857 | none | conceded to France (Guiana), c. 1857 |
| Constable island | 4°52'N 51°50'W | George R. Field Oct. 11, 1877 | none | conceded to France (Guiana), c. 1857 |
| Constable island | 4°52'N 51°50'W | James Jennett June 5, 1880 | none | conceded to France (Guiana), c. 1857 |
| Dangerous (Puka Puka, Motukoe, and Motukavata) islands | 10°S 165°56'W | U.S. Guano Co. Feb. 12, 1859 | No. 9 Feb. 8, 1860 | transferred to Cook islands by treaty (1980) |
| David's island | 0°40'N 170°10'W | U.S. Guano Co. Feb. 12, 1859 | No. 9 Feb. 8, 1860 | nonexistent |
| Ducie island | 24°40'S 124°48'W | John Daggatt March 10, 1867 | none | annexed by Great Britain, 1902 |

| islands, rocks, and keys (*denotes mining) | alleged location | discoverer or claimant, and filing date | bond number and date | disposition |
|---|---|---|---|---|
| Enderbury island* | 3°08′S<br>171°08′W | Phoenix Guano Co., March 14, 1859 | No. 6<br>Dec. 27, 1859 | transferred to the Republic of Kiribati by treaty (1979) |
| Enderbury island* | 3°08′S<br>174°14′W | U.S. Guano Co.<br>Feb. 12, 1859 | No. 9<br>Feb. 8, 1860 | transferred to the Republic of Kiribati by treaty (1979) |
| Fanning (America, Tabuaeran) island | | | | *see* America island |
| Farmers island | 3°S<br>170°50′W | U.S. Guano Co.<br>Feb. 12, 1859 | No. 9<br>Feb. 8, 1860 | nonexistent |
| Favorite island | 2°50′S<br>176°40′W | U.S. Guano Co.<br>Feb. 12, 1859 | No. 9<br>Feb. 8, 1860 | nonexistent |
| Flint island | 10°32′S<br>162°05′W | U.S. Guano Co.<br>Feb. 12, 1859 | No. 9<br>Feb. 8, 1860 | nonexistent |
| Flint island | 11°26′S<br>151°48′W | U.S. Guano Co.<br>Feb. 12, 1859 | No. 9<br>Feb. 8, 1860 | transferred to the Republic of Kiribati by treaty (1979) |
| Fox island | 51°N<br>59°W | William F. Lunt<br>May 1, 1899 | none | conceded to Canada 1899 |
| Frances island | 9°58′S<br>161°40′W | U.S. Guano Co.<br>Feb. 12, 1859 | No. 9<br>Feb. 8, 1860 | nonexistent |
| FRENCH FRIGATES SHOALS | 23°45′N<br>166°25′W | J.M. Brook | none | annexed to the U.S. with Hawaii, 1898 |
| Frienhaven island | 10°S<br>156°59′W | U.S. Guano Co.<br>Feb. 12, 1859 | No. 9<br>Feb. 8, 1860 | nonexistent |
| Gallego island | 1°42′N<br>104°05′W | U.S. Guano Co.<br>Feb. 12, 1859 | No. 9<br>Feb. 8, 1860 | nonexistent |
| Ganges island | 10°59′S<br>160°55′W | U.S. Guano Co.<br>Feb. 12, 1859 | No. 9<br>Feb. 8, 1860 | nonexistent |
| Gardner (Nikumaroro) island* | 4°40′S<br>174°52′W | U.S. Guano Co.<br>Feb. 12, 1859 | No. 9<br>Feb. 8, 1860 | transferred to the Republic of Kiribati by treaty (1979) |
| Gorda bank | 15°55′N<br>82°15′W | James Jennett<br>Feb. 19, 1887 | none | conceded to Honduras 1919 |
| Great island | 18°46′N<br>87°19′W | James Jennett<br>Jan. 8, 1887 | none | conceded to Mexico 1933 |
| Groninque island | 10°S<br>156°44′W | U.S. Guano Co.<br>Feb. 12, 1859 | No. 9<br>Feb. 8, 1860 | nonexistent |
| HOWLAND (Nowland) ISLAND* | 0°52′N<br>176°52′W | U.S. Guano Co.<br>May 2, 1857 | No. 4<br>Dec. 3, 1858 | unorganized U.S. territory |

| islands, rocks, and keys (*denotes mining) | alleged location | discoverer or claimant, and filing date | bond number and date | disposition |
|---|---|---|---|---|
| Hull (Orona) island* | 4°31′S 172°18′W | none (occupied and mined by Phoenix Guano Co.) | none | transferred to the Republic of Kiribati by treaty (1979) |
| Humphrey's (Manahiki) island | 10°40′S 160°52′W | U.S. Guano Co. Feb. 12, 1859 | No. 9 Feb. 8, 1860 | transferred to Cook islands by treaty (1980) |
| Huon island | 18°S 161°31′E | Andrew C. Cushing Jan. 23, 1877 | none | annexed by France, 1853 |
| JARVIS ISLAND* | 0°21′S 159°52′W | American Guano Co., Aug. 30, 1856 | No. 2 Oct. 28, 1856 | unorganized U.S. territory |
| JOHNSTON (Cornwallis) ATOLL* | 16°45′N 169°32′W | Pacific Guano Co. (Calif.), Aug 29, 1857 | No. 5 Sept. 6, 1859 | unorganized U.S. territory |
| Kemns (Kemmins, Gardners) island | 4°41′S 173°44′W | U.S. Guano Co. Feb. 12, 1859 | No. 9 Feb. 8, 1860 | *see* Gardners island |
| KINGMAN REEF (Dangers rock) | 6°30′N 162°23′W | U.S. Guano Co. Feb. 12, 1859 | No. 9 Feb. 8, 1860 | unorganized U.S. territory |
| Liderons island | 11°05′S 161°50′W | U.S. Guano Co. Feb. 12, 1859 | No. 9 Feb. 8, 1860 | nonexistent |
| Low islands | 9°33′S 170°38′W | U.S. Guano Co. Feb. 12, 1859 | No. 9 Feb. 8, 1860 | nonexistent |
| Macauley's island | 30°13′S 178°33′W | U.S. Guano Co. Jan. 11, 1859 | none | annexed by Great Britain, 1886 |
| Madison (Nukuhiva) island | 80°52′S 140°08′W | W.D. Porter Jan. 5, 1859 | none | annexed by France (Marquisas), 1842 |
| Makin (Mackin) island | 3°02′N 172°46′W | U.S. Guano Co. Feb. 12, 1859 | No. 9 Feb. 8, 1860 | nonexistent |
| Maldens (Independence) island* | 4°S 155°W | U.S. Guano Co. Sept. 13, 1858 | No. 8 Dec. 29, 1859 | transferred to the Republic of Kiribati by treaty (1979) |
| Marcus (Minami Tori Shima) | 24°14′N 154°E | Andrew A. Rosehill Oct. 14, 1889 | none | conceded to Japan 1902 |
| Mary Letitia's island | 4°40′S 173°20′W | U.S. Guano Co. Feb. 12, 1859 | No. 9 Feb. 8, 1860 | nonexistent |
| Mary's (Canton*, Abariringa) island | 2°53′S 172°W | U.S. Guano Co. Feb. 12, 1859 | No. 9 Feb. 8, 1860 | *see* Canton island |
| Mathew's island | 2°03′N 173°26′W | U.S. Guano Co. Feb. 12, 1859 | No. 9 Feb. 8, 1860 | nonexistent |

| islands, rocks, and keys (*denotes mining) | alleged location | discoverer or claimant, and filing date | bond number and date | disposition |
|---|---|---|---|---|
| McKeans island* | 3°35′S<br>174°17′W | Phoenix Guano Co.<br>March 14, 1859 | No. 6<br>Dec. 27, 1859 | transferred to the Republic of Kiribati by treaty (1979) |
| Monita island* | 18°N<br>68°W | Jacob Stokely<br>Feb. 25, 1859 | none | concede to Spain, 1859 (annexed to the U.S. with Puerto Rico, 1898) |
| Monita island* | | Patterson & Murguiondo<br>July 26, 1859 | none | conceded to Spain, 1857 (annexed to the U.S. with Puerto Rico, 1898) |
| Morant keys* | 17°26′N<br>77°55′W | James Jennett<br>May 24, 1869 | No. 13<br>Sept. 8, 1879 | conceded to Great Britain (Jamaica) 1862 |
| Nassau island | 11°30′S<br>165°30′W | U.S. Guano Co.<br>Feb. 12, 1859 | No. 9<br>Feb. 8, 1860 | annexed by Great Britain, 1888 |
| NAVASSA ISLAND* | 18°10′N<br>75°W | E.O and E.K. Cooper<br>Dec. 3, 1857 | No. 3<br>Aug. 31, 1858 | unorganized U.S. territory |
| PALMYRA ISLAND | 5°48′N<br>162°20′W | U.S. Guano Co.<br>Feb. 12, 1859 | No. 9<br>Feb. 8, 1860 | unorganized U.S. territory |
| PEAK (Pajaros) ISLAND | 20°02′N<br>145°10′E | Frederick Crocker<br>Dec. 6, 1859 | none | conceded to Spain 1860 (U.S. Trust Territory, Northern Marianas, 1947) |
| Pedro key | [18°N<br>78°W] | James Jennett<br>March 10, 1869 | No. 12<br>Nov. 22, 1869 | conceded to Great Britain (Jamaica) 1878 |
| Penrhyn (Tongareva) atoll | 8°55′S<br>158°07′W | U.S. Guano Co.<br>Feb. 12, 1859 | No. 9<br>Feb. 8, 1860 | transferred to Cook islands by treaty (1980) |
| Pescado island | 10°38′S<br>159°20′W | U.S. Guano Co.<br>Feb. 12, 1859 | No. 9<br>Feb. 8, 1860 | nonexistent |
| PETREL ISLAND* | [15°50′N<br>78°40′W] | James Jennett<br>Aug. 9, 1869 | No. 12<br>Nov. 22, 1869 | status unclear |
| Phoenix (Rawaki) island | 3°40′S<br>170°52′W | U.S. Guano Co.<br>Feb. 12, 1859 | No. 9<br>Feb. 8, 1860 | transferred to the Republic of Kiribati by treaty (1979) |
| Phoenix (Rawaki) island* | 3°47′S<br>170°55′W | Phoenix Guano Co.<br>May 14, 1859 | No. 6<br>Dec. 27, 1859 | transferred to the Republic of Kiribati by treaty (1979) |

| islands, rocks, and keys (*denotes mining) | alleged location | discoverer or claimant, and filing date | bond number and date | disposition |
|---|---|---|---|---|
| Prospect island | 4°42'N 161°38'W | U.S. Guano Co. Feb. 12, 1859 | No. 9 Feb. 8, 1860 | nonexistent |
| Quito Sueo island | [14°N 81°10'W] | James Jennett May 26, 1869 | No. 12 Nov. 22, 1869 | transferred to Colombia by treaty (1972) |
| Rierson's island | 10°10'S 160°53'W | U.S. Guano Co. Feb. 12, 1859 | No. 9 Feb. 8, 1860 | transferred to Cook islands by treaty (1980) |
| Rogewein's islands | 11°S 156°07'W | U.S. Guano Co. Feb. 12, 1859 | No. 9 Feb. 8, 1860 | nonexistent |
| Roncador island* | [13°15'N 80°40'W] | James Jennett May 26, 1869 | No. 12 Nov. 22, 1869 | transferred to Colombia by treaty (1972) |
| Roques island | 10°50'N 66°40'W | James Jennett May 28, 1869 | none | conceded to Venezuela, 1869 |
| Samarang islands (PALMYRA) | 5°10'N 162°20'W | U.S. Guano Co. Feb. 12, 1859 | No. 9 Feb. 8, 1860 | *see* Palmyra |
| Sarah Anne island | 4°N 154°22'W | U.S. Guano Co. Feb. 12, 1859 | No. 9 Feb. 8, 1860 | nonexistent |
| Serraña keys | 14°20'N 80°13'W | James Jennett June 30, 1866 | No. 11 Aug. 12, 1868 | transferred to Colombia by treaty (1972) |
| SERRANILLA KEYS* | 15°20'N 79°40'W | James Jennett May 24, 1869 | No. 14 Sept. 13, 1880 | U.S. reserves the right to claim |
| SERRANILLA KEYS* | 15°20'N 79°40'W | Pascal A. Quinan Oct. 25, 1882 | none | U.S. reserves the right to claim |
| Sombrero island* | 18°35'N 63°27'W | Copeland and Gowan Nov. 13, 1856 | none | annexed by Great Britain, 1904 |
| Starbuck (Barren) island* | 5°40'S 155°55'W | U.S. Guano Co. Feb. 12, 1859 | No. 9 Feb. 8, 1860 | transferred to the Republic of Kiribati by treaty (1979) |
| SWAINS (Quiros) ATOLL | 10°32'S 170°12'W | U.S. Guano Co. Feb. 12, 1859 | No. 9 Feb. 8, 1860 | assigned to American Samoa, 1925 (unorganized U.S. territory) |
| Swan islands* | 17°36'N 83°58'W | Atlantic & Pacific Guano Co., May 15, 1857 | No. 10 Dec. 30, 1862 | transferred to Honduras by treaty (1972) |
| Sydney (Manra) island* | 4°20'S 171°W | U.S. Guano Co. Feb. 12, 1859 | No. 9 Feb. 8, 1860 | transferred to the Republic of Kiribati by treaty (1979) |

| islands, rocks, and keys (*denotes mining) | alleged location | discoverer or claimant, and filing date | bond number and date | disposition |
|---|---|---|---|---|
| Verd key (Cayo Verde)* | 22°N<br>75°10′W | W.T. Kendall<br>May 24, 1859 | none | conceded to Great Britain (Bahamas), 1860 |
| Vivorilla (Vivorio) key* | | Julius Schultz<br>Sept. 14, 1887 | none | claimed by Honduras and Nicaragua |
| Vivorilla (Vivorio) key* | 15°50′N<br>83°18′W | P. Murguiondo<br>Aug. 16, 1882 | none | claimed by Honduras and Nicaragua |
| Vostok (Stavers) island | 10°05′S<br>152°16′W | U.S. Guano Co.<br>Feb. 12, 1859 | No. 9<br>Feb. 8, 1860 | transferred to the Republic of Kiribati by treaty (1979) |
| Walkers island | 3°58′N<br>149°10′W | U.S. Guano Co.<br>Feb. 12, 1859 | No. 9<br>Feb. 8, 1860 | nonexistent |
| Washington (Uahuga, Teraina) island | 4°40′N<br>160°07′W | U.S. Guano Co.<br>Feb. 12, 1859 | No. 9<br>Feb. 8, 1860 | annexed by Great Britain, 1892 |
| Western Triangle keys* | 20°54′N<br>92°13′W | James Jennett | No. 14<br>Sept. 13, 1880 | conceded to Mexico, 1894 |
| Woody key | 12°47′N<br>82°30′W | Pascal A. Quinan<br>Dec. 4, 1886 | none | nonexistent |
| York, Duke of (Atafu), island | 8°30′S<br>172°10′W | U.S. Guano Co.<br>Feb. 12, 1859 | No. 9<br>Feb. 8, 1860 | annexed by Great Britain, 1889 |

# NOTES

Citations follow scientific style. Complete references for each entry appear in the Bibliography.

## Preface

1. Skaggs (1975), *passim,* especially pp. 532-43.
2. A. Smith, pp. 325-590.
3. Bourgin, *passim.*
4. Gara, p. 149.

## Chapter 1: Supply, Demand, Price, and Politics

1. Brand, (MS.), p. 6; "Guano" (1867), p. 261; "Guano" (1989), VI: 911; Jacob, "Predecessors," p. 11; Nesbit, p. 13.
2. Collings, pp. 1-2; Lamer, pp. 1-6; Mather and Hart, p. 25; F.M.L. Thompson, p. 64.
3. Blakey, pp. 6-7; Collings, pp. 1-3; Lamer, pp. 36-37; Mather and Hart, pp. 25-27; M. W. Rossiter, pp. 10-28.
4. Blakey, pp. 6-7; Collings, pp. 1-3; Fairbanks and Berkey, pp. 93-94; Jacob, "History," pp. 21-22; Lamer, pp. 36-37; Liebig, pp. 213-21, 247-51, 371; Mather and Hart, pp. 25-27; Mokyr, pp. 120-21; Penrose, p. 21; Rasin, p. 6; M. W. Rossiter, pp. 10-28.
   Lawes's apatite was actually "coprolites," or petrified dung.
5. M. A. Smith (MS.), pp. 1-19; Wines (MS.), pp. 1-54; Craven, *passim*; Gras, pp. 191-92, 201, 205, 218, 292-93; Hedrick, pp. 346-47; Hesseltine, pp. 45, 277; M. W. Rossiter, pp. 3-9.
6. Gardiner (MS.), p. 49; Craven, p. 144; Rasmussen, p. 521.
7. Gardiner (MS.), pp. 28-29; Jordan, p. 211; Marti, pp. 28-31; Rasmussen, p. 521.
8. Skinner, p. 316.
9. Wines (MS.), pp. 81-85; U.S. Congress. H. Rept. 347. Serial 744, p. 5.
10. B[rowne], p. 91; Galarza, pp. 5-11; Hutchinson (1950), pp. 9-15; Levin, pp. 27-29; Liebig, p. 80; T. Moore, p. 45; Murphy (1925), pp. 45-70; Peck, pp. 153-73, 197-202; Tappy, pp. 186-87; U.S. Congress. H. Rept. 347. Serial 744, p. 6.
11. M. A. Smith (MS.), p. 24; A. J. Boyd, p. 4; B[rowne], p. 90; Fairbanks and Berkey, p. 93; Galarza, pp. 12-13; Haynes, p. 340; Hutchinson (1950), p. 3; Jacob, "Predecessors," p. 11; Jordan, p. 213; Levin, pp. 29-30; Penrose, p. 21; Tappy, p. 187; U.S. Congress. H. Rept. 347. Serial 744, p. 23.
12. Espinosa, p. 518; Levin, p. 30; Olinger (1980), p. 14.

13. Quoted in Levin, p. 30.

14. Howard, p. 235; Jacob, "Predecessors," p. 13; Levin, p. 30; Rasin, p. 5; U.S. Congress. H. Rept. 347. Serial 744, p. 23.

15. Mathew (1981), p. 25.

16. Jacob, "Predecessors," p. 13; Mathew (1981), pp. 22-25; Millington, p. 15.
Very early on *huano* (pronounced "wha-no" in Spanish) was rendered as "guano" (enunciated with a hard "g") in English. See Skinner, p. 316.

17. Mathew (1981), pp. 22-25; Werlich, pp. 80.

18. *Ibid.*, p. 27; Mathew (1977), p. 338.

19. Pike, p. 97.

20. Haynes, p. 341; Jacob, "Predecessors," p. 13; F.M.L. Thompson, p. 70.; Ant[on]y Gibbs & Sons, pp. 13-14.

21. F. M. L. Thompson, p. 70.

22. Kidd (1845), p. 327.
For other health risks related to guano, see also Kidd (1845-46); G. C. Watson (1845 and 1845-46); and Wearne.

23. Mathew (1981), p. 29.

24. Kann and David, pp. 163-64, 206; Penrose, p. 118.

25. Cochet, pp. 3-8; Levin, pp. 52-53; Mathew (1981), pp. 27-36; Pike, pp. 96-97; U.S. Congress. H. Rept. 347. Serial 744, p. 23.

26. Gardiner (MS.), pp. 63-64; Olinger (MS., 1973), p. 15; Gootenberg (1989), pp. 81-82, 128-30; Herring, p. 597; Mathew (1981), pp. 36-37; U.S. Congress. S. Exec. Doc. 25. Serial 981, pp. 72-75; Werlich, p. 81.

27. Mathew (1977), pp. 338-39.

28. Gardiner (MS.), pp. 23-24; B[rowne], pp. 95-96; Fuess, p. 1; L. C. Green, pp. 88-97; Jordan, p. 215; Mathew (1981), pp. 57-69; Penrose, pp. 21, 119.

29. B[rowne], pp. 95-96; Fuess, p. 1; L. G. Green, pp. 88-97; Mathew (1981), pp. 57-69.
Interestingly, Livingstone had learned of Ichaboe's existence by reading the memoirs of American mariner, Benjamin Morrell. See B. Morrell, pp. 293-94. Principal African Guano islands included Bird and St. Croix islands off Port Elizabeth, South Africa, Seal island in False bay, near Cape Town, Ichaboe and Dassen islands near Saint Helena bay, S.A., Seal island near Luderitz, Namibia, and Halifax island off Walis bay, Namibia.

30. Gardiner (MS.), pp. 29-30; Wines (MS.), p. 89; Jordan, p. 216; Mathew (1977), p. 338; Mathew (1981), pp. 57-69; Rutter, p. 43.
Rutter says 445 of the 700 tons went to Baltimore.

31. Wines (MS.), pp. 96-97.

32. Gardiner (MS.), pp. 31-33; Liebig, pp. 80-82, 188-90; Jordan, pp. 211-21; M. W. Rossiter, pp. 39, 43.

33. Washington, p. 464.

34. Quoted in M. A. Smith (MS.), pp. 52-53. See also R. H. Taylor (July 1953), pp. 305-11, and Eaton, pp. 180-81.

35. Jacob, "Predecessor," p. 13.

36. Decker (1986), p. 113.

37. Gardiner (MS.), pp. 33-38, 40-46; M. A. Smith (MS.), p. 46; Galarza, p. 3; Gates, p. 108.; Gras, p. 293; Millington, p. 15; U.S. Agriculture commissioner, p. 292.

38. Gardiner (MS.), pp. 64-66. 91; M. A. Smith (MS.), p. 44; Wines (MS.), p. 147; L. C. Gray, p. 701; Maryland (1858), pp. 215-18; Rutter, pp. 43-49; Robinson, pp. 80-83; U.S. Statistics bureau, "Compiled report for guano imported into the United States, 1848-67," in U.S. State department, *Records . . . relating to guano islands, 1852-1912* (1975), Reel 7, and U.S. Treasury department, *Foreign commerce and navigation,* annual reports commencing 1847.

39. Mathew (1977), p. 338; U.S. Statistics bureau, "Compiled report for guano imported into the United States, 1848-67," in U.S. State department, *Records . . . relating to guano islands, 1852-1912,* Reel 7; M. A. Smith (1942), p. 44.

40. B[rowne], p. 93.

41. *Ibid.*; Gardiner (MS.), pp. 57-61; Haynes, p. xliv; "Inspection laws," pp. 81-82; Jacob, "Predecessors," p. 14; Rutter, pp. 45-48; "Story of the fertilizer industry," p. 30.

42. B[rowne], p. 93; Haynes, p. xliv; "Inspection laws," pp. 81-82; Jacob, "Predecessors," p. 14; Rutter, pp. 45-48; "Story of the fertilizer industry," p. 30.

In 1854 the Maryland law was amended to require the classification and grading of guano by place of origin and nitrogen and phosphorus content. See Maryland (1858), pp. 215-19.

43. Gardiner (MS.), p. 61; U.S. Census bureau (1960), pp. 139, 278; U.S. Congress. S. Exec. Doc. 59. Serial 561, pp. 6-7.

44. U.S. Congress. S. Exec. Doc. 59. Serial 561, pp. 6-7.

45. Quoted in U.S. Congress. S. Exec. Doc. 80. Serial 562, p. 2.

46. U.S. Congress. S. Exec. Doc. 59. Serial 561, pp. 7-8.

47. Rasmussen, p. 521; U.S. Census bureau (1960), pp. 14, 141.

48. "Petitions to the 28th Congress regarding duties on guano," U.S. House Records, HR28A, G24.2, Record Group 233 (National Archives).

49. U.S. Treasury department, *Annual report: foreign commerce and navigation* (1848), p. 258.

50. Baxter, p. 473.

51. U.S. Congress. S. Exec. Doc. 59. Serial 561, p. 1.

52. Senate *Journal.* Serial 548, p. 386.

53. Nichols (1956), p. 158.

54. U.S. Congress. S. Exec. Doc. 58. Serial 561, p. 5. See also, U.S. State department, *Treaties* (1981), X: 999-1000.

55. Nichols (1956), p. 160.

56. U.S. Congress. S. Exec. Doc. 59. Serial 561, p. 2; U.S. Congress. H. Rept. 347. Serial 744, p. 32.

57. U.S. Congress. S. Exec. Doc. 59. Serial 561, pp. 3, 4; U.S. Congress. H. Rept. 347. Serial 744, p. 34.

58. Nichols (1956), p. 160.

59. U.S. Congress. H. Rept. 347. Serial 744, p. 39.

60. Nichols (1933), p. 521; Nichols (1956), pp. 160-61; Shewmaker, pp. 324-25; M. A. Smith (MS.), pp. 59-60; U.S. Congress. H. Rept. 347. Serial 744, pp. 17-36.

61. E. B. Smith, pp. 167, 220. See also Rayback, p. vii.
62. Nichols (1933), *passim.*
63. Shewmaker, pp. 324-25.
64. *Ibid.*, p. 325.
65. U.S. Congress. S. Exec. Doc. 80. Serial 562, pp. 1-2.
66. Nichols (1933), p. 521.
67. U.S. Congress. S. Exec. Doc. 80. Serial 562, pp. 1-2.
68. U.S. Presidents (1910), IV: 2619.
69. U.S. Congress. H. Rept. 347. Serial 744, p. 7.
70. Sam[ue]l K. George, Baltimore, to Dan[ie]l Webster, 3 Dec[embe]r 1850, in Webster *Papers,* reel 41. See also Werlich, p. 82.
71. George to Webster, 7 Dec[embe]r 1850, in Webster *Papers,* reel 41.
72. Boland (MS.), pp. 5-6; Gardiner (MS.), p. 33; Nichols (1956), p. 161; Olinger (1980), p. 15; Robinson, *passim*; Rutter, p. 41; Sherman, pp. 18-25; M. A. Smith (1943), p. 10; U.S. Congress. S. Exec. Doc. 25. Serial 981, p. 73. See also U.S. Congress. S. Rept. 397. Serial 891.

    About 1860, C. L. Bartlett again became agent for the Peruvian government, selling Chinca island guano in Boston. See Bartlett, *passim.*
73. Gootenberg (MS.), pp. 390-400; Olinger (1980), p. 16; Mathew (1977), pp. 337-70.

    Through special licenses and contracts, Gibbs & Sons continued to handle some Peruvian exports as late as 1861. See U.S. Congress. S. Exec. Doc. 25. Serial 981, pp. 6-8.
74. M. A. Smith (MS.), p. 44; U.S. Census bureau (1960), p. 285; U.S. Statistics bureau, "Compiled report for guano imported into the United States, 1848-67," in U.S. State department, *Records,* Reel 7; U.S. Congress. H. Rept. 347. Serial 744, p. 7.

## Chapter 2: The Entrepreneur and Daniel Webster

1. "Guano war."
2. Nichols (1956), pp. 192-93. See also Rayback, pp. 319-21; E. B. Smith, pp. 226-28.
3. Webster (1974-87), series 3, II: 716.
4. "Other deaths."
5. Benson's obituary in the *New York Times* gives his date of birth as 1804 whereas 1850 census data for Brooklyn, Kings County, New York, lists his age as forty-three, hence c. 1807. See "Other deaths"; U.S. Census bureau, *Manuscript census returns, 1850,* roll 517, p. 272.
6. "Other deaths"; U.S. Congress. H. Rept. 161. Serial 466, p. 1; U.S. Census bureau, *Manuscript census returns, 1850,* roll 517, p. 272; Webster (1974-87), series 1, VI: 344.
7. A. G. Benson, p. 19.
8. U.S. Congress. S. Rept. 319. Serial 593, p. 1.
9. A. G. Benson, p. 19.
10. U.S. Congress. H. Rept. 161. Serial 466, pp. 1-2.
11. A. G. Benson, p. 19; U.S. Congress. S. Rept. 319. Serial 593, p. 2.
12. A. G. Benson, p. 19.

13. U.S. Congress. S. Rept. 319. Serial 593, p. 1.

14. *Ibid,* p. 2; A. G. Benson, p. 19; Webster (1974-87), series 1, VI: 343-44.
According to editors of *The papers of Daniel Webster,* series 1, VI: 344, n. 1, the Bensons collected $10,792 in 1851 whereas Alfred Benson (p. 19) says he received $18,000.

15. "Other deaths."

16. Webster (1974-87), series 1, VII: 396.

17. G. P. Judd, IV (1960), p. 208.

18. Webster (1974-87), series 1, IV: 208.

19. Shewmaker, p. 336.

20. Benson, said by Webster's editors to be a "commercial merchant in New York [and] partner of Charles March" (Webster, 1974-87, series 1, IV: 208, n.1) clearly was not the same "Alfred G. Benson" identified by Webster's correspondence as March's business associate in 1809, when A. G. Benson of Lobos Affair fame would have been two-to-five years of age. Perhaps the elder A. G. Benson was the younger man's father as well as March's first Benson partner. See *ibid.,* I: 47, 110.

21. *Ibid.*

22. *Ibid.*, VI: 343-44.

23. Foner, pp. 56, 57.

24. Current, pp. 14-25.

25. *Ibid.*, pp. 25-26.

26. *Ibid.*, pp. 47-114.

27. Webster (1974-87), series 3, II: 760. See also Current, pp. 115-83.

28. Gardiner (MS.), p. 77; Stevers and Pendlebury, pp. 105-107; Murphy (1925), pp. 310-46; Shewmaker, pp. 322-23; Olinger (1973), p. 4; Herring, p. 597; Great Britain (1852), p. 73.
Lobos de Afuera (actually two islets separated by a narrow channel) is situated $7^{o}$ 3'S, $80^{o}$ 42'W, and Lobos de Tierra, $6^{o}$ 27'S, $80^{o}$ 52'W.

29. A. G. Benson, p. 3; M. A. Smith (1943), p. 10.

30. Great Britain (1852), p. 33. See also B. Morrell, 119ff.

31. Great Britain (1852), *passim.*

32. For examples, see "Guano on the Lobos"; "The Lobos guano islands"; "Guano at the Lobos"; and *New York Daily Times,* June 14, 1852, p. 1.

33. A. G. Benson, p. 4.
Aside from Benson's assertion, no other claim of continuous U.S. occupation of the Lobos islands has been found.

34. Quoted in *ibid.,* pp. 3-4; Webster (1974-87), series 3, II: 736; U.S. Congress. S. Rept. 397. Serial 891, p. 1.
It appears that Secretary Webster, like the public at large, did not learn of Benson's involvement in Jewett's Lobos enterprise until late August. See U.S. Congress. S. Rept. 397. Serial 891, p. 220.

35. Nichols (1933), pp. 523-24; Shewmaker, pp. 335-39.

36. Shewmaker p. 335.

37. A. G. Benson, pp. 4-6; Nichols (1933), p. 523; Shewmaker, p. 336; U.S. Congress. S. Rept. 397. Serial 891, p. 2; Webster (1974-87), series 3, II: 738.

38. A. G. Benson, pp. 4-6; Nichols (1933), p. 523; Shewmaker, p. 336; U.S. Congress. S. Rept. 397. Serial 891, p. 2; Webster (1974-87), series 3, II: 738.

39. A. G. Benson, pp. 19-20.

40. *Ibid.*, pp. 20. See also U.S. Congress. S. Rept. 397. Serial 891, p. 3.

41. R. E. Johnson, p. 106.

42. A. G. Benson, pp. 20, 7. See also U.S. Congress. S. Rept. 397. Serial 891, p. 3.

43. A. G. Benson, p. 27.

44. E. B. Smith, p. 226.

45. Rayback, p. 319.

46. A. G. Benson, pp. 7-8, 20; Shewmaker, pp. 326-27; U.S. Congress. S. Rept. 397. Serial 891, pp. 204-17, 258-60.

47. A. G. Benson, p. 6; Nichols (1933), p. 523.

48. Webster (1974-87), series 3, II: 739.

49. Gardiner (MS.), p. 79; A. G. Benson, pp. 9-10; Shewmaker, pp. 327-28; U.S. Congress. S. Rept. 397. Serial 891, pp. 3-5.

50. U.S. Congress. S. Rept. 397. Serial 891, pp. 30-32; U.S. Congress. S. Exec. Doc. 109. Serial 621, p. 3.

51. U.S. Congress. S. Rept. 397. Serial 891, p. 33; U.S. Congress. S. Exec. Doc. 109. Serial 621, p. 4.

52. U.S. Congress. S. Rept. 397. Serial 891, pp. 33-37; U.S. Congress. S. Exec. Doc. 109. Serial 621, pp. 1, 4-7.

53. Shewmaker, p. 328.

54. Webster (1974-87), series 3, II: 743.

55. *Ibid.*, p. 744. See also Sherman, pp. 25.

56. *Ibid.*, pp. 747, 748, 750-51; U.S. Congress. S. Rept. 397. Serial 891, 42.

57. "Lobos documents"; Webster (1974-87), series 3, II: 756-57.

58. "The guano war."

59. R. G. Ward, IV: 69.

60. "The Lobos islands." For a discussion of Webster's nicknames and public ethics, see Summers, p. 188.

61. Boland (MS.), p. 9.

62. Webster (1974-87), series 3, II: 755.

63. Millard Fillmore to Edward Everett, April 7, 1855 (Everett Papers).

64. Shewmaker, p. 332.

65. *Ibid.*; Nichols (1933), pp. 526-27; U.S. Congress. S. Exec. Doc. 109, part 2. Serial 621, p. 1; Fillmore to Everett, April 7, 1855 (Everett Papers).

Fillmore biographers R. J. Rayback, pp. 318-21, and E. B. Smith, pp. 226-27, have sanitized the president's contribution to this bumble in foreign policy by omitting any mention of Fillmore's initials of approval for Webster's flawed Lobos policy.

66. U.S. Congress. S. Exec. Doc. 109. Serial 621, p. 12; U.S. Congress. S. Rept. 397. Serial 891, p. 42.

67. U.S. Congress. S. Exec. Doc. 109, part 2. Serial 621, p. 2.

Graham had resigned as Navy secretary in order to become Winfield Scott's running mate in the election of 1852; they lost. See Coletta, I: 266, 269.

68. U.S. Congress. S. Rept. 397. Serial 891, p. 6. See also "The Lobos question; Mr. Webster's letter."

69. Webster (1974-87), series 3, II: 760.

70. Quoted in Gardiner (MS.), p. 82.

71. Webster (1974-87), series 3, II: 770.

72. A. G. Benson, p. 20.

73. Webster (1974-87), series 3, II: 774.

74. Quoted in "Mr. Webster."

75. "Mr. Benson."

76. Quoted in "Mr. Webster."

Although subsequently published in the *Daily Times,* Webster's September 30, 1852, letter to Benson is not included in Webster's published papers, which otherwise thoroughly covers the Lobos affair. See Webster (1974-87), *passim.*

77. Quoted in "Mr. Webster."

78. U.S. Congress. S. Rept. 397. Serial 891, pp. 169-70.

79. *Ibid.,* pp. 171-72; A. G. Benson, p. 24.

80. U.S. Congress. S. Rep. 397. Serial 891, p. 173.

81. A. G. Benson, p. 27.

For a list of Benson's guano fleet, see U.S. Congress. S. Rept. 397. Serial 891, pp. 258-60.

82. A. G. Benson, p. 27.

83. U.S. Congress. S. Rept. 397. Serial 891, pp. 230-38.

84. *Ibid.,* p. 283.

85. A. G. Benson, pp. 27-28.

86. "The function of private bills," pp. 329-333, 347. See also U.S. Congress. S. Miscellaneous Doc. 14. Serials 1945-1946, *passim.*

In the Fortieth Congress (1867-69), 415 (52.5 percent) were private bills, and in the Fifty-ninth Congress (1905-07), 6,249 (89 percent).

87. Quoted in "The function of private bills," p. 349. See also *Ibid.,* p. 346.

88. *Ibid.,* p. 340.

89. *Ibid.* pp. 345-47.

The nineteenth-century champion of the private veto was Grover Cleveland, who disapproved 482 measures, only three of which were overridden by Congress. During his twelve years in office, Franklin Roosevelt vetoed 497 private bills, none of which was overridden. Harry Truman, with 175 vetoes (and one override) in little more than a single year, was well on his way toward the record when, in 1946, the Legislative Reorganization Act banned the introduction of most categories of private legislation. *Ibid.,* pp. 329, 346.

90. U.S. Senate *Journal.* Serial 745, p. 177; U.S. Congress. S. Rept. 397. Serial 891, p. 27.

91. U.S. Senate *Journal.* Serial 745, p. 282.
92. U.S. Congress. S. Exec. Doc. 61. Serial 752, pp. 1-3.
93. U.S. Senate *Journal.* Serial 745, p. 314.
94. U.S. *Congressional globe* (33d Cong., 2d sess.), XXX: 1096.
95. *Ibid.,* 1086.
96. *Ibid.,* p. 1122.
97. *Ibid.,* p. 1122.

## Chapter 3: Turtles and Birds: Cases of Mistaken Identities

1. R. B. Morris," pp. 216-18.
2. U.S. Presidents, *Compilation,* IV: 2745.
3. Robinson, pp. 1-2.
4. Olinger (MS.), pp. 25-29; M. A. Smith (MS.), p. 44; "Birds do it," p. 1; "Casa Grace," p. 158; Gordon, p. 95; U.S. Congress. H. Exec. Doc. 70. Serial 723, p. 3; U.S. Treasury department, *Annual reports: foreign commerce and navigation,* (1852), p. 266, (1854), p. 276.
5. U.S. Congress. S. Miscellaneous Doc. 18. Serial 705, p. 1.
6. U.S. *Congressional globe* (33 Cong., 1st sess.), XXVIII (part 1): 336, 392.
7. U.S. Congress. H. Exec. Doc. 70. Serial 723, p. 1.
8. *Ibid.*, p. 4. See also U.S. Congress. S. Exec. Doc. 25. Serial 981, pp. 2-12.
9. U.S. *Congressional globe* (33d Cong., 1st sess.), XXVIII (part 1): 1144, 1194; U.S. Congress. H. Rept. 347. Serial 744), pp. 1-2. As to the size of Peru's guano reserves, see U.S. Congress. S. Exec. Doc. 25. Serial 981, pp. 14-18.
10. U.S. *Congressional globe* (33d Cong., 1st sess.), XXVIII (part 1): 1194.
11. U.S. Congress. H. Rept. 347. Serial 744, pp. 20-31. See also, U.S. Congress. H. Doc. 100-245 (Y1.1/7: 100-245), p. 299; U.S. Congress. S. Exec. Doc. 25. Serial 981, 2-12.
12. U.S. House of Representatives, Resolution 509, 33d Cong., 1st sess. (House Records). See also U.S. Congress. H. Rept. 347. Serial 744, p. 1.
13. House *Journal,* 33d Cong., 1st sess. (709), p. 1240.
14. Maryland, pp. 215-16.
15. Wines (MS.), p. 156.
16. *Ibid.,* pp. 156-57; Maryland, pp. 217-18.
17. Wines (MS.), pp. 156-57.
18. *Ibid.,* p. 155; Gruss, pp. 162, 165; Nichols (1933), pp. 532-33; Nichols (1956), p. 170.
19. Nichols (1933), p. 533; Nichols (1956), p. 171. See also, U.S. State department, Legal Adviser's office, "Sovereignty of islands claimed under the Guano Act" (MS.), p. 889, and Gruss, pp. 162-64.
20. U.S. Congress. S. Exec. Doc. 31. Serial 751, p. 10. See also B[rowne], p. 95.
21. Wines (MS.), pp. 154-55; Gruss, pp. 163, 166; Nichols (1933), pp. 533-34; Nichols (1956), p. 172.
22. Wines (MS.), pp. 154-55; Gruss, pp. 163, 166; Nichols (1933), pp. 533-34; Nichols (1956), p. 172.
23. Gruss, p. 165.

24. Gardiner (MS.), pp. 114-115; Wines (MS.), pp. 154-55; Gruss, pp. 164-69; Hurtado, p. 88; Nichols (1933), pp. 535-37; Nichols (1956), pp. 172-74.
25. Wines (MS.), pp. 154-55; Gruss, pp. 166-68; Nichols (1933), pp. 535-36; Nichols (1956), pp. 173-74.
26. Boland (MS.), p. 19; Gruss, p. 169; Nichols (1933), p. 536; Nichols (1956), p. 174; U.S. Senate *Journal.* Serial 745, p. 147; U.S. Congress. S. Exec. Doc. 31. Serial 751, *passim.*
27. Nichols (1958), p. 376.
28. Forbes, p. 50; U.S. Congress. S. Exec. Doc. 25. Serial 879, p. 62.
29. W. L. Harris (MS.), p. 6.
30. *Ibid.*, pp. 6-9; Gardiner (MS.), p. 119; M. A. Smith (MS.), p. 55; Wines (MS.), p. 161; Nichols (1933), p. 537; Nichols (1956), pp. 179-80; U.S. Congress. S. Ex. Doc. 10. Serial 1082, pp. 43, 72; U.S. Congress. S. Exec. Doc. 25. Serial 879, pp. 62-63, 87-88; U.S. State department, *Treaties and other international acts* (1948), VIII: 144.
    For a description of Aves island, see Bainbridge, *passim.*
31. U.S. Congress. S. Exec. Doc. 25. Serial 879, p. 63.
32. W. L. Harris (MS.), pp. 9-10; U.S. Congress. S. Exec. Doc. 25. Serial 879, p. 63.
33. W. L. Harris (MS.), pp. 11-12; W. J. Davis, pp. 114, 134, 149-50, 153, 263, 399; Forbes, p. 51; U.S. Congress. S. Exec. Doc. 10. Serial 1082, pp. 65-66, 142; U.S. Congress. S. Exec. Doc. 25. Serial 879, pp. 63, 88; [U.S.] Works Projects Administration, p. 137.
34. U.S. Congress. S. Exec. Doc. 25. Serial 879, pp. 65, 88. See also W. L. Harris (MS.), pp. 11-12, and U.S. Congress. S. Exec. Doc. 10. Serial 1082, pp. 65-67.
35. U.S. Congress. S. Exec. Doc. 10. Serial 1082, p. 67.
36. U.S. Congress. S. Exec. Doc. 25. Serial 879, p. 65.
37. *Ibid.*, pp. 65, 88-89.
38. *Ibid.*, pp. 2, 65, 73.
39. *Ibid.*; W. H. Gray, p. 73; Nesbit, pp. 10-12, 43; W. J. Taylor (March 1857), pp. 91-94; W. J. Taylor (September 1857), pp. 177-80; U.S. Agriculture department, *Report . . . for 1869,* pp. 74-75.
40. U.S. State department, *Treaties and other international acts* (1948), VIII: 154-55.
41. W. L. Harris (MS.), p. 14; U.S. Congress. S. Exec. Doc. 25. Serial 879, pp. 66, 91-93.
42. U.S. Congress. S. Exec. Doc. 25. Serial 879, p. 3. See also M. A. Smith (1943), p. 11.
43. U.S. Congress. S. Exec. Doc. 25. Serial 879, p. 6. See also U.S. State department, *Treaties and other international acts* (1948), VIII: 144.
44. W. L. Harris (MS.), pp. 51-52; W. H. Gray, p. 74; Nichols (1933), p. 537; Nichols (1956), p. 180; Morón, pp. 160-66; Rasin, p. 8; U.S. Congress. S. Exec. Doc. 25. Serial 879, p. 7.
45. U.S. Congress. S. Exec. Doc. 25. Serial 879, p. 68. See also W. L. Harris (MS.), p. 21.
46. W. L. Harris (MS.), 22-27; U.S. Congress. S. Exec. Doc. 10. Serial 1082, pp. 8-9, 22, 25; U.S. Congress. S. Exec. Doc. 25. Serial 879, pp. 11, 68-71, 74-75.
47. U.S. Congress. S. Exec. Doc. 25. Serial 879, p. 71. See also W. L. Harris (MS.), pp. 30-31.
48. W. L. Harris (MS.), pp. 28, 31-33; W. H. Gray, p. 74; Nichols (1933), pp. 537-38; Nichols (1956), pp. 179-80; U.S. Congress. S. Exec. Doc. 10. Serial 1082, pp. 26-28; U.S. Congress. S. Exec. Doc. 25. Serial 879, p. 72.

49. W. L. Harris (MS.), pp. 52-53; W. H. Gray, 74-76; Nichols (1933), p. 538; Nichols (1956), pp. 180-81; U.S. Congress. S. Exec. Doc. 10. Serial 1082, pp. 170-71; U.S. Congress. S. Exec. Doc. 25. Serial 879, pp. 7, 12-15.

50. W. H. Gray, p. 76; U.S. Congress. S. Exec. Doc. 25. Serial 879, pp. 21-25.

51. U.S. State department, "Sovereignty," pp. 435-36.

52. *Ibid.*, pp. 436-37; U.S. State department, *Digest of international law* (1906) I: 576-77.

53. U.S. Congress. S. Exec. Doc. 10. Serial 1082, p. 5.

54. *Ibid.*, p. 7.

55. U.S. Senate *Journal.* Serial 1948, VIII: 154-55; U.S. Congress. S. Exec. Doc. 10. Serial 1082, pp. 7, 37, 95; U.S. Congress. S. Exec. Doc. 25. Serial 879, p. 5; U.S. State department, *Treaties and other international acts* (1948) VIII: 140-45.

56. U.S. Congress. S. Exec. Doc. 25. Serial 879, p. 5.

57. *Ibid.*, pp. 5-13; W. L. Harris (MS.), pp. 47-51; U.S. State department, *Treaties and other international acts* (1948), VIII: 144-45.

58. W. L. Harris (MS.), pp. 49-51; U.S. Congress. S. Exec. Doc. 25. Serial 879, pp. 26-30; U.S. State department, *Treaties and other international acts* (1948) VIII: 145.

59. Quoted in W. L. Harris (MS.), p. 43.

60. *Ibid.*, pp. 35-36, 38-43.

61. U.S. Congress. S. Exec. Doc. 10. Serial 1082, pp. 21-25. See also *ibid.*, pp. 47-48.

62. *Ibid.*, pp. 25-26.

63. *Ibid.*, pp. 26, 38.

64. *Ibid.*, pp. 10-26; W. L. Harris (MS.), pp. 45-46.

65. W. L. Harris (MS.), p. 47, n. 20.

66. U.S. Congress. S. Exec. Doc. 25. Serial 879, p. 91.

67. *Ibid.*, pp. 82, 141; W. L. Harris (MS.), p. 62.

68. W. L. Harris (MS.), p. 63.

69. *Ibid.* pp. 62-66; U.S. Congress. S. Exec. Doc. 10. Serial 1082, pp. 103-107.

70. W. L. Harris (MS.), pp. 65-76; W. H. Gray, 75-77; Nichols (1933), p. 539; Nichols (1956), p. 182; U.S. Congress. S. Exec. Doc. 10. Serial 1082, pp. 82-93; U.S. Congress. S. Exec. Doc. 25. Serial 879, pp. 31-92; U.S. State department, *Treaties and other international acts* (1948) VIII: 162.

71. U.S. Congress. S. Exec. Doc. 10. Serial 1082, p. 80.

72. W. L. Harris (MS.), p. 67. See also Nichols (1958), *passim.*

73. U.S. Congress. S. Exec. Doc. 10. Serial 1082, pp. 129-31.

74. U.S. Congress. S. Exec. Doc. 25. Serial 879, pp. 93-95.

75. U.S. Senate *Journal.* Serial 809, p. 167; U.S. Congress. S. Miscellaneous Doc. 60. Serial 835, p. 2.

76. Although Shelton's petition was to die in the Senate, his nephew repeatedly traveled to Caracas over the ensuing two years, keeping the matter alive and, in the interim, buying the rival Lang & Delano claim against Caracas to consolidate the Aves island negotiations. On January 14, 1859, the American minister to Venezuela, Edward A. Turpin, negotiated the Aves Island

Convention, whereby the South American government agreed to pay U.S. guano miners $130,000 in compensation for their losses, the fourteenth and final installment due in 1864; however, because of numerous political changes in Venezuela, accompanied by assorted fiscal crises, Sanford, as principal heir of Shelton's estate, did not receive the final payment until 1904. See W. L. Harris (MS.), pp. 86-171.

## Chapter 4: Seward's Outhouse

1. U.S. Congress. H. Exec. Doc. 70. Serial 723; U.S. Congress. H. Rept. 347. Serial 744; U.S. Congress. S. Exec. Doc. 25. Serial 621; U.S. Congress. S. Exec. Doc. 31. Serial 751; U.S. Congress. S. Exec. Doc. 59. Serial 561; U.S. Congress. S. Exec. Doc. 61. Serial 752; U.S. Congress. S. Exec. Doc. 80. Serial 562; U.S. Congress. S. Exec. Doc. 109. Serial 621; U.S. Congress. S. Miscellaneous Doc. 18. Serial 705.
2. "Petitions to the 28th Congress regarding duties on guano," U.S. House Records, HR28A, G24.2, Record Group 233 (National Archives); U.S. Congress. H. Doc. 100-245 (Y1.1/7:100-245), p. 277.
3. U.S. Senate *Journal.* Serial 809, 76.
4. See U.S. Congress. S. Miscellaneous Doc. 14. Serials 1945-46, *passim.*
5. U.S. Congress. S. Rept. 397. Serial 891, p. 27.
6. *Ibid.*, pp. 28-283.
7. *Ibid.*, p. 23.
8. *Ibid.*
9. U.S. Senate bill 606 (Thirty-fourth Cong., 3d sess.), p. 1., in Senate Records (U.S. Senate, Office of the Secretary); U.S. Senate *Journal.* Serial 873, p. 221.
10. U.S. Senate *Journal.* Serial 809, p. 287.
11. *Ibid.*, p. 291.
12. *Ibid.*, p. 514; U.S. Congress. S. Exec. Doc. 25. Serial 879, p. 1; U.S. Congress. S. Miscellaneous Doc. 14. Serial 1946, p. 546.
13. U.S. Congress. S. Miscellaneous Doc. 60. Serial 835, p. 1. See also M. A. Smith (1943), p. 11; U.S. Senate *Journal.* Serial 809, p. 357; and U.S. *Congressional globe* (Thirty-fourth Cong., 1st sess.), p. 1297.
14. R. G. Ward, I: 182ff, III: 364ff.
15. Abstract of Title of American Guano Company to Jarvis and Baker islands in the Pacific ocean, n.d., p. 1, in "Baker and Jarvis file," U.S. State department, *Records . . . relating to guano islands,* reel 3. See also U.S. State department, Legal Adviser's office, "Sovereignty of islands claimed under the Guano Islands Act" (MS.), pp. 678-81, 694, 864-65, and U.S. Congress. S. Miscellaneous Doc. 60. Serial 835, pp. 2-3.

    Locations of all American appurtenances may be found in "Places Claimed and/or Acquired under the U.S. Guano Islands Act," in the Appendix.
16. R. G. Ward, I: 230.
17. U.S. State department, "Sovereignty," p. 694; Abstract of Title of American Guano Company to Jarvis and Baker islands in the Pacific ocean, n.d., p. 1, in "Baker and Jarvis file," U.S. State department, *Records,* reel 3; U.S. Congress. S. Miscellaneous Doc. 60. Serial 835, pp. 2-3, 8-9.

18. American Guano Company, Articles of Association, September 1, 1855, pp. 1, in "Baker and Jarvis file," U.S. State department, *Records,* reel 3.

19. *Ibid.*; American Guano Company (1855), pp. 3-5; *American Guano* v. *U.S. Guano,* p. 25; R. G. Ward, III: 367.

20. U.S. Congress. S. Miscellaneous Doc. 60. Serial 835, pp. 10, 12. See also, Gara, pp. 148-49.

21. Bertrand, p. 256.

22. R. G. Ward, III: 369-70.

23. *Ibid.,* p. 365.

24. U.S. Congress. S. Rept. 307. Serial 939, p. 2.

25. W. H. Seward, *passim*; U.S. Senate *Journal.* Serial 809, p. 257; U.S. *Congressional globe* (Thirty-fourth Cong., 1st sess.), p. 921.

26. Paolino, p. 38.

27. Paolino, pp. 106-16; Bailey, 366.

28. W. L. Harris (MS.), p. 72; U.S. *Congressional globe* (Thirty-fourth Cong., 1st sess.), p. 921; U.S. Senate *Journal.* Serial 809, 257; U.S. Congress. S. Exec. Doc. 25. Serial 879, pp. 93-95.

29. U.S. Congress. S. Exec. Doc. 25. Serial 879, pp. 93, 94.

    Although Senate bill 15 predated the submission of Shelton's memorial by thirteen days, it seems evident that Seward had been alerted to the proposal by his colleague Lafayette Foster of Connecticut.

30. *Ibid.,* pp. 94-95; U.S. *Congressional globe* (Thirty-fourth Cong., 1st sess.), p. 921; U.S. Senate *Journal.* Serial 809, p. 257.

31. U.S. *Congressional globe* (Thirty-fourth Cong., 1st sess.), p. 1696; U.S. Senate [bill] 339, pp. 1-2 [1st copy], in U.S. Senate Records (Record Group 46), Thirty-fourth Cong., 1st sess., file number Sen. 34a-B2 (National Archives).

32. U.S. State department, "Sovereignty," p. 317.

33. U.S. *Congressional globe* (Thirty-fourth Cong., 1st sess.), p.1697; U.S. Senate [bill] 339, pp. 3-5; U.S. *Congressional globe* (Thirty-fourth Cong., 1st sess.), p. 1697; U.S. Senate [bill] 339, pp. 1-2 [1st copy], in U.S. Senate Records (Record Group 46), Thirty-fourth Cong., 1st sess., file number Sen. 34a-B2 (National Archives).

34. U.S. Senate *Journal.* Serial 809, pp. 406, 464.

35. U.S. *Congressional globe* (Thirty-fourth Cong., 1st sess.), p. 1697.

36. *Ibid.*

37. A. A. Hayes, "Results of analysis . . . of a sample of guano from Islands belonging to the American Guano Co.," July 9, 1856, in "Baker and Jarvis file," U.S. State department, *Records,* reel 3. See also U.S. *Congressional globe* (Thirty-fourth Cong., 1st sess.), p. 1699, which cites Hayes figures without identifying them.

38. U.S. *Congressional globe* (Thirty-fourth Cong., 1st sess.), p. 1697.

39. Wines (MS.), pp. 170-71; Bourgin, *passim*; Skaggs (1975), *passim.*

40. U.S. *Congressional globe* (Thirty-fourth Cong., 1st sess.), pp. 1697-98.

41. *Ibid.,* p. 1698.

42. *Ibid.*

43. *Ibid.*

The legislation did not necessarily or automatically renounce U.S. ownership of guano islands once the material had been removed. See U.S. *Statutes at large* 11 (1856), p. 199, or Appendix, Guano Islands Act, section 4.

44. U.S. *Congressional globe* (Thirty-fourth Cong., 1st sess.), p. 1698.
45. *Ibid.*
46. U.S. Senate [bill] 339, pp. 3-5 [1st copy], pp. 3-6 [2nd copy], in U.S. Senate Records (Record Group 46), Thirty-fourth Cong., 1st sess., file number Sen. 34a-B2 (National Archives).
47. U.S. *Congressional globe* (Thirty-fourth Cong., 1st sess.), p. 1698.
48. *Ibid,* pp. 1698-99.
49. *Ibid.*, p. 1699.
50. *Ibid.*
51. *Ibid.*
52. *Ibid.*, p. 1700.
53. *Ibid.*, p. 1740.
54. *Ibid.*
55. *Ibid.*
56. *Ibid.*
57. *Ibid.*
58. *Ibid.*, pp. 1740-41.
59. *Ibid.*
60. *Ibid.*, p. 1741.
61. *Ibid.*
62. *Ibid,* p. 1742.
63. *Ibid.*
64. *Ibid.*, p. 1743.
65. *Ibid.*
66. *Ibid.*, pp. 2212, 2217, 2227; Gara, p. 149.

The complete text of the Guano Islands Acts (1856), as well as relevant amendments (1872), are reproduced in the Appendix.

Decatur, hero in numerous encounters with Barbary pirates as well as action in the War of 1812, was renown for his toast "Our country! In her intercourse with other nations may she always be in the right; but our country, right or wrong." He was killed by Captain James Barron, who was still smarting from his court-martial a dozen years before (following the infamous *Chesapeake-Leopard* encounter in which his vessel was attacked by a British man-of-war), suspension from duty, and reduction in rank, which he blamed on Decatur, a member of the court. See R. B. Morris, pp. 649-50.

## Chapter 5: Pacific Appurtenances, 1856-1865

1. Bolton and Marshall, pp. 5-11, 25, 78-96, 107-108; Dunmore, I: 57-112; Friis, *passim*; Manchester, pp. 61-85; Maude (1961), pp. 67-97; Maude (1968), pp. 84-121; Sharp, pp. 4-11, 48, 114-19, 128-46.

2. Caruthers, pp. 3-26, 71-80, 128-35, 161-71, 188-89; Cutler, pp. 3-59; Decker (1976), pp. 13-31; Dudden, pp. 3-5, 11-17; Levi, p. 55.
3. Bertrand, p. 262.
4. *Ibid.*, p. 262; U.S. Congress. H. Rept. 94. Serial 276, pp. 7-12.
5. U.S. Congress. H. Rept. 94. Serial 276, p. 13.
6. *Ibid.*, pp. 16-27.
7. Bertrand, p. 263.
8. Anne, Clipperton, Elizabeth's, Fanning, Gardner, Humphrey, Jarvis, Laysan, Malden, Marcus, Mary's [Canton], New Nantucket [Baker], Ocean, Riersons, Sidney [or Sydney], Starbuck, and Washington. Cf. U.S. Congress. H. Rept. 94. Serial 276, pp. 16-27, and U.S. Congress. S. Doc. 234. Serial 3858, pp. 15-16.
9. Bertrand, p. 263; Wilkes, I: 1.
10. Wilkes, *passim*, specifically, II: 130-31, 174-75, 196-202, for Birnie, Clarence, Danger, Duke of York (Oatufu), Enderbury, Flint, Hull, Jarvis, McKeans, Penrhyn, Stavers, Swains, and Washington islands.
11. Bertrand, p. 273.
12. *Ibid.*, p. 272; Dudden, pp. 19-20; R. E. Johnson, pp. 77-127.
13. Quoted in Hagan, p. 127.
14. Cutler, pp. 128-279; Morison, pp. 339-43; Rydell, pp. 56-57, 72-73, 132-43; [U.S.] Work Projects Administration, pp. 122-45.
15. Cutler, p. 128.
16. Rydell, p. 133.
17. Cutler, pp. 280ff; Safford, p. 98.
18. Quoted in Morison, p. 365.
19. Cutler, p. 320.
20. Rydell, p. 145.
21. U.S. Congress. S. Doc. 234. Serial 3858, pp. 15-16; U.S. Congress. S. Exec. Doc. 38. Serial 1316, p. 8.
22. Nichols (1958), p. 500; U.S. Congress. S. Rept. 307. Serial 939, pp. 1-2; Baker and Jarvis islands bond, August 28, 1856, in "Bonds of guano companies," in U.S. State department, *Records . . . relating to guano islands,* reel 7.
23. American Guano Company (1859), pp. 5-6; U.S. Congress. H. Exec. Doc. 2. Serial 944, pp. 574-75, or U.S. Congress. S. Exec. Doc. 11. Serial 921, pp. 574-75; U.S. Congress. S. Rept. 307. Serial 939, pp. 2-4.
24. U.S. Congress. S. Rept. 307. Serial 939, 5-10.
25. R. G. Ward, I: 206.
26. American Guano Company (1859), pp. 7-8.
27. Arthur W. Benson, affidavit, n.d., in "Howland file," U.S. State department, *Records,* reel 3; Charles H. Judd, affidavit, September 7, 1860, in *ibid.*; David L. Gregg to W. L. Marcy, March 10, 1857, document no. 208, and Gregg to Marcy, March 21, 1857, document no. 209, (Gregg Papers); *American Guano* v. *U.S. Guano, passim*; E. H. Bryan (1941), p. 29; Gregg, p. 394; "Polyps of coral," p. 20; United States Guano Company, pp. 27-29; R. G. Ward, I: 196.

Howland island was sometimes rendered as "Nowland island" on early lists. See U.S. Congress. S. Doc. 234. Serial 3858, p. 15.

28. U.S. State department, Legal Adviser's office, "Sovereignty of islands claimed under the Guano Act" (MS.), p. 712.

29. Gregg to Marcy, March 10, 1857, and Gregg to Marcy, March 21, 1857 (Gregg Papers); *American Guano* v. *U.S. Guano, passim*; Bryan (1941), p. 29; *passim*; Bryan (1941), p. 29; Gregg, p. 394; G. P. Judd, IV (1960), p. 222; United States Guano Company, p. 27; R. G. Ward, I: 196-97.

30. United States Guano Company, pp. 29-30.

31. *Ibid.*, p. 28; G. P. Judd, IV (1960), pp. 220-22.

32. *American Guano* v. *U.S. Guano,* pp. 24, 26. Arthur Benson's report is reproduced in R. G. Ward, I: 196-99.

33. U.S. State department, "Sovereignty," p. 712.

34. *American Guano* v. *U.S. Guano,* p. 24.

35. U.S. State department, "Sovereignty," pp. 712, 733, 862; affidavits, September 6, 1856, in "Howland file," in U.S. State department, *Records,* reel 3; affidavits, May 2, 1857, "Malden and Arthur file," in *ibid.,* reel 4; *American Guano* v. *U.S. Guano,* p. 26.

36. United States Guano Company, p. 9.

37. U.S. State department, "Sovereignty," p. 862.
The only place in the Pacific by that name is also known as Eniwetok, which is more than two thousand miles to the northwest in the Marshall islands.

38. U.S. State department, "Sovereignty," pp. 729-33; E. H. Bryan (1941), pp. 151-54; "Malden island to-day"; Sharp, p. 209.

39. E. H. Bryan (1941), p. 153; R. G. Ward, IV: 110.

40. U.S. State department, "Sovereignty," pp. 654-56.
Christmas island in the Pacific should not be confused with Christmas island ($10^{o}$ 3'S, $105^{o}$ 40'E) in the Indian ocean, which also came to be renowned for its phosphate deposits. See Rice (1987), pp. 444-53.

41. U.S. State department, "Sovereignty," pp. 656-58; assignment, May 11, 1857, in "Christmas island file," in U.S. State department, *Records,* reel 3.

42. The text of the law is reproduced in United States Guano Company, pp. 21-25.

43. Skaggs (1975), p. 290; United States Guano Company, p. 21.

44. American Guano Company, abstract of title, n.d., in "Baker and Jarvis file," in U.S. State department, *Records,* reel 3; *American Guano* v. *U.S. Guano,* pp. 24-25; United States Guano Company, pp. 1-6; R. G. Ward, I: 205-208, III: 263, 268, 395.

45. U.S. State department, "Sovereignty," pp. 658-59, 713, 733-35, 809-11. See also "Christmas island file," in U.S. State department, *Records,* reel 3; "Howland file," in *ibid.*; "Malden and Arthur file," in *ibid.* reel 4.

46. U.S. State department, "Sovereignty," pp. 658-59, 713, 733-35, 809-11; J. S. Black (1857), 30-32; U.S. Senate *Journal.* Serial 917, p. 234; U.S. Congress. S. Doc. 234. Serial 3858, p. 15; U.S. Treasury department, *Circular No. 1* .

47. America (Fanning), Annes, Barber, Bauman, Birnies Caroline, Clarence (Nukunonu), Dangerous islands (Pukapuka, Motukoe, and Motukavata), Dangers rock (Kingman reef), Davids,

Duke of York (Atafu), Enderburys, Farmers, Favorite, Flint, Flints (Flint), Frances (possibly Rakahanga or Monihiki), Frienhaven, Gallego, Ganges, Gardners (Kemins), Groninque, Humphreys (Manihiki), Kemns (possibly Gardner), Liderons, Low islands (possibly Fakaofu), Mackin (or Makin), Mary Lelitias (perhaps Gardner), Marys (Canton, Mary Balcouts, Swallow, Balcout, or Bulcot), Mathews (Maraki in the Gilberts), Nassau, Palmyros (Palmyra, Samarang), Penhuyns (Penrhyn, Tongareva), Pescado (perhaps San Bernardo, Solitaria), Phoenix, Prospect (Washington), Quiros (Swains, Gente Hermosa), Riersons (Rakaaanga), Rogeweins islands, Samarang (Palmyra), Sarah Anne, Sidneys (Sydney), Starbuck (Barren, Hero, Starve, Volunteer), Stavers (Vostok), Walkers, and Washington (New York, Prospect, Teraina). See U.S. Congress. S. Doc. 234. Serial 3858, pp. 15-16.

Place names are rendered as detailed on the State department's Number 9 bond list. Alleged locations for these (and other) islands, rocks, and keys claimed and/or acquired under the Guano Islands Act may be found in the Appendix.

48. E. H. Bryan (September 1939), p. 6.

49. Gardiner (MS.), pp. 166-67; U.S. State department, "Sovereignty," pp. 869-72; Maude (1968), p. 326; Bradford L. Thomas, Office of the Geographer, U.S. State department, Washington, D. C., to J.M.S., November 20, 1990.

50. Nichols (1956), p. 233.

51. U.S. State department, "Sovereignty," p. 873.

52. See U.S. Guano Co., Bond, February 8, 1860, in U.S. State department, *Records,* reel 7.

53. Behm, "Tafel 8."

54. G. P. Judd, IV (1961), p. 222.

55. Hague (1862), pp. 235-36.

56. Hague (1902), p. 660.

57. Jason L. Pendleton, affidavit, September 1, 1860, in "Howland file," U.S. State department, *Records,* reel 3.

58. C. S. Marshall to Lewis Cass, August 21, 1860, in "Howland file," U.S. State department, *Records,* reel 3.

59. Cass to A. G. Benson, June 14, 1860; Cass to J. S. Black, August, 31, 1860, in "Howland file," U.S. State department, *Records,* reel 3. See also U.S. State department, "Sovereignty," pp. 714-15.

60. See J. S. Black (1857), pp. 30-33; (1857), 128-29; (1859), pp. 364-71; and (1859), p. 406.

61. *American Guano* v. *U.S. Guano,* p. 29.

62. *Ibid.*

63. Speed (1865), pp. 401-402.

64. "The past guano company," (MS., n.d.), in historical miscellany file, Box 1 (Pacific Guano Company Collection); U.S. State department, "Sovereignty," pp. 720-24; Wines (MS.), p. 217; Pacific Guano Company. pp. 7-8, 18; E. H. Bryan (1941), p. 47.

65. U.S. State department, "Sovereignty," pp. 788-89; U.S. Congress. S. Doc. 234. Serial 3858, p. 15.

The location of these places are listed in the Appendix.

66. U.S. State department, "Sovereignty," p. 789; Decker (1970), p. 210; Decker (1973), pp. 113-14; Decker (1976), pp. 89-92, 166; Hague (1862), p. 242; Kuykendall, pp. 15, 164-65; U.S. Congress. S. Doc. 234. Serial 3858, p. 15; R. G. Ward, II: 80-81, III: 80-81, 344, 394-97, IV: 93-97, VI: 504-506.

67. Hague (1862), p. 242.

68. Decker (1973), p. 114; Phoenix Guano Company, pp. 3-5; R. G. Ward, III: 80-81, IV: 93-97.

69. Benson to Cass, July 7, 1860, in "Enderburys [sic] file," U.S. State department, Records, reel 3.
Undoubtedly Benson would also have specifically objected to Phoenix Guano's pretensions toward Barren or Starve island, had he been aware that it was the same place he knew as Starbuck.

70. U.S. State department, "Sovereignty," p. 798.

71. *Ibid.*, pp. 799-800; Sam[uel] Niles, Phoenix Guano attorney, to W. H. Seward, March 31, 1862, in "Enderbury file," U.S. State department, *Records,* reel 3; R. G. Ward, II: 272. See also, Skaggs (1989), p. 48.

72. R. G. Ward, IV: 110.

73. *Ibid.*, 104-108; U.S. State department, "Sovereignty," pp. 733-37.

74. U.S. State department, "Sovereignty," pp. 581-82; Emery, p. 1506; Nicholas, p. 628; Phillips, p. 608; Thorp, p. 5; agreement, November 21, 1904, in "Johnson [*sic*] and Agnes file," in U.S. State department, *Records,* reel 4.
Parker may also have been a physician; at least he is referred to as "Dr. W. H. Parker" in "Stock issued to Parker," 18 December 1858, in *ibid.*

75. U.S. State department, "Sovereignty," pp. 580-84; affidavit, December 28, 1857, in "Johnson [*sic*] and Agnes file," in U.S. State department, *Records,* reel 4; affidavit, December 4, 1858, in *ibid.*; R. G. Ward, III: 419.

76. U.S. State department, "Sovereignty," pp. 584-86; E. H. Bryan (June 1937), p. 16; Leff, pp. 24-26; Thorp, pp. 26-28; R. G. Ward, III: 421.

77. *U.S.* v. *Fullard-Leo* (133 F. 2d; 1943), p. 744.

78. U.S. State department, "Sovereignty," pp. 544-85; J. S. Black (1859), 365-66; Phillips, 608-609; Wm. H. Parker to Cass, January 24, 1859, in "Johnson [*sic*] and Agnes file," U.S. State department, *Records,* reel 4; Calhoun Benham to Cass, February 11, 1859, in *ibid.*; R. G. Ward, III: 424-34.

79. R. G. Ward, I: 214.

80. J. S. Black (1859), pp. 364, 368.

81. *Ibid.*, 370-71.

82. U.S. State department, "Sovereignty," pp. 594-605; U.S. Congress. S. Doc. 234. Serial 3858, p. 15; Proclamation, December 9, 1859, in "Johnson [*sic*] and Agnes file," U.S. State department, *Records,* reel 4.

83. U.S. State department, "Sovereignty," pp. 606-611.

84. *U.S.* v. *Fullard-Leo,* (133 F 2d; 1943), p. 775.

85. U.S. State department, "Sovereignty," p. 614.

86. U.S. State department, "Sovereignty," pp. 612-17; *U.S.* v. *Fullard-Leo,* (133 F. 2d; 1943), pp. 743-45, (66 F. Supp.; 1946), pp. 775-79, 783, (156 F. 2d.; 1946), p. 765 n. 3.
Although the U.S. government has generally conceded Palmyra to be part of Hawaii, it continues to be a legal curiosity. It was excluded from Hawaii's boundaries under the Hawaii Statehood Act and consequently falls outside that state's jurisdiction. See, E. H. Bryan (May 1937), p. 13; Bugliosi, pp. 128, 132; *U.S.* v. *Fullard-Leo,* (66 F. Supp.; 1946), *passim,* and (156 F. 2d.; 1946), *passim*; U.S. Interior department (1963), n.p.; and U.S. State department, *Digest* (1940), I: 489.

87. Olinger (MS.), pp. 17-22; Mathew (1981), pp. 122, 185-223.

88. Skaggs (1989), pp. 27, 41-45.
The first known American sighting of Clipperton was by mariner Benjamin Morrell. See B. Morrell, pp. 219ff.

89. U.S. State department, "Sovereignty," pp. 846-63; Dudden, pp. 15-16; Nichols (1958), p. 376; Richardson, IV: 2744; Skaggs (1989), pp. 45-82.

90. U.S. State department, "Sovereignty," pp. 831-34.

91. *Ibid.*, pp. 841-44; affidavit, January 28, 1860, "Bampton file," in U.S. State department, *Records,* reel 3.

92. U.S. State department, "Sovereignty," pp. 827-30.
As result of World War II, Uracas and the rest of the Marianas became part of the U.S. Trust Territory.

93. U.S. State department, "Sovereignty," pp. 649-50; "Fanning island" (1906), p. 125; Finney, pp. 7-72; McClellan (April 1940), p. 23; Parkhurst, p. 4; Ross (1947), p. 540.

94. McClellan (April 1940), pp. 23-24; Osbun, pp. 104-107.

95. U.S. State department, "Sovereignty," p. 649.

96. *Ibid.*, pp. 640-53; "Islands for sale," 5; Ross (1947), 540; R. G. Ward, VII: 503.
Washington island was also reportedly claimed by Dr. G. P. Judd on behalf of American Guano Company, but there is no evidence that the firm ever attempted to occupy or mine it. See McClellan (May 1940), p. 24.

## Chapter 6: Caribbean Appurtenances, 1856-1865

1. U.S. State department, Legal Adviser's office, "Sovereignty of islands claimed under the Guano Act" (MS.), pp. 482-83; Wines (MS.), p. 184; Bond, February 23, 1857, in "Sombrero file," U.S. State department, *Records . . . relating to guano islands,* reel 6; W. J. Davis, II: 282; Morfit, pp. 18-20.

2. U.S. State department, "Sovereignty," p. 483.

3. Quoted in Wines (MS.), p. 473.

4. U.S. State department, "Sovereignty," pp. 483, 485; J. S. Black (1857), pp. 128-29; Julien (1865), p. 375.

5. Quoted in U.S. State department, "Sovereignty," p. 483. See also, Bond, February 23, 1857, in "Sombrero file," U.S. State department, *Records,* reel 6.

6. U.S. State department, "Sovereignty," p. 484.
Curiously, Sombrero island was listed as a bonded American appurtenance on "Circular relative to the guano islands, appertaining to the United States," by Secretary of the Treasury Hugh McCulloch on August 23, 1867 (copy in "Sombrero file," U.S. State department, *Records,* reel 6), the earliest surviving official list of guano islands; however, McCulloch's compilation purported to be a "corrected list," thereby implying a previous listing, date unknown. For a discussion of Treasury department lists of guano islands, see Chapter 7.

7. Quoted in U.S. State department, "Sovereignty," p. 484.

8. *Ibid.*, p. 485.

9. Quoted in *ibid.*, pp. 485-86.

10. Quoted in *ibid.*, p. 486.

11. Quoted in *ibid.*, p. 488.

12. *Ibid.*, pp. 489-90.

13. *Ibid.*, p. 220.

14. *Ibid.*, pp. 220-21, 947-48; "In the case of J. W. Fabens, C. Stearns, & Duff Green," June 23, 1857, in "Swans file," U.S. State department, *Records*, reel 6.

15. U.S. State department, "Sovereignty," pp. 220-25; "Fabens, Joseph Warren."

16. J. S. Black (1857), pp. 30-31.

17. *Ibid.*, pp. 30-32.

18. Charles Stearns, New York, to Col. [J. W.] Fabens, n.p., May 30, 1857; J. W. Fabens, New York, to Gen. [Duff Green], n.p., June 1, 1857; Stearns to Green, June 1, 1857 (Green Papers); Wines (MS.), p. 186.

19. John Appleton to President [James Buchanan], June 24, 1857, in "Swans file," U.S. State department, *Records*, reel 6 (italics in the original). See also, "Green, Duff," pp. 540-42; F. M. Green, pp. 50-64.

20. Frances W. Ruggles, "In the matter of the New York Guano Company to have Swan islands considered as appertaining to the United States, &c., &c., &c.: supplemental report," February 6, 1863, [p. 2], in "Swans file," U.S. State department, *Records*, reel 6.

    Buchanan's memo, as well as numerous other relevant documents, has been lost by the State department. See U.S. State department, "Sovereignty," pp. 217-72.

21. Quoted in U.S. State department, "Sovereignty," p. 222, and in Ruggles, "In the matter of the New York Guano Company . . .: supplemental report," February 6, 1863, [p. 3], in "Swans file," U.S. State department, *Records*, reel 6.

22. U.S. State department, "Sovereignty," pp. 222-24; Ivey, Breyer, and Britton, p. 195; Lowe, pp. 18-23; U.S. Interior department (1971), p. 8; Wells, p. 57.

23. U.S. State department, "Sovereignty, pp. 223, 946-47; May, p. 401.

24. Pacific Guano Company, pp. 25, 28-29; Sargent, p. 510; Thomas P. Morgan, affidavit, December 31, 1862, in "Swan file," U.S. State department, *Records*, reel 6; Wells, p. 60.

25. Bailey, pp. 277-78; May, pp. 395-96.

26. May, pp. 390-91; U.S. Congress. S. Exec. Doc. 38. Serial 1316, p. 7; Webb and Carroll, I: 318, II: 122.

27. May, p. 386.

28. Connor, p. 88; May, pp. 390-91; Webb and Carroll, I: 318, II: 122.

29. May, p. 404, n. 41.

30. Connor, p. 88; May, pp. 387-90; Webb and Carroll, I: 318, II: 122.

31. May, pp. 399-400.

32. *Ibid.*, pp. 396, 403-405.

33. U.S. State department, "Sovereignty," pp. 223-24.

34. *Ibid..*, p. 426.

    Harvey Gardiner, "Guano in American agriculture" (MS.), p. 142, quotes U.S. Minister Charles Eames as saying that Philadelphia Guano abandoned Aves island as valueless sometime before 1856, but Gardiner's endnote for that paragraph is missing and his information is impossible to verify. Perhaps, as U.S. State department, "Sovereignty," p. 427, implies, the Americans encountered by Fowler were working for the Dutch government.

35. *Ibid.*, p. 427.

36. F. M. Green, p. 59.

37. Sargent, p. 510; Wells, p. 61.

Although the company by then was no longer in business, A&P lawyer J. S. Williams tried in 1866 to resurrect its claim to Aves, to no avail. Seward's State department would have none of it. See U.S. State department, "Sovereignty," pp. 427-28.

38. U.S. State department, "Sovereignty," pp. 224-26; Sargent, p. 510;U.S. Congress. S. Doc. 234. Serial 3858, pp. 15-16.

Wells, p. 59, among others, including U.S. Congress, Senate Report 606 (Serial 3364), p. 2, states that the Swans were the first islands claimed and occupied under the Guano Islands Act, which, as this study demonstrates, is incorrect.

39. Burne, Horsfield, and Robinson, pp. 110-11; Proctor, p. 49; U.S. State department, "Sovereignty," p. 375; U.S. Congress. S. Doc. 234. Serial 3858, p. 15.

Historian Roy Nichols (1933), p. 542, asserts that Navassa "is the oldest of American overseas possessions," which may have been technically correct at the time he wrote; however, inasmuch as Baker and Jarvis, abandoned by American miners during the 1870s, were reclaimed by the United States in 1935, Nichols's assertion is subject to argument. In any case, Navassa certainly qualifies as America's longest, uninterrupted overseas possession.

40. U.S. State department, "Sovereignty," p. 375; Burne, Horsfield, and Robinson, pp. 110-11; Navassa Phosphate Company, p. 6; Proctor, p. 49.

41. D'Invilliers, p. 77.

42. Wines (MS.), p. 127; Stancil, pp. 1-2; U.S. Congress. S. Exec. Doc. 37. Serial 1031, p. 3; "Notes on Navaza [*sic*] island: claims of Haiti . . . ," n.d., in "Navassa file," U.S. State department, *Records,* reel 5.

43. Nichols (April 1937), p. 507; U.S. Congress. S. Exec. Doc. 37. Serial 1031, p. 3.

T. C. J. Whedbee, p. 55, says Captain Edward K. Cooper of the bark *Abbotsford* discovered guano when he stopped off to bury a dead sailor on a island off the coast of Haiti, which he named Navassa. The report of discovering guano while burying a dead sailor is an oft-told tale, especially in the Pacific and, in the case of Navassa island, probably apocryphal. According to documents filed with the State department by the Coopers, E. O. Cooper purchased Duncan's rights to the island, which had been known by its present name (with variant spellings) for centuries. See U.S. State department, "Sovereignty," pp. 2-8.

44. Gardiner (MS.), p. 147; William J. Kelley, "Federal Hill story: the R. W. L. Rasin Company" (MS., n.d.), p. 1 (Kelley Collection); U.S. State department, "Sovereignty," p. 377; Logan, p. 361; Montague, p. 61; U.S. Congress. S. Exec. Doc. 37. Serial 1031, p. 4.

45. U.S. Congress. S. Exec. Doc. 37. Serial 1031, p. 8.

46. Montague, p. 62.

47. *Ibid.*

48. U.S. State department, "Sovereignty," pp. 377-78; Nichols (April 1933), p. 507; U.S. Congress. S. Exec. Doc. 37. Serial 1031, p. 12.

49. C. F. Howland, p. 117.

50. U.S. Congress. S. Exec. Doc. 37. Serial 1031, p. 8.

51. J. S. Black (1857), p. 33.

52. U.S. Congress. S. Exec. Doc. 37. Serial 1031, p. 10.
53. U.S. State department, "Sovereignty," p. 380; U.S. Congress. S. Exec. Doc. 37. Serial 1031, pp. 10-11, 15.
54. U.S. Congress. S. Exec. Doc. 37. Serial 1031, pp. 19-20.
55. *Ibid.*, pp. 24-25.
56. Quoted in U.S. State department, "Sovereignty," p. 382.
57. Montague, p. 64.
58. U.S. State department, "Sovereignty," p. 377.
59. U.S. Congress. S. Rept. 379. Serial 994, p. 2. See also, U.S. Congress. S. Miscellaneous Doc. 14. Serial 1945, p. 378.
60. U.S. State department, "Sovereignty," p. 380.
61. *Ibid*, pp. 380-81.
62. Navassa Phosphate Company, p. 13.
63. Kelley, "Federal Hill story: The R. W. L. Rasin Company," p. 2 (Kelley Collection). See also, "Story of the fertilizer industry," pp. 26-27.
64. *Ibid.*, pp. 593-632. See also Logan, pp. 310-12.
65. Kelley, "Federal Hill story: The R. W. L. Rasin Company," p. 3 (Kelley Collection); Navassa Phosphate Company, p. 14.
66. Kelley, "Federal Hill story: The R. W. L. Rasin Company," p. 3 (Kelley Collection). See also Rasin, p. 8, and "Alone on desert island."
67. See below, Chapter 10.
68. U.S. State department, "Sovereignty," p. 455; U.S. Congress. S. Rept. 280. Serial 1040, pp. 1-2, 15.
69. U.S. State department, "Sovereignty," p. 455; U.S. Congress. S. Rept. 280. Serial 1040, pp. 1-2, 15.
70. U.S. Congress. S. Rept. 280. Serial 1040, p. 15.
71. *Ibid.*, pp. 15-16.
72. *Ibid.*, p. 18.
73. *Ibid.*, pp. 16.
74. *Ibid.*, pp. 16-17.
75. Quoted in U.S. State department, "Sovereignty," pp. 456-57.
76. *Ibid.*, pp. 458-59.
77. J. S. Black (1859), p. 406.
78. Quoted in U.S. State department, "Sovereignty," p. 460.
79. U.S. Congress. S. Rept. 280. Serial 1040, pp. 1-4.
80. *Ibid.*, p. 2.
81. U.S. State department, "Sovereignty," p. 442.
82. *Ibid.*, p. 443; U.S. Congress. S. Exec. Doc. 38. Serial 1316, pp. 2-4.
83. U.S. State department, "Sovereignty," pp. 412-15; Chris Jeffries, Maryland Historical Society, to J.M.S., March 14, 1991.
84. Bemis (1965), p. 402; Bemis (1976), p. 91; Tansill, p. 287.

85. U.S. State department, "Sovereignty," p. 444-45; U.S. Congress. S. Exec. Doc. 38. Serial 1316, p. 4.
86. U.S. Congress. S. Exec. Doc. 38. Serial 1316, pp. 26-27.
87. *Ibid.*, pp. 32, 38-39, 45-46.
88. *Ibid.*, pp. 32-35.
89. *Ibid.*, pp. 5, 38, 47-48.
90. *Ibid.*, p. 49.
91. Nichols (1928), p. 397.

    Why Secretary Seward failed to champion his own legislation remains a mystery. His five-volume published works, which includes abbreviated memoirs, fail to mention the subject of guano or guano islands, thereby casting no light on the subject. See W. H. Seward, *passim.*
92. J. S. Black to W. H. Seward, March 27, 1861, in "Alta Vela file," U.S. State department, *Records,* reel 1.
93. U.S. State department, "Sovereignty," pp. 444-45; U.S. Congress. S. Exec. Doc. 38. Serial 1316, p. 50; J. S. Black (1857), p. 31.

    Of Attorney General Black's seven stipulated prerequisites for title, Patterson and Murguiondo fulfilled completely merely three: discovery, timely notification including location (but not description) of the island, and declaration of peaceable possession. They never submitted affidavits attesting that Alta Vela was without the lawful jurisdiction of any other government, that it was unoccupied at the time their agent had claimed it, and that it was not taken "out of the possession or occupation of any other people." Furthermore, the additional requirement imposed by the Buchanan administration that certificates attesting to both quantity and quality of guano be submitted was never met. See U.S. Congress. S. Exec. Doc. 38. Serial 1316, pp. 26-78.
94. J. S. Black (1859), p. 406.
95. Black to Seward, March 27, 1861, in "Alta Vela file," U.S. State department, *Records,* reel 1.
96. U.S. Congress. S. Exec. Doc. 38. Serial 1316, p. 8.

    Actually, Dominican President Pedro Santaña (facing continuous threats from neighboring Haiti) earlier that year had declared Santo Domingo to be a province of Spain, circumstances that prevailed for the following four years notwithstanding U.S. displeasure, perhaps because some American officials had designs on the island nation.
97. U.S. Congress. S. Exec. Doc. 38. Serial 1316, p. 8.
98. Bailey, pp. 361-63.
99. Tansill, p. 296.
100. U.S. Congress. S. Exec. Doc. 38. Serial 1316, p. 53.
101. U.S. State department, "Sovereignty," pp. 451-53; M. A. Smith (1943), p. 15; Tansill, p. 298-99; U.S. Congress. S. Exec. Doc. 38. Serial 1316, pp. 53-56.
102. U.S. Congress. S. Exec. Doc. 38. Serial 1316, p. 56.
103. E. Peshine Smith to Seward, September 19, 1867, in "Alta Vela file," U.S. State department *Records,* reel 1.
104. Tansill, p. 305.
105. *Ibid.*, p. 305. See also U.S. State department, *Treaties and other international acts* (1948) VIII: 179.
106. Tansill, p. 305.

107. *Ibid.*, p. 311; Gardiner (MS.), p. 185; Van Deusen, pp. 331-33.

108. Tansill, p. 311.

109. *Ibid.*, pp. 308, 310. See also U.S. Congress. S. Exec. Doc. 38. Serial 1316.

110. Quoted in *ibid.*, p. 312.

111. *Ibid.*, p. 312. See also U.S. Congress. H. Miscellaneous Doc. 10. Serial 1385.

112. *Ibid.*; Rehnquist, pp. 218, 226-29, 241-43, 246, 248.

113. Tansill, pp. 316-20.

114. Gardiner (MS.), p. 193; R. B. Morris, p. 683; U.S. Congress. H. Miscellaneous Doc. 10. Serial 1385, pp. 1-7.

U.S. Senate Miscellaneous Document 14 (Serials 1945-46), which purports to be "a list of private claims brought before the Senate of the United States from the commencement of the fourteenth Congress [1814] to the close of the forty-sixth [1881]," for some reason does not include Patterson and Murguiondo's appeal.

115. Tansill, p. 323. For a further assessment of Seward's ethics, see Summers, pp. 127, 153, 184, 189, 193, 212, 230-31, 263, 266-72, 277.

## Chapter 7: Shrinking Empire, 1866-1902

1. Bailey, pp. 422-27; Grattan, pp. 119-30; Leff, pp. 12-13, 21-22. When he annexed Midway for the United States, Commander Reynolds mistakenly expressed considerable pride "in taking possession of the first island ever added to the dominion of the

United States beyond our own shores. . . . " (Quoted in Leff, pp. 12-13.) Commander C. H. Davis of USS *St. Mary* had preceded him in that achievement by ten years at Baker island. See also U.S. Congress. H. Exec. Doc. 2. Serial 944, pp. 574-75; U.S. Congress. S. Exec. Doc. 11. Serial 921, pp. 574-75; U.S. Congress. S. Rept. 307. Serial 939, pp. 2-4.

2. U.S. State department, Legal Adviser's office, "Sovereignty of islands claimed under the Guano Act" (MS.), p. 699.

3. U.S. *Statutes at large* 11 (1856) 119. See also Appendix.

A draft of "Tariff Act of 1862, Last Proviso of Section Fifteen," n.d., is included in "Baker and Jarvis file," U.S. State department, *Records . . . relating to guano islands,* reel 3.

4. U.S. State department, "Sovereignty," p. 699.

5. *Ibid.*, pp. 699-700.

6. Bates, p. 31.

7. U.S. State department, "Sovereignty," p. 701; U.S. *Statutes* 13 (1865) 494.

For examples of Baker island guano shipments in foreign vessels, see R. G. Ward, I: 248, notwithstanding the law that stipulated such commerce "shall be regulated as in the coasting trade of the United States." (U.S. *Statutes* 11 (1856) 119). See also Appendix.

8. U.S. State department, "Sovereignty," pp. 701-702; Speed (1866), pp. 514-15.

9. U.S. *Statutes* 14 (1866) 328; 17 (1872) 48; 20 (1878) 30; 23 (1884) 11.

10. U.S. Congress. H. Rept. 4040. Serial 2890, p. 1.

11. U.S. State department, "Sovereignty," pp. 17-18; U.S. Congress. H. Rept. 252. Serial 2253, p. 1; U.S. Congress. H. Rept. 3989. Serial 2674, p. 1; U.S. Congress. H. Rept. 4040. Serial 2890, p. 1; U.S. Senate *Journal.* Serial 2891, p. 119.

12. U.S. *Congressional globe* (41st Cong., 2d sess.), pp. 2374, 3089; U.S. House *Journal.* Serial 1410, 72; Agnes [Parker] Burt, affidavit, December 27, 1870, in "Johnson [*sic*] and Agnes" file, U.S. State department *Records,* reel 4.

13. U.S. *Congressional globe* (41st Cong., 2d sess.), p. 3090.

14. U.S. State department, "Sovereignty," p. 588.

15. Quoted in *ibid.*, p. 589.

16. U.S. *Congressional globe* (41st Cong., 2d sess.), pp. 4427-33, 4453-58, 5610.

17. *Ibid.*, p. 5610.

18. *Ibid.*, p. 4458; U.S. Congress. S. Miscellaneous Doc. 14. Serials 1945-46, p. 279.

19. U.S. *Congressional globe* (41st Cong., 2d sess.), p. 5610.

20. *Ibid.*, p. 359.

21. *Ibid.*, pp. 360-61.

22. *Ibid.*, pp. 1981, 2045; U.S. *Statutes* 17 (1872), 48. See also Appendix.

23. Phillips, p. 609. See also J. S. Black (1859), pp. 364-71.

24. Phillips, p. 610.

25. U.S. State department, "Sovereignty," pp. 590-93.

    Nor did the *Revised statutes* assist Isabella Duncan, widow of Peter Duncan, to acquire title to his discoveries on Navassa. See *Duncan* v. *Navassa, passim,* and *Grafflin* v. *Nevassa* [*sic*] *Phosphate* Company, p. 476.

26. Quoted in U.S. State department, "Sovereignty," p. 593.

27. *Ibid.*, p. 598; Leff, pp. 26-27; *U.S.* v. *Fullard-Leo* (133 F. 2d; 1943), p. 744.

28. U.S. State department, "Sovereignty," p. 599.

29. "Other deaths."

30. U.S. State department, "Sovereignty," pp. 95, 491-94, 514-16; U.S. Congress. S. Exec. Doc. 151. Serial 2901, p. 5.

    Jennett also said he discovered guano on Booby and Woody keys, neither of which exist. See U.S. State department, "Sovereignty," pp. 536-37.

31. J. W. Jennett, n.p., to G. L. Walker, Washington, D.C., Nov[ember] 3, 1868, in "Serrana file," U.S. State department, *Records,* reel 5.

32. *Ibid.*

33. U.S. State department, "Sovereignty," pp. 60-67, 109-110, 405, 428-29, 440, 461-63, 473-75.

34. *Ibid.*, pp. 94-96.

35. Jennett, to Walker, Nov[ember] 3, 1868, in "Serrana file," U.S. State department, Records, reel 5.

36. James W. Jennett, "Bond for certain islands in the Caribbean," August 12, 1868, in "Bonds of Guano companies" file, *ibid.*, reel 7. Curiously, his bond was altered by someone evidently either in the State or Treasury department who scratched through both Jennett's name and the phrase "in the Caribbean Sea" and inserted instead "Andrew A. Rosehill" and "known as Marcus island in the North Pacific Ocean, longitude 150$^{o}$ East and latitude 24$^{o}$ 14' North." In 1889 Rosehill did initiate claim to Marcus, as discussed below, but there is no known connection between him and Jennett or their decidedly dissimilar claims half a world apart.

37. U.S. State department, "Sovereignty," pp. 65-66, 110, 405, 428, 462, 474, 495.

38. U.S. State department, *Digest* (1906), I: 562.

39. Tho[ma]s W. Cridler, State department, "*Confidential*" to Eugene T. Chamberlain, Bureau of Navigation, Treasury department, May 12, 1899, in "Correspondence related to lists of Guano Islands," U.S. State department, *Records.*, reel 7.

40. U.S. State department, *Digest,* (1940), I: 505.

41. U.S. State department, *Digest* (1906), I: 562, 564.

42. M. A. Smith (1943), p. 15. Allan Nevins, Hamilton Fish's principal biographer, does not address the issue of guano or the basis of Fish's antipathy toward American appurtenances. See Nevins, *passim.*

43. U.S. State department, *Digest* (1940), I: 502-24; U.S. State department, *Digest* (1906), I: 556-80.

44. U.S. State department, "Sovereignty," pp. 166-70; "Bonds of guano islands" file, U.S. State department, *Records,* reel 7.

Although the 1867 and 1869 lists were both printed, apparently only the second was made part of the public record as the department's *Circular No. 1, relative to the guano islands appertaining to the United States.* (See Bibliography.) Two independently published lists of American guano islands, supposedly carrying the rubric of government authenticity, differ slightly from the four official Treasury compilations. Charles E. Magoon's *Report on the legal status of the territories and inhabitants of the islands acquired by the United States . . .* (1900), pp. 15-16, lists fifteen bond groups, and the U.S. State department's *Digest of international law,* edited by J. B. Moore (1906), I: 567-68, contains an alphabetical list of seventy separate filings, four of which represent duplicate bonds by rival firms.

45. U.S. State department, "Sovereignty," pp. 60-67, 110-12, 407, 475, 429, 492, 494, 497-98; U.S. State department, *Digest* (1906) I: 567-68; U.S. Treasury department (1869).

46. U.S. State department, "Sovereignty," pp. 516, 526-27, 534-35; U.S. State department, *Digest* (1906) I: 567-68.

47. U.S. State department, "Sovereignty," p. 440.

48. According to Bardford L. Thomas, Office of the Geographer, U.S. State department, Washington, D.C., to J.M.S., November 20, 1990, "The United States reserves a right . . . to make a claim to Serranilla," while Petrel's status is unclear. See Chapter 11.

49. U.S. State department, "Sovereignty," pp. 65-67, 96, 410.

50. *Ibid.*, p. 408.

51. *Ibid.*, p. 67.

52. *Ibid.*, p. 100.

53. *Ibid.*, p. 466.

54. *Ibid.*, p. 112.

55. *Ibid.*, pp. 112, 157, 471; "Bonds of guano companies," in U.S. State department, *Records,* reel 7; U.S. Congress. S. Exec. Doc. 234. Serial 3858, p. 16.

56. U.S. State department, "Sovereignty," p. 471.

57. *Ibid.*, pp. 463-678; Ward H. Lamon to W[illia]m M. Evarts, Secretary of State, November 20, 1877, in "Morant file," U.S. State department, *Records,* reel 5.

58. U.S. State department, "Sovereignty," pp. 495-99, 512; Maryland Historical Society, Baltimore, to J.M.S., February 23, 1991; U.S. Congress. S. Exec. Doc. 234. Serial 3858, pp. 12, 16.

59. U.S. State department, "Sovereignty," p. 512.

60. *Ibid.*, p. 510.

61. *Ibid.*, p. 508.

62. U.S. Congress. S. Exec. Doc. 234. Serial 3858, p. 16; S. Wilke, Treasury department, to Collectors of Customs and others, November 21, 1894, in "Correspondence relating to lists of Guano islands," U.S. State department, *Records*, reel 7.

63. U.S. State department, "Sovereignty," pp. 115, 129, 141-44, 157-58, 429-30, 433-34, 499-505, 508-510.

64. *Ibid.*, pp. 60-62, 92-93, 151-55, 405-11, 481.

65. *Ibid.*, p. 69; *Petrel Guano Company and others* v. *Jarnette* [*sic*] *and others*, p. 675.

66. *Ibid.*, pp. 675-76.

67. U.S. State department, "Sovereignty," pp. 151, 410; "Prospectus," Caribbean Guano Company, n.d., in "Roncador file," U.S. State department, *Records*, reel 5.

68. U.S. State department, "Sovereignty," pp. 152-55, 410, 481.

69. *Ibid.*, p. 155.

70. *Ibid.*, p. 100.

71. Quoted in *ibid.*, pp. 105-106.

72. *Ibid.*, p. 91.

73. *Ibid.*, p. 77. Although Petrel bank was not mentioned by Columbia in a follow-up note in 1893, American diplomats presumed such was mere oversight. See *ibid.*, pp. 541-42.

74. *Ibid.*, pp. 78-89. See also Chapter 11.

75. *Ibid.*, p. 475.

76. *Ibid.*, p. 478.

77. *Ibid.*, p. 516.

78. *Ibid.*, p. 517.

79. *Ibid.*, pp. 518, 520. See also U.S. Congress. S. Exec. Doc. 151. Serial 2901, *passim*.

80. U.S. State department, "Sovereignty," pp. 532-33.

81. *Ibid.*, pp. 552-54.

    In 1904 and again in 1908, occupants of Swans islands in the Caribbean refiled on that site, but it was already considered to be an American appurtenance. See Chapter 11.

82. Quoted in *ibid.*, p. 555.

83. *Ibid.*, pp. 556-57.

84. *Ibid.*, pp. 556-68.

85. *Ibid.*, pp. 564-69.

86. *Ibid.*, pp. 813-15.

87. *Ibid.*, pp. 837-38.

88. Henry O'Connor, Memorandum, November 12, 1877, in "Huon file," U.S. State department, *Records*, reel 3.

89. U.S. State department, "Sovereignty," pp. 838-39.

90. *Ibid.*, pp. 846-61, 886; Avelar (1992), *passim*; Skaggs (1989), pp. 40-119, 142-51.

91. U.S. State department, "Sovereignty," pp. 816-18; Biddle, pp. 96-97; W. A. Bryan, p. 82.

92. Aiman (MS.), p. 22; North Pacific Phosphate and Fertilizer Company, "Minutes," pp. 9, 14-16, 44-45; Pacific Guano and Fertilizer Company, "Minutes," p. 88; E. H. Bryan (May 1938), p. 28; [King], pp. 18, 21.

93. U.S. State department, "Sovereignty," pp. 816-20; Marcus island bond, March 25, 1902, "Bonds on guano islands" file, U.S. State department, *Records,* reel 7; Biddle, pp. 96-97; W. A. Bryan, p. 82.

94. U.S. State department, "Sovereignty," p. 820.

95. *Ibid.,* pp. 820, 821.

96. Quoted in *ibid.,* pp. 823-24.

97. Quoted in *ibid.,* pp. 824.

Ironically, in 1927 the State department asked permission of Japan for the Western Union Telegraph Company to land a cable on the island, a request that was curtly rejected "on the grounds that the telegraph on Japanese territory was a government monopoly." See *ibid.,* p. 825.

98. *Ibid.,* p. 149.

99. W. P. Morrell, pp. 263-64; J. M. Ward, pp. 160-61.

100. "Malden island."

101. *Ibid.*; U.S. State department, "Sovereignty," pp. 729-37; E. H. Bryan (1941), pp. 151-54; Luke, p. 168; R. G. Ward, II: 272.

102. W. P. Morrell, p. 264.

103. U.S. State department, "Sovereignty," p. 661; W. P. Morrell, pp. 263-64; U.S. State department, *Foreign relations* (1888), pp. 712-13; J. M. Ward, pp. 160-61.

104. Ellis (1937), pp. 60-61; Leff, p. 51; Maude, p. 326; W. P. Morrell, p. 264; "Vostok history," p. 86-87.

105. U.S. State department, "Sovereignty," pp. 616, 685-86, 702-703, 719-24, 768, 771, 774, 777, 800; E. H. Bryan (1941), pp. 47, 50, 157; Ellis (1937), pp. 18-19, 24; Grattan, pp. 97-98; Leff, pp. 46-47; W. P. Morrell, p. 264.

In 1868 U.S. Guano had reportedly disposed of its rights on Howland to an unnamed English company, and it is entirely possible that Arundel traced his claim of title to the island to that transaction. In any case he occupied it until 1891 when, its phosphates exhausted, he abandoned it to its rats. See L. Howland, p. 105, and R. G. Ward, III: 320.

106. U.S. State department, *Foreign relations* (1888), p. 713.

Sources vary as to the spelling of "McFarlane." W. P. Morrell, pp. 266, 447, uses both MacFarlane and McFarlane; British diplomats say Macfarlane; and *The Times* says McFarlane. See "Pacific Islands Co. (Ltd.)," p. 11e, and U.S. State department, *Foreign relations* (1888), pp. 728.

107. U.S. State department, "Sovereignty," p. 667; Brigham, p. 157-58; E. H. Bryan (1941), p. 126; McClellan (April 1940), pp. 23-24; W. P. Morrell, pp. 426-27; Osborne, pp. 104-107.

108. "Pacific Islands Co. (Ltd.)," p. 11e.

109. Ellis (1937), p. 62.

110. *Ibid.,* p. 63.

111. Bailey, p. 425; "Bid of £575,000," p. 6b; Firth (1973), p. 25; Firth (1978), pp. 36-38; W. P. Morrell, p. 279; Oliver, pp. 214-15; Osborne, p. 463.

112. Ellis (1937), p. 19.

## Chapter 8: Peddling It: The Aroma of Profit

1. Mokyr, pp. 121, 138; Sauchelli (1965), pp. 1-3; Van Wazer, p. 5; Waggaman, pp. 15-17; U.S. Federal Trade Commission, p. 3.

2. Brand (MS.), pp. 6-17, 35-36, 39-43; Collings, pp. 115-16; B[rowne], p. 90; "Guano" (1867), p. 261; Jacob, "Predecessors," p. 11; Hutchinson (1950), pp. 3-4; Nelson, pp. 6-7; Penrose, p. 119; Zieman, pp. 1, 23.

   With a high nitrogen content, bat guano was an important source of saltpeter and was used in the manufacture of gunpowder as early as the War of 1812. It also found considerable use by Confederates during the American Civil War as raw material for explosives. See especially Collings, p. 115, and Zieman, p. 1.

   In *The American Pacific*, p. 66, Arthur Power Dudden implies that American appurtenances furnished "phosphates, nitrates, and potassium for high explosives," but there is no evidence that the output of American guano islands was used for anything other than that intended by law—fertilizer. Dudden does not cite a source for his assertion.

3. Hutchinson, pp. 4, 125; Palmer, p. 275; Penrose, p. 118.

4. B[rowne], p. 93; Hutchinson (1950), pp. 5-14, 76-125; Penrose, pp. 119-27.

5. Bentor, "Phosphorites," pp. 3-14; Fosberg, pp. 584-89; Lamer, p. 49; Oliver, pp. 214-15; Sauchelli, p. 32; Schlee, pp. 214-23; U.S. Navy, Intelligence Division, I: 16-17; Wiens, Atoll, p. 299.

   Calcium phosphate appears in nature in several guises: calcium mono-orthophosphate (as it is known to geologists, or to chemists as calcium dihydrogen phosphate monohydrate): Ca(H2PO4)2 H2O; calcium diorthophosphate (calcium monohydrogenphosphate dihydrate): CaHPO4 2H2O; calcium triorthophosphate (calcium phosphate): Ca3(PO4)2; anhydrous (or dry) calcium phosphate: Ca3(PO4)2; calcium hypophosphate (calcium hypophosphate dihydrate): Ca2P2O6 2H20; calcium metaphosphate: Ca(PO3)2; calcium pyrophosphate: Ca2P2O7; as well as the apatite or mineralized form: Ca5(F,Cl)(PO4)3

6. Principal Peruvian guano islands during the nineteenth century were Ballestas, Bermeja, the Chincas, Chipana, Colorada, Felix Gonzales, Guañape, Ferrol, Foca, Hormigas, Huanillos, Iquique, the Lobos, Macabi, Malabrigo, Marzoque, Pabellon de Pica, Patillos, Pelado, Pescadores, Puerto Ingles, Punta Corcobada, Punta Grande, Santa Tortuga, and Santo Martín. See Penrose, p. 119, and [Great Britain] (1852), pp. 67-75.

7. Wines (MS.), pp. 158-59; D'Invilliers, pp. 75-84; Jacob, "Predecessors," pp. 11, 14; Morfit, p. 2; Penrose, pp. 122-24; Shepard, pp. 96-99.

8. Dixon, "Notes," pp. 165-68; Hague (1862), pp. 224-43; Penrose, pp. 122-24; Wentworth, pp. 3-25.

9. Burstyn, p. 10; Rice (1972), pp. 299-300; Rice (1987) p. 446; Lamer, pp. 49-51; Sauchelli, p. 26-47; U.S. Congress. S. Doc. 190. Serial 6145, pp. 19-24, 50-64.

10. Collings, pp. 114-15; D'Invilliers, pp. 81-82; Dixon, "Guano," pp. 176-79; Dixon, "Notes," p. 172; "Guano," (1867), p. 263; Hayes, pp. 300-301; Haynes, I: 340; Julien, "Metabrushite," p. 368, 370-72, 374-76, 378; Nesbit, pp. 5-49; Palmer, pp. 274-75; Penrose, pp. 117-19; Phipson, pp. 277-78; Piggot (1856), pp. 299-300; Piggot (1857), pp. 120-22; Shepard, pp. 96-97; Skaggs (1989), pp. 84, 167; U.S. Agriculture commissioner, pp. 74-75; Wentworth, pp. 5-21; Wiens, *Atoll*, pp. 298-301.

11. American Guano Company (1860), pp. 11-27; Phoenix Guano Company (1860), *passim.*

12. Nesbit, p. 10.

13. *Ibid.*, pp. 11, 16-21; Penrose, pp. 118-22.

James J. Higgins, Maryland's first state chemist, was less generous in his appraisal of Chincan guano, assessing its chemical value at merely $45 a ton. See "Story of the fertilizer industry," p. 4.

14. Nesbit, pp. 32-45.

Not included by Nesbit were the products of several other islands, rocks, and keys either claimed or mined by Americans, whose approximate value per ton can be calculated with his formula: Alta Vela, £6 18s ($34.50); Christmas island (in the Pacific), £4 12s; ($23); Clipperton island, £3 6s ($16.50); Howland island, £6 ($30); Johnston, £2 4s ($11); Malden, £4 18s ($24.50); Monks, £4 ($20); Quito Sueño, £3 12s ($18), Pedro key £4 12s ($23), Phoenix, £6 ($30), and Sombrero, £1 5s ($6.25). For chemical content of specific island guano, see Dixon, "Notes," p. 172; Hague (1862), pp. 229, 233; Piggot (1857), p. 121; Penrose, p. 123; Phipson, p. 277; Skaggs (1989), p. 84; U.S. Agriculture commissioner, p. 75; U.S. Congress. S. Exec. Doc. 38. Serial 1316, p. 29; and "Analyses [of Christmas and Malden island guano]," n.d., in "Christmas island" file, U.S. State department, *Records . . . relating to guano islands,* reel 3.

15. R. G. Ward, II: 138.

16. U.S. Treasury department, *Foreign commerce and navigation* (1855), XIV: 276; *ibid.* (1858) XV: 295; *ibid.*, (1860) p. 294; *ibid.* (1863), XVII: 223; *ibid.* (1867), p. 270; *ibid.* (1869) p. 142. See also Rutter, p. 43.

17. Levin, pp. 107-108; "Life," p. 114; Millington, pp. 15-21; Pike, p. 134; *The Times,* August 5, 1875, p. 7d.

18. Hague (1902), p. 659.

19. Hayes, pp. 300-301; Higgins and Bickell, pp. 121-22; Julien, *passim*; Phipson, 277-78.

20. North Pacific Phosphate and Fertilizer Company, "Minutes," pp. 20, 64.

American firms were far from alone in employing scientific expertise. For examples, see works by W. A. Dixon, regarding British exploitation of Malden island, and Albert F. Ellis, regarding British geological studies generally in the Pacific.

21. Gardiner (MS.), p. 20; Haynes, I: 343; "Kettlewell's," pp. 99-105; Rasin, p. 6; "Story of fertilizer industry," p. 27; U.S. Federal Trade Commission, pp. 3-5.

22. Wines (MS.), pp. 234-47; U.S. Federal Trade Commission, pp. 4, 76-85.

23. Pacific Guano Company, p. 8.

24. William J. Kelley, "Federal Hill story: Liebig & Gibbons," n.d., p. 1 (Kelley Collection); "Brimstone, sulphuric acid, guano and fish went in: out came fertilizer and tremendous smell," unidentified newspaper clipping, n.d., in Scrapbook, Box 2 (Pacific Guano Company Collection); anonymous and untitled history of Pacific Guano Company (MS., n.d.), in historical miscellany file, Box 1, *ibid.*; Wines (MS.), p. 217; Pacific Guano Company, pp. 13, 19; Rasin, p. 6; "Story of the fertilizer industry," p. 28.

25. John S. Reese (1866), n.p., c.1. See also John S. Reese & Co. (n.d.).

26. Pacific Guano Company, p. 13.

27. John S. Reese (1866), n.p., c.1.

28. Pacific Guano Company, pp. 13, 18.

29. *Ibid.*, p. 30.

30. "Swan-Island Bulletin for 1866, 1867, and 1868" (Krupnick Collection); Pacific Guano Company, pp. 27, 34; U.S. Congress. S. Exec. Doc. 37. Serial 1031, p. 4.

31. Blackly, pp. 11-12; Haynes, I: 344, 348; Morfit, pp. 20-24; Pacific Guano Company, pp. 31-45; U.S. Congress. S. Doc. 190. Serial 6145, p. 21.
32. U.S. Congress. S. Rept. 606. Serial 3364, pp. 1-4.
33. Wines (MS.), p. 221.
34. *Mosquito,* "Ship's manifest," January 7, 1886 (Krupnick Collection); Pacific Guano Company, pp. 7, 25-30; U.S. Congress. S. Rept. 606. Serial 3364, p. 2; U.S. Federal Trade Commission, p. 193; Wells, p. 61.
35. Armour, pp. 192-94; Clemen, pp. 366-67; Morfit, pp. 25-27; "R. W. L. Rasin," p. 8; "Story of the fertilizer industry," p. 30.
36. "Story of the fertilizer industry," pp. 33-36.
37. *Ibid.*; Howard, pp. 235-41; Rutter, pp. 48-49; Whedbee, pp. 54-56.
38. Kelley, "The Federal Hill story; The R. W. L. Rasin Company," p. 3 (Kelley Collection); Haynes, I: 345; "R. W. L. Rasin," p. 8.
39. U.S. Federal Trade Commission, p. 11.
40. Howard, p. 236.
41. Nichols (1956), p. 192.
42. Skaggs (1973), pp. 371-408, 455-68.
43. Haynes, I, xliv; "Inspection laws," 80-90; Jacob, "Predecessors," p. 14; Maryland, 215-19; Rutter, pp. 45-48.
44. Blakey, pp. 1-35; Haynes, I: 346-50; Hesseltine, p. 556; U.S. Congress. S. Doc. 190. Serial 6145, pp. 19-24; U.S. Federal Trade Commission, pp. 94-101.
45. Armour, pp. 191-92; Clemen, pp. 367-68; Markham, p. 70; "Story of the fertilizer industry," p. 36; U.S. Federal Trade Commission, pp. 200-203, 209-11.
46. Sinclair, pp. 150-59.
47. Caribbean Guano Company, "Prospectus," c. 1912, in "Roncador" file, U.S. State department, *Records,* reel 5.
48. Markham, p. 62; Pike, p. 134.

    In 1991 Grace abandoned the fertilizer business altogether, focusing instead on specialty chemical and health-care businesses. See Hicks, pp. D1, D5.
49. Haynes, I: 346-48.
50. U.S. *Statutes* 17 (1873) 48.
51. U.S. Congress. H. Rept. 252. Serial 2253, p. 1; U.S. Congress. H. Rept. 4040. Serial 2890, p. 1.
52. Markham, p. 35.
53. Palmer, p. 278.

    Palmer cites unpublished data from the U.S. Treasury, Bureau of Statistics, which a diligent search has not uncovered. In any case, it appears that no one in government ever compiled figures concerning "guano brought from islands appertaining to the United States" prior to 1869.
54. U.S. Commerce and Labor department, *Circular* 132 (1906), 54.
55. Haynes, I: 350-51; U.S. Federal Trade Commission, pp. 170-244.
56. U.S. Agriculture department, *Agriculture yearbook, 1923,* p. 1188; U.S. Federal Trade Commission, pp. 8, 25-31, 86-87.

57. *Ibid.*, pp. 91, 181-211.
As late as 1930—well after the "guano mania" in the United States had subsided—American fertilizer companies continued to use the term guano, no fewer than 236 products employing the word in their trade names. See Brand, pp. 67-75.

58. Palmer, p. 278.
No official data are available for the years 1857 through 1868, which was the period of most feverish mining activity, especially in the Pacific; however, it seems reasonable to assume that output for 1857-1868 was at least equal to average shipments to the U.S. in the years 1869 through 1898, or 9,462 tons annually. Such extrapolation yields an estimated additional production of 113,548 tons. In all probability the total was far larger. Neither Palmer's figures nor simple extrapolation takes into account rock guano shipments from American appurtenances directly to Europe, which occurred illegally before the Civil War and, afterwards, legally until 1889. None of these exports was ever officially counted or unofficially estimated.

59. U.S. Congress. H. Rept. 347. Serial 744, p. 7.
W. R. Grace, who hauled guano from Peru to the United States, eventually made a fortune from the carrying and chemical trade, but he neither prospected for nor mined American guano islands.

60. A. G. Benson, p. 27.

61. U.S. Congress. S. Exec. Doc. 10. Serial 1082, pp. 7, 95.

62. U.S. Congress. S. Exec. Doc. 38. Serial 1316, pp. 38-39; U.S. Congress. S. Rept. 280. Serial 1040, pp. 3-4.

63. Caribbean Guano Company, "Prospectus," n.d., in "Roncador file," U.S. State department, *Records,* reel 5.

64. U.S. Congress. S. Exec. Doc. 151. Serial 2901, p. 10.

65. Whedbee, p. 56.

66. Gaussoin, p. 14; Navassa Phosphate Company, pp. 26-27; "Story of Wm. James."

67. Nichols (1956), p. 233.

68. "Other deaths."

69. U.S. State department, Legal Adviser's office, "Sovereignty of islands claimed under the Guano Act" (MS.), pp. 155, 466.

70. Decker (1973), p. 114.

71. North Pacific Phosphate and Fertilizer Company, "Minutes," pp. 25-26, 28, 31; Pacific Guano and Fertilizer Company, "Minutes," pp. 53, 57, 64-65.

72. Whedbee, p. 56.

73. Gardiner (MS.), p. 51; A. J. Boyd, p. 8.

74. G. C. Watson (1845/46), p. 48.

75. R. G. Ward, VIII: 14.

76. "Life," p. 118; R. G. Ward, I: 222-93.

77. "Brimstone, sulphuric acid," in Scrapbook, Box 2 (Pacific Guano Company Collection); E. H. Bryan (1941), p. 34; Pacific Guano Company, pp. 19; Skaggs (1989), pp. 58-61; R. G. Ward, II: 269-320, 404-11, 429, III: 98, IV: 91, 98, 112, VI: 510.

78. R. G. Ward, III: 409.

79. North Pacific Phosphate, "Minutes," p. 25. See also, Gardiner (MS.), p. 51.

80. *Whiton* v. *Albany*, p. 24.

81. *Ibid.*, p. 25.

82. *Ibid.*, pp. 30-31.

83. *Ibid.*

## Chapter 9: Shoveling It: Life and Labor on Guano Islands

1. A. J. Boyd, p. 8; "Guano island," p. 555; Kam, p. 41; Levin, p. 88; Robinson, p. 77; Stewart, p. 96; "Visit," pp. 434-35; Werlich, pp. 81-82.

2. Gardiner (MS.), pp. 51-53; A. J. Boyd, p. 8; "Guano island," pp. 554-55; Peck, pp. 210-11; Pike, p. 97; Robinson, 78; Stevers and Pendlebury, 106; Stewart, p. 96; "Visit," pp. 434-35; Werlich, pp. 81-82.

3. Kidd (1845), pp. 327-28, (1845-46), pp. 128-29; G. Smith, p. 8; Stewart, pp. 96-98; Watson (1845), pp. 467-68, (1845-46), pp. 48-49; Wearne, pp. 774-75.

4. Gardiner (MS.), pp. 53-54; A. J. Boyd, p. 9; Kam, p. 41; L. G. Green, pp. 26, 54-55; T.R. Moore, p. 48; Stewart, 97; G. Smith, p. 8; Schwendinger, p. 42; Watson (1845-46), p. 48.

5. Stewart, p. 5.

6. Pike, pp. 65-66.

7. Stewart, p. 6.

8. *Ibid.*, p. 8.

9. *Ibid.*, pp. 12-13; Gootenberg (1990), pp. 57, 74, 84, 98-99, 123; Levin, pp. 85-87.

10. Stewart, *passim.*

11. *Ibid.*, pp. 13-54; Schwendinger, pp. 38-40; G. Smith, p. 8.

12. Schwendinger, p. 39; G. Smith, p. 9.

13. Kam, p. 41; Levin, pp. 87-88; Pacific Guano Company, p. 21; Peck, p. 208; Schwendinger, pp. 38-40, 42; Stewart, pp. 21-24, 97-98.

14. Brookes, pp. 294-95; I. C. Campbell, pp. 103-111; Furnas, pp. 223, 240, 306, 347; Oliver, pp. 212-15; Siegel, p. 42; Wiens, *Pacific*, p. 25.

15. Boddam-Whetham, pp. 187-92; Brookes, 294; Burnett, pp. 42-46; I. C. Campbell, pp. 111-12; Furnas, 305-306, 357-66; Michener and Day, 213-47; Scarr, 5-7, 10-11, 16-17; Siegel, 42-45.

16. Bolton, pp. 50-53; Brookes, pp. 294-96; E. H. Bryan (1941), p. 126; I. C. Campbell, p. 111; Furnas, pp. 359-60; Levin, pp. 89-90; Luke, pp. 240-41; Michener and Day, p. 230; Shlomowitz, pp. 45-47.

17. Brookes, p. 295; Levin, p. 89; Schwendinger, p. 42; Stewart, pp. 14, 25-28.

18. Brookes, p. 385; Harrop, pp. 201-202; Levin, pp. 89-90; Petukhov, pp. 79-94; Schwendinger, p. 44; Shann, pp, 322-23; Sharp, p. 332; Stewart, pp. 138-205, 216-17.
    Distracted by the Civil War, the U.S. government was powerless to invoke the Monroe Doctrine, as with a contemporary intervention in Mexico by Great Britain, France, and Spain supposedly to collect foreign debts, but which actually led to the French-backed Maximilian regime.

19. Benians, pp. 347-50; Brookes, pp. 296, 370-72, 385-86; A. J. Campbell, p. 124; I. C. Campbell, pp. 111-12; Dixon, pp. 180-81; Ellis (1937), pp. 44-45, (1946), pp. 101-102; Firth

(1973), pp. 14, 25-28 (1978), pp. 36-52; Furnas, pp. 364-67; Loud, pp. 114-16; W. P. Morrell, pp. 171-86; Purcell, pp. 189-211; Siegel, pp. 44-47; J. M. Ward, pp. 219-23; R. G. Ward, V: 82-87, 92.

20. Hague (1902), p. 660; "Life," p. 115; R. G. Ward, II: 272, III: 391.
21. Hague (1902), p. 660.
22. U.S. State department, Legal Adviser's office, "Sovereignty of islands claimed under the Guano Act" (MS.), p. 784; E. H. Bryan (May 1938), p. 28; Hague (1862), pp. 225-39, (1902), p. 666; "Life," pp. 114-15, 118; Skaggs (1989), pp. 55-56; U.S. Interior department, *Other* (1992), pp. [1-9]; Wentworth, pp. 5-21.
23. U.S. State department, "Sovereignty," p. 818; E. H. Bryan (1941), p. 47.
24. W. L. Harris (MS.), pp. 17-18.
25. Donald Emerson Glidden, "The story of Swan island [*sic*]," (MS., 1960), p. 8 , in Box 2 (Pacific Guano Company Collection); Ethel M. Crowell, "Return to Swan island," (unidentified newspaper clipping, c. 1960), in Scrapbook, *ibid.*
26. Glidden, "The story of Swan island," p. 8, in *ibid.*
27. North Pacific Phosphate and Fertilizer Company, "Minutes," p. 15.
28. "Agreement," between Sam Elliott and Cecil Roberts and James Jennett, October 5, 1869, in "Rogues file," U.S. State department, *Records . . . relating to guano islands,* reel 4.
29. Petition, December 9, 1859, in *Hanuu, et al.,* v. *C. A. Williams, et al.,* First Circuit Law no. 365 (Hawaii State Archives).
30. Petition, February 7, 1868, Judgment, April 25, 1868, in *Kaona* v. *C. A. Williams, et al.,* First Circuit Law no. 531, in *ibid.*; Susan Shaner, Hawaii State Archives, January 3, 1991, to J.M.S.
31. A. F. Judd, et al., pp. 32, 41; Hague (1862), pp. 239-40, (1902), pp. 664-65; L. Howland, pp. 99-101, 103; R. G. Ward, I: 230.
32. Skaggs (1989), pp. 55-78, 90.
33. E. H. Bryan (1941), pp. 34, 58; Sauchelli (1942), p. 28; R. G. Ward, III: 431-32.
34. Pacific Guano and Fertilizer Company, "Minutes," p. 47; R. G. Ward, II: 272.

    At least some residents of the Swan islands were counted in the U.S. census of 1960, but this was long after guano mining had ceased throughout American appurtenances. See Chapter 11.
35. U.S. State department, "Sovereignty," pp. 69-70.
36. William J. Kelley, "Federal Hill story: The R. W. L. Rasin Company," (MS., n.d.), p. 1 (Kelley Collection); Skaggs (1989), p. 96.

## Chapter 10: Navassa Island

1. U.S. State department, Legal Adviser's office, "Sovereignty of islands claimed under the Guano Act" (MS.), pp. 385-87; Nichols (1933), pp. 508-509. For details of Alta Vela and Key Verd, as well as early American occupation of Navassa, see Chapter 6.
2. U.S. State department, "Sovereignty," p. 375; Burne, Horsfield, and Robinson, pp. 110-11; D'Invilliers, pp. 75-78; Gaussoin, *Memoir,* pp. 7-10; Navassa Phosphate Company, pp. 7-10.
3. D'Invilliers, p. 78.
4. Proctor, p. 50.

5. D'Invilliers, p. 77; Gaussoin, *The island of Navassa,* pp. [2-3].
6. Neil Hurley, "Navassa island light," (MS., n.d.), [p. 5], in U.S. Coast Guard Records (Commandant's Office); U.S. Coast Guard Historian's office, "History of Navassa island lighthouse" (MS., n.d.), p. 3 in *ibid.*; D'Invilliers, pp. 77, 82-84; Gaussoin, *Memoir,* pp. 5-6; "'That is the man'"; "Roby's great pluck"; "Story of Wm. James."
7. Kelley, "Federal Hill story: The R. W. L. Rasin Company," p. 2 (Kelley Collection); D'Invilliers, p. 84; "Navassa Murders"; Navassa Phosphate Company, p. [6].
8. Gaussoin, *Memoir,* p. 6; Navassa Phosphate Company, [p. 4].
9. Zinn, p. 204.
10. Gutman (1976), p. 442.
11. Carroll and Noble, p. 275.
12. Brackett, pp. 28-33.
13. W. H. Harris, p. 19.
14. *Jones* v. *U.S.,* p. 208. According to Prisoners' Record, 1879-1894, items 6798-6820, in Maryland House of Correction Records (Maryland State Archives), only four of twenty-three laborers convicted of rioting on Navassa in 1889 could read.
15. Gallilean [*sic*] Fishermen, pp. 17, 19, 27; "Navassa murders"; "Navassa rioters confess."
16. D'Invilliers, pp. 76, 80, 82-84; Navassa Phosphate Company, p. 14; "Story of Wm. James"; "'That is the man.'"
17. "'That is the man.'"
18. D'Invilliers, p. 82.
19. D'Invilliers, pp. 81-84; "'That is the man.'"
    According to D'Invilliers, p. 81, miners dug one test hole that commenced on the upper plateau 248 feet above sea level and extended 251 feet downward, mostly through pure limestone, before being abandoned with twelve to thirty-six inches of salt water at its bottom.
20. D'Invilliers, pp. 79, 83-84.
21. "'That is the man.'"
22. "Story of Wm. James." See also Gaussoin, *The island of Navassa,* plates V-VI.
23. D'Invilliers, pp. 82-84.
24. Hurley, "Navassa island light," [p. 2] (U.S. Coast Guard Records); D'Invilliers, p. 84; "'That is the man.'"
25. "Story of Wm. James."
26. *Ibid.*; Hurley, "Navassa island light," [p. 4] (U.S. Coast Guard Records); "In the Caribbean," pp. 7-8; "Navassa rioters confess"; R. J. O'Brien, p. 58; "Roby's great pluck"; "This was the motive"; E. K. Thompson, p. 174.
27. "Navassa rioters confess."
28. E. K. Thompson, p. 174.
29. Quoted in U.S. State department, *Digest* (1906) I: 558.
30. "Defense begins"; "Navassa murders"; "Story of Wm. James"; "This was the motive"; "'That is the man'"; E. K. Thompson, p. 174.
31. "Defense begins"; "Roby's great pluck"; "Story of Wm. James"; "This was the motive."

32. "Defense begins."
33. "Roby's great pluck."
34. *Ibid.*; "Story of Wm. James"; "'That is the man.'"
35. Quoted in "Defense begins."
36. *Ibid.*
37. "Roby's great pluck."

    As was typical of American newspapers during the late nineteenth century, journalists writing for the *Baltimore Sun* routinely deleted profanity and expletives from quotations. Court transcripts for the resulting legal cases have not been preserved, and it is impossible to know whether interpolated wording provided (for purposes of readability) in this and other quotations in this chapter are accurate. For certain they are far from being the only possible choices or interpretations.
38. "Navassa murders"; "'That is the man.'"
39. "Defense begins"; "Navassa murders"; "'That is the man.'"
40. "Navassa murders."
41. "'That is the man.'"
42. *Ibid.*; "Roby's great pluck."
43. "Defense begins"; "Roby's great pluck"; "'That is the man.'"
44. "Defense begins."
45. "Roby's great pluck"; "'That is the man.'"
46. "Navassa murders"; "'That is the man.'"
47. "'That is the man.'"
48. "Roby's great pluck."
49. *Ibid.*; "'That is the man.'"
50. "Roby's great pluck."
51. "Arguing to the jury"; "Navassa murders"; "Rioters from Navassa"; "Story of Wm. James"; "Was there a plot?"
52. "Roby's great pluck."
53. "'That is the man.'"
54. *Ibid.*; "Confessed one murder"; "Jury still out"; "Navassa island murders"; "Story of Wm. James."
55. "Roby's great pluck."
56. *Ibid.* See also Gallilean [*sic*] Fishermen, p. 27.
57. "Roby's great pluck"; "'That is the man.'"
58. "Roby's great pluck"; "'That is the man.'"
59. "Defense begins"; "'That is the man.'"
60. "'That is the man.'"
61. *Ibid.*; "Defense begins"; "Jury still out."
62. "Another Navassa murder trial"; "Defense begins"; "Jury is still out"; "Navassa jury locked up"; "'That is the man'"; "Was there a plot?"

63. "Defense begins"; "Navassa murders"; "Story of Wm. James."

64. "Roby's great pluck"; "'That is the man.'"

65. "Roby's great pluck"; "'That is the man.'"

66. "'That is the man.'"

67. *Ibid.*; E. K. Thompson, p. 173.

68. E. K. Thompson, pp. 173-74.

69. McGuinn, p. 151.

70. *Ibid.*; "Galena arrives"; "Riot at Navassa"; "Rioters from Navassa"; "More Navassa rioters expected today"; R. J. O'Brien, p. 57.

71. "Indicted on five separate charges"; "Key guilty of murder"; McGuinn, p. 151.
    Alleged accessories to murder were Alfred Brown, Edmund ("Blueball") Francis, James Johnson (alias, Thomas Welch), Alfred ("Texas Shorty") Jones, Amos Lee, James Phillips, James H. ("Snow") Robinson, James Tasker (or Tascar), Moses ("Dakota") Williams, Edward Woodfork, and Norman ("Juggler") Wooster. See "Convictions in Navassa murder trial."

72. "Story of Wm. James"; "'That is the man'"; "This was the motive."
    For a detailed explanation of federal court procedure prior to 1891, see Warren, pp. 240-45.

73. Brackett, pp. 52-54; Gallilean [*sic*] Fishermen, p. 3; "Jurisdiction over Navassa island"; McGuinn, pp. 147, 151-52; "Navassa rioters confess"; "Navassa rioters' trial postponed"; "This was the motive."

74. "Defense begins"; "Navassa island murders"; "Story of Wm. James"; "'That is the man.'"

75. "Story of Wm. James."

76. *Ibid.*; "Defense begins"; "Navassa island murders"; "'That is the man'"; "Was there a plot?"

77. "Arguing to the jury"; "Defense begins"; "Navassa murders."

78. "Arguing to the jury"; "Navassa rioters confess."

79. "Was there a plot?"

80. "Key guilty of murder"; "Navassa rioters."

81. "Another Navassa murder trial"; "Confessed one murder"; "Jury still out"; "Navassa murder trial progressing rapidly."

82. "United States Circuit Court."

83. "Navassa jury locked up all night."

84. "Convictions in Navassa murder trial"; "Third Navassa trial."

85. "Convictions in Navassa murder trials"; Navassa rioters"; "Navassa rioters convicted."

86. "Fate of Navassa rioters."

87. Prisoners' Record, 1879-1894, items 6798-6820, in Maryland House of Correction Records (Maryland State Archives); Sue McDonough, Civil Reference Branch, National Archives, Washington, D.C., to J.M.S, June 13, 1990; "Fate of Navassa rioters"; "Navassa rioters sentenced."
    "Navassa rioters sentenced," *New York Times,* February 21, 1890, p. 7, says the men were to be incarcerated "in the Albany (N.Y) Penitentiary"; however, according to Mark E. Shepard, New York State Department of Corrections, May 15, 1991, to J.M.S, New York has never maintained a prison at Albany. Likely the men were sent to New York's Auburn State Penitentiary, but, their fates likely will forever be unknown, because (according to William Gorman, New York State Archives, to J.M.S., January 3, 1992) state prison records are

incomplete, many of them having been destroyed before the Archives was given authority over the documents during the 1970s.

88. *Jones* v. *U.S.*, pp. 203-24; *Key* v. *U.S.*, p. 224; *Smith* v. *U.S.*, p. 224; U.S. *Stats.* 25 (1889), 656.

89. Fred Carter, Navassa island, Mar[ch] 6, 1891, to President [Benjamin Harrison] (photocopy; O'Brien Collection); McGuinn, pp. 152-53; "Navassa rioters."

Carter's original letter, housed in U.S. Navy Records, has been misplaced, perhaps misfiled after being photocopied during the 1970s for Lt. Col. Richard J. O'Brien, who was researching the U.S. Marine Corps landing on the island in 1891.

90. Harrison to B. F. Tracy, April 10, 1891, in Harrison Papers (Series 1), Reel 31.

91. Bancroft Gherardi to Horace Elmer, April 27, 1891, in U.S. Navy, *Area file . . . records,* reel 217; R. J. O'Brien, p. 56.

92. Horace Elmer to Secretary of the Navy [Tracy], May 4, 1891, in *ibid.*

93. Elmer to Lieut. Commdr. Charles Belknap, et al., April 30, 1891, in *ibid.*

94. Charles Belknap, et al., to Elmer, April 30, 1891, pp. 1-3, in *ibid.*; F. M. Everett to Belknap, April 30, 1891, in *ibid.*

95. Charles Belknap, et al., to Elmer, April 30, 1891, pp. 1-3, in *ibid.*

96. *Ibid.*

97. Everett to Elmer, May 2, 1891, in *ibid.*

98. R. J. O'Brien, p. 57.

99. Elmer to [Tracy] May 4, 1891, in U.S. Navy, *Area file . . . records,* reel 217.

100. Quoted in Elmer to Tracy, May 14, 1891 (decoded courtesy of Center for Cryptological History, Fort George G. Meade, Mary.), in *ibid.*

101. Quoted in *ibid.*; "Kearsarge at Key West."

102. *Ibid.*

103. Elmer to Tracy, May 14, 1891, in *ibid.*

104. Elmer to Navy Secretary [Tracy], May 18, 1891, in *ibid.*; USS *Kearsarge,* Deck Log, May 12, May 13, 1891, in U.S. Navy Records, Record Group 45 (National Archives).

105. Jno. H. Fowler, Navassa Phosphate, Baltimore, to Tracy, May 20, 1891, in U.S. Navy, *Area file . . . records,* reel 217.

106. Elmer to [Tracy], May 18, 1891, in *ibid.*

107. Quoted in Elmer to [Tracy], June 2, 1891, in *ibid.*

108. Elmer to [Tracy] June 20, 1891, in *ibid.*; "Kearsarge at Key West"; R. J. O'Brien, p. 58.

In 1929, Bates and his detachment were awarded the Marine Corps' new Expeditionary Medal for their landing at Navassa. See R. J. O'Brien, pp. 57-58.

109. "Slaves under our flag."

110. "Recent troubles at Navassa island."

111. Quoted in "Navassa rioters: President Harrison's. . . . "

Harrison's version of Elmer's report, as published by the *New York Times,* is at variance with the original; one passage attributed by Harrison to Elmer, as published in the newspaper, reads: "that the discipline maintained on the island seems to be that of a convict establishment, without its comforts *and clean linen,*" the italicized matter *not* appearing in the original. See *Ibid.*, and Belknap to Elmer, April 30, 1891, *Area file . . . records,* reel 217.

112. Quoted in "Navassa rioters: President Harrison's. . . ."
113. *Ibid.*
114. Criminal Docket Book A, p. 48, U.S. Circuit Court, Fourth Circuit (Maryland), Mid-Atlantic Region, in U.S. District Court Records, Record Group 21 (National Archives).
     Although the story of Harrison's commutation of sentences was prominently featured by the *New York Times,* the *Baltimore Sun* failed to mention it. For example, see, "From Washington."
115. U.S. Presidents, *Compilation,* VIII: 5625.
116. U.S. State department, "Sovereignty," pp. 391-92. The title "governor" was similarly employed elsewhere, as on Clipperton island circa 1896. See Skaggs (1989), pp. 63-64.
117. Quoted in "All quiet at Navassa."
118. "All quiet at Navassa"; R. J. O'Brien, p. 58.
119. U.S. State department, "Sovereignty," pp. 392-93.
120. U.S. State department, "Sovereignty," pp. 394-95; "Island sold at auction"; "To be rescued from Navassa island."
121. U.S. State department, "Sovereignty," pp. 394-95; "Alone on desert island"; "To be rescued from Navassa island."
     The *New York Times* description of the island resemble an exercise in creative writing. According to "Alone on desert island," Navassa "was destitute of vegetation," and the blacks who revolted there in 1889 believed "that the white men in charge of them were deliberately withholding provisions, [and] attacked and killed every white man on the island."
122. Quoted in "To be rescued from Navassa island."
123. U.S. State department, "Sovereignty," p. 395-96; "To be rescued from Navassa island."
124. Shipman, p. 190.
125. "The lesson of the humble guano islands."
126. *Downes* v. *Bidwell,* pp. 245-46.

## Chapter 11: Guano Happens

1. Nichols (1933). For assorted other treatments of American "guano diplomacy," see Duniway; W. H. Gray; Logan; Montague; J. B. Moore, pp. 241-42; Nichols (1928); Shewmaker; Stearns; M. A. Smith (1943); and Tansill.
2. U.S. State department, Legal Adviser's office, "Sovereignty of islands claimed under the Guano Act" (MS.), pp. 413-18, 606-611; W. F. Johnson, p. 74; U.S. Congress. S. Doc. 159. Serial 4912, pp. 7-9. See Chapters 5 and 7, herein.
3. W. Q. Graham to Secretary of the Treasury [John G. Carlisle], January 14, 1895, in "Letters regarding bonds of guano companies" file, U.S. State department *Records . . . relating to guano islands,* reel 7.
4. Tho[ma]s W. Cridler, "*Confidential*" to Eugene T. Chamberlain, May 12, 1899, in *ibid.*
5. S. Y. Smith to [A. A.] Adee, December 28, 1904, in "Christmas island" file, *ibid.*, reel 3.
6. Quoted in U.S. State department, *Digest* (1940), I: 512-13.
7. *Ibid.*, p. 513.
8. U.S. *Congressional record* (63d Cong., 1st sess.), L: 1922-23; U.S. *Statutes at large* 38 (1913) 224.

9. U.S. State department, *Digest* (1940) I: 513.

10. U.S. *Statutes at large* 39 (1917), part 2, p. 1763.

11. Neil Hurley, "Navassa island light" (MS., n.d.), [p. 3] (U.S. Coast Guard Records); Putnam, pp. 402-403.

12. Putnam, p. 403.

13. Hurley, "Navassa island light," [p. 4] (U.S. Coast Guard Records); Stancil, p. 4; Douglas, p. 54.

14. T. Michael Peay, Assistant Legal Adviser for Inter-American Affairs, U.S. State department, Washington, D.C., August 24, 1992, to J.M.S.; Hurley, "Navassa island light," [pp. 4-5] (U.S. Coast Guard Records); Captain R. D. Peterson, U.S. Coast Guard District 7, Miami, to J.M.S., 29 August 1990; Stancil, pp. 2-4; Kaplan, p. 195; "In the Caribbean," p. 7-8; U.S. Navy, Hydrographic Office, *List of lights,* p. 190; U.S. State department, "Sovereignty," pp. 402-404; U.S. Interior department, *Territorial areas,* p. 9.

15. U.S. State department, "Sovereignty," pp. 84-133; U.S. State department, *Digest* (1940) I: 520-24; Douglas, pp. 54-55; U.S. Navy, Hydrographic Office, *List of lights,* p. 216.

16. U.S. State department, "Sovereignty," pp. 133-40; U.S. State department, *Digest* (1940), I: 524.

17. U.S. State department, *United States treaties,* XXXIII, part 2: 1405-1433.

18. U.S. Congress. S. Rept. 606. Serial 3364, pp. 1-3.

19. U.S. State department, "Sovereignty," pp. 228; J. W. Davis, pp. 216-17; U.S. State department, *Digest* (1940), I: 516; Wells, 61-62.

    Although Adams's and Swan Island Commercial's incomplete filings came well after Andrew Rosehill's on Marcus island in 1902, which is usually considered to be the last such request for recognition under the Guano Act, Adams's and Commercial's applications did not seek to expanding the list of U.S. appurtences but, rather, to transfer possession of one that already existed.

20. U.S. State department, "Sovereignty," pp. 228-32; J. W. Davis, pp. 217-18; U.S. State department, *Digest* (1940), I: 516.

21. Wells, pp. 62-63, 65.

22. J. W. Davis, p. 216.

23. U.S. State department, "Sovereignty," pp. 301-315; U.S. State department, *Digest* (1940), I: 516-19; Wells, pp. 63-64.

24. U.S. State department, *Digest* (1940), I: 517.

25. Sargent, p. 515.

26. U.S. State department, "Sovereignty," pp. 325-26.

27. Donald Emerson Glidden, "The story of Swan island [*sic*]" (MS., 1960), pp. 28ff, Box 2 (Pacific Guano Company Collection); U.S. State department, *Foreign relations* (1940), pp. 927-40; Wells, pp. 65-66.

28. U.S. State department, *Digest* (1940), I: 520.

29. "Memorandum of points and authorities in support of defendant's motion for summary judgment," September 17, 1970, pp. 12-13, in *Sumner Smith* v. *U.S.* (1971), Civil Action 68-429-C, U.S. District Court for Massachusetts (copy in Krupnick Collection); U.S. Navy, Hydrographic Office, *List of lights,* p. 215; Wells, p. 66.

30. Kneitel, pp. 53; Wells, p. 67; Wise and Ross, pp. 328-29.

31. Richard Severo, "Future of Swan islands as obscure as beginning," unidentified newspaper clipping, in Scrapbook, Box 2 (Pacific Guano Company Collection); "Caribbean: disputed territory"; "Census"; Wise and Ross, pp. 328-32.

32. Wells, p. 67; Wise and Ross, p. 54.

33. Wise and Ross, pp. 54, 335-36.

34. "Swan islands treaty."

35. Dillon, pp. 177, 180-81, 212-13.

36. "Complaint," "Defendant's answer, first defense," "Memorandum and authorities in support of defendant's motion for summary judgment," and "Stipulation of dismissal," in *Sumner Smith* v. *U.S.* (copies in Krupnick Collection); Severo, "Future of Swan islands as obscure as beginning," Scrapbook, Box 2 (Pacific Guano Company Collection); Cornelius F. Hurley, "U.S. pulls tiny isle from under his feet," unidentified newspaper clipping in *ibid.*; "Mr. Smith says U.S. gave his islands away," unidentified newspaper clipping in *ibid.*; *Duncan* v. *Navassa Phosphate Company,* pp. 651-52.

37. U.S. State department, "Sovereignty," p. 409.

38. Interestingly, Baja Nuevo (Petrel) was among a half dozen "Gulf" islands leased by Mexico to one Francisco F. Ogilve in 1909. Contracto, 29 enero de 1909, in Secretaría de Fomento Documentos, Caja 908(3) (México, Archivo Gubernación).

39. U.S. State department, "Sovereignty," pp. 109-114; U.S. State department, *Digest* (1940), I: 520-21.

40. U.S. State department, "Sovereignty," p. 108. See also, U.S. State department, *Digest* (1940), I: 520.

    As discussed above, the United States and Columbia exchanged notes in 1928 regarding Roncador, Quito Sueño, and Serraña whereby the two nations acknowledged their conflicting interests but agreed to respect each other's property on and possible rights to these places without prejudice. The document was never submitted to either nation's legislature for ratification; hence, it never carried the legal force of a "treaty."

41. Bradford L. Thomas, Office of the Geographer, U.S. State department, Washington, D.C., to J.M.S., November 20, 1990.

42. James D. Hague, New York, to Secretary John Hay, February 9, 1900, in "Letters regarding bonds of guano companies, 1856-1912," file, U.S. State department *Records,* reel 7.

43. Levi, p. 60.

44. *Ibid.,* pp. 60-61.

45. *Ibid,* p. 61.

46. Holbrook, pp. 8-12; Levi, p. 61.

    Inclusions of Marcus, long since conceded to Japan, and Johnston, resolutely defended as U.S. property since 1859, as well as Palmyra, are curious. Levi fails to cite his source for this study, and on this point Holbrook cites Levi. Efforts to identify and locate Levi's source(s) have been fruitless.

47. U.S. Navy, Hydrographic office (1918), *passim.*

48. Levi, p. 61.

49. Geo[rge] P. Wickham, General Land Office, to Commissioner of Navigation [E.T. Chamberlain], Department of Commerce, July 27, July 28, 1921, in General Correspondence and Related Records, File #123815, Commerce department, Marine Inspection and Navigation bureau, Records, Record Group 41 (National Archives).

50. Charles E. Hughes to Secretary of Commerce [Herbert Hoover], August 27, 1921, in *ibid.*

51. U.S. State department, "Sovereignty," p. 630.

52. U.S. State department, "Sovereignty," pp. 628-30; E. H. Bryan (July 1939), pp. 5; Leff, pp. 35-37; Stephenson, p. 361-62.

53. E. H. Bryan (July 1939), p. 5; Leff, pp. 37-38; Stephenson, p. 363; U.S. State department, *Digest* (1940), I: 482.

54. U.S. State department, "Sovereignty," p. 631.

55. Stephenson, pp. 357-61.

56. U.S. State department, "Sovereignty," pp. 632-34.

57. U.S. State department, *Digest* (1940) I: 483.

58. U.S. State department, "Sovereignty," p. 634.

59. Quoted in U.S. State department, *Digest* (1940) I: 484.

60. "America annexes Swain's island," p. 27; Bryan (July 1939), p. 7; Leff, p. 42; U.S. *Statutes* 43 (1925) 1357; U.S. State department, *Digest* (1940) I: 485-86.

61. U.S. State department, "Sovereignty," *passim.*

62. *Ibid.*, p. 149.

63. U.S. *Code,* Title 48, Ch. 8, sections 1411-19.

64. Aiman (MS.), p. 58; U.S. State department, "Sovereignty," pp. 623-24, 875-76; Biddle, p. 24; Emory (1934), p. 7; W. E. Kingman; Leff, pp. 27-28; McClellan (March 1940), pp. 13-14; Nicholas, p. 626; Orent and Reinsch, p. 446; Padgett, pp. 9, 29; Parkhurst, p. 5; Sharp, pp. 182-83.

65. U.S. State department, "Sovereignty," p. 625.

66. "Kingman reef," p. 21; Padgett, pp. 9, 29; U.S. State department, *Digest* (1940) I: 511.

67. U.S. State department, "Sovereignty," p. 876.

68. U.S., *Code of federal regulations,* Executive Order 6935; [U.S. Presidents], *Presidential executive orders,* p. 584; U.S. Navy, *Report to the United Nations,* p. 55.

69. "Annexed by U.S.A."; R. B. Black, pp. 210-11; Dodge, pp. 192-95; DuPuy, pp. 59-61; Ellis (1937), p. 17; "Howland, Jarvis, and Baker"; McClellan (October 1936), pp. 5-6, 29; "Not annexed"; "Pacific dots," pp. 708; U.S., *Code of federal regulations,* Executive Orders 7358, 7568; U.S. Interior department, *Highlights,* p. 16; U.S. Interior department, *Other,* pp. [1-3]; Welty, pp. 24, 56-58; John Williams, pp. 409-410; "Wings," pp. 33-34.

70. "Agreement over Canton," pp. 521-23; R. B. Black, pp. 211-12; "Friendly rival," p. 9-10; Hall, pp. 65-76; Hobbs, p. 86-87; Reck, 671-72; "Tropical pawn," p. 15; U.S., *Code of federal regulations,* Executive Orders 7828 and 8616; U.S. Congress. H. Rept. 2573. Serial 10443, pp. 1-2; U.S. Congress. S. Rept. 536. Serial 10294, p. 1; U.S. State department, *Digest* (1940) I: 508-11; John Williams, pp. 409-410.

71. Follett, p. 80; John Williams, pp. 409-411; U.S. Interior department, *Other,* pp. [1-2].

In 1992 The International Group for Historic Aircraft Recovery (TIGHAR) claimed to have found remains of Earhart's aircraft and other artifacts about 350 miles to the southeast of Howland in the Phoenix group on Nikumaroro (Gardner) island, which was also once claimed as an American appurtenance.

72. *U.S.* v. *Fullard-Leo* (1940) pp. 775-80; (1943), pp. 745, 747; (1944) pp. 784-85.

It is not clear from whom Pacific Navigation acquired its rights to the island.

73. Rock (1929), p. 366.

74. *U.S.* v. *Fullard-Leo* (1943), pp. 746-48.

75. *Ibid.*, p. 750.

76. E. H. Bryan (May 1937), p. 13; Chong, pp. 1-2; Cooper, pp. 446-48; McClellan (February 1940), p. 22; "Palmyra islands base"; "Rejects claim to island"; U.S., *Code of federal regulations,* Executive Order 8616; U.S. Interior department, *Highlights,* p. 18; U.S. Interior department, *Other United States insular areas,* p. [7]; U.S. State department, *Digest* (1940), I: 487-91; "U.S. seeks Pacific islands"; *U.S.* v. *Fullard-Leo* (1940) p. 782; *ibid.* (1944) p. 784; *ibid.*, 156 Fed. Rep. (1946) p. 760; *ibid.*, U.S. (1946) p. 100.

77. "American bases"; E. H. Bryan (June 1937), pp. 16, 30; [Coletta], (1947), I: 27-29; Thorp, p. 29; U.S., *Code of federal regulations,* Executive Orders 4467, 8682; John Williams, pp. 409-411.

78. Braisted, pp. 175-76; [Coletta], (1947), II: 156-58; Shaplen; Thorp, p. 28.

79. Follett, p. 80; Hobbs, pp. 77-78; U.S. Interior department, *Canton* (1954), p. 2; U.S. Interior department, *Highlights,* p. 15; U.S. Interior department, *Territorial responsibilities,* p. 30.

80. Guzmán, pp. 135-82; Rossfelder, 190-267; Skaggs (1989), pp. 48-262.

81. "U.S. requests Britain cede three islands."

82. "Malden island"; Maude, pp. 31, 37; Luke, p. 167; Robson, pp. 48, 57-58; Rougier, pp. 289-93.

83. U.S. Interior department, *Territorial areas,* p. 17; "U.S. to drop claims."

84. U.S., *Friendship and territorial sovereignty: treaty with . . . Tuvala,* p. 3; U.S., *Friendship and territorial sovereignty: treaty with . . . Kiribati,* pp. 3, 5; U.S., *Maritime boundaries: treaty [with] . . . Cook islands,* pp. 3, 6. See also U.S., *Maritime boundaries: treaty [with] . . . New Zealand,* p. 5, by which that nation recognized U.S. sovereignty over Swains island.

85. Bradford L. Thomas, Office of the Geographer, U.S. State department, Washington, D.C., September 22, 1992, to J.M.S.

86. U.S. Interior department, *Other* (1990, pp. [1-3]; *ibid.*, pp. [1-3]; U.S. Interior department, *Territorial areas,* p. 23.

87. Bugliosi, *passim*; U.S. Interior department, *Highlights,* p. 18.
The television miniseries "And the Sea Will Tell" was originally broadcast by CBS on February 24 and 26, 1991.

88. Chong, pp. 1-2; U.S. Interior department, *Other* (1990), p. [7]; *ibid.* (1992), p [7]; U.S. Interior department, *Territorial areas,* p. 21.

89. Thorp, p. 1.

90. U.S. Interior department, *Other,* p. [4].

91. U.S. Defense department, p. [2].

92. *Ibid.* p. [2]; Columbia Broadcasting System evening news, June 8, 1993.

93. Cheri E. Abdelnour, Public Affairs Office, Defense Nuclear Agency, Alexandria, Va., November 21, 1990, to J.M.S.
In *The American Pacific,* p. 270, Arthur Power Dudden states unequivocally that "lonely Johnson Atoll stored chemical and nuclear weapons," but Dudden cites no source for this assertion.

94. "Storm."

95. Rear Admiral P. J. Coady, Director, Politico-Military Policy and Current Plans Division (OP-61), Office of the Chief of Naval Operations, Washington, D.C., 4 Aug[ust] 1990, to J.M.S.; "Chemical arms"; Scherer; U.S. Defense department, p. [2]; "U.S. starts pullout."
96. Scherer.
97. U.S. Presidents, *Weekly compilation,* 26 (No. 44), 1684.
98. U.S. Congress, Senate bill 3119, 101 Congress, 2d session (1990), in U.S. Congress, Senate Records (Office of the Secretary); U.S. *Congressional record* (101 Cong., 2d sess.), CXXXVI: S12129-30, S14543-44, S15319.
99. "Company selected"; "Raytheon Services"; "Time bomb"; U.S. Defense department, p. [1].
100. U.S. *Code of federal regulations,* Executive Order 9633. See also, Corey (April 1947), pp. 43, 45; Corey (December 1947), pp. 62, 64.
101. Gardiner (MS.), p. 195.
102. Bourgin, *passim*; Skaggs (1975), *passim.*
103. B. Gardiner (MS.), *passim.*
104. Skaggs (1989), pp. 41-46.

## Appendices: Guano Island Act(s)

1. U.S. *Statutes at large* 11 (1856), 199-20.
2. "Revision," p. 2.
3. U.S. *Statutes* 17 (1873) 48; U.S. *Revised statutes* (1873) 5570-5578.
4. U.S. *Code* (1989), I, vii.
5. For temporary suspensions, see U.S. *Statutes at large* 13 (1865) 494; 14 (1866) 328; 17 (1873) 48; 20 (1878) 30; 23 (1884) 11.
6. U.S. *Statutes* 17 (1873) 48 actually suspended the prohibition for ten years, commencing July 14, 1867, thereby providing *ex post facto* sanction for exports after the expiration of the 1866 law.

# Bibliography

The following list contains all works consulted and cited. Modern library style is used throughout the unabridged entry format, except for those items that contain *q.v.* (*quod vide*), which refer the reader to a complete citation elsewhere. To facilitate the location of often elusive public documents, SuDocs (U.S. Superintendent of Documents) and/or U.S. government serial set numbers are appended where appropriate.

## Unpublished Material


Adikes, Anna Maria. "The American interests in the Pacific." M.A. thesis, Columbia University, 1915.

Aiman, Eliece. "American acquisition and development of minor Pacific islands." M.A. dissertation, University of Chicago, 1944.

Boland, Brian. "Colonies and connections: American interests in guano, Santo Domingo and Haiti, 1849-1869." M.A. thesis, Northern Illinois University, 1978.

Brand, Charles J. "The significance of the word 'guano' in fertilizer terminology." National Fertilizer Association, *amicus curiae* brief in the matter of Patuxent Guano Co., Docket No. 1939, before the U.S. Federal Trade Commission, 1931. Copy in Library, University of Minnesota, St. Paul.

Everett, Edward. Papers. Massachusetts Historical Society, Boston.

Gardiner, Harvey Nelson. "Guano in American agriculture, politics and diplomacy during the mid-nineteenth century." M.A. thesis, Southern Illinois University, 1970.

Green, Duff. Papers. Southern Historical Collection, Library, University of North Carolina, Chapel Hill.

Gregg, William L. Collection. Special Collections, Hawaii State Archives, Honolulu.

Gootenberg, Paul Eliot. "Merchants, foreigners and the state: the origins of trade policies in post-independence Peru." Ph.D. dissertation, The University of Chicago, 1985.

*Hanuu, et al.,* v. *C. A. Williams, et al.* (1859). Hawaii State Archives, Honolulu.

Harris, William Lane. "The Aves island claims: a study of claims technique." M.A. thesis, Vanderbilt University, 1963.

Hawaiian Fertilizer Company, Ltd. Records. Special Collections, Hawaii State Archives, Honolulu.

Holbrook, Francis X. "United States national defense and trans-Pacific commercial air routes, 1933-1941." Ph.D. dissertation, Fordham University, 1969.

Hunt, Shane J. "Growth and guano in nineteenth century Peru." Woodrow Wilson School Research Program in Economic Development, Discussion Paper No. 34, Princeton University, 1973.

*Kaona* v. *C. A. Williams, et al.* (1868). Hawaii State Archives, Honolulu. Kelley, William J. Collection. Maryland Historical Society, Baltimore.

Krupnick, Jon E. Collection of Swan island papers. Fort Lauderdale, Florida.

Maryland House of Corrections. Records. Maryland State Archives, Annapolis.

Mexico. Secretaría de Fomento. Documentos. Archivo Gobernación, Mexico, D.F.

O'Brien, Richard J. Collection. Marine Corps Historical Center, Washington Navy Yard, Washington, D.C.

North Pacific Phosphate and Fertilizer Company. Records. Special Collections, Hawaii State Archives, Honolulu.

Olinger, John Peter. "Dreyfus Frères, guano and Peruvian government finance, 1869-1880: a chapter in economic imperialism." Ph.D. thesis, State University of New York at Binghamton, 1973.

Pacific Guano Company. Collection. Special Collections, Baker Library, Graduate School of Business Administration, Harvard University, Boston.

Pacific Guano & Fertilizer Company. Records. Special Collections, Hawaii State Archives, Honolulu.

Smith, Marshall Abbott. "The relationship of fertilizer to the American farmer and his soil during the nineteenth century." Senior thesis, Princeton University, 1942.

United States Coast Guard. Records. Office of the Commandant, Washington, D.C.

U.S. Commerce department. Marine Inspection and Navigation bureau. Records. National Archives, Washington, D.C. U.S. Congress. House of Representatives. Records. Office of the Clerk, U.S. House of Representatives, Washington, D.C.

———. Records. National Archives, Washington, D.C.

U.S. Congress. Senate. Records. Office of the Secretary, U.S. Senate, Washington, D.C.

———. Records. National Archives, Washington, D.C.

U.S. District Courts. Records. National Archives, Washington, D.C.

U.S. Navy. Records. National Archives, Washington, D.C.

U.S. State department. Legal Adviser's office. "Sovereignty of islands claimed under the Guano Act and of the northwestern Hawaiian islands, Midway and Wake." Typescript; 3 vols. [continuously paginated] 1932-33. Library, U.S. State department, Washington, D.C. JX239.1856

Wines, Richard A. "From recycled wastes to commercial fertilizers: the evolution of a technological system in the eastern United States, 1800-1880." Ph.D. thesis, Brown University, 1981.

## Published Material

"All quiet at Navassa: necessity of government interference shown by recent events." *New York Times,* July 1, 1891, p. 9.

"Alone on desert island: reported unhappy plight of four American contract workmen; went to Navassa, in the Caribbean sea, for the purpose of laboring in the phosphate beds." *New York Times,* January 29, 1901, p. 5.

"America annexes Swain's island: romantic little atoll comes into limelight." *Pacific island monthly* 5 (June 25, 1935) 26-28.

"American bases: building protective screen for Hawaii." *Pacific islands monthly* 10 (March 1940) 60.

"American discoverers of guano." *New York Daily Times,* August 19, 1856, p. 2.

"American guano [advertisement]." [Washington, D.C.] *Daily Intelligencer,* February 22, 1859, [p. 4].

American Guano Company. *Prospectus.* New York: John F. Trow, Printer, 1855.

———. *Report of experiments with American Guano.* New York: W. H. Arthur & Co., Printers and Stationers, 1859.

*American Guano Company* v. *United States Guano Company and others* 44 (1865) 23-30. In *Reports of cases in law and equity in the Supreme Court of the state of New York,* compiled and edited by Oliver Lorezo Barbour. Albany: Gould, Banks & Gould, n.d.

"Annexed by U.S.A.: Baker, Howland and Jarvis is[lands]." *Pacific island monthly* 6 (October 24, 1935) 5.

"Another Navassa murder trial: Carsar [*sic*] Fisher and Henry Jones accused of killing bookkeeper Thomas N. Foster." *Baltimore Sun,* December 14, 1889, p. 4.

Ant[on]y Gibbs & Sons. *Guano: its analysis and effects, illustrated by the latest experiments.* London: William Clowes & Sons, 1843.

*Appleton's cyclopaedia of American biography,* James Grant Wilson and John Fiske, eds. New York: D. Appleton and Company, 1889.

"Arguing to the jury: prayers of the prosecution; ruling of Judges Bond and Morris; the district attorney's opening argument; six speeches for the defense; court will be in session today." *Baltimore Sun,* November 28, 1889, p. 6.

Armagnac, Alden P. "Uncle Sam's new ocean empire." *Popular science monthly* 132 (June 1938) 22-25, 107.

Armour, J. Ogden. *The packers, the private car lines, and the people.* Philadelphia: Henry Altemus Company, 1906.

Arundel, John T. "The Phoenix group and other islands of the Pacific." [Auckland] *New Zealand Herald,* July 5, 12, 1890, n.p.

Avelar, Miguel Gonzáles. *Clipperton, isla mexicana.* [Ciudad] México: Fondo de Cultura Económica, 1992.

———. "La isla Clipperton." M. R. Vayssade, *Cartografía histórica de las islas Mexicanas,* q.v.

Bailey, Thomas A. *A diplomatic history of the American people.* 6th ed. New York: Appleton-Century-Crofts, Inc., 1958.

Bainbridge, J. S., Jr. "Five weeks on a magnet." *Audubon* (January 1991), 72-81.

*Baltimore Sun,* December 16, 1889, p. 4; December 19, 1889, p. 4; December 23, 1889, p. 6; February 10, 1890, p. 4.

Bancroft, Hubert Howe. *The new Pacific.* Rev. ed. New York: The Bancroft Company, Publishers, 1913. Bancroft, Frederick. *The life of William H. Seward.* 2 vols. New York: Harper & Brothers Publishers, 1900.

[Bartlett, C. L.]. *Guano: a treatise on the history, economy as a manure, and modes of applying Peruvian guano, in the culture of the various crops of the farm and garden.* Boston: C. L. Bartlett, 1860.

Bates, Edward. "Case of Delano and Russell." U.S. Justice department *Official opinions of attorneys general* 11 (1863) 30-31, q.v.

Baxter, Maurice C. *One and inseparable: Daniel Webster and the union.* Cambridge, Massachusetts: The Belnap Press of Harvard University Press, 1984.

Bear, Firman E., ed. *Chemistry of the soil.* New York: Reinhold Publishing Company, 1955.

Behm, Von E. "Das Amerikanisches Polynesien: und die politischen Verhaltnisse in den ubrigen Theilen des Grossen Oceans im J. 1859." *Petermann's geographische mittheilungen* 5 (1859), 173-94.

Belmont, Perry. *An American diplomat: the recollections of Perry Belmont.* 2d ed. New York: Columbia University Press, 1941.

Bemis, Samuel Flagg. "Alta Vela claim." *Dictionary of American history.* I (1976) 91, q.v.

———, ed. *American secretaries of state and their diplomacy.* 10 vols. New York: Alfred A. Knopf, 1927- 29.

———. *A diplomatic history of the United States.* 5th ed. New York: Holt, Rinehart and Winston, Inc., 1965.

———. *The Latin American policy of the United States: an historical interpretation.* New York: W. W. Norton & Company, Inc., 1943.

Benians, E. A. "The western Pacific, 1788-1885." J. H. Rose, ed., *Cambridge history of the British empire,* VII, part 1 (1933), 325-364, q.v.

Bennett, Frederick Debell. *Narrative of a whaling voyage round the globe, from the year 1833 to 1836: comprising sketches of Polynesia, California, and the Indian archipelago, etc., with an account of the southern whales, the sperm whale fishery, and the natural history of the climates visited.* 2 vols. London: Richard Bentley, 1840.

[Benson, Alfred G.] *Memorial of Alfred G. Benson to the Senate and House of Representatives of the United States.* N.p.: n.p., [1855].

[Benson, George.] "Sketch of Christmas island." *Hawaiian Spectator* 1 (1838) 64-68.

Bentor, Y. K., ed. *Marine phosphorites: geochemistry, occurrences, genesis.* Tulsa, Oklahoma: Society of Economic Paleontologists and Mineralogists Special Publication No. 29 (1980).

———. "Phosphorites, the unsolved problem." In Y. K. Bentor, ed., *Marine phosphorites* (1980), 3-18, q.v.

Bernstein, Joseph. "El Niño is trouble-maker." *Nature* 51 (1958) 461-64.

Bertrand, Kenneth J. "Geographical exploration by the United States," pp. 256-91, in Herman R. Friis, ed., *The Pacific basin,* q.v.

"'Best fertilizer' source recovers under control." *Science news letter.* 67 (May 7, 1955) 296.

"Bid of £575,000: shipping company's huge purchase of shares." *The Times,* July 27, 1917. p. 6b.

Biddle, Clement. "Some Pacific ocean islets appertaining to the United States: a brief historical and descriptive narrative." Geographical Society of Philadelphia *Bulletin* 16 (1918) 18-26.

"Birds at work in Peru." *The Economist* 197 (October 1, 1960), p. 58.

Black, Jeremiah S. "Cayo Verde." U.S. Justice department *Official opinions of attorneys general* 9 (1859) 406, q.v.

———. "Guano islands." U.S. Justice department *Official opinions of attorneys general* 9 (1857) 30-33, q.v.

———. "Johnson's [*sic*] island." U.S. Justice department *Official opinions of attorneys general* 9 (1859) 364-71, q.v.

———. "Sombrero island." U.S. Justice department *Official opinions of attorneys general* 9 (1857), 128-29, q.v.

Black, Richard B. "American equatorial islands." *The American year book* (1938) 210-12.

Blakey, Arch Fredric. *The Florida phosphate industry: a history of the development and use of a vital mineral.* Cambridge, Massachusetts: Harvard University Press, 1973.

Boddam-Whetham, J. W. *Pearls of the Pacific.* London: Hurst and Blackett, Publishers, 1876.

Boggs, S. Whittmore. "American contributions to geographical knowledge of the central Pacific." *Geographical review* 28 (April 1938) 177-92.

Bolton, Herbert Eugene, and Thomas Maitland Marshall. *The colonization of North America.* New York: The Macmillan Company, 1920.

Bolton, W. W. "Tragedy of the *Moroa:* fierce fight aboard labour vessel in 1869." *Pacific islands monthly* 8 (September 1937) 50-53.

Bonilla, Heraclio. *Guano y burguesía en el Perú.* Lima: Instituto de Estudios Peruanos, 1974.

Bourgin, Frank. *The great challenge: the myth of laissez-faire in the early republic.* New York: George Braziller, 1989.

Boyd, A. J. "Reminiscences of Chinca islands." Royal Geographical Society of Australia, Queensland Branch, *Proceedings and transactions* 8 (1892-93) 3-12.

Boyd, Andrew, comp. *Boyd's New London directory, 1874-5.* New London, Connecticut: C. Allyn, 1874.

Brackett, Jeffrey R. *Notes on the progress of the colored people of Maryland since the war: a supplement to The negro in Maryland, a study of the institution of slavery.* Baltimore: Publication Agency of the Johns Hopkins University, 1890.

Braisted, William R. "Johnston island, U.S. naval facility, 1941-1948." P. E. Coletta, ed., *United States Navy and Marine Corps bases, overseas* (1985), 175-76, q.v.

Brigham, William T. *An index to the islands of the Pacific ocean: a handbook to the chart on the walls of the Bernice Pauahi Bishop Museum of Polynesian ethnology and natural history.* Honolulu: Bishop Museum Press, 1900.

Brookes, Jean Ingram. *International rivalry in the Pacific islands, 1800-1875.* Berkeley: University of California Press, 1941.

Brooks, Thomas R. *Toil and trouble: a history of American labor.* New York: Dell Publishing Co., Inc., 1964.

Brown, Norman D. *Daniel Webster and the politics of availability.* Athens: University of Georgia Press, 1969.

Brown, Philip Marshall. "Frederick T. Frelinghuysen." In S. F. Bemis, ed., *The American secretaries of state and their diplomacy* VIII, q.v.

B[rowne], D.J. "Fertilizers: guano, its history, sources, qualities, and applications." U.S. Congress. S. Exec. Doc. 42, part 3. Serial 755, pp. 90-102, q.v.

Bryan, Edwin H., Jr. *American Polynesia: coral islands of the Central Pacific.* Honolulu: Tongg Publishing Company, 1941.

———. *American Polynesia and the Hawaiian chain.* Honolulu: Tongg Publishing Company, 1942.

———. "Bennett's description of Caroline island." *Paradise of the Pacific* 51 (1939) 19-21.

———. "Johnston island, an island of Hawaii." *Paradise of the Pacific* 49 (June 1937) 16, 30.

———. "Laysan, an island of Hawaii." *Paradise of the Pacific* 50 (May 1938) 21, 28-29.

———. "Natural history of the Phoenix islands." Bernice P. Bishop Museum *Special publications* 34 (1939) 6-7.

———. "Palmyra, part of Hawaii." *Paradise of the Pacific* 49 (May 1937) 13.

———. *Panala'au memoirs.* Honolulu: Bernice P. Bishop Museum, 1974.

———. "Swains island, U.S.A." *Paradise of the Pacific* 51 (July 1939) 5-8.

———. "Phoenix guano islands: eclipse mecca." *Paradise of the Pacific* 49 (April 1937) 27, 31-32.

———. "What were the guano islands?" *Paradise of the Pacific* 51 (September 1939) 5-7; (October 1939) 18-20.

Bryan, William Alanson. "A monograph of Marcus island." Bernice P. Bishop Museum *Occasional papers* 2 (1902) 77- 124.

Bryce, James. *South America: observations and impressions.* Detroit: Bay View Reading Club, 1912.

Buell, Raymond Leslie. "Our colonial empire imposes a huge administrative task: in the Pacific as well as in the Caribbean, to be visited by the president, it presents a variety of governmental problems." *New York Times,* March 22, 1931, XX, 3.

Bugliosi, Vincent, with Bruce B. Henderson. *And the sea will tell.* New York: W. W. Norton, 1991.

Bunting, W. H., compiler and annotator. *Portrait of a port: Boston, 1852-1914.* Cambridge, Massachusetts: The Belknap Press of Harvard University, 1971.

Burne, R. V., W. T. Horsfield, and E. Robinson. "The geology of Navassa island." *Caribbean journal of science,* 14 (December 1974), 109-114.

Burnett, Frank. *Through tropical seas.* London: Francis Griffiths, 1910.

Burr, Robert N. *By reason or force: Chile and the balancing of power in South America, 1830-1905.* Berkeley: University of California Press, 1965.

Burstyn, Harold L. "Science pays off: Sir John Murray and the Christmas island phosphate industry, 1886-1914." *Social studies of science* 5 (1975) 5-34.

Callahan, James Morton. *American relations in the far East, 1784-1900.* Johns Hopkins University *Studies in historical and political science* 19 (1901) 9-175.

Cameron, Frank K. *A preliminary report on the fertilizer resources of the United States.* U.S. Congress. S. Doc. 190. Serial 6145, q.v.

Campbell, A. J. "Notes from Malden island." *The Victorian naturalist* 7 (1889) 123-26.

Campbell, Charles S. *The transformation of American foreign relations, 1865-1900.* New York: Harper & Row, Publishers, 1976.

Campbell, I. C. *A history of the Pacific islands.* Berkeley: University of California Press, 1989.

"Canton island." *Newsweek* 16 (October 16, 1940) 15.

"Caribbean: disputed territory." *Time* 75 (May 2, 1960) 24.

Carrillo y Ancona, Crescencio. *La isla de Arenas: apuntes para la defensa de la integridad del territorio nacional, con relación á dicha isla, y á otras muchas que con ella se enlazan en las costas de Yucatan.* [Cuidad México]: Mérida de Yucatan, 1886.

Carroll, Peter N., and David N. Noble. *The free and the unfree: a new history of the United States*. 2d ed. New York: Penguin Books, 1988.

Caruthers, J. Wade. *American Pacific ocean trade: its impact on foreign policy and continental expansion, 1784-1860*. New York: Exposition Press, 1973.

"Casa Grace." *Fortune* 12 (December 1935) 94-101, 157-58, 161.

Caulkins, Frances Manwaring. *The history of New London, Connecticut: from the first survey of the coast in 1612, to 1852*. New London: The Author, 1852.

"Census spotlights old pirate lair." *U.S. news & world report* 48 (April 25, 1960) 16.

"Chemical arms disposal late, report says." *Washington Post*, August 30, 1990, p. A4.

Chong, Jerry. "Palmyra: peril of Polynesia." *Honolulu Advertiser*, June 6, 1948, pp. 1-2.

"Christmas island." Pacific Science Association Sixth Congress *Proceedings* 4 (1940) 502.

Ciba Foundation. *Phosphorus in the environment: its chemistry and biochemistry*. Amsterdam: Excerpta Medica, 1979.

Clemen, Rudolf Alexander. *The American livestock and meat industry*. New York: The Ronald Press, 1923.

Closson, Mabel H. "Under the southern cross." *Overland monthly* 21 (1893) 205-16.

[Cochet, Alexander]. *Truth demonstrated and culumny defeated: brief historical abridgment of the facts which prove the titles of Alexander Cochet to obtain the prize which, as true discoverer of the value of guano, has been awarded to him by the Committee on Prizes of the Congress of 1849*. Lima: Printing House of *El Correo*, 1851.

Coker, Robert E. "Regarding the future of the guano industry and the guano-producing birds of Peru." *Science* 28 (July 10, 1908) 58-64.

Cole, Fred. "Guano." *Dictionary of American history* 3 (1976) 230, q.v.

Coletta, Paolo E., ed. *American secretaries of the Navy*. 2 vols. Annapolis, Maryland: Naval Institute Press, 1980.

[Coletta, Paolo E.] *Building the Navy's bases in World War II: the history of Bureau of Yards and Docks and Civil Engineer Corps, 1940-46*. 2 vols. Washington, D.C.: United States Government Printing Office, 1948. D795.U6bA48, or N21.2:B86/2/v.2

———, ed. *United States Navy and Marine Corps bases, overseas*. Westport, Connecticut: Greenwood Press, 1985.

Collings, Gilbeart H. *Commercial fertilizers: their sources & use*. 3d ed. Philadelphia: The Blakiston Company, 1941.

"Colonial concessions." *The Times*, July 21, 1910, p. 6c.

C[olumbia] B[roadcasting] S[ystem]. *Evening news*, May 30, 1990; June 8, 1993.

"Company selected for big DOE contract." *Raytheon News*, May 1990, p. 1.

"Confessed one murder: Henry Jones tells of his crime on Navassa island." *Baltimore Sun*, December 18, 1889, p. 4.

Connor, Seymour V. *Adventure in glory: the saga of Texas, 1836-1849*. Austin: Steck-Vaughn Company, 1965.

"Convictions in Navassa murder trial." *Baltimore Sun*, February 13, 1890, p. 6.

Cooling, Benjamin Franklin. *Benjamin Franklin Tracy: father of the modern American fighting navy.* Hamden, Connecticut: Archon Books, 1973.

Cooper, Henry E. "My Palmyra." *Mid-Pacific magazine* 10 (1915) 446-51.

Corey, Herbert. "A legal key to Davy Jones' locker." *Science digest* 42 (December 1947), 62-66.

———. "A legal key to Davy Jones' locker: a forgotten murder provides a background for our announced right to seek oil in the Gulf of Mexico." *Nation's business* 35 (April 1947), 43-45.

Craven, Avery Odelle. *Soil exhaustion as a factor in the agricultural history of Virginia and Maryland,, 1606- 1860.* Champaign: University of Illinois Press, 1926.

Cufley, C. F. H. *Ocean freights and chartering.* London: Staples Press, 1962.

Current, Richard N. *Daniel Webster and the rise of national conservatism.* Boston: Little, Brown and Company, 1955.

Cutler, Carl C. *The story of the American clipper ship: greyhounds of the sea.* New York: Halcyon House, 1930.

Daniel, Hawthorne. *Islands of the Pacific.* New York: G. P. Putnam's Sons, 1943.

Davis, John W. "Sovereignty over Swan islands." U.S. Justice department *Official opinions of attorneys general* 31 (1918) 216-224, q.v.

Davis, William J. *Professional and industrial history of Suffolk County, Massachusetts.* 3 vols. Boston: The Boston History Company, 1894.

Dawson, E. Yale. "Changes in Palmyra atoll and its vegetation through the activities of man, 1913-1958." *Pacific naturalist: contributions from the Beaudette Foundation for Biological Research* 1 (1959) 1-51.

"Death of Central Pacific pioneer [James Morgan Ellis]." *Pacific island monthly* 11 (September 1940) 47.

"Died: [Abram P.] Patterson." *Baltimore Sun,* April 5, 1893, p. 4.

Decker, Robert Owen. *The New London merchants: the rise and decline of a Connecticut town.* New York: Garland Publishing, Inc., 1986.

———. *The whaling city: a history of New London.* Chester, Connecticut: Published for the New London Historical Society by the Pequot Press, 1976.

———. *Whaling industry of New London.* York, Pennsylvania: Liberty Cap Books, 1973.

"Defense begins: evidence in Navassa trial; had the officers been drinking? Witnesses say there was rum on the island; was it a conspiracy or a strike? The attack of Francis on Mr. Roby." *Baltimore Sun,* November 26, 1889, p. 6.

Deneger, Otto, and Edwin Gillaspy. "Canton island, South Pacific." *Atoll research bulletin* 41 (1955) 1-41.

*Dictionary of American history.* Rev. ed. New York: Charles Scribner's Sons, 1976.

Dill, Homer R., and W[illia]m Bryan. *Report of an expedition to Laysan island in 1911.* U.S. Agriculture department Biological Survey Bulletin No. 42 (1912).

Dillon, Sam. *Comandos: the CIA and Nicaragua's contra rebels.* New York: Henry Holt and Company, 1991.

D'Invilliers, Edward V. "The phosphate deposits of the island of Navassa." Geological Society of America *Bulletin* 2 (January 27, 1891) 75-84.

Dixon, W. A. "The guano and other phosphatic deposits occurring on Malden island." Royal Society of New South Wales (Sydney, Australia) *Journal and proceedings* 11 (1877) 176-81.

———. "Notes on the meteorology and natural history of a guano island." Royal Society of New South Wales (Sydney, Australia) *Journal and proceedings* 11 (1877) 165-75.

Dodge, Ernest S. *Islands and empires: western impact on the Pacific and east Asia.* Minneapolis: University of Minnesota Press, 1976.

*Downes* v. *Bidwell* (1901). 182 U.S. 244-392.

Douglas, Edward M. *Boundaries, areas, geographical centers and altitudes of the United States and the several states, with a brief record of important changes in their territory and government.* 2d ed. Washington, D.C.: United States Department of the Interior, Geological Survey *Bulletin* 817 (1930). I19.3:817

Dudden, Arthur Power. *The American Pacific: from the old China trade to the present.* New York: Oxford University Press, 1992. Dulles, Foster Rhea. *America in the Pacific: a century of expansion.* New York: Houghton Mifflin Company, 1938.

*Duncan* v. *Navassa Phosphate Company* (1891). 137 U.S. 647-54. See also, *Grafflin* v. *Nevassa* [*sic*] *Phosphate Company.*

Duniway, Clyde Augustus. "Daniel Webster (second term)" S. F. Bemis, *American secretaries of state and their diplomacy* 6 (1928) 77-113, q.v.

Dunmore, John. *French explorers in the Pacific.* 2 vols. Oxford: At the Clarendon Press, 1965.

DuPuy, William Atherton. "Our new islands: three new American possessions, small but of future importance." *Current history* 45 (February 1937) 58-64.

Eaton, Clement. *The growth of southern civilization, 1790- 1860.* New York: Harper & Row, Publishers, 1961.

Ellis, Albert F. *Adventuring in coral seas.* Sydney: Angus & Robertson Limited, 1937.

———. *Mid-Pacific outposts.* Auckland: Brown and Stewart, 1946.

———. *Ocean island and Nauru: their story.* Sydney: Angus and Robertson Limited, 1936.

Emery, K. O. "Marine geology of Johnston island and its surrounding shallows, Central Pacific ocean." Geological Society of America *Bulletin* 67 (1956) 1505-19.

Emory, Kenneth P. *Archaeology of the Pacific equatorial islands.* Bernice P. Bishop Museum Bulletin 123, 1934.

———. "Additional notes on the archaeology of Fanning island." Bernice P. Bishop Museum *Occasional papers* 15 (1939) 179-89.

"England in the Pacific (from an occasional correspondent)." *The Times,* September 6, 1906, p. 10a.

Espinosa, Antonio Vázques de. *Compendium and description of the West Indies,* trans. by Charles Upson Clark. *Smithsonian miscellaneous collections* 102 (1942): SI1:7:102.

Etzold, H. Thomas. *The conduct of American foreign relations: the other side of diplomacy.* New York: New Viewpoints, 1977.

Evans, Henry Clay, Jr. *Chile and its relations with the United States.* Durham, North Carolina: Duke University Press, 1927.

"Fabens, Joseph Warren." *National cyclopaedia of American biography* 7 (1897) 178.

Fairbanks, Helen R., and Charles P. Berkey. *Life and letters of R. A. F. Penrose, Jr.* New York: Geological Society of America, 1952.

"Fanning island." Polynesian Society *Journal* 15 (1906) 125.

"Fanning island." Pacific Science Association Sixth Congress *Proceedings* 4 (1940) 501.

"Fate of Navassa rioters: three to be hanged and others sentenced to prison and hard labor." *Baltimore Sun,* February 21, 1890, p. 5.

"Father Rougier: memories of one of Pacific's notable personalities." *Pacific islands monthly* 13 (July 1943) 1.

"Feathered factories." *Américas* 4 (May 1952) 24-8.

Finney, Ben R. "Recent finds from Washington and Fanning islands." *Journal of the Polynesian Society* 67 (1958) 70-72.

Firth, Stewart. "German firms in the western Pacific islands." *The journal of Pacific history* 8 (1973) 10-28.

———. "German labour policy in Nauru and Angaur, 1906-1914." *The journal of Pacific history* 13 (1978) 36-52.

"Fliers on an isle, is hope of expert: Miss Earhart's adviser tells her husband she may have set up radio on atoll." *New York Times,* July 4, 1937, p. 3.

"Flint island." Pacific Science Association Sixth Congress *Proceedings* 4 (1940) 503.

Forbes, H. O. "The Peruvian guano islands." *Ibis,* Series 10, vol. 1 (1913) 709-13.

Follett, Helen. *Ocean outposts.* New York: Charles Scribner's Sons, 1942.

Foner, Philip S. *Business & slavery: the New York merchants & the irrepressible conflict.* New York: Russell & Russell, 1968.

Forbes, Frank H. "The old Boston water front." W. S. Rossiter, ed., *Days and ways in old Boston* (1917) 45-59, q.v.

"Foreign corporations: under laws of the United States for particular territory or District of Columbia." *American jurisprudence.* 2d ed. Rochester, New York: The Lawyers Co-operative Publishing Company, 1968. 36: 24-25.

Fosberg, F. R. "Description and occurrence of atoll phosphate rock in Micronesia." *American journal of science* 255 (October 1957) 584-92.

Frankfurter, Felix, and James M. Landis. *The business of the Supreme Court: a study in the federal judicial system.* New York: The Macmillan Company, 1928.

Freedley, Edwin T. *Philadelphia and its manufacturers: a hand-book of the great manufacturers and representative mercantile houses of Philadelphia in 1867.* Philadelphia: Edward Young & Co., 1867.

Freeman, Otis W., ed. *Geography of the Pacific.* New York: John Wiley & Sons, Inc., 1951.

"Friendly rival claims for Canton island: British official party now in possession there," *Pacific islands monthly* 8 (March 24, 1938) 9-18.

Friis, Herman R., ed. *The Pacific basin: a history of its geographical exploration.* New York: American Geographical Society Special Publication No. 38, 1967.

"From Washington: a swarm of official callers at the White House; President Harrison's busy day." *Baltimore Sun,* May 18, 1891, p. 6.

Fuess, John C. "Guano islands, Union of South Africa." U.S. Department of the Interior *Fishery leaflet* 305 (May 1948) 1-6.

"The function of private bills." *Congressional quarterly's guide to the Congress of the United States: origins, history and procedures.* Washington, D.C.: Congressional Quarterly Service, 1971.

Furnas, J. C. *Anatomy of Paradise: Hawaii and the islands of the South Seas.* New York: William Sloane Associates, Inc., 1947.

Galarza, Mae. *The guano islands [of Peru].* Washington, D.C.: The Pan-American Union with the cooperation of the Office of the Coordinator of Inter-American Affairs, 1942. PA1.2:G9314

"Galena arrives: nine prisoners on board; accused of murder and mutiny; they are now in the Baltimore jail; latest news from Navassa; the flagship's officers; cruise of the Ewing." *Baltimore Sun,* October 28, 1889, p. 4.

Gallilean [*sic*] Fishermen. *The Navassa island riot.* 1st ed. Baltimore: The American Job Office, 1889.

"Ganges island: Japanese naval surveyors report it has disappeared." *New York Times,* June 28, 1933, p. 1.

Gara, Larry. *The presidency of Franklin Pierce.* Lawrence: University Press of Kansas, 1991.

Gardner, Brian. *The East Indian Company: a history.* New York: Dorset Press, 1971.

Gardner, Irvine C. "Crusoes of Canton island: life on a tiny Pacific atoll that has recently flashed into world importance." *National Geographic* 73 (June 1938) 749-66.

Gates, Paul W. *The farmer's age: agriculture, 1815-1860.* New York: Harper & Row, 1960.

Gaussoin, Eugene. *The island of Navassa, illustrated from sketches by Eugene Gaussoin.* Baltimore: s.n., 1866.

———. *Memoir on the island of Navassa (West Indies).* Baltimore: J. B. Roise & Co., 1866.

Gibbs, Ant[on]y, & Sons. See Ant[on]y Gibbs & Sons.

Gifford, Bill. "My country 'tis of me." *Washington City Paper,* April 26, 1991, pp. 21-28.

Gigot, Paul A. "The smallest nation has a rare problem: too much wealth: Nauru phosphate income fell from the sky, bringing much laziness and waste." *Wall Street Journal,* September 22, 1983, pp. 1, 14.

Gill, William. *Gems of the Pacific: or, incidents of contrast between savage and Christian life of the South Seas islanders.* 2 vols. London: Ward and Co., 1956.

Gómez, Francisco González. "Islas de norponiente de Yucatán." M. R. Vayssade, *Cartografía histórica de la islas Mexicanas,* q.v.

Gootenberg, Paul. *Between silver and guano: commercial policy and the state in postindependence Peru.* Princeton, New Jersey: Princeton University Press, 1989.

Gordon, Wendell G. *The economy of Latin America.* New York: Columbia University Press, 1950.

Graebner, Norman A., ed. *Manifest destiny.* New York: The Bobbs-Merrill Company, Inc., 1968.

*Grafflin* v. *Nevassa* [*sic*] *Phosphate Company* (1888). 35 Fed. Rep. 474-77. See also, *Duncan* v. *Navassa Phosphate Company.*

Gras, Norman Scott Brien. *A history of agriculture in Europe and America.* New York: F. S. Crofts & Co., 1925.

Grattan, C. Hartley. "Our unknown Pacific islands." *Harper's* 182 (April 1941) 523-32.

———. *The United States and the southwest Pacific.* Cambridge, Massachusetts: Harvard University Press, 1961.

Gray, Lewis Cecil. *History of agriculture in the southern United States to 1860.* New York: Peter Smith, 1941.

Gray, William H. "The human aspect of Aves diplomacy." *The Americas* 6 (July 1949) 72-84.

[Great Britain.] *Correspondence respecting the guano islands of Lobos de Tierra & Lobos de Fuera, 1833-1852: presented to the House of Commons, by command of Her Majesty, in pursuance of their address of May 14, 1852.* London: Printed by Harrison and Son, [1852].

———. Colonial Office. *Gilbert and Ellice islands colony and the central and southern Line islands: report for the years 1954 and 1955.* London: Her Majesty's Stationery Office, 1957.

———. *Gilbert and Ellice islands colony and the central and southern Line islands: report for the years 1968.* London: Her Majesty's Stationery Office, 1969.

[Gregg, David Lawrence.] *The diaries of David Lawrence Gregg: an American diplomat in Hawaii, 1853-1858,* edited by Pauline King. Honolulu: Hawaiian Historical Society, 1982.

———. House of Commons. *Debates.* 1852.

"Green, Duff." *Dictionary of American biography* 7 (1931) 540- 42.

Green, Fletcher Melvin. "Duff Green: industrial promoter," in *Democracy in the old South, and others essays,* edited by J. Isaac Copeland. [Nashville:] Vanderbilt University Press, 1969.

Green, Lawrence G. *Panther head: the full story of the bird islands off the southern coast of Africa, the men of the islands, and the birds in their millions.* London: Stanley Paul and Co., Ltd., 1955.

Greenhill, Robert. "Merchants and the Latin American trades: an introduction," pp. 159-97, in D. C. M. Platt, ed., *Business imperialism* (1977), q.v.

Gruss, Louis. "The 'Mission' to Ecuador of Judah P. Benjamin." *Louisiana historical quarterly* 23 (1940), 162-69.

"Guano." *The land we love* 2 (1867) 261-66.

"Guano." *The Oxford English dictionary* 6: 911. 2d ed.; 20 vols. Oxford: Clarendon Press, 1989.

"Guano: its history and uses." *DeBow's review* 16 (1853) 459-63.

"Guano at the Lobos islands." *The Times,* May 26, 1852, p. 8d.

"Guano island." *National* 3 (1853) 553-56.

"Guano islands." U.S. *Code* (1989), Title 48, Ch. 8, Sect. 1411-1419, q.v.

"Guano islands." U.S. *Revised statutes* (1873), Title 72, Sec. 5570-78, or, U.S. *Statutes at large* 18, part 1 (1873), Sec. 5570-78, q.v.

"Guano islands." U.S. Justice department *Digest of the official opinions of the attorneys-general* (1885) q.v.

"Guano islands." U.S. State department, *Digest of international law* 1 (1940) 503-24. S7.12:940/1 q.v.

"Guano islands." U.S. State department, *Digest of international law* 1 (1906) 556-80. S7.12:906/1 q.v.

"Guano on the Lobos islands." *The Times,* May 13, 1852, p. 8f.

"The guano question." *The Times,* June 26, 1852, p. 8b.

"Guano war: decisive diplomacy of Secretaries Webster and Graham." *New York Daily Times,* August 18, 1852, p. 1.

Gunderson, Gerald. *The wealth creators: an entrepreneurial history of the United States.* New York: Truman Talley Books, 1989.

Gutman, Herbert G. *The black family in slavery and freedom, 1750-1925.* New York: Pantheon Books, 1976.

———. *Power & culture: essays on the American working class.* New York: Pantheon Books, 1987.

Guzmán, Teresa Arnaud de. *Tragedia de Clipperton (la isla de Pasión).* Mexico City: N.p., 1982.

Haas, William H., ed. *The American empire: a study of the outlying territories of the United States.* Chicago: University of Chicago Press, 1940.

Hagan, Kenneth J. *American gunboat diplomacy and the old navy, 1877-1889.* Westport, Connecticut: Greenwood Press, 1973.

Hague, J. D. "On phosphatic guano islands of the Pacific ocean." *American journal of science and arts* 34 (September 1862) 224-43.

———. "Our equatorial islands: with an account of some personal experiences." *Century* 64 (September 1902) 653-70.

———. "Some coral islands and islanders." *Atlantic monthly* 22 (July 1868) 36-51.

Hall, Russell E. "Conflicting interests in Pacific islands." *Far eastern survey* 7 (March 23, 1938) 65-67.

Halstead, Murat. *Pictorial history of America's new possessions: the isthmian canals* [*sic*] *and the problem of expansion; comprising six books in one volume; being a history and description of each of Porto Rico, Cuba, Hawaii, the Philippines, isthmian canal, and a discussion of the problem of expansion.* Chicago: The Dominion Company, [c. 1898].

Harris, J. A. "Bat-guano cave environment." *Science* 169 (September 1970) 1342-3.

Harris, William H. *The harder we run: black workers since the Civil War.* New York: Oxford University Press, 1982.

Harrison, Benjamin. *Papers.* 151 reels; Washington, D.C.: Library of Congress Microfilm, c 1960.

Harrop, A. J. "New Zealand and the empire, 1852-1921." J. H. Rose, ed., *Cambridge history of the British empire* VII, part 2 (1933), 201-224, q.v.

Hart, Thomas C. "The United States and the Pacific islands." American Academy of Political and Social Science *Annals* 225 (1948) 115-23.

Hayes, A. A. "On Monks island guano." *American journal of science and arts* 22 (1856) 300-301.

Haynes, William. *American chemical industry,* [*a history:* 6 vols. (1945-54), Vol. I] *background and beginnings, 1609- 1911.* New York: D. Van Nostrand, 1954.

Hedrick, Ulysses Prentiss. *A history of agriculture in the state of New York.* New York: Hill and Wang, 1966.

"Helicopter builds an aerial span to guano cave in Grand Canyon: big vacuum cleaner to be used to mine deposits left by giant, meat-eating bats millions of years ago." *New York Times,* March 27, 1957, pp. 43, 47.

Henshaw, Henry W. "Our mid-Pacific bird reservation." U.S. Agriculture department, *Yearbook . . . 1911* (1912), 155-64, q.v.

Herring, Hubert. *A history of Latin America: from the beginnings to the present.* 3d ed. New York: Alfred A. Knopf, 1968.

Hesseltine, William B. *The South in American history.* New York: Prentice-Hall, Inc., 1943.

Hicks, Jonathan P. "New Grace strategy plans a $1.5 billions sale of units." *New York Times*, November 8, 1991, pp. D1, D5.

Higgins, James, and Charles Bickell. "On Colombian guano: its composition and character." *American journal of science and arts* 23 (May 1857) 121-22.

Hobbs, William Herbert. *The fortress islands of the Pacific.* Ann Arbor, Michigan: J. W. Edwards, 1945.

Holden, E. S. "Caroline island: history." National Academy of Science *Memoirs* 2 (1883) 20-22.

"Honorable Charles Augustus Williams, 1829-1899." New London [Conn.] Cemetery Association *Cedar Grove Cemetery* 1 (1936), 15.

"How Canton island got its name." *Pacific island monthly* 11 (September 1940) 29-30.

Howland, Charles F. *American relations in the Caribbean: a preliminary issue of section I of the annual survey of American foreign relations, 1929.* New York: Arno Press & the *New York Times*, 1970.

Howland, Llewellyn. "Howland island, its birds and rats, as observed by a certain Mr. Stetson in 1854." *Pacific science* 9 (1955) 95-106.

"Howland island claimed for U.S. two years ago." *New York Times*, July 3, 1937, p. 3.

"Howland, Jarvis and Baker islands: America's claim not to be disputed." *Pacific island monthly* 6 (March 19, 1936) 21.

Howard, George W. *The monumental city: its past history and present resources.* Baltimore: J. D. Ehlers & Co., 1873.

Hurtado, Osvaldo. *Political power in Ecuador*, translated by Nick D. Mills, Jr. Boulder, Colorado: Westview Press, 1985.

Hutchinson, George Evelyn. *The biochemistry of vertebrate excretion.* New York: American Museum of Natural History Monograph No. 3, 1950.

———, Harry G. Albaum, Harold C. Hodge, Jacob Sacks, and Henry A. Lardy. *The biochemistry of phosphorus.* [East Lansing:] Michigan State College Press, 1952.

Ihde, Aaron J. "Fertilizers." *Dictionary of American history* III (1976) 16, q.v

"In the Caribbean: hams and goats." *Time* 119 (May 3, 1982), 7-8.

Inder, Stuart, ed. *Pacific islands year book.* 12th ed. Sydney: Pacific Publications, 1977.

"Indicted on five separate charges." *Baltimore Sun*, November 15, 1889, p. 4.

"Inspection laws." *The southern planter*, 16 (March 1856) 80- 90.

"Island expedition French: Christmas island occupation permit granted; aim not given." *New York Times*, February 22, 1937, p. 8.

"Island sold at auction: Navassa, in Caribbean sea, goes to only bidder for $25,000; transaction to be investigated for stockholders of the company that owned the property." *New York Times*, September 22, 1900, p. 1.

"Islands for sale: romantic story of Fanning and Washington." *Pacific islands monthly* 5 (July 1935) 5.

Ivey, M. L., Jr., J. A. Breyer, and J. C. Britton. "Sedimentary facies and depositional history of the Swan islands, Honduras." *Sedimentary geology*, 27 (1980), 195-212.

Jacob, K. D. "History and status of the Superphosphate industry." U.S. Agriculture department, Agriculture Research Service, *Superphosphate: its history, chemistry, and manufacture* (1964) 19-94, q.v.

———. "Predecessors of Superphosphate." U.S. Agriculture department, Agriculture Research Service, *Superphosphate: its history, chemistry, and manufacture* (1964) 8-18, q.v.

John S. Reese & Co. *General agents for Soluble Pacific Guano in the southern states. Richmond Enquirer* supplement, July 1866, 2pp.

[———]. *The testimony of five hundred farmers concerning Soluble Pacific Guano, which, with letters heretofore published, amount to over 3,000, showing its uniform quality and superior excellence: warranted fine and dry for application by the drill.* [Baltimore: John S. Reese & Co., n.d.]

Johnson, Robert Erwin. *Thence round Cape Horn: the story of United States naval forces on Pacific station, 1818-1923.* Annapolis, Maryland: United States Naval Institute, 1963.

Johnson, Willis Fletcher. *America's foreign relations.* 2 vols. New York: The Century Co., 1921.

*Jones* v. *United States* (1890). 137 U.S. 202-24.

Jordan, Weymouth T. "The Peruvian guano gospel in the old South." *Agricultural history* 23 (1949) 211-21.

Judd, Albert Francis, [G. P. Judd, and C. H. Judd]. *The guano islands: diary of A. Francis Judd's voyage to Jarvis island, 1858; memorandum journal of G. P. Judd, voyage to Jarvis, Barker, and Howland islands, 1859; letter of C. H. Judd to J. O. Carter, Dec[ember] 7, 1859, written from Baker.* Honolulu: A. F. Judd 2nd, 1935.

Judd, Gerrit P., IV. *Dr. Judd, Hawaii's friend: a biography of Gerrit Parmele Judd (1803-1873).* Honolulu: University of Hawaii Press, 1960.

———. *Hawaii: an informal history.* New York: Collier Books, 1961.

Julien, A. A. "Observations on the Sombrero guano." *The American journal of science and arts* 36 (1863) 424-26.

———. "On metabrushite, zeugite, ornithite and other minerals of the key of Sombrero." *The American journal of science and arts* 40 (1865) 367-79.

———. "On two varieties of sponge-spicules." *The American journal of science and arts* 40 (1865) 379-83.

"Jurisdiction over Navassa island." *Baltimore Sun,* November 7, 1889, p. 4.

"Jury still out: trying to reach a verdict in the Navassa murder trial; an unexpected incident in court; a juror's mother dies and he is overcome." *Baltimore Sun,* December 21, 1889, p. 4.

Kann, Robert A., and Zdenêk V. David. *The peoples of the eastern Habsburg lands, 1526-1918.* Seattle: University of Washington Press, 1984.

Kam, Katherine. "Through Chinese eyes." *Oceans* 14 (1981) 41.

Kaplan, H. R. "The unluckiest island." *Motor boating* 117 (March 1966), 193-95.

"Kearsarge at Key West: she reports phosphate company strikers bound for Baltimore." *New York Times,* June 27, 1891, p. 1.

Kelly, Alfred H., and Winifred A. Harbison. *The American constitution: its origins and development.* 3d ed. New York: W. W. Norton & Company, Inc., 1963.

Kemble, John Haskell, ed. *To California and the South Seas: the diary of Albert G. Osbun, 1849-1851.*

Kennedy, J. N. "A little-known bird colony in the Gulf of Mexico." *Ibis* 5 (1910) 41-43.

Kerr, James Edward. *The insular cases: the role of the judiciary in American expansion.* Port Washington, New York: Kennikat Press, 1982.

"Kettlewell's Manipulated Guano," [advertisement] *American farmer* (5th series) 2 (September 1860) 99-106.

"Key guilty of murder: Williams declared not guilty; a disagreement as to the others." *Baltimore Sun,* December 3, 1889, p. 1.

*Key* v. *U.S.* (1890). 137 U.S. 224.

Keyte, G. S. "Fanning's island: an incident." [Honolulu] *Friend,* May 1, 1861, 35.

Kidd, Charles. "Poisonous effects of guano." *Medical times* 12 (1845) 327-28.

———. "The toxic agency of guano." *Medical times* 13 (1845/46) 128-29.

Kilman, Scott. "Seeds of change: farmers, eying costs and the environment, limit use of chemicals, but evolving attitudes mean hard times for a dealer in fertilizer and pesticides; new era for an Iowa elevator." *Wall Street Journal,* May 30, 1990, pp. A1, A4.

[King, Robert D.] *Index to the islands of the Territory of Hawaii, including other islands under the sovereignty of the United States scattered in the North Pacific ocean.* [Honolulu: Office of Territorial Surveyor, 1931.]

Kingman, W. E. "Letter to the editor." [Honolulu] *Friend,* September 29, 1855, p. 69.

"Kingman reef, or 'Antipodes here we come'." *Paradise of the Pacific* 49 (1937) 21, 31.

Kiste, Robert C. "Termination of the U.S. trusteeship in Micronesia." *The journal of Pacific history* 21 (1986) 127-38.

Kneitel, Tom. "Radio Swan: the thorn in Castro's side." *Popular electronics* 14 (March 1961) 52-54.

Knox, Dudley W. *A history of the United States Navy.* New York: G. P. Putnam's Sons, 1936.

Kolodny, Y. "The origin of phosphorite deposits in light of occurrences of recent sea-floor phosphorites." Y. K. Bentor, ed., *Marine phosphorites* (1980), 249, q.v.

Krauss, N. L. H. *Bibliography of the Line islands, central Pacific.* Honolulu: N. L. H. Krauss, 1970.

———. *Bibliography of the Phoenix islands, central Pacific.* Honolulu: N. L. H. Krauss, 1970.

———. *Bibliography of Swains island, American Samoa.* Honolulu: N. L. H. Krauss, 1970.

———. *Johnston island (central Pacific) bibliography.* Honolulu: N. L. H. Krauss, 1969.

Kuykendall, Ralph S. *The Hawaiian kingdom, 1854-1874.* Honolulu: University of Hawaii Press, 1953.

LaFeber, Walter. *The new empire: an interpretation of American expansion, 1860-1898.* Ithaca, New York: Cornell University Press, 1963.

Laing, Edith M. "The guano birds of Peru." *Nature magazine* 35 (April 1942) 204.

Lamer, Mirko. *The world fertilizer economy.* Stanford, Calif.: Stanford University Press, 1957.

Laxton, P. B. "Nikumaroro." [Auckland] New Zealand Polynesian Society *Journal* 61 (1952) 62-89.

Leary, Paul M. *The Northern Marianas covenant and American territorial relations.* Institute of Governmental Studies Research Report 80-1, University of California, Berkeley, 1980.

Leeson, Ida. *A bibliography of bibliographies of the South Pacific.* London: Oxford University Press, 1954.

Leff, David N. *Uncle Sam's Pacific islets.* Stanford, California: Stanford University Press, 1940.

"The lesson of the humble guano islands." *New York Sun,* November 8, 1900, p. 6.

Levi, Werner. "American attitudes toward Pacific islands, 1914-1919." *Pacific historical review* 17 (1948) 55-64.

Levin, Jonathan V. *The export economies: their pattern of development in historical perspective.* Cambridge, Massachusetts: Harvard University Press, 1960.

Lewis, C. Bernard. "The history of the Pedro and Morant cays." *Jamaican historical review* 1 (1948) 1-9.

———. "Treasure on the Pedro bank." *Jamaican historical review* 2 (1949) 26-32.

Liebig, Justus. *Organic chemistry in its applications to agricultural physiology.* 2d American ed., with introduction, notes, and appendix by John Y. Webster. Cambridge: John Owen, 1841.

"Life on a guano island." *The nautical magazine and naval chronicle* 39 (1870) 113-18.

Lindley, M. F. *The acquisition and government of backward territory in international law: being a treatise on the law and practice relating to colonial expansion.* London: Longmans, Green and Co., Ltd., 1926.

"Lobos documents: Mr. Webster to Capt. Jewett of the Philomela." *New York Daily Times,* August 12, 1852, p. 1.

"The Lobos guano islands." *New York Daily Times,* July 15, 1852, p. 4.

"The Lobos guano islands." *The Times,* May 14, 1852, p. 8b.

"The Lobos islands." *New York Daily Times,* August 20, 1852, p. 1.

"The Lobos question: the correspondence." *New York Daily Times,* August 31, 1852, p. 1.

"The Lobos question: Mr. Webster's letter." *New York Daily Times,* August 25, 1852, p. 4.

Logan, Rayford W. *The diplomatic relations of the United States with Haiti.* Chapel Hill: University of North Carolina Press, 1941.

Loud, Emily S. "A day on a guano island." *Californian* [illustrated magazine] 3 (January-June, 1881) 113-16.

Lowe, Percy R. *A naturalist on desert islands.* London: Witherby & Co., 1911.

Luke, Harry. *Britain and the South Seas.* Rev. ed. London: Longman, Green and Co., 1949

———. *Islands of the South Pacific.* London: George G. Harrap & Co., Ltd., 1962.

Mackie, Marshall. "British-American Pacific islands." *Paradise of the Pacific* 52 (June 1940) 11, 22.

Magdoff, Harry. *The age of imperialism: the economics of U.S. foreign policy.* New York: Monthly Review Press, 1969.

[Magoon, Charles E.] *Legal status of the territory and inhabitants of the islands acquired by the United States during the war with Spain, considered with reference to the territorial boundaries, the constitution, and laws of the United States.* See U.S. Congress. S. Doc. 234. Serial 3858, q.v.

Malcomson, Scott L. "Stranger than paradise." *Mother Jones* 14 (January 1989) 19-21, 51-54.

"Malden island to-day: uninhabited barren rock was once world's most valuable guano deposit." *Pacific island monthly* 8 (October 1937) 30.

Manchester, Curtis A., Jr. "The exploration and mapping of the Pacific," pp. 61-88, in O. W. Freeman, ed., *Geography of the Pacific* (1951), q.v.

Maples, Glynn. "Peru's guano industry is imperiled as flocks of cormorants shrink: offshore islands yielding less fertilizer." *Wall Street Journal,* September 3, 1969, p. 1.

Markham, Jesse W. *The fertilizer industry: study of an imperfect market.* Nashville: Vanderbilt University Press, 1958.

Marshall, Bailey S. "Christmas island of the United States." *Paradise of the Pacific* 51 (March 1939) 11-12, 15.

Marti, Donald B. "Agricultural journalism and the diffusion of knowledge: the first half-century in America." *Agricultural history* 54 (1980), 28-37.

Maryland. House of Delegates. *Journal of proceedings at the January session, eighteen hundred and fifty-eight.* Annapolis: Thomas J. Wilson, 1858.

Mather, Eugene, and John Fraser Hart. "The geography of manure." *Land economics* 32 (1956) 25-38.

Mathew, W. M. "Antony Gibbs & Sons, the guano trade and the Peruvian government, 1842-1861," pp. 337-70, in D. C. M. Platt, ed., *Business imperialism* (1977) q.v.

———. *The house of Gibbs and the Peruvian guano monopoly.* London: Royal Historical Society, 1981.

Maude, H. E. "The colonization of the Phoenix islands." New Zealand Polynesian Society *Journal* 61 (1952) 62-89.

———. *Of islands and men: studies in Pacific history.* Melbourne: Oxford University Press, 1968.

———. "Post-Spanish discoveries in the central Pacific." New Zealand Polynesian Society *Journal* 70 (1961) 67-111.

———. "Spanish discoveries in the central Pacific." New Zealand Polynesian Society *Journal* 68 (1959) 284-326.

———. "Sovereignty over Christmas island." *Australian outlook* 11 (1957) 31-37.

May, Robert E. "Lobbyists for commercial empire: Jane Cazneau, William Cazneau, and U.S. Caribbean policy, 1846-1878." *Pacific historical review* 48 (1979) 383-412.

McClellan, Edwin North. "The American island of Washington." *Paradise of the Pacific* 52 (May 1940) 19, 24.

———. "Is Fanning an American island?" *Paradise of the Pacific* 52 (April 1940) 23-24.

———. "Jarvis to Baker to Howland." *Paradise of the Pacific* 52 (1940) 19-20, 29.

———. "Kingman reef of the United States." *Paradise of the Pacific* 52 (March 1940) 13-14.

———. "Under three flags: Palmyra island." *Paradise of the Pacific* 52 (February 1940) 22.

McGuinn, Henry J. "Equal protection of the law and fair trials in Maryland." *Journal of Negro history* 24 (April 1939) 143-66.

McIntire, Elliot G., comp. *Canton island, Phoenix islands: a library brochure,* edited by William L. Thomas. N.P.: Prepared for the Pacific Missile Range, Point Mugu, California, by the University of California, 1960.

McKinley, Albert Edward. *Island possessions of the United States: volume twenty, the history of North America.* 20 vols. Philadelphia: George Barrie & Sons, 1907.

Merk, Frederick. *Manifest destiny and mission in American history: a reinterpretation.* New York: Alfred A. Knopf, 1963.

———. *The Monroe doctrine and American expansionism, 1843- 1849.* New York: Alfred A. Knopf, 1966.

Michener, James A., and A. Grove Day. *Rascals in paradise.* New York: Random House, 1957.

Miller, Rory. "British firms and the Peruvian government, 1885-1930," pp. 371-94, in D. C. M. Platt, *Business imperialism* (1977) q.v.

Millington, Herbert. *American diplomacy and the war of the Pacific.* New York: Columbia University Press, 1948.

Mokyr, Joel. *The lever of riches: technological creativity and economic progress.* New York: Oxford University Press, 1990.

Monberg, Torben. *The reaction of people of Bellona island towards a mining project.* Copenhagen: International Work Group for Indigenous Affairs, 1976.

Montague, Ludwell Lee. *Haiti and the United States, 1714- 1938.* Durham, North Carolina: Duke University Press, 1940.

Monteón, Michael. *Chile in the nitrate era: the evolution of economic dependence, 1880-1930.* Madison: University of Wisconsin Press, 1982.

Moore, John Bassett. *American diplomacy: its spirit and achievements.* New York: Harper & Brothers Publishers, 1905.

———. *The principles of American diplomacy.* New York: Harper & Brothers Publishers, 1918.

Moore, Tui de Roy. "Guano." *Oceans* 14 (1981), 45-50.

"More Navassa rioters expected today." *Baltimore Sun,* November 1, 1889, p. 4.

Morfit, Campbell. *Practical treatise on pure fertilizers: and the chemical conversions of rock guanos, maristones, coprolites, and the crude phosphates of lime and alumnia generally, into various valuable products.* New York: D. Van Nostrand, Publishers, 1872.

Morison, Samuel Eliot. *The maritime history of Massachusetts, 1783-1860.* Boston: Houghton Mifflin Company, 1921.

Morón, Guillermo. *A history of Venezuela,* translated and edited by John Street. New York: Roy Publishers, Inc., 1964.

Morrell, Benjamin, Jr. *A narrative of four voyages to the South Seas, north and South Pacific ocean, Chinese sea, Ethiopic and southern Atlantic ocean, Indian and Antarctic ocean, from the year 1822 to 1831: comprising critical surveys of coats and islands, with sailing directions, and an account of some new and valuable discoveries, including the Massacre islands, where thirteen of the author's crew were massacred and eaten by cannibals, to which is prefixed a brief sketch of the author's early life.* New York: J. & J. Harper, 1832.

Morrell, W. P. *Britain in the Pacific islands.* Oxford: At the Clarendon Press, 1960.

Morris, Charles. *Our island empire: a hand-book of Cuba, Porto Rico, Hawaii, and the Philippine islands.* J. B. Lippincott Company, 1899.

Morris, Penrose Clibborn. "How the Territory of Hawaii grew and what domain it covers." Hawaiian Historical Society *42nd annual report* (1933) 13-19.

Morris, Richard B., ed. *Encyclopedia of American history.* New York: Harper & Brothers, Publisher, 1953.

Motteler, Lee S. *Pacific island names: a map and name guide to the new Pacific.* Honolulu: Bishop Museum Miscellaneous Publication 34, 1986.

Mowat, Charles L. "The entry of the southwest Pacific into world politics." *Southwest Pacific and the war.* Berkeley: University of California Press, 1944.

"Mr. Benson, the Evening post, and Col. Thomas." *New York Daily Times,* November 8, 1852, p. 5.

"Mr. Webster, Mr. Benson, and the Evening post." *New York Daily Times,* November 6, 1852, p. 1.

Murphy, Robert Cushman. *Bird islands of Peru: the record of a sojourn on the west coast.* New York: G. P. Putnam's Sons, 1925.

———. "Peru profits from sea fowl." *National Geographic* 115 (March 1959) 395-413.

———, Robert J. Niedrach, and Alfred M. Bailey. *Canton island.* Denver Museum of Natural History *Museum pictorial* No. 10. (1955).

National Fertilizer Association. *Code of trade practices of the fertilizer industry, amended and revised December 1929.* Washington, D.C.: National Fertilizer Association, n.d.

*National geographic atlas of the world.* 5th ed. Washington: National Geographic Society, 1981.

*Navassa Guano Company* v. *Chicago, Milwaukee & St. Paul Railway Company et al.* Case No. 6901, in U.S. Interstate Commerce Commission, *Reports* 39 (1916) 171-72, q.v.

"Navassa island murders." *Baltimore Sun,* November 25, 1889, p. 6.

"Navassa jury locked up all night." *Baltimore Sun,* February 12, 1890, p. 6.

"Navassa murder trial postponed until Friday." *Baltimore Sun,* December 11, 1889, p. 4.

"Navassa murder trial progressing rapidly." *Baltimore Sun,* December 17, 1889, p. 4.

"Navassa murders: nearly all the testimony in; the arguments may begin today; what took place before the riot according to the prisoners' side of the story; not uneasy as to the result." *Baltimore Sun,* November 27, 1889, p. 6.

Navassa Phosphate Company. [Prospectus]. New York: Navassa Phosphate Company, 1864.

"Navassa rioters." *New York Times,* February 16, 1890, p. 10.

"Navassa rioters: President Harrison's sharp denunciation of the company. *New York Times,* May 3, 1891, p. 3.

"Navassa rioters confess: they will tell all about the murders; jurisdiction of the island." *Baltimore Sun,* November 8, 1889, p. 9.

"Navassa rioters convicted." *New York Times,* February 15, 1890, p. 4.

"Navassa rioters sentenced." *New York Times,* February 21, 1890, p. 7.

"Navassa rioters' trial postponed." *Baltimore Sun,* November 12, 1889, p. 4.

Nelson, Edward W. "Bats in relation to the production of guano and the destruction of insects." U.S. Department of Agriculture *Bulletin* 1395 (March 1926) 1-12.

Nesbit, J. C. *The history and properties of the different varieties of natural guanos.* London: Rogerson and Tuxford, 1860.

Newbury, C. W. "The South Pacific islands." In Charles Osborne, ed., *Australia, New Zealand and the South Pacific,* 455-74, q.v.

Nevins, Allan. *Hamilton Fish: the inner history of the Grant administration.* Rev. ed. 2 vols. New York: Frederick Ungar Publishing Co., 1957.

"New Pacific Coal & Oil, Ltd., plans 1-for-5 reverse split." *Wall Street Journal,* January 13, 1960, p. 17.

*New York Evening News,* November 24, 1852, p. 1.

*New York Times,* June 14, 1852, p. 1; March 16, 1919, p. 7; October 1, 1931, p. 12; November 22, 1934, p. 4; September 1, 1935, p. 7; February 22, 1937, p. 8.

Nicholas, William H. "American pathfinders in the Pacific." *National Geographic* 89 (May 1946) 617-40.

Nichols, Roy F. *Advance agents of American destiny.* Philadelphia: University of Pennsylvania Press, 1956.

———. *Franklin Pierce: young hickory of the granite hills.* Philadelphia: University of Pennsylvania Press, 1958.

———. "Jeremiah Sullivan Black." S. F. Bemis, ed., *American secretaries of State and their diplomacy* 6 (1928) 387-406, q.v.

———. "Latin American guano diplomacy." A. Curtis Wilgus,

———, ed. *Modern hispanic America.* Washington, D.C.: The George Washington University Press, 1933, pp. 517-43.

———. "Navassa, a forgotten acquisition." *American historical review* 38 (April 1933) 505-10.

———. *A short history of American democracy.* New York: D. Appleton-Century Company, 1943.

Nicholson, J. Shields. *A project of empire: a critical study of the economics of imperialism, with special reference to the ideas of Adam Smith.* London: Macmillan and Co., Limited, 1909.

"Not annexed." *Pacific islands monthly* 6 (October 24, 1935) 5.

Nufer, Harold F. *Micronesia under American rule: an evaluation of the strategic trusteeship (1947-77).* Hicksville, New York: Exposition Press, 1978.

O'Brien, Richard J. "The landing at Navassa, 1891: a little known episode in Marine Corps history." *The Marine Corps gazette* 61 (1977) 56-58.

O'Brien, Robert Lincoln. "Advertising in Boston, 1847-1914." W. S. Rossiter, ed., *Days and ways in old Boston* (1915) 77-81, q.v.

Olinger, John Peter. "The guano age in Peru." *History today* 30 (June 1980): 13-18.

Oliver, Douglas L. *The Pacific islands.* 3d ed. Honolulu: University of Hawaii Press, 1989.

"Operation of the agriculture bureau of the patent office." *DeBow's review* 23 (1857) 77-85.

Orent, Beatrice, and Pauline Reinsch. "Sovereignty over islands in the Pacific." *American journal of international law* 35 (July 1941) 443-61.

Osborne, Charles, ed. *Australia, New Zealand and the South Pacific: a handbook.* New York: Praeger Publishers, 1970.

Osma, J[uan] Y. de. *Vindication of the policy of the Peruvian government in the management of the guano trade, in a letter from the Peruvian minister, Washington, to a gentleman in Philadelphia, first published in the "North American and United States Gazette"," of that city, on the 26th of May, 1856.* N.p.: n.p., n.d.

O'Sullivan, James L. "The trust territory of the Pacific." *American foreign service journal* 26 (December 1949), 16-17, 44, 46, 48.

"Other deaths: Mr. Alfred G. Benson." *New York Times,* April 20, 1878, p. 8.

"Pacific dots: islets coveted as aviation prepares for antipodes." *Literary digest* 123 (January 23, 1937) 7-8

Pacific Guano Company. *The Pacific Guano Company: its history, its products and trade, its relation to agriculture; exhausted guano islands of the Pacific ocean; Howland's island, Chincha islands, etc., etc.; the Swan islands; the marl beds and phosphate rock of South Carolina; chisolm's island phosphate; the menhaden.* Cambridge: Printed for The Pacific Guano Company by The Riverside Press, 1876.

"Pacific Guano and Fertilizer Company, for 1936." *New York Times,* June 6, 1937, p. 43.

"Pacific Islands Co. (Limited)." *The Times,* April 20, 1899, p. 11e.

"Pacific phosphate." *The Times,* October 31, 1912, p. 19f.

"Pacific phosphate: a romantic enterprise." *The Times,* May 22, 1913, p. 17d.

"Pacific Phosphate Company." *The Times,* December 19, 1912, p. 11b.

"Pacific Phosphate Company (Limited)." *The Times,* May 7, 1906, p. 13e.

Padgett, John L. "Kingman reef becomes American." *Paradise of the Pacific* 49 (May 1937) 9, 29.

Palmer, T. S. "A review of economic ornithology in the United States." U.S. Agriculture department *Yearbook, 1899* (1899) 259-292. A1.10:899

"Palmyra island." U.S. State department *Digest of international law* 1 (1940) 487-91, q.v.

"Palmyra islands base for navy gets setback." *New York Times,* December 24, 1940, p. 7.

Paolino, Ernest N. *The foundations of the American empire: William Henry Seward and U.S. foreign policy.* Ithaca, New York: Cornell University Press, 1973.

Parkhurst. Joseph L., Jr. "*Betsey's* voyage of Pacific discovery." *Pacific discovery* 12 (September-October 1959), 4-5.

Paynter, Raymond A., Jr. "Birds of the Swan island." *Wilson bulletin* 68 (June 1956), 103-110.

Peck, George W. *Melbourne and the Chincha islands: with sketches of Lima, and a voyage around the world.* New York: Charles Scribner, 1854.

Penrose, R. A. F., Jr. "Nature and origin of deposits of phosphate of lime." U.S. Geological Survey *Bulletin* 46 (1888) 475-617. I19.3:42-46

"Peruvian guano." *The Times,* June 12, 1852, p. 8d.

*Petrel Guano Co. and others* v. *Jarnette* [*sic*] *and others.* 1885. 25 Fed. 675-79.

Petukhov, V.I. "Poslediyaya interventsiya Ispanii v yzhoi Amerike (1863-1866)." *Voprosy istorill* 7 (1970) 79-94.

Phillips, Samuel F. "Guano islands in the Pacific." U.S. Justice department *Official opinions of attorneys general* 14 (1873) 608-11, q.v.

Phipson, T. L. "On Sombrerite." Chemical Society of London *Journal* 15 (1862) 277-78.

"Phoenix group: now included in Gilbert and Ellice colony." *Pacific islands monthly* 7 (May 1937) 64

[Phoenix Guano Company.] *Phoenix guano from McKean's island, Pacific ocean, imported by the Phoenix Guano Company.* New London, Connecticut: Starr & Farnham, Book and Job Printers, 1860, 1866.

Pierpoint, J. B. "The natural." *Baltimore business journal* 7 (September 11-17, 1989) 1, 15.

Piggot, A. Snowden. "Hard guano of Monks island." *American journal of science and arts* 23 (1857) 120-23.

———. "Monks island or Colombian guano." *American journal of science and arts* 22 (1856) 299-300.

Pike, Frederick B. *The modern history of Peru.* New York: Frederick A. Praeger, Publishers, 1969.

Pittman, G. A. *Nauru: the phosphate island.* London: Longmans, 1959.

Platt, D. C. M., ed. *Business imperialism, 1840-1930: an inquiry based on the British experience in Latin America.* Oxford: At the Clarendon Press, 1977.

———. *Finance, trade, and politics in British foreign policy, 1815-1914.* Oxford: Clarendon Press, 1968.

———. "Introduction." D. C. M. Platt, ed., *Business imperialism* (1977), pp. 1-14, q.v.

Points, Betty Lou. *America the beautiful: a popular guide to travel in the United States and its possessions for everyone who wants to see America first.* New York: Greenwich Book Publishers, 1957.

*Poisoned winds of war.* Public Broadcasting System, *Nova,* 1990.

"Polyps of coral and guano gave us Howland." *Paradise of the Pacific* 49 (February 1937) 20, 31.

Pomeroy, Earl S. "American policy respecting the Marshalls, Carolines, and Marianas, 1898-1941." *Pacific historical review* 17 (1948) 43-53.

———. *Pacific outpost: Americn strategy in Guam and Micronesia.* Stanford, California: Stanford University Press, 1951.

———. *The territories and the United States, 1861-1890: studies in colonial administration.* Seattle: University of Washington Press, 1947.

Pratt, Julius W. *America's colonial experiment: how the United States gained, governed, and in part gave away a colonial empire.* New York: Prentice-Hall, Inc., 1950.

"Present status of the guano islands." *New York Sun,* November 16, 1900, p. 6.

Proctor, George R. "Observations on Navassa island." *Geonotes: quarterly newsletter of the Jamaica Group of the Geologists' Association,* 2 (1959), 49-54.

"Productive guanay." *Time* 66 (October 24, 1955) 85.

Purcell, David C., Jr. "The economics of exploitation: the Japanese in the Mariana, Caroline and Marshall islands, 1915-1940." *The journal of Pacific history.* 11 (1976), 189-211.

Putnam, George R. "An important new guide for shipping: Navassa light, on a barren island in the West Indies, is the first signal for the Panama Canal." *National Geographic* 34 (1918), 401-406.

"R. W. L. Rasin, Ph.D." *The American fertilizer* 1 (July 1894) 8.

Rasin, R. W. L. "Growth of the fertilizer industry." *The American fertilizer* 1 (July 1894) 5-8.

Rasmussen, Wayne D., ed. *Agriculture in the United States: a documentary history.* 4 vols. New York: Random House, 1975.

Rayback, Robert J. *Millard Fillmore: biography of a President.* Buffalo: Published for the Buffalo Historical Society by Henry Stewart, Incorporated, 1959.

"Raytheon Services Nevada begins work at DOE test site." *Raytheon News,* December 1990, pp. 1-2.

"Recent troubles at Navassa island." *Baltimore Sun,* May 15, 1891, p. 4.

Reck, Daisy D. "Gentlemen's agreement in the South Seas." *American foreign service journal* 17 (1940) 671-707.

Reese, John S. & Co. See John S. Reese & Co.

Reeves, J. S. "Editorial comment: agreement over Canton and Enderbury islands." *American journal of international law* 33 (July 1939) 521-26.

Rehnquist, William H. *Grand inquests: the historic impeachments of Justice Samuel Chase and President Andrew Johnson.* New York: William Morrow and Company, Inc., 1992.

"Rejects claim to island: Supreme Court won't review dispute of U.S. Palmyra title." *New York Times,* May 11, 1943, p. 15.

"Revision of the statutes." *New York Times,* July 14, 1871, p. 2.

"Rhodes super phosphate of lime [advertisement]." [Washington, D.C.] *Daily Intelligencer,* February 23, 1859, [p. 4.]

Rice, A. L. [Tony]. *Deep-sea challenge: the John Murray/Mabahiss expedition to the Indian ocean, 1933-34.* Paris: UNESCO, 1986.

———. "H.M.S. *Challenger:* midwife to oceanography." *Sea frontiers* 18 (1972) 291-305.

———. "Oceanography on stamps: the Christmas Island Phosphate Company." *Sea frontiers* 33 (1987) 444-53.

"Riot at Navassa: a number of Americans killed; the Galena ordered to the scene." *Baltimore Sun,* September 20, 1889, p. 1.

"Rioters from Navassa: participants and witnesses; the Romance and Alice arrive; how the Negroes were arrested, brought to the city and lodged in jail; curious crowds on the streets." *Baltimore Sun,* November 2, 1889, p. 2.

Rippy, J. Fred. *British investment in Latin America, 1822- 1949: a case study in the operations of private enterprise in retarded regions.* Minneapolis: University of Minnesota Press, 1959.

Roberts, Stephen H. *The history of French colonial policy, 1870-1925.* Hamden, Connecticut: Archon Books, 1963.

Robertson, James Oliver. *America's business.* New York: Hill and Wang, 1985.

Robinson, Solon. *Guano: a treatise of practical information for farmers, containing plain directions how to apply Peruvian guano to the various crops and soils of America, with a brief synopsis of its history, locality, quantity, method of procurement, prospect of continued supply, and price; an analysis of its composition, and value as a fertilizer, over all other manures.* New York: Solon Robinson, 1853.

Robson, R. W. "Rougier: missionary who became king of the atolls." *Pacific islands monthly* 18 (December 1947) 48, 57-58.

"Roby's great pluck: wounded but full of fight: the Navassa island murder trial; testimony of four of the officers; the rioters were determined and blood-thirsty; individual encounters." *Baltimore Sun,* November 23, 1889, p. 6.

Rock, Joseph F. *Palmyra island, with a description of its flora.* College of Hawaii Publications *Bulletin* 4, 1916.

———. "The voyage of the Luka to Palmyra island." *The Atlantic monthly* 144 (1929) 361-66.

Rose, J. Holland, et al., eds. *The Cambridge history of the British Empire.* 8 vols. Cambridge: At the University Press, 1929-59.

Ross, S. G. "Dengue fever at Fanning island (central Pacific)." 2 *The medical journal of Australia* (1948) 63- 66.

———. "Fanning island (central Pacific): its past and present." *The medical journal of Australia* 2 (1947) 540- 48.

———. "Preliminary report on fish poisoning at Fanning island (central Pacific)." *The medical journal of Australia* 2 (1947) 617-21.

Rossfelder, André. *Clipperton, l'île tragique.* Paris: Albin Michel. 1976.

Rossiter, Margaret W. *The emergence of agricultural science: Justus Liebig and the Americans, 1840-1880.* New Haven: Yale University Press, 1975.

Rossiter, William S., [ed.] *Days and ways in old Boston.* Boston: R. H. Stearns and Company, 1915.

Rougier, Emmanuel. "My diary of Christmas island." *Mid- Pacific* 9 (1915) 289-93.

Rutter, Frank R. *South American trade of Baltimore.* Baltimore: The Johns Hopkins University Press, 1897.

Rydell, Raymond A. *Cape Horn to the Pacific: the rise and decline of an ocean highway.* Berkeley: University of California Press, 1952.

Sachet, Marie-Hélène, and F. Raymond Fosberg. *Island bibliographies: micronesia botany; land environment and ecology of coral atolls; vegetation of tropical Pacific islands.* Washington: National Academy of Sciences- National Research Council Publication 335, 1955.

———. *Island bibliographies supplement. . .* Washington: National Academy of Sciences, 1971.

Safford, Jeffrey J. "The United States merchant marine in foreign trade, 1800-1939." International Conference on Business History *Proceedings* 11 (1985) 91-118.

Sargent, John G. "Sovereignty over Swan islands." U.S. Justice department *Official opinions of attorneys general* 34 (1925) 507-15, q.v.

Sauchelli, Vincent. *Manual on phosphates in agriculture: general information for fertilizer salesmen, county agent, agricultural teacher, farmer and fertilizer dealer.* Baltimore: The Davidson Chemical Corporation, 1942.

———. *Phosphates in agriculture.* New York: Reinhold Publishing Corporation, 1965.

Scaife, Walter B. "The development of international law as to newly discovered territory." American Historical Association *Papers* 4 (1890) 269-93.

Scarr, Deryck. "Recruits and recruiters: a portrait of the Pacific islands labour trade." *The journal of Pacific history* 2 (1967) 5-24.

Scherer, Ron. "US chemical-weapon plan divides Pacific." *Christian Science monitor,* August 10, 1990, p. 5.

Schlee, Susan. "The curious controversy over coral reefs." *Sea frontiers* 17 (1971) 214-23.

Schwendinger, Robert J. "Coolie trade: the American connection." *Oceans* 14 (1981), 38-40, 42-44.

Seward, Frederick W. *Seward at Washington as senator and secretary of State: a memoir of his life, with selections from his letters.* 3 vols. New York: Derby and Miller, 1891.

[Seward, William H.] *The works of William H. Seward,* edited by George E. Baker. 5 vols. New York: Redfield, 1853- 84.

Shann, E. O. G. "Economic and political development, 1860-1885." J. H. Rose, ed., *Cambridge history of the British empire* VII, part 1 (1933), 297-323, q.v.

Shaplen, Robert. "Cherchez la femme: it's a feast or a famine." *Newsweek* 23 (June 12, 1944) 44.

Sharp, Andrew. *The discovery of the Pacific islands.* Oxford: At the Clarendon Press, 1960.

Shepard, Charles U. "Five new mineral species." *American journal of science and arts* 22 (1856) 96-99.

Sherman, Frederick Barreda. *From the Guadalquivir to the golden gate by way of Lima, Baltimore, Newport, Washington, London, Paris and Cuajiniquilapa; being the story of the lives of Frederico Luciano Barreda y Aguilar and Matilde Laverrerie y Barreda, his wife, with certain information concerning the ancestors and descendants.* Mill Valey, California: Privately Published by Hall and Smith Company, 1977.

Shewmaker, Kenneth E. "'Untaught diplomacy': Daniel Webster and the Lobos islands controversy." *Diplomatic history* 1 (fall 1977) 321-40.

Shipman, Paul R. "Webster on the territories." *Yale law journal* 9 (March 1900), 185-206.

Shlomowitz, Ralph. "Mortality and the Pacific labour trade." *The journal of American history* 22 (1987) 34-55.

"Sidney guano." Chemical Society of Great Britain *Abstracts* 48 (1885) 429.

Siegel, Jeff. "Origins of Pacific islands labourers in Fiji. *The journal of Pacific history* 20 (1985) 42-55.

Sinclair, Upton. *The jungle.* Toronto: McLeod & Allen, Publishers, 1906.

Skaggs, Jimmy M. *Clipperton: a history of the island the world forgot.* New York: Walker and Company, 1989.

———. *An interpretive history of the American economy.* Columbus, Ohio: Grid, Inc., 1975.

[Skinner, John S.] "Guano, a celebrated manure used in South America." *American farmer* 6 (December 24, 1824) 316-17.

"Slaves under our flag: a strike at the Navassa phosphate island; the government looking into charges against the methods of the company; an agreement which bears hard upon laborers." *New York Times,* May 14, 1891, p. 9.

Smith, Adam. *An inquiry into the nature and causes of the wealth of nations.* New York: P.F. Collier & Sons, 1909.

Smith, Elbert B. *The presidencies of Zachary Taylor & Millard Fillmore.* Lawrence: University Press of Kansas, 1988.

Smith, Gaddis. "Agricultural roots of maritime history." *The American neptune* 44 (winter 1984) 5-10.

Smith, Jean Edward [comp. and ed.]. *The Constitution and American foreign policy.* St. Paul, Minnesota: West Publishing Company, 1989.

Smith, Marshall A. "Guano on the American diplomatic scene." *Fertilizer review* 18 (Fall 1943) 10-11, 15.

*Smith* v. *U.S.* (1890). 137 U.S. 224.

Sorrenson, Laurel. "Scientists study the climatic effects of el Niño, a fickle warm-sea phenomenon in the Pacific." *Wall Street Journal,* March 24, 1983, p. 56.

Spate, O. H. K. *Monopolists and freebooters.* Minneapolis: University of Minnesota Press, 1983.

Speed, James. "Application of American Guano Company." U.S. Justice department *Official opinions of attorneys general* 11 (1865) 397-403, q.v.

———. "Exportation of guano." U.S. Justice department *Official opinions of attorneys general* 11 (1866) 514-15, q.v.

Stampp, Kenneth M. *America in 1857: a nation on the brink.* New York: Oxford University Press, 1990.

Stancil, Arnold T. *History of Navassa island.* Mimeograph. Washington, D.C.: U.S. Coast Guard, Public Information Division, 1967.

Stearns, Foster. "Edward Everett." S. F. Bemis, ed., *American secretaries of State and their diplomacy* 6 (1928) 115-41, q.v.

Stephenson, C. S. "Historical note on Swains island." U.S. Navy *Medical bulletin* 35 (1937) 361-64.

———. "Sanitary report on Swains island, 1934." U.S. Navy *Medical bulletin* 35 (1937) 357-61.

Stevenson, Mrs. Robert Louis [Fanny Van de Grift]. *The cruise of the "Janet Nichol" among the South Seas islands.* New York: Charles Scribner's Sons, 1914.

Stevers, Martin D., and Jonas Pendlebury. *Sea lanes: man's conquest of the ocean.* Garden City, New York: Garden City Publishing Co., Inc., 1938.

Stewart, Watt. *Chinese bondage in Peru: a history of the Chinese coolie in Peru, 1849-1874.* Durham, North Carolina: Duke University Press, 1951.

———, and Harold F. Peterson. *Builders of Latin America.* New York: Harper & Brothers Publishers, 1942.

"Storm found to spare atoll weapons stores." *New York Times,* August 22, 1984, p. A12.

"Story of the fertilizer industry in Baltimore." *Commercial fertilizer* 56 (June 1938) 24-36.

"Story of Wm. James: the Navassa island murders: trial in the United States court; a number of witnesses testify as to the incidental particulars; how the horrible plot was fully developed." *Baltimore Sun,* November 21, 1889, p. 6.

Streets, Thomas H. *The American naturalist* 11 (1877) 63-72.

Summers, Mark W. *The plundering generation: corruption and the crisis of the union, 1849-1861.* New York: Oxford University Press, 1987.

"Swains island." U.S. State department *Digest of international law* 1 (1940) 482-87, q.v.

"Swan islands treaty with Honduras enters into force." U.S. Department of State *Bulletin* 67 (1972) 326.

Tansill, Charles Callan. *The United States and Santo Domingo, 1798-1873.* Baltimore: The Johns Hopkins Press, 1938.

Tappy, Elizabeth P. "Peruvian guano." U.S. Agriculture department *Foreign agriculture* 7 (August 1943) 185-92. A67.7:7

Taylor, C. R. H. *A Pacific bibliography: printed matter relating to the native peoples of Polynesia, Melanesia and Micronesia.* 2d ed. Oxford: At the Clarendon Press, 1965.

Taylor, Rosser. H. "Fertilizers and farming in the southeast, 1840-1950: part I: 1840-1900, introduction of guano." *North Carolina historical review* 30 (July 1953) 305-28.

———. "Fertilizers and farming in the southeast, 1840- 1950: part II: 1900-1950, the state of agriculture at the turn of the century." *North Carolina historical review* 30 (October 1953) 483-523.

Taylor, W[illiam] J. "Investigation on the rock guano from the islands of the Caribbean sea." Academy of Natural Sciences of Philadelphia *Proceedings* (March 1857), 91- 100.

———. "Investigation on the rock guano from the islands of the Caribbean sea." *American journal of science and arts* (2d series) 24 (November 1857) 177-88.

Ten Have, Ton, Wim Heijnen, and Enno Nickel. "Alterations in guano phosphates and mio-Pliocene carbonates of Table Mountain, Santa Barbara, Curacao." *Sedimentary geology* 31 (1982) 141-65.

"'That is the man': how Key shot Mr. Mahon: Dr. Smith's graphic statement; clearest and most comprehensive story yet told of the Navassa island riot and murders; the other witnesses; 'That is the man who shot Mr. Mahon.'" *Baltimore Sun,* November 22, 1889, p. 6.

"Third Navassa trial: one person guilty of murder and others guilty of manslaughter." *New York Times,* February 13, 1890, p. 1.

"This was the motive: Navassa's horrible murders: the government's view of the case; District Attorney Hayes says the men wanted to leave the island because they were indebted to the company." *Baltimore Sun,* November 20, 1889, p. 6.

Thompson, Edgar K. "Navassa: a forgotten acquisition." *The American neptune* 26 (1966) 171-76.

Thompson, F. M. L. "The second agricultural revolution, 1815- 1880." *Economic historical review* 21 (April 1968) 62-77.

Thorp, Thomas E., comp. *Johnston island: a library brochure,* edited by William L. Thomas. Mimeograph. N.P.: Prepared for the Pacific Missile Range, Point Mugu, California, by the University of California, 1960.

"Three men on an island." *Mid-Pacific* 21 (1921) 74-79.

"Time bomb." *Sixty minutes.* New York: Columbia Broadcasting System, 1992.

*The Times.* May 29, 1852, p. 6d; August 5, 1875, p. 7; June 24, 1914, p. 13a; July 7, 1917, p. 13d; July 19, 1917, p. 12c; July 30, 1917, p. 11b.

"To be rescued from Navassa island: steamship Alps to take off the four men abandoned there; have had to shift for themselves since December—aided by a British cruiser and a United States yacht." *New York Times,* May 31, 1901, p. 1.

"Tropical pawn: British reclaim Christmas island, once seized by American [*sic*]." *Literary digest* 123 (March 12, 1937) 15-16.

Truman, Harry S. *Public papers.* Washington, D.C.: United States Government Printing Office, 1961. AE2.114:year

"Twenty million pets." *Time* 50 (September 15, 1947), 67.

Ullmann, Herbert S. "The most prosperous bird colony: guano islands' cormorants and gannets thrive but fishing may imperil food supply." *Audubon* 65 (May-June) 1965: 151- 52.

United States Guano Company. *Report to the stockholders.* New York: United States Guano Company, 1859.

"United States Circuit Court." *Baltimore Sun,* December 23, 1889, p. 6.

*United States of America* v. *Fullard-Leo et al.* 133 Fed. Rep. (2d series; 1943) 743-52; 156 Fed. Rep. (2d series; 1946) 756-69.

———. 66 Fed. Supp. (1940) 744-82; 66 Fed. Supp. (1944) 782-88.

———. 329 U.S. (1946) 697.

United States of America. *Code, 1988 edition: containing the general and permanent laws of the United States, in force on January 3, 1989.* Washington: Government Printing Office, 1989. Y1.2/5:988.

———. *Code of federal regulations.* Title 3 (the President). Washington, D.C., Office of the Federal Register, 1943. GS4.108/2:years.

———. *Revised statutes of the United States, passed at the first session of the forty-third Congress, 1873-'74: embracing the statutes of the United States, general and permanent in their nature, in force on the first day of December, one thousand eight hundred and seventy-three, as revised and consolidated by commissioners appointed under an act of Congress.* Washington, D.C.: Government Printing Office, 1873. S7.10.

———. *Statutes at large.* 11 (1856) 119-20; 13 (1865) 494; 14 (1866) 328; 17 (1872) 48; 18, part 1 (1873), 1080-81, part 3 (1873-74), 1045; 20 (1878) 30; 23 (1884) 11; 25 (1889) 655-56; 35 (1909) 1143; 38 (1913) 208, 224; 39 (1917) 1763; 43 (1925) 1357. AE2.111:[vols.].

———. *Friendship and territorial sovereignty: treaty between the United States of America and Tuvalu, signed at Funafuti February 7, 1979.* Washington: Treaties and other international acts series, 10776, [1985]. S9.10:10776.

———. *Friendship and territorial sovereignty: treaty, with agreed minute, between the United States of America and Kiribati signed at Tarawa September 20, 1979.* Washington: Treaties and other international acts series, 10777 [1985]. S9.10:10777.

———. *Maritime boundaries: treaty between the United States of America and the Cook islands signed at Rarotonga June 11, 1980.* Washington: Treaties and other international acts series, 10774 [1985]. S9.10:10774.

———. *Maritime boundaries: treaty between the United States of America and New Zealand signed at Atafu December 2, 1980.* Washington: Treaties and other international acts series, 10775 [1985]. S9.10:10775.

U.S. Agriculture commissioner. *Report for the year 1869.* Washington: Government Printing Office, 1870. A1.1:869.

U.S. Agriculture department. *Agriculture yearbook.* Washington: Government Printing Office, annual. [title varies] A1.10:year.

———. Agriculture Research Service. *Superphosphate: its history, chemistry, and manufacture.* Washington: U.S. Government Printing Office, 1965. A77.2:Su7.

U.S. Census bureau. *Abstract of the twelfth census of the United States, 1900.* New York: Arno Press, 1976.

———. *Historical statistics of the United States, colonial times to 1957.* Washington, D.C.: U.S. Government Printing Office, 1960. C3.134/2: H62/957.

———. *Manuscript census returns, 1850.* Washington: National Archives Microfilm Publication M-517, 1965.

———. *The statistical history of the United States: from colonial times to the present.* Stamford, Connecticut: Fairfield Publishers, Inc., 1965.

U.S. Commerce department. *Magnetic hourly values: Jarvis island, 1957-58.* Washington: Coast and Geodetic Survey, 1960. C4.40:J158.

U.S. Commerce and Labor department. *Circulars.* Washington: Government Printing Office, serial C1.4.

U.S. Congress. *The congressional globe, containing the debates, proceedings, laws, etc., of . . . Congress.* 33d Cong., 1st sess. (1853-54), parts 1-3, X103:33/1-3; 33d Cong., 2d sess. (1854-55) X107:33/2; 34th Cong., 1st sess. (1855-56), parts 1-2, X111:34/1-2; 34th Cong., 3d sess. (1856-57) X113:34/3; 42d Cong., 1st sess. (1871), part 1, X169:42/1; 41st Cong., 2d sess. (1869-70), part 2, X164:41/2; 42d Cong., 2d sess. (1871-72), parts 2, X171.42/2.

———. *Congressional record.* 51st Cong., 2d sess. (1890-91) Vols. 22-23 (pts. 3-5), X297:51/2 ; 62nd Cong., 1st Sess (1911) Vol. 47 (pt. 2), X454:62/1; 63rd Cong., 1st sess. (1913), Vol. 50 (pt. 5), X78:63/1; 84th Cong., 2d sess. (1956), Vol. 102 (pts. 7-8, 12), X84/2:102/pts. 7-8, 12; 87th Cong., 2d sess. (1962), Vol. 108 (pt. 6), X.87/2:108/pt. 6; 91st Cong., 2d sess. (1970), Vol.116, (pt. 17), X.91/2:116/pt. 17; 101st Cong., 2d sess. (1990), Vol. 136, (nos. 103, 104, 121, 128, 138), X/a:136/013, 136/104/pt. 3, 136/121, 136/128, 136/138.

———. *Digest of public bills and selected resolutions with index.* 84th Cong., 2d sess. (1956). LC14.6:84-L/4.

U.S. Congress. House of Representatives. Document 100-245. *Records of the United States House of Representatives at the National Archives, 1789-1989.* 100th Congress, 2d sess. (1989). Y1.1/7: 100-245.

———. Executive Document 2. *Report of the secretary of the Navy.* 35th Cong. 1st sess. (1857-58). Serial 944.

———. Exec. Doc. 4. *Letter from the secretary of State . . . [regarding the] commercial relations of the United States with foreign nations for the year ending September 30, 1859.* 36th Cong., 1st sess. (1859-60). Serial 1044.

———. Exec. Doc. 70. *The guano trade.* 33d Cong., 1st sess. (1853-54). Serial 723.

———. Exec. Doc. 105. *Letter from the secretary of the Navy regarding the Pacific ocean and South Seas. . . .* 23d Cong., 2d sess. (1834-35). Serial 273.

———. Exec. Doc. 161. *Letter from the secretary of the Navy, transmitting a report from the Bureau of Construction, &c., relative to contracts entered into with A. G. & A. W. Benson.* 28 Cong., 2d sess. (1844-45). Serial 466.

———. *Journal.* 33d Cong., 1st sess. (1853-54). Serial 709; 33d Cong., 2d sess. (1854-55). Serial 776; 34th Cong., 1st sess. (1855-56). Serial 839; 41st Cong., 2d sess. (1869-70). Serial 1410; 42d Cong., 1st sess. (1871). Serial 1469; 48th Cong., 1st sess. (1883-84). Serial 2180.

———. Miscellaneous Document 10. *Memorial of Patterson and Murguiondo, citizens of Baltimore, relative to the claims of the government and citizens of the United States to the island of Alta Vela.* 40th Cong., 3d sess. (1868-69). Serial 1385.

———. Rept. 94. *Explore Pacific ocean, &c.* 23d Cong., 2d sess. (1834-35). Serial 276.

———. Rept. 252. *Guano islands.* 48th Cong., 1st sess. (1883-84). Serial 2253.

———. Rept. 347. *Trade between the United States and the republic of Peru.* 33d Cong., 1st sess. (1853-54). Serial 744.

———. Rept. 1790. *Report . . . relative to certain missing papers from the files of the Department of State and also directing inquiries to be made as to the connection of one or more ministers plenipotentiary of the United States with business transactions. . . .* 47th Cong., 1st sess. (1881-82). Serial 2070.

———. Rept. 2573. *Extending jurisdiction of the United States district court, territory of Hawaii, over the Midway and other islands.* 76th Cong., 3d sess. (1940). Serial 10443.

———. Rept. 3989. *Guano islands.* 50th Cong., 2d sess. (1888-89). Serial 2674.

———. Rept. 4040. *Guano islands.* 51st Cong., 2d sess. (1890-91). Serial 2890.

U.S. Congress. Senate. Document 100-34. *Biographical directory of the United States Congress, 1774-1989.* 100th Congress, 2d Session (1989). X1.1/3:100-34.

———. Doc. 159. *Ordinances of executive council of Porto Rico.* 59th Cong., 1st sess. (1905-06). Serial 4912.

———. Doc. 190. *Fertilizer resources of the United States.* 62d Cong., 2d sess. (1911-1912). Serial 6145.

———. Doc. 194. *The history and growth of the United States census, prepared . . . by Carroll D. Wright. . . .* 56th Cong., 1st sess. (1899-1900). Serial 3856.

———. Doc. 234. *Legal status of the territory and inhabitants of the islands acquired by the United States during the war with Spain, considered with reference to the territorial boundaries, the constitution, and laws of the United States* 56th Cong., 1st sess. (1900). Serial 3858.

———. Doc. 551. *The fertilizer industry.* 64th Cong., 1st sess. (1916). Serial 6447.

———. Executive Document 10. *Message from the President of the United States communicating . . . information respecting Aves island.* 36th Cong., 2d sess. (1860-61). Serial 1082.

———. Exec. Doc. 11. *Report of the secretary of the Navy.* 35th Cong., 1st sess. (1857-58). Serial 921.

———. Exec. Doc. 25. *Message from the President of the United States communicating . . . the correspondence between the governments of the United States and Peru regarding the Lobos islands.* 32 Cong., 1st sess. (1851-52). Serial 621.

———. Exec. Doc. 25. *Message from the President of the United States communicating . . . information respecting the Aves or Bird islands. . . .* 34th Cong., 3d sess. (1856-57). Serial 879.

———. Exec. Doc. 25. *Message of the President of the United States . . . [communicating] information in relation to the guano trade.* 35th Cong., 2d sess. (1858-59). Serial 981.

———. Exec. Doc. 31. . . . *[regarding] E. N. Horsford's . . . analysis of guano.* 33d Cong., 2d sess. (1854-55). Serial 751.

———. Exec. Doc. 37. *Message from the President of the United States . . . in regard to the occupation by American citizens of the island of Navasa* [*sic*], *in the West Indies.* 36th Cong., 1st sess. (1859-60). Serial 1031.

———. Exec. Doc. 38. *Message of the President of the United States . . . in relation to a claim to the guano on Alto Velo, an island in the vicinity of Saint Domingo.* 40th Cong., 2d sess. (1867-68). Serial 1316.

———. Exec. Doc. 42, part 3. *U.S. Commissioner of Patents: report on agriculture.* 33d Cong., 2d sess. (1854-55). Serial 755.

———. Exec. Doc. 58. *Message from the President of the United States . . . relative to the payment of the Peruvian indemnity.* 31st Cong., 1st sess. (1849-50). Serial 561.

———. Exec. Doc. 59. *Report of the secretary of State respecting the trade in guano.* 31st Cong., 1st sess. (1849-50). Serial 561.

———. Exec. Doc. 61. *Message of the President of the United States. . .* [conveying] *a copy of a letter from the Minister of Peru to the secretary of State, of November 17, 1852, relative to the Lobos islands.* 33d Cong., 2d sess. (1854-55). Serial 752.

———. Exec. Doc. 69. *Message from the President of the United States communicating a report of the secretary of State . . . on the subject of guano.* 35th Cong., 1st sess. (1857-58). Serial 930.

———. Exec. Doc. 80. *Report from the secretary of State respecting Peruvian guano,* 31st Cong., 1st sess. (1849-50). Serial 562.

———. Exec. Doc. 109. *Message from the President of the United States . . . regarding the Lobos islands.* 32d Cong., 1st sess. (1851-52). Serial 621.

———. Exec. Doc. 109, part 2. *Message from the President of the United States in further compliance with a resolution of the Senate relative to the Lobos islands, a report of the Secretary of State, and a copy of the orders given to the commander of the United States squadron in the Pacific.* 32d Cong., 1st sess. (1851-52). Serial 621.

———. Exec. Doc. 151. *Message from the President of the United States in relation to guano deposits on Arcas cay.* 52d Cong., 1st sess. (1891-92). Serial 2901.

———. Exec. Doc. 234. *Report on the legal status of the territory and inhabitants of the islands acquired by the United States during the war with Spain. . . .* 56th Cong., 1st sess. (1899-1900). Serial 3858.

———. *Journal.* 33d Cong., 2d sess. (1853-54). Serial 745; 34th Cong., 1st sess. (1855-56). Serial 809; 34th Cong., 3d sess. (1856-57). Serial 873; 41st Cong., 2d sess. (1869-70). Serial 1404; 42d Cong., 1st sess. (1871). Serial 1465; 52nd Cong., 1st sess. (1891-92). Serial 2891.

———. Miscellaneous Document 14. *List of private claims brought before the Senate of the United States from the commencement of the fourteenth Congress to the close of the forty-sixth Congress . . . in two volumes.* (46th Cong., 3d sess.). Serials 1945-46.

———. Miscellaneous Doc. 18. *Resolutions of the legislature of Maryland in favor of some arrangement with the Peruvian government by which the monopoly in the sale of guano may be removed.* 33d Cong., 1st sess. (1853-54). Serial 705.

———. Miscellaneous Doc. 60. *Memorial of the American Guano Company, praying the recognition and protection of all islands discovered and settled by Americans, as well as other islands or lands which may hereafter be discovered and settled by them, and which contain guano.* 34th Cong., 1st sess. (1855-56). Serial 835.

———. Miscellaneous Doc. 267. *Papers in relation to a cargo of guano received by Schuyler Livingston. . . .* 35th Cong., 1 sess. (1857-58). Serial 937.

———. Rept. 280 *[regarding] the memorial of William T. Kendall, of Baltimore, asking indemnity for property seized and confiscated by the alleged authority of the British government, and for the value of guano claimed under the act of August 18, 1856. . . .* 36th Cong., 1st sess. (1859-60), serial 1040.

———. Rept. 307. *Report . . . ascertaining the correctness of certain discoveries of guano on Jarvis and Baker's islands. . . .* 35th Cong., 1st sess. (1857-58). Serial 939.

———. Rept. 319. *Report [of the] . . . Committee on Naval Affairs . . . [concerning] the memorial of A. G. & A. W. Benson.* 31st Cong., 2d sess. (1832-33). Serial 593.

———. Rept. 379. *Report . . . to accompany S. Bill 531 . . . entitled "An act to allow Edward K. Cooper and his assigns, being citizens of the United States, the exclusive right of occupying the island or key of Navassa, in the Caribbean sea, for the purpose of obtaining and selling guano therefrom. . . .* 35th Cong., 2d sess. (1858-59). Serial 994.

———. Rept. 397. *Report . . . [regarding] Alfred G. Benson. . . .* 34th Cong., 3d sess. (1856-57). Serial 891.

———. Rept. 536. *Extending the jurisdiction of the United States district court for Hawaii.* 76th Cong., 1st sess. (1939). Serial 10294.

———. Rept. 606. *Light house on Swan island.* 54th Cong., 1st sess. (1895-96). Serial 3364.

U.S. Commission on Organization of the Executive Branch of Government [Hoover commission]. *Administration of overseas affairs: a report to the Congress by the Commission . . . March 1949.* [Washington: Government Printing Office, 1949]. Y3:Or3:20v2.

U.S. Federal Communications Commission. *New plain English rules: citizens band radio service.* Washington: Government Printing Office, 1983.

U.S. Federal Trade Commission. *The fertilizer industry.* U.S. Congress. S. Doc. 551. Serial 6447, q.v.

[U.S. Defense department.] Defense Nuclear Agency, Field Command [FCDNA]. "Johnson atoll." *Fact sheet.* Public Affairs Office, Kirtland Air Force Base, New Mexico, October, 1990. [No SuDocs.]

U.S. Guano islands acts. See U.S. *Code*; or, U.S. *Statutes at large.*

U.S. Interior department. *American Samoa: fact sheet.* Mimeograph. Washington, D.C.: Office of the Secretary, 1990. I35.2:date

———. *Other United States insular areas: fact sheet.* Mimeograph. Washington, D.C.: Office of the Secretary, 1990. I35.2:date

———. *Other United States insular areas: fact sheet.* Mimeograph. Washington, D.C.: Office of the Secretary, 1992. I35.2:date

———. *Canton and other equatorial islands.* Washington: Interior Duplicating Section, 1954, 1955, 1957. I35.2:c16/2/date

———. *Highlights: Office of Territories.* [Washington: Government Printing Office, 1970.] I35.2:H53.

———. *Territorial areas administered by the United States.* Washington: U.S. Government Printing Office, 1971. I35.2:T27/2/971

———. *Territorial responsibilities.* Washington: U.S. Government Printing Office, 1963. I35.2:R31

U.S. Interstate Commerce Commission. *Reports.* Washington: Government Printing Office, annual. IC1.6/1:vol.

U.S. Justice department. *Digest of the official opinions of the attorneys-general of the United States, comprising all of the published opinions contained in volumes I to XVI inclusive and embracing the period 1789 to 1881,* [comp. and ed.] by A. J. Bentley. Washington, D. C.: Government Printing Office, 1885. J1.6:885

———. *Official opinions of the attorneys general of the United States advising the President and heads of departments in relation to their official duties.* Washington, D.C.: Government Printing Office, serial. J1.50:vol

U.S. Navy. *Area file of naval records collection, 1775-1910.* Washington, D.C.: National Archives Microfilm Publication M625, 1965.

———. *Report to the United Nations on Guam, American Samoa and other island possessions administered by the Navy department.* [Washington, D.C.] Assistant Chief of Naval Operations (Island Government), July 1946. N27.2:G93

———. Hydrographic Office. *List of lights and fog signals.* Washington, D.C.: United States Government Printing Office, 1960. N6.8:30.

———. *Notes on the guano islands of the Pacific ocean.* [Washington, D.C.]: Prepared for the [U.S.] Department of State, 1918. DU22N67.1918.

———. Intelligence division. *Pacific islands.* 4 vols. [Washington, D.C.:] Geographical Handbook Series, B. R. 519, 1943-45.

[U.S. Presidents.] *A compilation of the messages and papers of the presidents,* edited by James D. Richardson. 11 vols. N.p.: Bureau of National Literature and Art, 1910.

———. *Presidential executive orders: numbered series (1862-1938).* Wilmington, Delaware: Michael Glazier, Inc., 1981.

———. *Weekly compilation of presidential documents.* [Washington, D.C., Serial.] AE2.109:vol/no.

U.S. State department. *Digest of international law,* [compiled and edited] by Green Haywood Hackworth. 8 vols. Washington: Government Printing Office, 1940. S7.12:vol.

———. *A digest of international law as embodied in diplomatic discussions, treaties, and other international agreements, international awards, the decisions of municipal courts, and the writings of jurists, and especially in documents, published and unpublished, issued by presidents and secretaries of State of the United States, the opinions of attorneys-general, and the decisions of courts, federal and state,* [compiled and edited] by John Bassett Moore. 8 vols. Washington: Government Printing Office, 1906. S7.12:date/vol.

———. *Foreign relations of the United States: diplomatic papers.* Serial. Washington: United States Government Printing Office, annual. S1.1:vol/date.

———. *Records of the Department of State relating to guano islands, 1852-1912.* 7 reels. Washington, D.C.: National Archives Microfilm Publication M974, 1975.

———. *Treaties and other international acts of the United States of America,* edited by Hunter Miller. 8 vols. Washington: Government Printing Office, 1931-48. S9.5/1:vol.

———. *Treaties and other international agreements of the United States of America, 1776-1949.* 13 vols. [Washington: Government Printing Office, 1968-76. S9.12/2:vol.

———. *Treaties in force: a list of treaties and other international agreements of the United States in force on January 1, 1981.* [Washington: Government Printing Office, 1981.] S9:14:981.

———. *United States treaties and other international agreements.* Washington: Government Printing Office, serial. S9.12:vol.

———. Foreign Commerce bureau. *Commercial relations of the United States with foreign countries during the year 1898.* 2 vols. Washington: Government Printing Office, 1899.

———. Intelligence and Research bureau. "United States and outlying areas." *Geographic bulletin* 5 (April 1965), 1-16. S1.11.9/2:5.

U.S. Treasury department. *Circular No. 1, relative to the guano islands appertaining to the United States.* Washington: Government Printing Office, 1869. T1.4:869.

———. *Annual reports: foreign commerce and navigation.* Washington, D.C.: Government Printing Office, serial. T37.1:(date).

[U.S.] Works Projects Administration. [Federal Writers' Project]. *Boston looks seaward: the story of the port, 1630-1940.* Boston: B. Humphries, 1941.

*U.S. overseas: Puerto Rico, territories, cumulative index.* New York: Time-Life Books, 1969.

"U.S. requests Britain cede three islands in the Pacific." *New York Times,* May 12, 1946, pp. 1, 25.

"U.S. seeks Pacific islands: suit for title to Palmyra group is entered at Honolulu." *New York Times,* December 13, 1939, p. 4.

"U.S. starts pullout of chemical arms: 30-mile convoy in West Germany is 1st leg to destruction in the Pacific." *Washington Post,* July 27, 1990, pp. A1, 32.

"U.S. to drop claims on 25 Pacific isles: most of them to be transferred to the former Ellice and Gilbert chains, now independent." *New York Times* May 19, 1980, p. A7.

Urofsky, Melvin I. *A march of liberty: a constitutional history of the United States.* New York: Alfred A. Knopf, 1988.

Van Alstyne, R[ichard] W. *The rising American empire.* New York: W. W. Norton, 1974.

Van Cleve, Ruth G. "Trust Territory of the Pacific." *Dictionary of American history* VII (1976) 124-25, q.v.

Van Deusen, Glyndon G. *Thurlow Weed: wizard of the lobby.* Boston: Little, Brown and Company, 1947.

Van Wazer, John R. "Phosphorus and mankind's problems today." Ciba Foundation, *Phosphorus in the environment* (1979), 5-21, q.v.

Vayssade, Martín Reyes, coordinador. *Cartografía histórica de las islas Mexicanas.* [Cuidad México]: Secretaría de Gobernación, 1992.

"Venezuela: January 14, 1859." U.S. State department, *Treaties and other international acts.* 8 (1948) 137-88, q.v. S9.5/1:8.

Villiers, Alan. *The way of a ship: being some account of the ultimate development of the ocean-going square-rigged sailing vessel, and the manner of her handling, her voyage-making, her personnel, her economics, her performance, and her end.* New York: Charles Scribner's Sons, 1953.

"Visit to a guano island." *Leisure hour* 2 (July 7, 1853) 433- 36.

"Vostok island." Pacific Science Association Sixth Congress *Proceedings* 4 (1940) 502.

"Vostok island's history is yet to be made." *Pacific islands monthly* 37 (1966) 87.

Waggaman, W[illia]m H. *Phosphoric acid, phosphates and phosphatic fertilizers.* 2d ed. New York: Reinhold Publishing Corporation, 1952.

———. "Phosphate rock, our greatest fertilizer asset." U.S. Agriculture department, *Yearbook . . . 1917* (1918), 177-83, q.v.

Walker, Howell. "Air age brings life to Canton island." *National Geographic* 107 (January 1955) 117-32.

Ward, John M. *British policy in the South Pacific (1786- 1893).* Westport, Connecticut: Greenwood Press, Publishers, 1976.

Ward, R[alph] Gerard, ed. *American activities in the Central Pacific, 1790-1870: a history, geography and ethnography pertaining to American involvement and Americans in the Pacific taken from contemporary newspapers, etc.* 8 vols. Ridgewood, New Jersey: The Gress Press, 1966-67.

Warner, Richard E. "Recent history and ecology of the Laysan duck." *The condor* 65 (1963) 3-23.

Warren, Charles. *A history of the American bar.* New York: Howard Fertig, 1966. "Was there a plot? A question for the jury: defense view of Navassa murders; arguments in the United States Circuit Court; were the men so exasperated that they acted on impulse?" *Baltimore Sun,* November 29, 1889, p. 6.

Washington, John A. [Uses of guano.] *Prairie farmer* 12 (October 1852) 464-65.

Watson, G. C. "On the noxious effects of ammoniacal vapours disengaged from guano." *Medical times* 12 (1845) 467-69.

———. "Toxicological effects of guano." *Medical times* 13 (1845/46) 48-49.

Watson, J. S. "Feral rabbit populations on Pacific islands." *Pacific science* 15 (1961) 591-93.

Wearne, J. "Presumed poisonous effects of guano." *Lancet* 1 (1850) 774-75.

Webb, Walter Prescott, and H. Bailey Carroll, eds. *The handbook of Texas.* 2 vols. Austin: Texas State Historical Association, 1952.

Webster, Daniel. *The papers of Daniel Webster,* edited by Charles M. Wiltse. 15 vols. Hanover, New Hampshire: University Press of New England, 1974-87.

———. *Microfilm edition of the papers of Daniel Webster,* edited by Charles M. Wiltse. 41 reels. Ann Arbor, Michigan: University Microfilms in collaboration with Dartmouth College Library, 1971.

Weinberg, Albert K. *Manifest destiny: a study of national expansionism in American history.* Baltimore: The Johns Hopkins Press, 1935.

Wells, Tom Henderson. "The Swan islands dispute." *Journal of inter-American studies* 6 (1964) 57-68.

Welty, Earl. "Finders keepers." *Collier's* (October 7, 1939) 24, 56-58.

*Wenberg* v. *a cargo of mineral phosphate and another* (1883). 15 Fed. Rep. 285-88.

Wenkam, Robert. *The great Pacific rip-off: corporate rape in the far east.* Chicago: Follett Publishing Company, 1974.

———, and Byron Baker. *Micronesia, the breadfruit revolution.* Honolulu: East-West Center Press, 1971.

Wentworth, Chester K. "Geology of the Pacific equatorial islands". Bernice P. Bishop Museum *Occasional papers* 9 (1931) 3-25.

———, and H. S. Ladd. "Pacific island sediments." University of Iowa *Studies in natural history* 13 (1931) 2-47.

Werlich, David P. *Peru, a short history.* Carbondale: Southern Illinois University Press, 1978.

"Wetmore, Prosper M." *Appleton' cyclopaedia of American biography.* VI: 445, q.v.

Whedbee, T. Courtney. *The port of Baltimore in the making, 1828 to 1878.* Baltimore: Privately printed to mark the twenty-fifth anniversary of the founding of F. Bowie Smith & Son, Inc., 1953.

*Whiton* v. *Albany and Narragansett Insurance Companies* (1871). 109 Massachusetts 24-31.

Wiens, Harold J. *Atoll environment and ecology.* New Haven, Connecticut: Yale University Press, 1962.

———. *Pacific island bastions of the United States.* New York: D. Van Norstrand Company, Inc., 1962.

Wilkes, Charles. *Narrative of the United States exploring expedition during the years 1838, 1839, 1840, 1841, 1842.* 2 vols. London: Ingram, Cooke, and Co., 1852.

Williams, John. "More American air bases." *Asia* 37 (1937) 409-13.

Williams, William Appleman. *The roots of the modern American empire: a study of the growth and shaping of social consciousness in a marketplace society.* New York: Random House, 1969.

Willoughby, William Franklin. *Territories and dependencies of the United States: their government and administration.* New York: Century, 1905.

"Wings: Pacific air-bases; U.S. security key; from Hawaiian 'crossroads,' planes scout for phantom foes." *Literary digest* 122 (November 7, 1936) 33-34.

Wise, David, and Thomas B. Ross. *The invisible government.* New York: Random House, 1964.

Zans, V. A. "The Pedro cays and Pedro bank: report on surveys of the cays, 1955-57." Jamaican Geological Survey *Bulletin* 3 (1958) 1-47.

Zieman, Mark. "Birds do it, bats do it, but the issue is, Who does it better? Peruvian export finds U.S. is fertile field, but firms here refuse to cave in." *Wall Street Journal,* July 24, 1984, pp. 1, 23.

Zinn, Howard. *A people's history of the United States.* New York: Harper & Row, Publishers, 1980.

# INDEX